JAGUAR

A tradition of sports cars

Bernard Viart   Michel Cognet

JAGUAR

A tradition of sports cars

Foulis

Haynes

ISBN 0 85429 456 2

A FOULIS Motoring Book

This edition first published 1985

© E.P.A., Paris 1984
Published by:
Haynes Publishing Group
Sparkford, Yeovil, Somerset BA22 7JJ,
England.

CONTENTS

Jaguar Cars Exports Limite

PO Box No 81
Browns Lane
Allesley
Coventry CV5 9DR
England

Telephone: 0203 402121
Telex: 31622

Je salue aujourd'hui avec joie l'initiative française qui me permet d'admirer l'épreuve définitive du livre sur les Jaguar de sport.

Il y avait déjà en effet de nombreux ouvrages sur la marque Jaguar en langue anglaise, mais c'est la toute première fois qu'un livre français parle avec un tel bonheur de la marque que j'ai créée voilà maintenant plus de 60 ans.

C'est bien plus qu'un livre en français, c'est un livre français.

C'est aussi un moment très émouvant, car j'ai à l'égard de la France des liens très particuliers qui en font pour moi un pays extrêmement cher. J'ai eu des rapports infiniment cordiaux et amicaux avec toute la famille Delecroix qui distribua ma marque en France pendant tant d'années avec la même fidélité et le même enthousiasme.

Le passionnant ouvrage de Bernard Viart et Michel Cognet me rappelle avec émotion ces années fabuleuses grâce à cette richesse iconographique que je croyais disparue et qui m'étonne encore par sa diversité et sa nouveauté.

Je souhaite bonne chance à ce remarquable exploit d'édition et je profite de l'occasion qui m'est offerte pour saluer à travers ce livre tous les amoureux de la marque Jaguar qui ont su transmettre le feu sacré de leur passion tout au long de ces années si fertiles en création automobile.

W Lyons

Sir William Lyons

Sir William Lyons died on friday february 8th, 1985, whilst this english language edition was in preparation. He continued to have a strong interest in Jaguar after his retirement and lived long enough to see the company he co-founded regain its strength and pride. This book is now a lasting tribute to a great man.

Sir William Lyons and the authors at Wappenbury Hall, near Coventry.

Translation to Foreword

As can be seen opposite, Sir William Lyons' foreword to the original French edition was, itself, written in French and typed on Jaguar headed note-paper. Because it is felt that the sentiments expressed still stand, the foreword has been retained.

It is with great pleasure that I welcome the French initiative which has enabled me to admire the final proofs of the book on Jaguar sports cars.

Many English books have dealt with the Jaguar marque, but this is the very first time that a French work has portrayed so well the marque which I created more than 60 years ago.

It is much more than a book written in French: it is a French book.

This is a very emotional moment for me, for I have some very special connections with France which have made that country particularly dear to me. I have had extremely warm and friendly relations with all the Delecroix family who have distributed my cars in France for so many years with unflagging loyalty and enthusiasm.

This fascinating volume by Bernard Viart and Michel Cognet brings back all the excitement of those fabulous years through the wealth of illustrations, many of which I thought had long disappeared, and which still surprise me with their variety and newness.

I wish good luck to this remarkable publishing venture, and I should like to take this opportunity to greet, through these pages, all the lovers of the Jaguar marque who have passed on their passion to others down these years which have been so rich in new automobile creations.

Sir William Lyons in 1969.
A living industrial legend, a man of vision and a creative genius, Sir William Lyons left his indelible mark on automobile history by offering non-standard cars at the price of series production models.

THE PRIDE OF LYONS

A UNIQUE CAR CONCEPT

In the early decades of this century the words 'free enterprise' conjured up visions of wild-west escapades and deeds of derring-do, so that any young man with guts and talent was happy to invest his last penny in the great industrial adventure.

Motor car history is full of these larger-than-life geniuses whose names live on in their creations: Beau de Rochas with his four-stroke cycle; De Dion's suspension; Panhard's front-mounted engine; Clément and his Bayard; Jeantaud; Cottin; Desgouttes; Rolls; Royce... and then, of course, there is Jaguar and its originator, Lyons.

The story of Jaguar is so closely entwined with that of the meteoric rise to success of the marque's creator, Sir William Lyons, that it is difficult to separate the two.

In a sense, Jaguar's history is the story of one man; but it is also a tale of the staunch loyalty and friendship which united a band of men, brought together through their exceptional engineering talents and through a mutual passion for the motor car.

The names of these men crop up time and time again: William Heynes, Claude Baily, Walter Hassan, Harry Weslake, and F.R.W. 'Lofty' England. Remember them, for you will be meeting them again at the turning-points in the company's history.

This is also a tale of people who had unshakable faith in Lyons from the moment they met him: the first holder of the Jaguar concession and the first importers.

And at the centre of our story is William Lyons, the Blackpool lad obsessed by motorcycles and racing whose uncanny business flair led him to go into the manufacture of sidecars just as they were becoming popular with the middle class.

As early as 1921 Lyons designed and built his first sidecar, using his father's garage as a workshop. He even received firm orders for more, although this is not so surprising, considering that his sidecars were much more attractive and sleek than the average production model. To put it plainly, they had class.

Lyons was limited in his construction methods by the size of his diminutive workshop, so he used aluminium panels on an ash frame.

In 1922, on the day he came of age, he signed the documents to take a lease on a factory; this was a young man in a hurry. By now he had found a partner in the equally dedicated William Walmsley.

So, by his twenty-first birthday, this tall, determined young man was running his own business: the Swallow Sidecar Company. Not bad going when you think that most of his contemporaries were studying and still wondering what to do with their lives!

The business took off from the word go and, for the next three years, orders flooded in with the result that the fledgling business was already outgrowing the new factory.

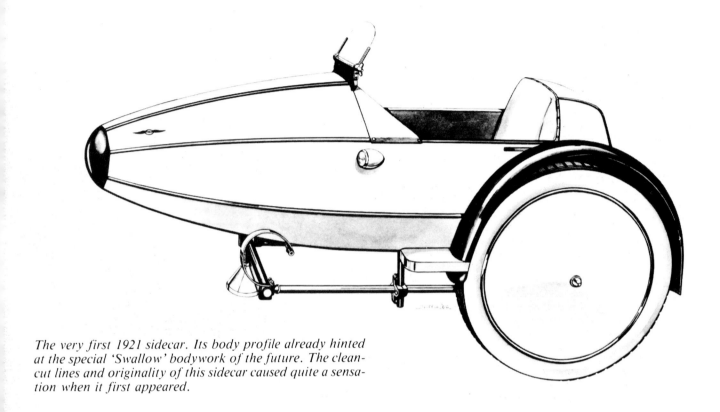

The very first 1921 sidecar. Its body profile already hinted at the special 'Swallow' bodywork of the future. The clean-cut lines and originality of this sidecar caused quite a sensation when it first appeared.

Swallow sidecars enjoyed some success in the Isle of Man TTs. This brought the firm to the public's attention and young Lyons soon realised the value of publicity, whether it be in newspaper and magazine articles, through sporting events, or in the form of personal testimonies, as in his first brochures... all was grist to the mill of the Swallow Sidecar Company.

In 1926 Bill Walmsley's father bought some industrial premises on the corner of Cocker Street and Exchange Street — still in Blackpool, of course. The two young businessmen gratefully took on the lease, since they would now have more space to meet the evergrowing demand.

However great the success of their elegant, comfortable and weatherproof sidecars, it was not long before Lyons and Walmsley began to set their sights higher. They were to make their way into the world of car production through the tradesmen's entrance.

For some time the Swallow Company had been dealing in coachpainting, trimming and hood manufacture. As they examined, stripped, repainted and trimmed cars, with requests from the customers for 'that little extra something to make the car special', Lyons and Walmsley came to the conclusion that it would not be a bad idea if they were to build complete bodies, using other manufacturers' chassis as a base.

William Lyons thought that the average production car was singularly uninspiring, and he was hooked on the idea of putting a new body on the popular Austin Seven chassis, thereby transforming it into an open two-seater sports car.

The long and the short of it was that he took delivery of the first chassis in January 1927 and that the first Austin-Swallow was seen by the public in May of the same year.

But let us put flesh on the bare bones of the story. Just after his marriage on September 15 1924, Lyons had bought a second-hand Austin Seven which was barely two years old. As soon as he sat behind the wheel he began to think about the hundred and one ways in which he could improve the car.

The innovative sports car sold like hot cakes; the public took this loveable, original little car to its heart, and for a year the factory buzzed like a beehive with the men's efforts to keep pace with the demand.

Then, one fine day, Herbert ('Bertie') Henly, the most important car distributor in Britain, took a look at the precocious pair's product and, on the spur of the moment, placed an order for 500 Austin Swallows — half of them open two-seaters and the rest saloons! It was no joke: Henly was in deadly earnest. The two associates looked at each other in mute astonishment, as though Henly had

The 1928-32 747 cc Austin Seven Swallow saloon: the start of it all. By comparing a Swallow body with the original ex-works design, you could tell that the new company was on the right road.

asked a saucepan manufacturer to produce a core for a nuclear reactor. Lyons at last broke the silence, saying, 'Well, I'm game. How about you?'

Bill Walmsley, shaking with terror, replied, 'You must be mad!'

He had a point, for it was a crazy thing to do, to accept such a mammoth order when you were only a midget in the giant industrial world. But Lyons' instinct told him that the time had come to start thinking big, both financially and technologically, no matter how many sleepless nights such a step would entail.

The Blackpool stationmaster's face was a picture when he saw a trainload of Austin chassis pulling in, addressed to that small-time coachbuilding factory. At first he must have thought that someone was pulling his leg, but he realised that this was no joke when Lyons turned up to discuss the possibility of unloading the chassis as and when the workmen needed them. Since there was no room for storage at the Swallow factory, this was the only solution short of piling the chassis up in the road! For some weeks, therefore, the small Blackpool railway station was transformed into an annexe of the Swallow company.

*Even the Swift marque was given the Swallow treatment.
The result is shown here, together with Andrew Whyte
who, at the time of the photograph (1972), was chief of
public relations at Jaguar. Andrew Whyte, Paul Skilleter
and Chris Harvey are the marque's greatest historians.*

Space was now the overriding problem and so it was that,
in November, the Swallow Sidecar and Coachbuilding
Company made another move. In the Blackpool workshops
they had been able to turn out only fourteen cars a week . . .
and a little mental arithmetic will tell you how long it would
have taken them to fill Henly's order at that rate!

So the company moved lock, stock and barrel to Coventry, where Bill Lyons took on upwards of a thousand men.
The assembling of Austin- and Morris-Swallows continued
apace in the new headquarters. The 'Swallowing' mania
spread to Fiats with Fiat-Swallows, and then reached epic
proportions with Swift-Swallows, Wolseley-Swallows and
Standard-Swallows following in quick succession.

With the advent of the Standard-Swallow there was a lull
in the introduction of new designs. Relations between
Swallow and Standard's managing director, Captain (later
Sir) John Black, were to be very close; so close, in fact, that
in 1930 the longstanding, respected Coventry firm agreed to
produce a special chassis for Swallow, built to the exact
specification which Lyons had just laid on the MD's desk.

'What's this new car to be called, then?' asked Captain
Black.

William Lyons fixed Black with his steel-blue eyes and
replied, 'The Swallow-Sport, of course!'

'Stuff and nonsense!' retorted Black. 'It'll be the
Standard-Special!'

Happily, whatever the outcome of this discussion, the
initials were identical — 'SS' — and an unspoken agreement settled the problem to the satisfaction of both parties.
So the 'SS' it was, although Lyons never shed any light on
what the two initials stood for; those who are so inclined
can therefore put forward their versions and argue the toss
until they are blue in the face, without fear of contradiction.

The first SS — later referred to, naturally enough, as the
SS1 — was to be revealed to the world with due pomp and
ceremony at the jubilee-period 1931 motor show at
Olympia. Press and public were so impressed by the new car

*The manufacturer's name was often shown underneath the
car (centre) and on the rear wings (bottom). The model
name was there for all to see. On the Austin Swallow (top)
it was plumb in the centre of the radiator grille.*

The giant industrial Jaguar complex covers thousands of acres. This birds-eye view of the Browns Lane factory in the Coventry suburbs was taken in 1970.

The Jaguar works is a quarter of a mile along on the right.

The cockpit of an SS1 Tourer. It is an impressive sight, and the instrumentation was remarkably comprehensive for the period.

The 6-cylinder side-valve Standard engine was soon given a new lease of life so that it could match up to William Lyons' ambitions. This large unit was fitted with just one RAG carburettor.

The SS1 coupé, with its imitation-leather top and dummy hood irons looks as elegant today as it did on its first appearance.

A 1934 SS1 fixed-head coupé. This was, in effect, the very first 'Jaguar' and had some features which were to become the marque's trademarks.

Anything the Jaguar factory produces has to come through these gates.

The administration block at Browns Lane. It was behind the third window from the left on the first floor that, for decades, William Lyons ruled over his industrial empire.

that for a long time it bore the nickname 'Olympia'. The magnificent SS1 captured the romance of motoring: it was low, elegant and seemingly built for speed. The bonnet seemed to go on for ever, and all the classic ingredients were there. William Lyons' masterstroke made the headlines and the recipe — if there ever was one — was to be applied to every new model for decades afterwards: advanced styling, a super-luxury finish, and a very modest price-ticket for such a magnificent vehicle.

Lyons always insisted on this last point, saying that one should always make the customer feel that he is getting value for money. The SS1 might, in today's terms, be thought of as a 'flash' car, with the feeling of speed created by its low lines and interminable bonnet.

The press acclaimed this newcomer to the motoring scene. The *Daily Express* screamed: '"Dream" car unveiled — a £1,000 look for only £310!'

The company's own advertising emphasised the unique nature of the SS; witness this extract from a full-page advertisement in the July 1931 edition of *Autocar*:

'Wait: The SS is coming!

'S.S. is the new name of a new car that is going to thrill the hearts of the motoring public and the trade alike. It's something utterly new... different... better! Long... low... very low... and very FAST!'

There is no doubt that the 'value for money' aspect helped to make the SS series an overwhelming success for, by 1939, there were no less than 20,000 SS of all types on the roads of Britain. Full marks to our adventurous duo!

All this was in the future. First, there was the SS2, a shorter and more conventional version based on the Standard Nine, which was to gain itself a large slice of the sales cake at the lower end of the market.

The success of the SS phenomenon was no flash in the pan; SS Cars Limited became a subsidiary of the Swallow Coachbuilding Company and, in 1933, Lyons called a halt to the production of Swallow cars, for these 'hybrids', although profitable, were a distraction from the real business of SS production.

In 1934 William Walmsley handed over control and sold his shares in the company to Lyons, who was now in sole charge.

January 1935: the year started well, for the company went public when their shares were floated on the stock exchange. The Swallow Coachbuilding Company was now a subsidiary of SS Cars Ltd, reflecting the change in emphasis. 1935 was to continue as an eventful year in the company's history. One of the landmarks was to be the arrival of one William Heynes; a brilliant young engineer who brought with him exciting, innovative ideas, of which more later...

The world-record-breaking driver John Cobb provided a testimonial which praised the merits of the SS1. The Airline had a short production life, despite its stylish good looks. (A 1935 advertisement which the Jaguar distributors, Henlys, inserted in The Motor.)

The radiator shell and headlights made a harmonious unit. This front view of an SS1 highlights the elegance of the Coventry cars.

The SS Generation

SS 90

MAY—SEPTEMBER 1935

SS 100

MARCH 1936—NOVEMBER 1941

THE CREATION OF AN ARCHETYPE

"One day in 1935, I got a telephone call from a fairly new but lively company which had opened up not far from the Triumph works in Foleshill, Coventry. They were working on a new range of cars for '36, but the lack of power was giving them some headaches. The unit in question was the Standard side-valver which was barely producing 70 bhp, despite its 2½ litres-plus capacity.''

These are the reminiscences of Harry Weslake, an outstanding consultant engineer who already had the reputation of being able to pull extra horsepower out of thin air. Among his scalps were the Coventry-Climax engines fitted to the Southern Cross and Gloria Triumphs, and collaboration with the great W.O.Bentley on the Lagonda AJS, not to mention the Sunbeam.

Harry Weslake was always to work with, rather than for, Jaguar: they were to ask his advice on many other occasions and, looking into the future, he was to be in with Heynes, Hassan and Baily on the creation of the world-famous XK engine. His name would become synonymous with hemispherical combustion chambers, the wide-angle cylinder head and the straight-port head of the XK 150S.

That historic telephone call came from none other than William Lyons, and the company in question was, of course, SS Cars Ltd.

Harry Weslake continues: "I had just had the devil of a row with Cecil Kimber of M.G. and I was wondering how best to put the spanner in the Abingdon works... As the new SS saloons seemed perfectly capable of standing up to M.G.'s SA range, Lyons' invitation was a splendid opportunity for getting my own back.

"The most obvious way of pepping up the Standard block was by simply shoving the valves upstairs..."

And so began a remarkable motoring story.

SS Cars Ltd had gone public in October 1934, like any other worthy, respectable concern, which was the direct result of a lot of hard work and remarkable determination.

William Lyons knew what he wanted: that his cars should be the talk of the automobile world so that sales would rocket. The solution sounds simple, but it was easier in theory than in practice. He set out to make non-standard cars for the same price as production cars and, if possible, a little more cheaply; to win races, thereby gaining valuable publicity; and to be technologically streets ahead of the opposition!

By 1934 the factory was already pushing out 1,500 cars a year but, so far, the models' only two selling points had been their low price and their attractive styling. However, Lyons' first real sensation was around the corner: the SS 90.

Earls Court, in March 1935, saw the launching of this new SS baby, alongside the famous drophead coupé version of the SS 1. One of the pair was to earn itself a place in

This very rare 1935 SS1 drophead coupé (only 100 were built) with its foldaway hood, shared many features with the model which was to appear only a few weeks later: the SS1 90.

The SS1 90, commonly called the SS90 because of its top speed potential, first appeared in 1935. The rear of the car had duck-tail styling which housed the spare wheel. The SS90 was a typical 1930s and '40s open two-seater with its miniscule passenger accommodation and extended bonnet.

Jaguar history through its effect on the marque's development and image; the other was favourably received, but it was to be eclipsed by the new infant prodigy.

As you have probably guessed, the shining star on the SS stand was the '90'. It was so successful that they soon had to give it extra horsepower to satisfy the speed merchants among their customers.

As it turned out only 23 were produced and, exactly ten months later, the SS 100 came out, of which, in its 2½-and 3½-litre versions, 308 were made. Not bad as a total, when you realise that its production life spanned only from March 1936 to November 1941, with two years deducted for the war.

The SS 90 was really just a patchwork job, using a shortened SS 1 chassis; the frame was ash clothed with aluminium panels. Nevertheless, the result was a minor miracle of balance, breeding and raciness: superbly designed long wings embraced a seemingly infinite bonnet which gave the optical illusion of being lower than the wings themselves. It had a very stylish and aggressive radiator surround which, combined with two enormous QBD.66.5 (or P85) Lucas headlights, made the SS 90 look even more like a wild beast ready to pounce on its prey.

The severely cut-away doors, in pure vintage style, came down to the level of the rear wheels and gave an instant indication of the sporting nature of the new car.

The prototype featured a duck's-tail back with the spare wheel set at an angle of 45 degrees in a recess in the tail.

When the car went into production the petrol tank was moved into a vertical position with the spare wheel mounted vertically on it.

Apart from the body itself and the shortening of the chassis by removing a section towards the rear, most of the SS 1's features were retained in the SS 90 including, among others, the track, suspension and steering.

It was an archetypal sports car with the components given most space and the passengers having to squeeze in as best they could. One of its main objectives was to provide a guaranteed 90 mph (144 km/h) so that potential customers knew that, if they wanted speed, SS Cars Ltd was the company to approach.

To help them reach this top speed, SS Cars took on a young engineer who was to prove to be the Coventry firm's *deus ex machina* — William M. Heynes. Together with Harry Weslake he was to transform the rather sluggish Standard 20 engine by ridding it of its most basic defect: its side valves. But, before reaching the final solution, they exploited the unit to the full in its side-valve configuration, with a new cylinder head and camshaft which gave better gas-flow at high speeds, an increased fuel supply, and a stronger crankshaft with a greatly improved dynamic balance. All these measures yielded the princely bonus of an extra 15 bhp from the revered, but lazy, Standard block and they were now within range of the necessary 90 bhp.

So the new car now had its innards, in the shape of the gingered-up power unit, and William Lyons, who was blessed with an innate understanding of style, fashions and aesthetics, could begin to fashion the body. It was to be an open two-seater and its real name was the SS1 90. Although its production life was fated to be short, the SS 90 would live on in the future models it inspired, for one cannot forget one of the most handsome sports cars of all time that easily!

As often happens in such cases, the manufacturers had been a little over-optimistic about the new car's potential, and it was soon obvious that there was no point in trying to reach the magic figure of 90 which was displayed proudly on a lozenge in the centre of the headlight tie-bar. True, some drivers came close to it, but the speedometer needle stayed tantalisingly short of the mark. Even if it had been possible it is unlikely that many motorists would have been so rash as to attempt it for, although the bodywork was superbly designed, the basic structure might not have been sound enough to take the stress.

Be that as it may, the SS 90 caused a sensation when it appeared in public in May 1935. The production model was even more impressive than the prototype, thanks to the redesigned rear with the vertical 14-gallon (70-litre) tank plus spare wheel.

So many features contributed to its charisma: the folding windscreen; the instrument board; the overall interior finish; the huge 18-inch diameter spoked Rudge wheels; the handsome, long, louvred bonnet; the low silhouette; the cat-like grace of it all...

Just one glance told you that this car had class. It was fortunate that the exterior had such an impact since once the bonnet was raised you heaved a great sigh on recognising the antiquated, dyspeptic, side-valve Standard 20 engine. It had been given a face-lift, granted, but there it was still, and, inexorably, on its side!

To put this in perspective, there are three main engine configurations: side valves; overhead valves actuated by a side camshaft; and overhead valves and overhead camshaft, with or without rockers.

The first of these stands for a simple but archaic system, with L- or T-shaped combustion chambers and inefficient gas flow. The second gives a pretty good volumetric efficiency, but engine speed is limited due to the inertia of the moving parts, notably the long push-rods. The third option is synonymous with class, high performance and prestige, especially if there are two camshafts, rather than just one.

There is good reason for this little explanation, since the Jaguar marque was to progress through three stages of evolution: side valves until 1935, overhead valves until 1945 and twin overhead camshafts thereafter.

So the SS 90 represents the last part of the first stage in Jaguar engine development for, by the end of that 1935 summer, the Heynes-Weslake pairing, later to be joined by Walter Hassan, had finally had enough of seeing the antiquated Standard block lurking under the bonnet of such a handsome sports car.

The scene was set for the second act in the technological revolution at SS Cars Ltd. The era of overhead valves and rockers in the cylinder head had at last arrived.

Between May and September 1935 — in those days paid holidays were still just a dream — 23 cars were produced, giving an average of about five per month.

The SS 90 may not be the best-remembered car among connoisseurs of old cars, but its successor has left a much greater mark: the SS 100.

But before the SS 100 appeared there was a transitional period from September 1935 to March 1936, during which the SS sports assembly line had a short doze. The reason for this was that, rather than put the new overhead engine into the SS 90 body, William Lyons preferred to provide a new engine and new coachwork to maximise the impact.

This six-month hibernation paid off handsomely for, like the phoenix rising from its ashes, an open two-seater emerged into the daylight in the spring of 1936, only this time the name was SS 100. And this time it was a sports car through and through; you only had to take a short drive in one to convince yourself of the fact.

The Standard 20 still served as a base for the new power unit, but a completely new cylinder head had transformed it almost beyond recognition: the Weslake-designed head with overhead valves.

Let's start with some statistics. It was a 2,663 cc 6-cylinder engine with a 73 mm bore and 106 mm stroke producing 104 bhp; the firing order was the (later invariable) 1, 5, 3, 6, 2, 4.

Two 1¾-inch SU carburettors supplied the head on the left side. There was a manual choke which acted mechanically on the carburettor main jet to give a richer mixture. From 1937 onwards this choke was an electro-magnetically controlled system, working on the obscure principle of an auxiliary mini-carburettor in which a valve is opened by a solenoid with a plunger controlled by a thermostat which measures the water temperature in the induction tube.

Two electric fuel pumps were mounted horizontally on the engine bulkhead.

I have already mentioned the classic firing order of the

Cutaway view of the SS90. You can see that the valves were still mounted on the side of the engine, but not for long. The mechanical arrangement hints at the layout for the SS 100 which was announced shortly afterwards.

pistons, and the sparks were supplied by the equally classic Joseph Lucas concern, with a distributor and high-tension coil supplying the spark for combustion via the 14 mm plugs. A manually controlled advance and retard was still offered to customers.

The chassis was largely the same as the SS 90's with an identical track and wheelbase, but there were significant improvements in the suspension and braking systems.

The brakes were efficient and resilient, thanks to large-diameter Millenite drums, and fins which gave better heat dispersal. Careful rod adjustment was needed, however, to get the full benefit of this efficiency.

The original SS 1 had been fitted with a Bendix cable system, and the substitution of the Girling rod-operated mechanism was a welcome event. These Girling brakes, provided that they have been meticulously adjusted, can still surprise the modern driver with their reliability.

The use of wire wheels was another aid to cooling and, for those who like to know every detail, the brake linings were Ferodo BZs.

The SS 90 had used Marles-Weller steering — infamous for its woolliness and stiffness — but, happily, the SS 100 was given a worm and nut Burman-Douglas Box, in common with other British cars of the period.

Front and rear suspension was by perfectly conventional semi-elliptical springs, but a less conventional introduction was the mix of Luvax hydraulic shock-absorbers at the rear and Hartford friction absorbers on the front. The two

Luvax units more or less damped the spring movements... less rather than more, according to many who have had experience of them!

The splined hubs were supplied by Dunlop rather than Rudge and one could choose between 550 x 18 or 525 x 18 tyres. There were 60 spokes on each wheel, in case you have never counted them.

There were other detail differences between the 90 and the 100: the 100's radiator shell was slightly more impressive, and the chrome-plated grille which protected the radiator proper was now set back under the edge of the shell. The lights were large QK596s from Lucas; this is an important detail for keen restorers since, all too often, you can see SS 100s fitted with monstrous P100s which were never intended for this model. The explanation for this aberration is that the P100s have been pirated from SS saloons!

The larger surface area of these lamps does not improve lighting anyway, despite their sensational appearance.

The design of the rear part of the front wings was slightly more rounded than on the SS 90. A red badge with the chrome legend '100' was mounted in the centre of the headlamp tie-bar.

Bear with me for one last detail. A winged motif bearing the initials 'SS' stood proudly on top of the radiator shell, whereas the 90 bore no such identification mark.

The instrumentation on the dash was pretty comprehensive for its time: petrol gauge; water temperature gauge; ammeter; oil-pressure gauge; clock; speedometer; ignition warning light; trafficator warning light; key-operated ignition switch; screen wiper knob; lamp switch; panel light switch; cigar lighter; fog-light switch; reserve fuel tank tap; manual retard and advance control; horn on the steering-wheel boss and adjustable steering wheel. Not bad, was it?

The bucket seats were covered in leather, as were the doors, and the luggage space was luxuriously carpeted. The high-quality fabric hood was easy to erect but it was better left down, for an SS 100 with the hood up is an incongruous and rather unpleasant sight. In contrast, when the hood is tucked tidily away in its cover, the SS 100 is the eighth wonder of the world.

Judged to perfection. This splendid body was to be the epitome of British sports car design for years to come. The SS 100 was launched in 1937 and became a favourite all over the world.
Note the two plaques to the right of the wooden front doors; one bears the legend 'Swallow Coachbuilding Company' and the other 'SS Cars Ltd Registered Office'.

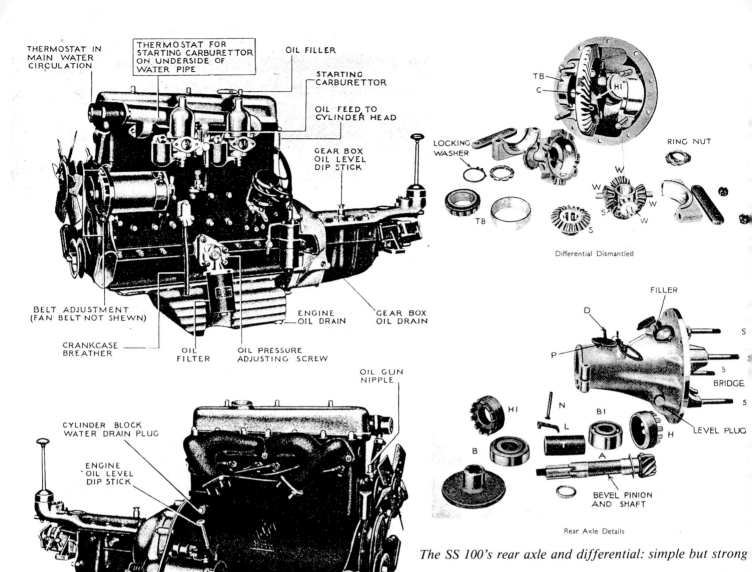

THERMOSTAT IN MAIN WATER CIRCULATION

THERMOSTAT FOR STARTING CARBURETTOR ON UNDERSIDE OF WATER PIPE

OIL FILLER

STARTING CARBURETTOR

OIL FEED TO CYLINDER HEAD

GEAR BOX OIL LEVEL DIP STICK

BELT ADJUSTMENT (FAN BELT NOT SHEWN)

CRANKCASE BREATHER

OIL FILTER

OIL PRESSURE ADJUSTING SCREW

ENGINE OIL DRAIN

GEAR BOX OIL DRAIN

LOCKING WASHER

TB

C

HI

TB

W

W

W

S

W

S

RING NUT

Differential Dismantled

FILLER

D

P

N

L

B

HI

B1

A

H

S

S

BRIDGE

S

LEVEL PLUG

BEVEL PINION AND SHAFT

Rear Axle Details

The SS 100's rear axle and differential: simple but strong

OIL GUN NIPPLE

CYLINDER BLOCK WATER DRAIN PLUG

ENGINE OIL LEVEL DIP STICK

The main difference between the engines in the SS 90 and the SS 100 was the decisive change to an overhead-valve design. This move gave the old Standard unit the extra power it needed to push the SS 100 along at its title speed. It was a minor engineering miracle, made possible by Harry Weslake's new cylinder head (above).

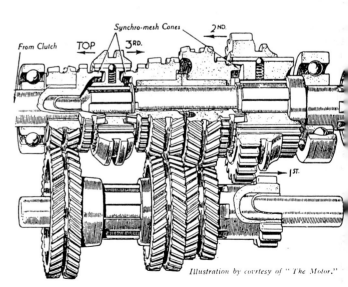

Synchro-mesh Cones

2ND.

From Clutch

TOP

3RD.

1 ST.

Illustration by courtesy of " The Motor."

The almost prehistoric gearbox. It was unsynchronised noisy, tough and slow, but it could take a lot of punish ment.

The car was constructed in a classic, not to say conservative, fashion. Two massive side-members were joined by cross-members to form the chassis; the ash frame was built directly on this base by a very skilled team of carpenters; and, finally, the skeleton was covered with aluminium panels which were shaped by hand, then pinned to the ash frame.

The only pressed sections were the bonnet panels, in which the louvres were pressed out individually, and the rear wings.

William Lyons called on the services of a sub-contractor who specialised in aluminium pressings: Cooke and Sons of Nottingham.

According to a British expert in such matters, it seems that the wooden jigs are still stored at the Cooke factory so that, if you ever need a set of SS 100 wings, you have only to ask!

Back to the engine — that Standard 20 block whose valves had been shifted overhead. It was now a cohesive whole, though some traces of its sideways existence still remained in the casting from which the block was produced. The bottom end of the engine was the bedrock on which the structure depended, and a robust, seven-main-bearing crankshaft in forged steel ensured durability. The connecting rods and pistons were made from aluminium to make the power unit that much lighter.

The engine was co-operative, flexible and long-lasting, and its theoretical output led to hopes that 100 mph would soon be a realistic objective although, as things were, short of a great deal of arduous preparation, this figure was not yet in SS sights. The figures show that the SS 100, in its 2½-litre version, just managed to overtake the title figure of its predecessor with 92 mph (147 km/h).

We shall have to wait for Tommy Wisdom and his hyper-prepared 115 bhp SS 100, which achieved 104.4 mph (167.04 km/h) in October 1938 with the windscreen lowered and the chassis drilled as full of holes an an Emmental cheese.

But, when the SS 100 appeared, sordid details such as top speeds were of little importance compared with the appearance and overall performance of the car. It was a beautiful, intoxicating motor with some powerful acceleration up its sleeve. The SS 100 more than measured up to the contemporary opposition: Rileys, Aston Martins, M.G.s, Bentleys, or A.Cs. Its French rivals were Talbots, in Germany there was the Mercedes SSK, and in Italy the Alfa Zagato 1750.

September 1937 was a key month, first because the SS range was boosted by the arrival of the new magnificent saloons, and secondly because the works announced the long-awaited appearance of the new 3½-litre engine.

At last the SS 100's heart was to be a match for its exterior, and about time too!

Although it had been described as a new engine, the only true novelty lay in the 3½-litre displacement. There was no question but that this unit was in direct line of descent from the old Standard block; some people even said, rather unkindly, that SS Cars Ltd were past masters at using up left-overs.

True though this may be, it was a management technique which paid dividends for the burgeoning company.

This 'new' 3½-litre engine had an exact capacity of 3,485 cc, produced with a bore of 82 mm and a stroke of 110 mm.

But, just a minute! If you compare these figures with the 73 x 106 of the 2½-litre, you can see that both figures have changed. The diameter of the pistons has been increased by 9 mm, which is standard practice when you want to boost an engine's displacement, but if the stroke has been increased by 4 mm, this means that the crankshaft must have been changed. And that *is* a significant fact, even if a potential customer didn't notice it at first glance. The new crankshaft turned out to be even heavier, better designed, fitted with a forward damper to absorb torsional vibration — and the balance of its seven main bearings had been improved. This, indeed, was the really new aspect of the 3½-litre engine.

Aluminium had been scrapped for the connecting rods, to be replaced by steel — a wise choice for several reasons, including durability.

The faithful Weslake cast-iron cylinder head was again in evidence, with its rocker-operated overhead valves. As for the exhaust manifold, it was now split into two distinct groups of three cylinders each. They had done themselves proud.

The giant dial on the test bench indicated 125 bhp or, in other words, 25 more with an increase of 800 cc at a maximum engine speed of 4,500 rpm and with a compression ratio of 7.2:1.

All they had to do now was to drop this new 3½-litre into the SS 100 chassis and discover whether it could at last live up to its name. The two motoring giants of journalism, The Autocar and The Motor, turned out to put the new combination through its paces and, in so doing, to ask it some very searching questions.

The road tests were conclusive: SS could at last lay claim to 100 mph! A little over 101 mph (161.6 km/h) in fact, and this result confirmed beyond all doubt that the SS was now a member of the élite group of cars which could break that magic psychological 100 barrier. For a car costing between £395 and £445, it was little short of a miracle.

Even more amazing than its top speed was its acceleration: 0-60 mph in 10.4 seconds.

Nevertheless, The Autocar had one reservation. The test driver could only break the 100 barrier with the windscreen lowered and, if it was up (even with the hood down), on the best runs he could only manage 97 mph (155 km/h). Some people are never happy!

The test driver from The Motor, on the other hand, had no trouble in reaching 101 mph (162 km/h) with the windscreen in a position to screen him from the wind! One should not draw any hasty conclusions from these results except, perhaps, for the fact that weather conditions play a very important part in testing a car which has no true aerodynamic styling.

With the aim of making best use of the extra power and the new torque, two new final drive ratios were offered on the 3½-litre model: 4.25:1 and 3.8:1; the 2½-litre version stuck with 4.5:1 and 4:1.

Leaving aside a speedometer graduated to 120 mph (190 km/h), a new flywheel, clutch and differential housing, there were no other major differences between the 3½- and 2½-litre versions of the SS 100. The 3½ did not, in fact, replace the 2½, for the two were produced concurrently, with the 2½ gaining a few valuable extra bhp thanks to the dual exhaust from the 3½.

SS 100 production began to slow down once the Second World War got under way, and in 1941 production was stopped completely. The 2½-litre ground to a halt first in March 1941, after 190 had been built. As to the SS 100 3½-litre, 118 were assembled in all, which may seem a paltry sum for a car which left such a mark on automobile history, but in those days many other sports cars were produced in even smaller runs, and this has never stopped them becoming legends! When all is said and done, 308 SS 100s is quite a respectable total.

When the works came up for air at the end of the war, it decided not to give the SS 100 an artificial new lease of life. The model's inclusion in catalogues had no source other than the advertising department's optimism and the firm's desire to offer a full range of options for the motorist.

The initials 'SS' had sinister connotations after the war anyway, and they had already been substituted with the name 'Jaguar' on its own, right across the range.

Competition successes enhanced the reputation of the SS 100, and it was thanks to this model that Coventry acquired a sporting image. International rallies, hill climbs, track records and circuit racing over three or four years proved sufficient to link the Jaguar name with motor racing success.

As early as 1936, Tommy Wisdom and Sammy Newsome took a 2½-litre '100' to the model's first major victory by winning a Coupe des Alpes in the International Alpine Trial, ahead of some top-flight drivers and makes with established reputations in competition motoring. They also won the event overall. This astonishing performance, together with the car's good looks, was to have commercial and advertising spin-offs from which the whole Jaguar range benefited. Tommy Wisdom described the SS 100 as being 'too good to be true; it looked like the sort of dream car which a very talented art student might sketch.'

As far as competition was concerned, William Lyons was very cautious at first about having his name linked with sporting events in which victory was not guaranteed. It took several wins to convince him that giving his sanction to works involvement was not such a bad idea.

When he eventually came round to the idea it was more as a result of pressure put on him by those around him than through inner conviction. And even then, at the beginning, he could only bring himself to countenance the possibility of taking part in local endurance events of the trial or rally variety — circuit racing was out.

Newsome's first victory in the Alpine Rally (driving what was to become the most famous SS 100 of all time) played a decisive part in settling Jaguar's destiny as a sporting marque. This 2½-litre had chassis number 18008 and earned the affectionate nickname of 'Old Number 8', in recognition of the fact that it was the eighth of the model to be produced.

This historic car is now, along with three other '100's, the property of Dr Philippe Renault, honorary president of the French Jaguar Drivers' Club and probably the greatest Jaguar collector in the world.

'Number 7' experienced its own hour of glory at the Rheims Grand Prix in July 1936, in the capable hands of the Australian driver McEvoy, competing in the 2-3-litre class.

Competition successes came thick and fast in 1937. The year began with the world-famous RAC Rally in which Tommy Wisdom and Bill Rankin, Jaguar's publicity chief, came second behind another SS 100 entered privately by Jack Harrop.

July saw the Welsh Rally, with E.Jacob taking top honours in a '100'. In September it was Newsome's turn at Shelsley Walsh, the oldest and most famous hill-climb course in England, but this time 'Old Number 8' had been fitted with a 3½-litre engine.

Many experiments were carried out on SS 100s during their lifespan, with varying degrees of expertise... everyone seemed to want to have a go at giving them that extra bit of muscle which would enable them to overtake Bugattis, Talbots, or BMW 'Mille Miglia' 328s, to name but a few.

'Number 8' was subjected to one of the most ambitious modifications of the 3½-litre overhead block. The first stage was to produce some very exclusive pistons, which were extremely light and produced a compression ratio of 13.9:1 — no mean feat in itself! The next item on the agenda was a bronze-coated cylinder head, which could make a better job of coping with the intense heat produced through the use of a special fuel mixture based on methanol. Then came a high-performance Scintilla magneto instead of the 33-pound (15-kg) battery. Now the real weight-saving programme started: all non-essential parts were stripped from the body and the chassis was heavily drilled. The wheels were fitted with 525 x 17 racing tyres on the front and 650 x 16 racing on the rear, and in October 1937 it was off to Brooklands, near Weybridge, to see what they would see!

Tommy Wisdom was the man to do the honours, and honours he did. He achieved the astonishing lap-speed of 118 mph (189 km/h), winning the First October Long Handicap by some 12 seconds.

This was by no means the end of Jaguar's experiments with the 3½-litre-engined 'Old Number 8'. The car gradually lost more and more weight, via its wings and spare wheels and other bits and pieces. Eventually it gained the name 'Brooklands' after the circuit on which it had made the Scintilla sparks fly.

It was at about this time that Walter (Wally) Hassan was taken on by SS Cars Ltd, and Tommy Wisdom recalls the hazy, crazy days during which they collaborated with Bill Heynes in working on that exotic engine.

"Hassan was hooked by the bait which Lyons had cast. He went to Coventry where, working with Heynes, he immersed himself in the development of a super-powerful engine. With this end in view, they engineered a special bronze cylinder head which had a compression ratio of at least 17.5:1. The standard coil ignition was replaced by a magneto. They gave the engine a high-lift camshaft and extended the overlap..."

With a compression ratio in the region of 17.5:1, they of course had to use an alcohol-based fuel, but consumption using methanol was rather sobering to say the least — something close to 1 mpg! In those days methanol cost 17 shillings (87½p) per gallon, so it was an expensive exercise.

Obviously, this pepped-up SS 100 was not your everyday runabout. Can you imagine it being driven up your local high street?

This amazing 'Brooklands' SS 100 established many

*'Old number 8'. The most highly tuned and outlandish of
all the race-prepared SS 100s (Crystal Palace, 1938).*

records in its time, of which the most outstanding were a top speed of 140 mph (225 km/h) and a lap average of 125 mph (201 km/h) set at Brooklands.

Not surprisingly, there is no record of how many crankshafts 'Old Number 8' worked its way through!

The winning run continued in 1938, including the RAC Rally in May and the Welsh Rally in July. There were many similar victories or placings in rallies and hill climbs, some of which were prestige events while others were more local affairs.

Numerous further attempts were made to improve 3½-litre SS 100s the length and breadth of the land, such as Truett's 'Number 15' where the chassis was so full of holes that one wondered whether it was possible to climb into the car without it disintegrating.

In those golden days, when nerve and talent were more valuable than money, fanatics were trying their hand left, right and centre. Really crazy recipes for the mixture to use with a 12:1-plus compression ratio went the rounds! The words 'combustion engine' had never been more

appropriate: cylinder heads softened, clutches shredded, gearboxes spewed out teeth and the sturdiest crankshafts collapsed, with oil-soaked entrails littering the circuits. Those were the days!

Marques and teams became locked in bitter rivalry so that, from 1937 to 1940, the duel between BMW 328s and SS 100s dominated the race track.

There is a little anecdote which tells how William Lyons discovered one day that a private team had entered a 2½-litre SS 100 in the RAC classic, the Tourist Trophy, which was to be run at Donington. Knowing that the car had no chance of winning, Lyons opted for refunding the two drivers' entry fees in preference to seeing them damage the marque's image. (The Trophy was won by Gérard in a Delage.) His laconic comment, once the affair was over, was: 'We knew its limitations'.

One of Lyons' most indomitable characteristics is illustrated by this story: his determination to have what he wanted and never to fail.

Having read so much about racing triumphs, you are

The SS 100 was a favourite with rally drivers, too. Three line up for the local paper's photographer at Swansea.

probably burning to know the answer to one particular question: 'What about Le Mans?'

Well, this was another area in which Lyons did not want to make a mistake by being too hasty. He was content to hold his horses, for he knew that the time would come and, when it did, the rest wouldn't know what had hit them.

We can therefore dismiss the rumours about three 3½-litre SS 100s being destined to line up at Sarthe in 1938. 'There was never any question of it!' declared Lyons categorically.

The Second World War came and with it a deathly silence fell on the circuits, and deadly bombs on the towns. Enthusiasts had to wait for 1945 to see the revival of automobile sport and motor car construction.

Gradually, when the war ended, the whirl of motor racing started up again, despite appalling problems with supplies. From short sprints to prestige rallies, there was an inexorable progression towards one of the SS 100's most spectacular successes: the 1947 Coupe des Alpes. From that year this famous name was inextricably linked with that of a driver so that when one thinks of the Alpine Rally one immediately thinks of Ian Appleyard, and at the mention of Ian Appleyard the Alpine Rally springs immediately to mind.

This distinguished son of a Leeds car dealer was to stupefy the rallying world with his virtuosity, daring and verve by finishing third in a car which was almost ten years old. True, it had not seen much action during the war, but it was still ten years since it had emerged from the SS works, which is more than a lifetime for a racing car! First place, on this occasion, was taken by a Type 43 Bugatti which had enjoyed an unadventurous, but penalty-free, run.

It was in the following year that the Jaguar-Appleyard-Alpine epic really began.

William Lyons wanted to give young Appleyard a first-class car, for he knew Ian's father well and was very impressed by the lad's spirit. As it turned out, Lyons entrusted the young man not only with a priceless car but also with his daughter, Patricia. Since the SS 100 was no longer in production by that time, Lyons hit on the ideal solution. For the duration of the war he had kept a brand-new 2½-litre SS 100 in storage at his home, Wappenbury Hall. The car in question bore chassis number 49010 and the famous LNW 100 number-plate. In 1947 Lyons brought it out from its wartime wraps to be fitted with a brand-new hotted-up 3½-litre engine.

He made Ian Appleyard a present of this package, asking one favour in return: that Ian should go out and win to make sure that Jaguar's colours would fly high.

So this was how a pristine SS 100 was not registered until 1947, despite the fact that none of this model had been produced for six years. LNW 100 was just ready in time for the 1948 Alpine, an event which is recorded in automobile history as the one which Appleyard would have won were it not for his kindness. In fact, Appleyard stopped to help the Hiskin-Marsden pairing who had had a very nasty accident in their Sunbeam Talbot, caused by the atrocious weather conditions.

Despite this dramatic incident, Ian Appleyard showed his driving ability, as well as his selflessness, by finishing first in his class.

The next year, after twelve months crammed with all sorts of rallies, LNW 100 was once more lined up for the start of the Alpine, although its place should have been taken by the new XK 120, which had appeared some months before but which was not race-ready in time for the rally.

The long and the short of the 1949 Alpine was that Ian Appleyard would have won had not a fiendish level-crossing barrier thrown his hopes to the winds by remaining stubbornly lowered for some interminable minutes. He came a good second, nevertheless.

Rallies, circuit races and record breaking had done a great deal for the sporting prestige of the Jaguar marque, but the Jaguars' sensational styling must have done even more, for, if you look objectively at the racing results, there are not as many successes as you might expect. England has a very strong tradition of rallies, hill-climbs and trials, many of which draw their spectators from only the local areas. On average there could be slightly more than a hundred such events annually. Bearing this in mind one can more easily understand why the SS 100 managed to build

such a reputation for itself in competition circles, thanks to the proliferation of these local events, where the publication of results was usually restricted to the regional newspaper or, perhaps, only passed on by word of mouth in the pub that night. Such events included the Blackpool Rally, JCC Eastbourne Rally, Lancashire Rally, Morecambe Rally, London Rally, *Daily Mirror* Rally, Silverstone Touring Car Race, Bournemouth Hill-Climb, et al.

Exporting, as such, was virtually non-existent in the pre-war period; the 308 SS 100s and 23 SS 90s were practically all taken up by the domestic market and a few anglophile countries, not all of them in the Commonwealth.

Had anyone in France heard of the SS 100 in 1937? Most people had not, though a few had, and the word had not spread far outside the inner circle of motoring enthusiasts. The odd example was spotted at international rallies, but the car was as foreign to the French as those from Asia or Communist China are to us today.

How many were sold in France during the production years of the SS 100/90? One and one only (a 90)!

Of course, you have to remember that there was no shortage of handsome, sporty cars in France in those days, so there was no reason for the French to buy such models in from abroad when they already had access to Bugattis, Talbots, Salmsons, Delahayes and Delages at home.

A breakdown of the home and export figures for the SS 100 during its production life gives the following result: England 259; South Africa 7; Czechoslovakia 6; Switzerland 5; Belgium 4; Holland 3; Argentina 2; Rumania 2; United States 2; Germany 2; Austria 2; Singapore 2; Java 2; Portugal 2; Australia 2; Palestine 1; France 1; Hong Kong 1; Nyasaland 1; Poland 1.

I am indebted to the Jaguar company historian, Andrew Whyte, for this research.

Analysis of these sales figures reveals some surprises; why so few sold to America and such a relatively large number to a country like Rumania? You had better keep a look out if you are a globetrotter, especially if you are ever in Rumania or Indonesia!

Nowadays, many of these SS 100s are to be found in the United States, and one of the most important American clubs, the Classic Jaguar Association, spent several years compiling a register of the 100s still in existence. This is how the figures work out: United States 121; England 45; Australia 16; Canada 6; France 6; South Africa 5; Switzerland 4; New Zealand 3; Germany 2; Sweden 2.

Each of the following countries is listed as having one example: Holland, Mexico, Argentina, Greece, Denmark, Ireland, Japan, Scotland, Hong Kong.

So, thanks to this Herculean labour, 219 SS 100s have been located and logged throughout the world. If we add to this figure those cars which must have been preserved but which have defied the CJA's attempts to locate them, then the percentage still extant is very impressive indeed.

The problems of restoring an SS 100 are common to the model, whether the car is now in America, Britain, France — or Australia. Almost without exception the most titanic difficulty is posed by the ash frame... it rots. You therefore have to strip down the entire body, bit by bit. The reason for this dire defect is that almost all the cars were originally used in Britain, with its heavy rainfall and salted winter roads. As you know, once moisture gets into wood it

One of the most successful and widely photographed SS 100s, LNW 100 romped home to victory in British and foreign rallies in the capable hands of Ian Appleyard. These wins included the 1947 and '48 Coupe des Alpes.

stays there for a long, long time, especially if air cannot get to it to dry it out. And so the slow, unseen process of rotting begins, with the car's owner probably remaining in blissful ignorance.

Every now and then, of course, you will hear strange squeaks, creaks and grinding noises. The frame moves out of true by a fraction, the doors don't close properly any more, and there are horrendous noises as the car jolts along a bumpy road. Then one day, just like a boneless body, the poor aluminium panels find themselves pinned to thin air because the ash frame underneath is no more than a decayed memory. This is the moment when you ought to start worrying!

This deterioration is inevitable considering the open body of the car into which the rain can stream to its heart's content, even (dare I say it?) with the hood up. You must also remember that aluminium is very susceptible to corrosion and has an understandable aversion to being pinned to soggy wood. Fortunately aluminium will take a lot more punishment of this type than will steel.

Although aluminium has advantages such as light weight, relative resistance to rusting and its malleability for the production of largely hand-made cars, it has the disadvantage of not withstanding cold hammering.

The alloy becomes brittle as it ages, so that knocking it into shape is a very dicey project. This difficulty is exacerbated by the fact that aluminium is not easy to weld and paint does not adhere to it very well.

This brittleness explains why the body panels sometimes develop a network of hairline stress cracks.

Anyone who wants to restore an SS 100 is therefore confronted with an apparently insoluble problem. The body is not that rusty, but what can he do about the small cracks which riddle the surface at the stress points. The wooden structure is probably rather overripe by now, to put it politely, so one has to remove all the pinned panels which, again, probably means replacing the lot.

So, any proper restoration of an SS 100 has to begin with the car being stripped down to the bare chassis. This is followed by reconstruction of the ash frame to within a millimetre of the original and by major surgery on the aluminium — strengthening, welding and replacing it where necessary.

If you are going to do the job properly, you then have to rebuild the engine and chassis and it is scarcely surprising that, for this job, you need the skills of a carpenter, aluminium panel-beater, coachbuilder, upholsterer, trimmer, hood-manufacturer and more, besides those of an expert mechanic!

This adds up to months and maybe years of hard work, not forgetting the inevitable treasure hunt for replacements for missing or broken parts, since the minimum requirement for a proper restoration is that the car should be fitted with an original engine; not one from any old SS saloon or even Mark V, as was often done some twenty years ago when too many amateurs settled for a quick patch-up job.

33

Obviously it would be much quicker and cheaper to buy a saloon and to cannibalise it for the parts you need to make your SS 100 roadworthy.

I am probably stating the obvious, but an SS 100 is only worthy of the name if it is in exactly the same state as the one in which it left the factory. That is to say, it should have all the right accessories, right down to the tool box (with nothing missing), maintenance manual and log book.

The car must also have all the other authentic parts, from the instruments down to the fuel pump, coil or distributor. And that is not all. The paintwork must adhere precisely to the original colour-scheme, and you should know every detail of the car's history: all the owners, any crashes or modifications — and there might have been some competition successes, too. It's not much to ask, is it?

It is particularly in this area that the various owners' clubs play a vital role, for they have the machinery and expertise to delve into a car's history, whether it be by making inquiries at the works, from dealers, or from the many Jaguar collectors and enthusiasts all round the world.

Some cars have such engrossing histories that they could almost make the basis for a novel — 'Old Number 8', for example. And some owners are so passionately bound up in their cars that their stories smack more of romantic fiction than of a factual account of a hunk of machinery!

In France the few catalogued cars are shared between four fortunate people. Dr Philippe Renault comes out top with no less than four SS 90/100s: 18008, the 'Old Number 8' which won the Alpine Rally in 1938; 180012, which had a recorded top speed of 107.5 mph (172 km/h); 390012, from 1937 with a bronze-coated cylinder head; 39021, which was rebuilt with a new chassis in 1951; 49065, a 3½-litre; and a 1935 SS 90, the only one imported into France (chassis No 249479).

Yves Anselin, Philip Vosolov and Guy Martinez each own a 3½-litre SS 100. Martinez' car was rebuilt with such meticulous attention to detail and is now so beautifully authentic that it is rightly considered as one of the most handsome of its kind in France — and perhaps in the world.

These marvellous cars are now so rare that we see them less and less frequently in displays of veteran and vintage cars. This is a great pity, but one can easily understand why when one thinks that the slightest collision would assume the importance of a national catastrophe! This applies to other cars besides the SS 100, of course; it is the sad fate of so many exquisite and very rare cars, which we shall one day be able to see only in museums or private collections, occasionally in major *concours* events, but never again in road rallies.

Speed addicts, however, seem to take incredible risks with even more expensive cars. How can they bring themselves to race their wonderful machines at Croix-en-Termois, Bois-Guyon, Mogaro, Dijon, Zandvoort, or the Nürburgring? The owners have a ready answer; they would much rather take the calculated risk of bringing their cars out to race against experienced drivers than face the unpredictability of Sunday-afternoon pootlers on a three-lane main road!

The SS 100 is an aggressive animal which will not submit to being tamed by any Tom, Dick or Harry. You need to be pretty experienced to discover all its little ways and to appreciate its finer points. If you want to drive it flat out

Restored to its former glory, LNW 100 pays a visit to Paris for a rally organised by the British Jaguar Drivers' Club. In this 1968 photograph you can see F.R.W.England, at that

you will need strong nerves but, once you have recovered from the initial qualms and cold sweats, there is nothing like it on earth.

The car has a tendency to oversteer, but it is genuine and responsive as long as you treat it indulgently. You can steer the car to within an inch on even the tightest bends; the back end has the engaging habit of sliding off line, but this can easily be controlled. This habit is accentuated by the unusual tyre layout — an 18-inch diameter rim by only 4½ inches wide (45.72 cm x 11.43 cm)! They are more like motorbike tyres, and they make it positively foolish to lark about while you are trying to keep the car on line. I won't mention the antediluvian tyre profiles and the ghastly squeals you hear as you are taking a bend, in case it gives you nightmares!

Although such characteristics might seem a trifle alarming, the SS 100 is in no way a dangerous vehicle — on the contrary, it is an honest animal with no nasty surprises to spring on you when you least expect them. This responsiveness is due, to a large extent, to the excellent weight distribution and to the very good brakes, even though they may seem a little timid in modern traffic conditions.

The less reassuring side of the SS 100 is its basic structure, which is not really suited to sporting activity. The chassis, in fact, is of too mixed a composition to be firm

time Jaguar's after-sales manager, and Ch.-J. Delecroix, the French Jaguar distributor.

enough for this open two-seater. Consequently there is a degree of flexibility which sometimes gives you the disconcerting feeling that you have lost control of the car and that it is steering you, rather than the other way round! As the steering itself is not a paragon of precision, you can easily imagine the worrying 'floating' feeling which communicates itself to your wrists at such moments.

The driving position is very 'vintage', which is hardly surprising when you consider the car's birth date. You sit bolt upright with the steering wheel at chest level, elbows back and your right arm outside the car as there is no room for it inside.

The gear lever knob is in exactly the right position, so that your hand finds it unerringly. And, as you look to the front, there, a long way ahead, is the radiator cap.

The most important factor in driving the SS 100 is familiarity. Within a thousand miles or so you will feel perfectly at home and supremely confident. A vital contributor to the pleasure of being at the wheel of this car is the engine with its fabulous power, flexibility and spirit. It growls and roars at you, but always obeys. This savage side is accentuated by the gear ratios and the short axle. One must admit, however, that the gearbox is not that amenable to sudden bursts of acceleration!

If you lower the windscreen and make do with the sym-bolic 'Brooklands' aero-screen for wind protection, at 50 mph (80 km/h) you feel the exhilaration of being out in a storm, the intoxication of the mountain tops: the wind distorts your face; all you can hear is the roaring of the wind mixed with the roaring of the engine; you cling to the steering wheel for dear life; for a few seemingly endless seconds you fly into a kind of heaven, leaving the earth far behind you; you are convinced that everything is dissolving, falling apart, cracking up, that the car is about to spew out its insides and you with it; you are sure that you are airborne but, if you dare to take your eyes off the road for an instant to look at the speedometer, you find that you are only doing 80 mph (128 km/h). Go on, then — put your foot down and watch the needle move round! This is when things start to go sour and you are back on earth with a bang. Before you know it you are stone cold sober and that blissful experience might never have been. To put it bluntly, you start to feel fear in the pit of your stomach and soon come to the conclusion that anybody who has the guts to put his foot down to the floor at 100 mph should be canonised. At any speed above 80 mph you have to hang on like grim death to the reinforced ebonite steering wheel, seemingly your only link with reality and the only way you can exert any influence at all on the wild animal that has you in its thrall.

As soon as you begin to ease off with your right foot, you start to relax and enjoy yourself again, providing, that is, that the road surface is even; otherwise you are in for a long and harrowing tussle with the jolting, twisting, bucking steering wheel.

This type of behaviour is not, of course, the prerogative of the SS 100. Anyone who has ever driven a Lagonda, Alvis, Invicta, Aston Martin or M.G. could tell you that it is commonplace and only to be expected. All the British open sports cars of that era have similar problems which stem from their chassis, the mix of materials used in their construction and the lack of rigidity caused by the open bodies. The SS 100 is nothing out of the ordinary in that respect — it is even a slight improvement on the rest of the bunch. You only have to ask an old-car enthusiast about the Invicta and its tendency to come to grief...

The petrol consumption varies from 23½ to 16½ mpg (12 to 17 litres per 100 km), depending on speed. Despite the current cost of petrol no one would object to purchasing an SS 100 today, even if it only did one mile to the gallon, for how often would one dare to drive the thing, anyway?

Few coachbuilders showed any interest in converting the SS 100, probably because they did not feel that they could improve on the original. It was such a stunning car in the first place that to alter even so much as a handle might have seemed like sacrilege.

However, Sammy H.Newsome, the racing ace, did feel tempted to give two SS 100s a different dress, and asked the New Avon company of Warwick to produce two drophead coupés from his own designs. The first had the chassis number 39109 and the second 39115.

The end results were fairly impressive and there are perfectly understandable reasons for wanting all-weather protection, especially when you are planning to take your wife out for a drive, for example. The most fundamental modifications were to the front wings, where the wheel arches were much more curved, following the shape of the wheels; to the back wings which were fitted with spats, and to the boot which acquired a saloon-like styling. There were proper wind-up windows sunk into the doors, and the tops of the doors came level with the bonnet and boot, giving the car a continuous waistline. A luxurious, fully-lined, watertight hood gave protection worthy of a fixed-head coupé. But the design still retained the original sports flavour through the folding windscreen and the two aero-screens.

Two other conversions of this type were ordered by Emile Frey, to be carried out on chassis number 39092 (from Willy Bernath) and number 39113. These were not such happy conversions as Newsome's, being rather too heavy and streamlined.

In 1945, Vanden Plas did their best with chassis No 49064 in an attempt to give the car a French flavour with faired-in headlights for the Brussels Motor Show, but this version was also a little too heavy and voluminous to have universal appeal.

The most important and the most successful conversion was carried out by Jaguar itself, not by an independent coachbuilder, and it produced the famous SS 100 fixed-head coupé, based on chassis number 39088. The prototype was built specially for the 1938 Earls Court Motor Show.

This astonishing design foreshadowed what was to come ten years later. Its first owner was Gordon March, followed by a ten-year spell in the United States, a return to England where it became the jewel of Robert Danny's collection, then back across the Atlantic once again into David Barber's ownership.

If you look at a side-view of this SS 100 coupé, you cannot help but see something of the style and personality of the magical model which was to succeed it: the XK 120. All the ingredients were there to a greater or lesser extent — a smaller and more rounded cockpit, flowing curves at the back, the proportions of the wings.

This prototype was never put into production because of the war, which broke out soon after. When peace returned, the XK 120 project erased all memories of this brilliant design, which can clearly be seen as the missing link between the SS and XK generations.

It played the part of the link in the chain of Jaguar sports cars for a long, long time, for it was not until 1948 that great sports cars would again be turned out by the Coventry works... seven long years during which one might have started to think that Jaguar had lost all interest in sports cars. But anyone who thought that was very much mistaken!

After having read the impressions of driving an SS 100 which appeared earlier in this chapter, you may enjoy the detailed road-test report which *The Autocar* published in the issue dated 9 September 1938, and which is reprinted below in full.

"In the 3½-litre 100 model open two-seater, SS Cars Ltd. have certainly produced a machine to covet, and a star performer, particularly in acceleration. This is all the more remarkable at a price well below £500. Not least, it is of satisfying appearance. It is not intended as a racing car, or to be developed into one, and it exhibits much of the docility of an ordinary type of car.

"During an unusually extensive test that extended to 1,400 miles — the bulk of which was covered in three days

A driver's view of the SS 100. Everything was designed to make him feel part of the car and the sports experience.

— this car displayed its versatility in conditions as diverse as the traffic of London and of provincial cities, some of the best main-road stretches in England and Scotland, tracks such as the average tourist avoids, and finally on Brooklands for the testing of performance.

"It can be driven quietly and not attract undue attention, and it is not a machine that calls for any trick methods of control. A driver who uses the indirect gears will obviously obtain the most from it, when it is seen that third can give over 80 mph and second over 50 mph, but it is surprisingly flexible in top gear.

"About 10 mph is possible, though anyone who appreciates a car of this type is likely to engage second gear at so low a speed. Top gear acceleration is strong, even fierce in a controlled fashion, right through the range.

"Third is a wonderful gear. A burst on this ratio for overtaking purposes sends the car shooting forward, and it is up into the 60 to 70 mph range extremely rapidly. In this connection, the acceleration test figures best tell the story. They are a striking set, and some of these results have not been equalled in *The Autocar* tests by what may be termed a normal car.

"The gears are quiet, especially third and second, the use of which is scarcely noticed as regards gear audibility. Also, the gear change is an excellent one. The synchromesh provided on all gears except first gives a virtual certainty of quiet changes, up or down, and the movements of the short and rigid remote-linkage lever are smooth and light. Changes can be made quickly. The lever could with advantage be slightly nearer as regards first and third gear positions.

"Reserve of power is one of this machine's great features, derived from the use of the 3½-litre SS engine in a short-wheelbase chassis as compared with the saloon model. In this country it is obviously not often feasible to let it right out, but if the car is given any chance by traffic conditions the average speed can be outstanding, and so vivid is the acceleration away from obstacles and up even appreciable gradients that adverse conditions do not cause a poor average in the generally recognised sense.

"Up to about 60 mph the engine is scarcely noticed, except for increasing exhaust note during rapid acceleration on the indirect gears. It is then a hard note, but this is little heard at fast cruising rates. There is some slight pinking when pulling away from low speed, controllable by the ignition lever on the steering wheel.

"Beyond about 65 mph the fact of travelling fast is conveyed, not so much by special noise or harshness in the engine — for it is smooth and fairly quiet mechanically — as by the general characteristics of its behaviour. Above that figure the speed may as well be 80 as 70 mph for the difference apparent.

"At increasing speeds as acquaintance is gained with the machine it goes round bends close to the left-hand side, in an exact swing, and the feeling experienced at all times of positive connection between the steering wheel and the front wheels is worth more than even exceptional performance. The steering is high geared, only 2¼ turns of the wheel being needed from lock to lock.

"Possessed of high maximum speed and terrific acceleration as it is, the SS 100 is still a real pleasure for gentle motoring, not only because the engine is docile, but also because the car is under definite control in every way and

This unique SS 100 fixed-head coupé was built specially for the 1938 London Motor Show. It bore an uncanny resemblance to the later XK 120 but this prototype was never put into production due to the Second World War.

the driver has first-class visibility. He is seated comfortably behind a wheel placed at the correct height and angle for confidence.

"The right degree of damping is afforded by the shock absorbers — hydraulic and friction in combination at the front and hydraulic only at the rear. But the riding is decidedly not harsh by sports car standards. Movement of the road wheels caused by surface variations is quickly dealt with, no acute reactions being felt.

"A slightly unusual tribute can be paid to the Girling brake system in that, after the brakes had given the utmost confidence during the long road test, they achieved an altogether exceptional emergency stopping figure from 30 mph. They have great power, but are not fierce or sudden, and want only moderate pedal pressure. Also, these brakes are entirely safe from high speed.

"The hand-brake lever is conveniently placed, and is of normal pattern, not the fly-off ratchet type. It holds securely on a steep hill, and it is interesting that, although first gear is a high ratio, there is sufficient power to spin the rear wheels when restarting on a 1 in 4 gradient.

"No criticism of the driving position can reasonably be made except that more room for the left foot when off the clutch pedal would be appreciated. The seat cushions have coil springs with Dunlopillo overlay. They are not notable for softness, but give firm support, and the curved backrests are also particularly good in this respect.

"Driver and passenger sit well down inside the body, and the driver has a comfortable right arm position. The steering wheel is telescopically adjustable. Rev counter and speedometer are immediately in front of the driver. The speedometer proved to be faintly slow at 30, and almost accurate at 40, 50, 60, 70 and 80, when checked over the measured mile on the racing tyres that were used as a precaution during prolonged testing of the maximum speed of this very fast car.

"The best figure shown of 101.12 mph was taken with the main windscreen lowered, the highest speedometer reading being approximately 102 (4,750 rpm). With the main windscreen up, a quarter-mile was timed at 96.77 mph, the speedometer reading 98.

"Detail work is better than is sometimes the case in this type of car. Concealed screenwipers are fitted, and these do their work well. On the instrument board is a reserve petrol tap; and a reversing lamp works in conjunction with the gear lever.

"Due to the small clearance of the bonnet over the top of the o.h.v. engine, it is necessary to open one side to read the oil level, and the other side to replenish the sump, but the filler is particularly convenient. Automatic mixture control is provided for cold starting. The engine fires at once, and quickly settles down from cold; also it starts at a touch of the switch when warm, and is not at all apt to stall.

"There is good luggage space behind the seats, under the protection of the tonneau cover, which is of that valuable kind capable of being extended over the front compartment. The horn note is exactly right, and the headlamp beam satisfactory, if not superlative in relation to the car's speed. The bonnet strap is not standard equipment. The hood goes up and down quickly, and leaves adequate room when up."

The XK Generation

XK 120

22 OCTOBER 1948 — SEPTEMBER 1954

THE GOLDEN AGE OF THE OPEN TWO—SEATER

'What does that 120 mean, then?' Harold Hastings asked William Lyons on 14 October 1948, exactly two weeks before the opening of the London Motor Show.

'Miles per hour, of course!' replied Lyons, haughtily. I should perhaps explain that Harold Hastings was at that time one half of the famous automobile magazine *The Motor,* and that cars capable of reaching 120 mph were not thick on the ground in a depressed post-war England. The same economic gloom hung over the rest of Europe, with people struggling to make ends meet. Reclamation and cobbling together were more the order of the day and, as British constructors brought old models out of storage, the odour of mothballs filled the air. Now that factories were freed from the strictures of contributing to the war effort, they began to assemble cars as best they could. Toolings were worn-out and the only vehicles rolling off the production line were the result of rushed camouflage jobs, attempting to hide the true age of the models. The most modern one dated from 1938, and just looking at them made you think of warmed up fish and chips! It was the same story right through the alphabet, from A.C., Alvis, Armstrong-Siddeley and Austin, to Wolseley; everyone was having to cope with the same lack of capital investment and shortage of raw materials.

Automobile development had been on the back boiler for years and, after the severe deprivation and suffering of the war, customers could not afford to be too choosy — having four wheels was a blessing in itself.

Export was now the golden word in British industry, and it was 'export or bust'. The main target was the United States of America, the source of invaluable dollars which were the passport to purchasing steel, copper, oil and rubber, and the quickest way to put British business back on the right rails. This preoccupation with exporting was almost an obsession. Lord Attlee, Chancellor of the Exchequer, decided that he would give financial support only to those firms which pledged 50 per cent or more of their production to export. William Lyons therefore put his best foot forward and went to plead Jaguar's case with George Turner, the Under-Secretary of State for Industry. Lyons was nothing if not a superb salesman, and he succeeded in selling Turner a product which had not yet passed the drawing-board stage — impressive stuff! The project he plugged was for a sports car and fast saloon, and he undertook to export 80 per cent of the production to the United States, Australia, South Africa and New Zealand.

He had everything there in black and white: the production schedule was detailed, comprehensive and, more importantly, credible. Lyons had complete and utter faith in the project and this faith communicated itself to everyone else, until they were just as enthusiastic as he was. Only he could have sold a luxury product to a socialist Secretary of State during a depression...

It was during this industrial slump that the general public first became aware of the Jaguar name through a typically dare-devil feat performed by Major Goldie Gardner, a

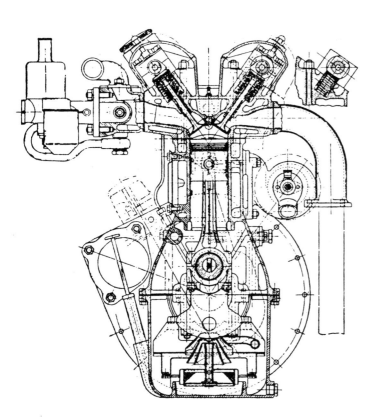

One of the technological links in the XK engine's development; the XK 4-cylinder unit already had twin overhead camshafts (1,360 cc displacement), with a 66.5 mm bore and 98 mm stroke.

Right: The dohc 4-cylinder XK engine which was intended to power the XK 100 — a model which only ever existed in the catalogues. This 2-litre XK unit featured exactly the same arrangement as its 6-cylinder big brother. The factory decided not to offer its customers this under-powered model. Bore: 80.5 mm; stroke 98 mm; capacity 1,995 cc, output 95 bhp at 5,000 rpm. Roland Urban collection.

The BMW 328 engine had a considerable influence on this XG experimental engine, with its overhead valves and hemispherical head . . . but with side camshafts and rockers.

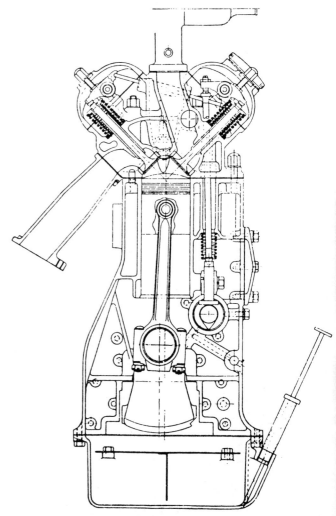

specialist in automobile speed records. This ex-army driver was now 58 years old and made a habit, as well as a profession, of pushing docile cars to their limits by the simple expedient of keeping the throttle wide open at all times!

His most memorable achievement had been in 1939 when he drove a tiny 1,100 cc car at 200 mph (320 km/h) under the eagle-eyed gaze of some Nazi officers. He had also been Cecil Kimber's official test driver at M.G. since 1930, which explains why he treated himself to the celebrated record-breaking M.G. called 'Magic Magnette', which he subsequently rebodied with such an outrageously low layout that the poor driver had to be almost prone on the side-members.

On 14 September 1948 the venue was a stretch of disused motorway at Jabbeke, not far from Ghent in Belgium. It was here that an engine codenamed XJ powered a car and its driver to 176.25 mph (282 km/h) over the flying kilometre. The car body was that of the ultra-low and ultra-lightened M.G., which was just strong enough to carry the Jaguar power unit. This XJ engine was the baby of a young and enthusiastic Jaguar engineering team and was the source of a sensationally successful and glittering future.

At Browns Lane there were four, rather than three, musketeers: William Lyons, the boss; Bill Heynes, chief engineer and co-responsible for the conception of the engine; Wally Hassan, in charge of development; and Claude Baily, chief engine designer. More or less by themselves they gave birth to a generation of cars whose designation was to become known throughout the world: the XKs. Other contributors to the XK's phenomenal future were Harry Weslake, the freelance engineer who specialised in head-design; Philip Weaver who took charge of competition preparation; the distinguished engineer Harry Mundy, and a little later on Lofty England, who became racing manager.

The cast was now assembled for the play. The opening scene took place during the war, while Hitler's *Blitzkrieg* brought death from the skies. The works had been requisitioned by the Ministry of Defence for the manufacture of light combat vehicles. This was tame stuff compared with cars and, in the evenings after a hard day's work, the team would stay up into the early hours, discussing and perfecting, in their minds and on paper, the new generation of cars which they would reveal to the world once peace came.

Each man had his own special part to play. Weslake was the monarch of the hemispherical combustion chamber; he knew more about gas flow than any man alive. Heynes was a firm believer in double overhead camshafts. Hassan championed special steels and thin-wall bearings. So they each had their own little field and, by 1946, the basics had been ironed out. Their plans revolved around a single, but mind-blowing specification, for they were tackling the puzzle of how to produce enough power to shift a luxurious, sturdy saloon, weighing almost two tons, at 100 mph (160 km/h).

This power had to be produced at about 5,000 rpm, and such a unit was guaranteed to put such a car way out in front of any average production touring car.

One of the models used by the engineers during their deliberations was the very powerful BMW 328. They gave

Chassis No 660001. Body No F.1001. **The** *car of the 1948 Earls Court Motor Show. It was the very first off the line and was to bear the famous HKV 455 registration number. Given a metallic bronze finish for the Motor Show, the car was later painted birch grey as a works test car and ended its days with Dunlop as a test model for brake systems. It was subsequently broken up for spare parts.*

each of their successive designs a code-name beginning with the letter 'X', and worked through the alphabet for the second letter of the code. When they reached 'XF' they came up with a design which had several interesting features, despite the fact that they soon shelved it and moved on. This engine already had twin overhead camshafts, with a capacity of 1,360 cc (66.5 mm bore x 98 mm stroke). It was also useful in that it served to test the efficiency of the camshaft chain drive and the gas flow in the new head.

This design was followed by the XG engine. There were still four cylinders, but the capacity was 1,706 cc, with 73 mm bore and 106 mm stroke. The valves were actuated by a camshaft which was placed very low in the block, and the whole unit was so obviously inspired by the BMW engine that Jaguar could have been had up for industrial piracy had they put the XG into production.

As it happened, the XG arrangement was not good enough for the team: the large number of moving parts made it much too noisy; there was too much inertia due to the length of the pushrods; and the gas flow was far inferior to that in the XF study; the vertical inlet ports taking the

fuel mixture into the head did not lead to such good volumetric efficiency and blending of the mixture as in the XF's cylinder head with its horizontal ports.

Logically enough, the next experimental engine was called the XJ. There were still four cylinders, but now the displacement was 1,996 cc and the bore/stroke proportion was getting squarer — 80.5 x 98 mm. This XJ engine was the one which really led to the XK, as it bore most of the hallmarks of the masterpiece to follow. The head was given hemispherical chambers with a valve arrangement which produced maximum turbulence. There were chain-driven twin cams, the design of the crankshaft was similar, and the special pistons gave a compression ratio of 12:1. This unit registered a figure of 146 bhp at 6,000 rpm on the test-bed, with an upper limit of 6,500 rpm. The XJ, coming just under the 2-litre limit (class E) was fitted in Major Goldie Gardner's EX 135 M.G., when he pulverised the flying-kilometre speed record.

There were two versions of the XJ: the four-cylinder one, and an enlarged six-cylinder model which gave a 3.2-litre capacity by means of a slight increase in the bore to 83 mm, resulting in an even squarer proportion than the original

XJ. It was the ideal engine on paper, and it looked as though the replacement for the old 2½- and 3½-litre blocks had at last been found.

However, when it came to full-scale tests, the team was let down by the low torque produced at low revs, and the stroke had to be modified at the last minute, so that the bore/stroke measurements were now 83 x 106 mm. Now, of course, a new crankshaft had to be designed and manufactured. Once the revised unit had been assembled, the results they had been waiting for appeared: the 83 x 106 mm bore/stroke figures produced the 3,442 cc capacity which is now world-famous.

This, then, was the XK engine with its new crankshaft and 106 mm stroke. This latter gave rise to some very lively 'debates' among the engineers, some of whom were put off by the archaic implications of the long-stroke solution. The supporters of the square or even over-square ratio stressed the advantages of their own preference for all they were worth: it would cause less engine wear and would enable much higher engine speeds to be achieved through the consequent reduction in the linear speed of the pistons.

Bill Heynes opted for the long-stroke XK solution, since

he was a realist and knew that they would never be able to combine the 'ideal' solutions for each component in one engine. When he presented a now-famous paper to the Society of Mechanical Engineers, describing the genesis of the XK engine, he explained the advantages of the design:

1) Valve throat flow was extremely efficient, both during the induction and the exhaust phase.

2) There was excellent exhaust-valve cooling: a good flow of water to the seat was made possible by the open angle of the head surface with the valve inside the water jacket.

3) Machining was straightforward, as it required just one single form cutter.

4) Ease of access: the cylinder head could be removed complete without disturbing the distributor or valve adjustment.

5) There was optimum combustion due to the central spark plug and gas turbulence.

6) Running-on was virtually non-existent.

7) Apart from the high rate of heat conduction of the DTD 424 aluminium alloy, it had the additional advantage of being very light: the head tipped the scales at only 50 pounds (23 kilos) 'bare', whereas it would have weighed 120

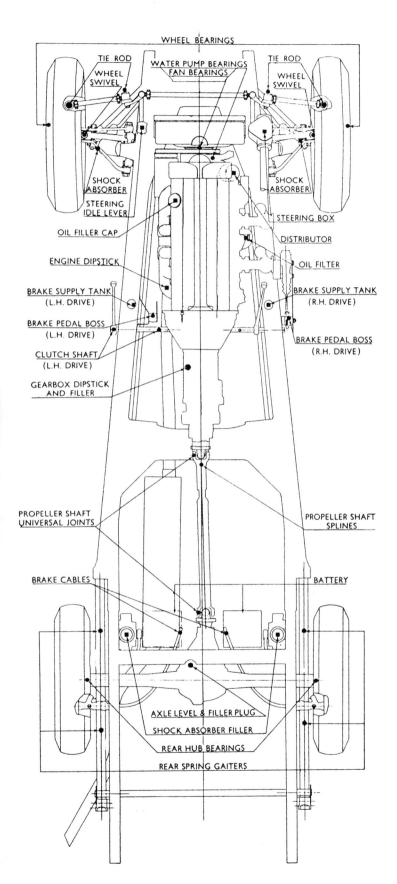

WHEEL BEARINGS

TIE ROD
WHEEL SWIVEL

WATER PUMP BEARINGS
FAN BEARINGS

TIE ROD
WHEEL SWIVEL

SHOCK ABSORBER

SHOCK ABSORBER

STEERING IDLE LEVER

STEERING BOX

OIL FILLER CAP

DISTRIBUTOR

ENGINE DIPSTICK

OIL FILTER

BRAKE SUPPLY TANK
(L.H. DRIVE)

BRAKE SUPPLY TANK
(R.H. DRIVE)

BRAKE PEDAL BOSS
(L.H. DRIVE)

CLUTCH SHAFT
(L.H. DRIVE)

BRAKE PEDAL BOSS
(R.H. DRIVE)

GEARBOX DIPSTICK
AND FILLER

PROPELLER SHAFT
UNIVERSAL JOINTS

PROPELLER SHAFT
SPLINES

BRAKE CABLES

BATTERY

AXLE LEVEL & FILLER PLUG

SHOCK ABSORBER FILLER

REAR HUB BEARINGS

REAR SPRING GAITERS

Right: You would have been hard put to it to find a more comprehensive and efficient dashboard layout in 1951. The XK 120 open two-seater's instrumentation would have satisfied even the most demanding customer.

This drawing of a 6-cylinder XK engine still bears the characteristic signs of the first few to be assembled: long 'chimney' carburettor, five-blade fan in magnesium alloy, absence of fixing studs on the front part of the cam covers, Mark V-style distributor, geared oil pump, old-style starter, and auxiliary starting carburettor solenoid.

Lubrication diagram for the XK 120. Lubrication was an important factor in cars of the period.

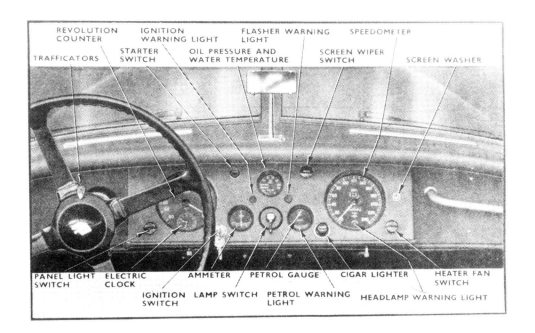

REVOLUTION COUNTER   IGNITION WARNING LIGHT   FLASHER WARNING LIGHT   SPEEDOMETER

TRAFFICATORS   STARTER SWITCH   OIL PRESSURE AND WATER TEMPERATURE   SCREEN WIPER SWITCH   SCREEN WASHER

PANEL LIGHT SWITCH   ELECTRIC CLOCK   AMMETER   PETROL GAUGE   CIGAR LIGHTER   HEATER FAN SWITCH

IGNITION SWITCH   LAMP SWITCH   PETROL WARNING LIGHT   HEADLAMP WARNING LIGHT

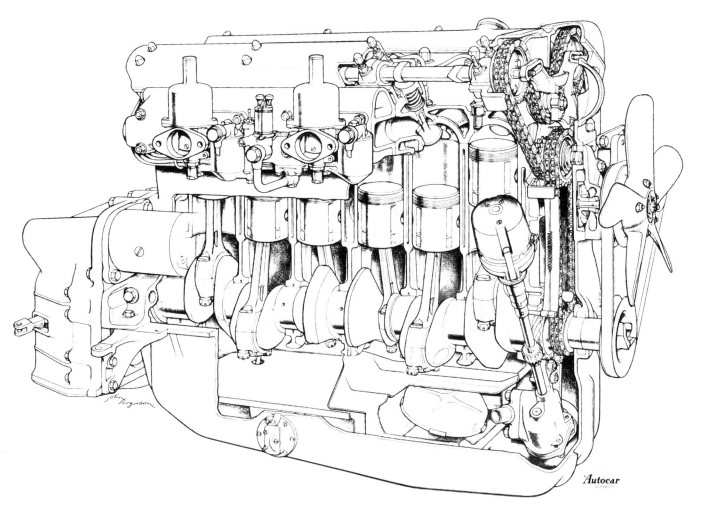

Autocar

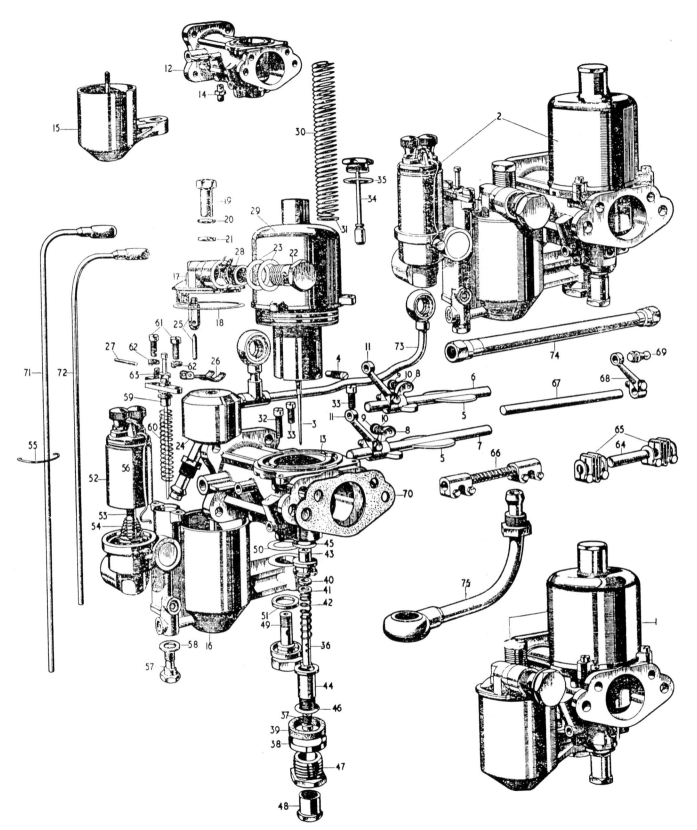

As British as mint sauce, these SU (Skinner Union) H6 carburettors were second-generation models and were fitted on the XK 120. The '6' in H6 indicates that the throttle opening measured 1¾ inches in diameter.

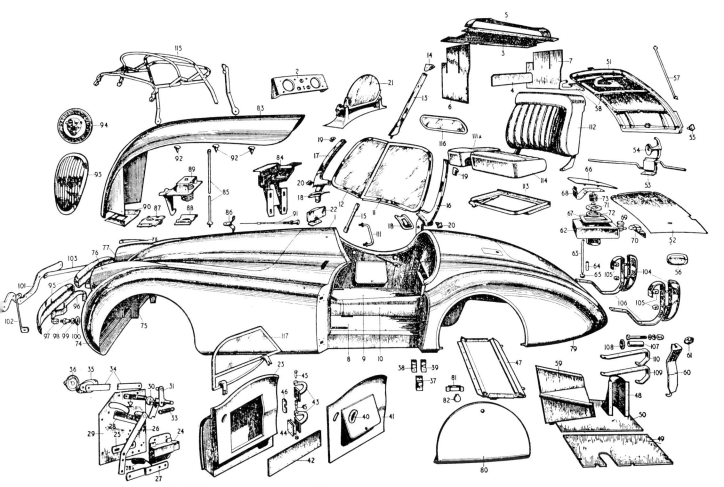

Body components for an XK 120 open two-seater. This technical drawing, taken from a parts catalogue, shows the complexity of the XK 120's construction.

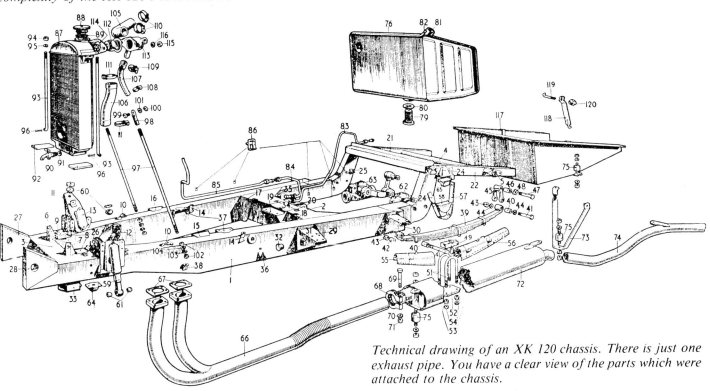

Technical drawing of an XK 120 chassis. There is just one exhaust pipe. You have a clear view of the parts which were attached to the chassis.

The impressive sight of a highly polished double row of camshafts.

An original angle on an XK 120 radiator with a starting handle socket at the bottom, reminiscent of the Mark V Jaguar.

pounds (54 kilos) in cast iron. Also, since this alloy has good machining characteristics, production costs could be kept down.

8) The valve seats were of high nickel austenitic cast iron, and were inserted in the head after it had been heated to a temperature of 232°C. The valve guides were fitted at only 80°C.

The bedrock of this magnificent piece of machinery was the crankshaft: with its seven large main bearings, each 2¾ inches (76 mm) in diameter, and its counterweights for balancing, it was an eminently reliable and impressive mechanical unit. First the crankshaft was dynamically balanced separately, then the crankshaft-flywheel assembly was balanced statically. The damper, fitted at the front, took the form of a steel plate bonded to a floating weight through a rubber disc. This was designed to absorb the torsional vibrations produced by the crankshaft during high-speed operation. Another interesting detail was that the crankshaft was made of EN 16 steel which was heat-treated before machining to strengthen it. The thin-wall bearings were made from steel lined with babbit or indium-coated lead-bronze which gave them a pinkish colour. The journals and crankpins were ground and hand-lapped to give a final finish of ten microns and the holes of the oil-ways were smoothed off and countersunk as a lead-in for the oil.

These feed holes were drilled at right-angles through the crankpins which were themselves drilled diagonally to form a sludge trap; these holes were sealed with taper-threaded grub screws which were secured by centre-punching the crank web.

Compared with these intricate and minute refinements, the block itself was extremely simple: the cylinders were bored straight into the block and wear was minimal, thanks mainly to the generally even temperature which the design produced. Bore wear was reduced by at least 50 per cent by the use of a chromium-plated top piston ring.

From the outset this mechanical masterpiece was planned for both 6-cylinder (3.4 litres) and 4-cylinder (2 litres). Bill Heynes' notebooks even showed a V configuration which would have produced a V8 and a V12. The V8 version fell by the wayside, but both the 4-cylinder and the V12 survived beyond the drawing-board stage, although the 4-cylinder had rather an abortive career and was never to power a production car. The 6-cylinder version looked like having more potential, so the development team decided to concentrate on this configuration.

Only five examples of the 4-cylinder engine still exist, and it is likely that little more than 50 were ever produced. One of these can be seen in Jaguar's own marque museum; a second is in the impressive collection at Donington museum; a third in Guy Griffith's personal collection; a fourth in the York automobile museum; and the fifth is the property of the enthusiastic Jaguar collector Roland Urban, the president of the French Jaguar Drivers' Club.

Jaguar was taking quite a risk, straight after the war, in producing a twin-overhead-cam engine for public consumption. Few garage mechanics knew enough about this sort of engine, at that time, to be able to service or repair it. Lyons was well aware of the problem, and had therefore insisted that the engine be ultra-reliable. He knew that if the new unit were to show the slightest sign of an Achilles heel it could never be a commercial success.

Overall view of the main Coventry assembly shop. This is a fascinating photograph since it shows how large a part hand-building played in construction techniques. On the left you can see a Mark V drophead coupé, some XK 120 open two-seaters, and a Mark VII saloon. Body panels seem to be lying any old how in a state of ordered chaos. Dated October 1951, this picture gives positive proof that Mark V drophead coupés, XK 120s, and Mark VIIs were all in production at the same time.

A stunning procession on the Rheims circuit for the 1952 motoring Tour de France. Three XK 120 fixed-head coupés are surrounded by Ferraris, Aston Martins, Porsches, Gordinis, Delahayes, and... a Renault 4CV. Flanked by fixed-head 120s in the centre of the photograph is a Jaguar-based 'special' named 'Oblin' after the Belgian coach-builder who fashioned it in the style of a Ferrari 166. This 'Oblin' made a good showing in the 1951 Liège-Rome-Liège when it finished second for the Herzet/Baudouin pairing.

This astonishing works photograph shows, once more, the combined production of drop-head coupé Mark Vs and XK 120s. Virtually bare chassis wait patiently for their mechanics, while fitters are mounting the ENV differential and transmission shaft. This illustration throws some interesting light on XK 120 construction.

The Browns Lane production lines in 1951, just before the trim stage. You can make out some Mark VII bodies. The wings lack parking lights which were integral on some cars and projected on others. This detail proves that one cannot use these lights as a criterion for dating a Mark VII Jaguar.

A view of the Coventry paint line. The cars were fixed to a gigantic revolving cradle to ensure that every little recess was given its layer of paint. This photograph was taken in 1951.

Lyons was not disappointed by the reaction of the public at the Earls Court Motor Show on 27 October 1948. All eyes were on the extraordinary car which had been given pride of place in the centre of the Jaguar stand. The XK 120 was breathtaking. Jaguar's new baby had style, balance, subtlety, class and air of barely controlled aggression. Before they had even found out what was under the bonnet, the crowds were won over by the magic of the new car. Its body was perfect — the kind dreams are made of. The XK 120 was an undeniably 'British' car, but at the same time it was unique and almost ahead of its time.

This lack of regard for fashion, and strict refusal to go along with the latest Italian bodystyling, made it a truly daring original. Most other cars seemed to be following the pontoon style which had first appeared some years before, as exemplified by the new body which Howard Darrin had produced for the Kaiser 6-cylinder.

Nevertheless, when you took a closer look at the XK 120, you could see that this sports car had used ingredients from many sources which the designers had played around with and modified to produce a masterpiece. There was a vague suggestion of... an impression of... a slight resemblance to... But, at the same time, it could only have come from the Jaguar stable with that sort of positive personality which makes a Jaguar instantly identifiable as such, even in thick fog.

There were still those who claimed that it reminded them of the Bugatti Atlantic, a BMW 327, perhaps A.C., with a touch of Riley, a trace of Lagonda — and so it went on. But this did not stop the XK 120 from being the star of the show, and we must look for the reasons for its success else-where.

It is worth remembering that William Lyons was very talented as a body designer. He seemed to have a sixth sense when it came to gauging the direction of styling fashions, or feeling the mood of the public, and could turn his instincts into commercially successful and supremely attractive cars, as witness the SS1 and SS 100.

The XK 120, however, came about through a slightly more complicated design procedure which consisted of brilliant flashes of intuition and serendipitous discoveries rather than methodical development by a team of design engineers locked in the R & D department. The 120 body, in fact, was such an almost makeshift production that the Jaguar works was caught short by the demand for the new car and had to alter its production schedule radically to cope with it. The XK 120 might even never have been there on the Jaguar stand in 1948 at all, since the only reason for its hasty creation was that the great showpiece car which should have been in its place was not ready in time!

To tell the truth, the 120 prototype body was built merely to cover the new XK engine while it was being road-tested — standard practice in the automobile industry. No one could ever have dreamed that such a haphazard design would produce a classic car! The only real difference bet-ween this and a run-of-the-mill body produced for road-testing a new unit was that, since Jaguar knew that it would be on show at Earls Court, more care had been taken with the finish and the works had tried to make it attractive.

From the outset, the XK 120's success was astonishing. It stole the limelight from all Jaguar's other products, and the original intention of making only a small number of this

The eve of the official opening of the 1950 Paris Motor Show. This XK 120 proudly displayed its hallmarks: the curved windscreen mounting, circular spat keyhole and black steering wheel (below and opposite).

model soon went out of the window. The car's instant appeal meant that the Browns Lane workforce was working flat out, with orders pouring in left, right and centre. For once the critics were unanimous: trade reporters, sceptical journalists, hardy test-drivers, the public at large... everyone agreed that, with the XK 120, Jaguar had hit on a magic formula.

Although luck may have played its part, we must not underestimate the exceptional team of men who had slaved away in the Coventry works. Those chiefly responsible for this coup — Lyons, Heynes, Baily and Hassan — had been working at full stretch since 1938 and had accumulated enough new ideas in their notebooks to produce several revolutionary cars. There are very few, if any, secrets in the automobile world — new developments spread like wildfire — and combining even the most perfected components in one car is no guarantee of success. What counts in the long run is having the right instincts, an almost clairvoyant knowledge of what will work and what will not, and the attributes of a poker player. It was Lyons who, in the last resort, settled differences of opinion and held the casting vote as to which technical solution should be adopted when there was little to choose between them. He was a decisive character with fixed ideas about what was needed to make any car into a commercially successful proposition. One of his top priorities, therefore, was a high-level public-relations operation which would keep the press interested by not hiding too much, but which could also keep the public on tenterhooks by not giving too much away.

The figures achieved on the Jabbeke-Aeltre stretch of motorway were the first weapon in the publicity department's armoury, and the second was to be the selling price of the car: £998, just two pounds below the vital £1,000 limit. Back in 1940 the government had introduced the dreaded purchase tax, a sort of early form of VAT, and a variable tax which was applied to cars and other goods, depending on their ex-works price. As long as a vehicle was priced at under £1,000 this tax was restricted to 26.5 per cent, but over that figure it jumped viciously to 66.6 per cent.

So, with the XK 120's price of £998, a customer could get away with paying a total of about £1,265. If Jaguar had asked £1,001 for the new car, the unhappy purchaser would have been lumbered with an invoice for £1,668. Consequently, one of the original specifications for the XK 120 had been that it must come under the £1,000 limit if it was to sell.

These vital financial considerations meant that there had to be no wastage during manufacture and that management had to keep a tight rein on the costings. Because of this, Lyons must occasionally have seemed like the embodiment of Ebeneezer Scrooge. It was as though he had eyes in the back of his head: nothing must be mislaid; the least wastage tortured him, the slightest delay haunted him. He tried to be a father figure, but at the same time he had to be a ruthless manager.

It was only by dint of watching every penny that Lyons could charge such a small amount for so exceptional a car; it was a quarter of the price of a Bugatti 57 SC, and half that of a 3-litre Alfa Romeo! The experts could not help

A fashionable symbol of social standing and eccentricity, the XK 120 soon became the darling of film stars and personalities, who rushed to be photographed with their new set of wheels. Françoise Sagan and her 1950 open two-seater were one of the Paris sights in those exciting years.

wondering how he had managed to pull it off, and felt that there had to be some nasty surprises somewhere in the car; it was just too good to be true!

William Lyons had always been a firm believer in giving the customer the impression that he was getting a real bargain, and that no other manufacturer could sell him a similar car for less than twice the price of a Jaguar and still provide the same reliability, accessories, refinements, sophisticated design, comfort, luxury, line, speed, power or roadholding. It was the sense of value for money which gave a man that delicious and indescribable feeling that someone had made a mistake with the price and that he had pulled a fast one on the salesman.

Lyons was a bold and imaginative businessman, a knowledgeable and innovative technician, but also an impressive leader of men who could be counted on to get the best out of his workforce — from top management to the youngest apprentices. He was the ruler of a small and autocratic kingdom, a bustling hive of industry in which engineers of all grades would willingly work all the hours that God sent to make sure that a project was completed in an impossibly short time — as was the case with the XK 120.

We have seen that great stress was laid on keeping costs to a minimum, but even more important was that the end result should give the impression that money had been lavished on the car; whistling for the moon, perhaps? With this objective in view, the lucky XK 120 purchaser (who, as we have seen, already thought that he had the snip of the century), was to be treated to genuine leather upholstery from Connolly Brothers and to all the refinements you would expect to find in much more expensive cars. Before he had even put his key in the ignition, our typical customer would feel that he was already a member of the most élite club in the world.

But it did not stop there, not by a long way. Once the car was on the move and taken to a relatively straight stretch of road, our by now ecstatic new Jaguar owner began to feel that something extraordinary was about to happen and that the seductive bodywork was hiding something even more intoxicating. It could not be otherwise when you think of the technological level of car production of that time in general, and of English cars in particular, compared with this 3½-litre 6-cylinder miracle with its twin overhead camshafts, and independent torsion-bar front suspension. What other firm could offer a genuine 120 mph (193 km/h) in 1948? If you really looked hard enough you might come up with the Bugatti 57SC, the 3-litre Alfa Romeo and the Delahaye 135 MS.

Let's just go back a few months to the time when Jaguar was planning the XK 120. As you know, the XK engine had been designed with the aim of powering a 2-ton saloon to a cruising speed of 100 mph (160 km/h), and the design of the saloon was well advanced, as the Coventry team had already decided on its main components — the chassis, independent front suspension, torsion-bars, hydraulic brakes and new steering.

As far as the body was concerned, they had entrusted its manufacture to a company which had vast experience in this field, the Pressed Steel Company, which was already responsible for the production of 60 per cent of British car bodies.

The saloon was to be an innovative, completely up-to-date car which would be sent off to capture the American market with some aces up its sleeve. However, the best laid plans... Lyons ran out of luck on this occasion, for Pressed Steel had some problems with tooling up and was incapable of delivering the body panels to Jaguar in the time given.

This was a real body-blow for Browns Lane. For several days there was a general mood of gloom and despondency, as everyone knew that it was no use trying to launch a new car without the London Motor Show as a platform. This crisis led directly to the birth of two new models: the first would be called the Mark V and the other the XK 120.

The Mark V was a transition car since, although it adopted the new independent front suspension with torsion-bars, hydraulic brakes and the new chassis, it retained a rather old-fashioned body which featured faired-in headlights as the only concession to fashion. From the outside the Mark V looked just like the pre-war 3½-litre, except that the enormous P100 headlamps had been replaced by Lucas' famous PF 770 tripods, which were also used on the 120.

Now it was fairly obvious that, if Jaguar hoped to make the most of the newly evolved twin cam, they could not profitably use the Mark V body, with its slightly old-fashioned air, for the new engine's début. This combination would have been incongruous and would have detracted from the novelty value of the XK. Consequently, the Mark V stuck to the overhead 3½-litre unit (with 2½ litres as an option) from its predecessor, a block which had been keeping the Jaguar flag flying ever since the SS 100. The 3½-litre overhead block still showed signs of its Standard ancestry and had enjoyed an eventful and chequered career. The Mark V was to be its last renaissance and it would

*Humphrey Bogart posing with his Americanised XK 120
open two-seater: impact-absorbers on the bumpers fore-
shadow the XK 140's accessories, and note American headlamps and white-walled tyres.*

*When the XK 120 fixed-head coupé appeared in 1952 it
created a sensation. It was a perfect balance of the flowing
curves of the roof and the more brutal aggression of the rest
of the body. The XK 120 fixed-head coupé remains a classic
design, and still attracts admiring glances today.*

Cutaway view of the first XK 120 fixed-head coupé.

The **Autocar**
COPYRIGHT

Complete with spats, which cover the rear wheels, and its tiny, bulbous roof, the XK 120 fixed-head coupé was a wonderful blend of sportiness and the unabashed luxury of a comfortable, weatherproof cockpit.

The passenger compartment in the XK 120 fixed-head coupé would not have disgraced a luxury saloon. It also boasted a very sporty dashboard. The adjustable steering wheel is a Jaguar speciality.

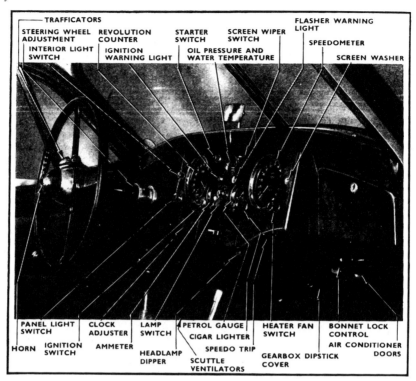

TRAFFICATORS
STEERING WHEEL ADJUSTMENT
INTERIOR LIGHT SWITCH
REVOLUTION COUNTER
IGNITION WARNING LIGHT
STARTER SWITCH
SCREEN WIPER SWITCH
OIL PRESSURE AND WATER TEMPERATURE
FLASHER WARNING LIGHT
SPEEDOMETER
SCREEN WASHER

PANEL LIGHT SWITCH
HORN
IGNITION SWITCH
CLOCK ADJUSTER
AMMETER
LAMP SWITCH
HEADLAMP DIPPER
PETROL GAUGE
CIGAR LIGHTER
SCUTTLE VENTILATORS
SPEEDO TRIP
HEATER FAN SWITCH
GEARBOX DIPSTICK COVER
BONNET LOCK CONTROL
AIR CONDITIONER DOORS

eventually be laid to rest in 1951, after an impressive production run of 10,466 cars.

The other car, the XK 120, which was the product of bad luck (Pressed Steel) and necessity (the London Motor Show), was therefore designed in somewhat unseemly haste and with but one objective — to dazzle the Earls Court crowds to such an extent that they would forget all about the fast saloon that should have been on display. William Lyons therefore decided to give them a dream car with a heavenly bodyline which would knock the public sideways. The Browns Lane team proceeded to hand-build a superb sports car, working frantically against the clock. Since time was so short there was no alternative but to do everything in-house. They started off with a Mk V chassis with the suspension, brakes and steering already fitted, shortened it by 18 inches (46 cms), removed the central cross-bracing and replaced it with a box-section cross-member because of the gearbox problem. The result was a chassis which was 5 inches (13 cms) narrower and which had a wheelbase of 8 feet 6 inches (2.6 metres). Some alterations were made to the wishbones, torsion-bars and ball-joints of the suspension; an anti-roll bar was fitted between the two lower wishbones, as well as a pair of Newton telescopic shock absorbers.

Steering was assured through the Burman-Douglas recirculating ball box, which was much lighter in use than the

worm and nut type. The gearbox was the equally classic four-gear Moss, with syncromesh on the top three. Since first gear was straight cut, it could only be engaged when the car was stationary, unless the driver was a genius at double-declutching and had a rev counter in his right foot! It was a reliable box, needing no special maintenance, but one had to be quite aggressive in using it. You would have to be patient with the slow changes, particularly the one from first to second which required a seemingly interminable pause in neutral. But, apart from its frustrations, the Moss gearbox posed no problems, providing that you lubricated it with thicker oil as the years passed to offset a tendency towards noisiness.

The rear wheels weere connected to an ENV axle with spur and bevel gearing. The live rear axle was in turn linked to a one-piece prop shaft and fitted with universal joints. The wheels were those of the Mark V, measuring 16 inches (41 cms) in diameter by only 6.00, attached by five bolts. One of the reasons which later led to the replacement of the ENV with a Salisbury differential was the impossibility of fitting the car with wire wheels. Now, in 1950, many owners wanted to have the handsome Dunlop 54-spoke wheels with their splined hubs and eared knock-off caps; this was because the wire option gave better flexibility, a reduction in the unsprung weight, improved brake-drum cooling and, above all, in many people's opinion, a more attractive

result than the disc wheel. If you wanted wire wheels you had to remove the rear spats, since there was not enough room for the eared cap. In later years the Americans solved the problem by cutting away part of the spats to accommodate the knock-off cap and five-bolt wire wheels on XK 120s which still had the old ENV axle. But more of the Americans later!

The clutch was the Mark V's classic Borg and Beck with fingers and graphite block. A single 10-inch (25-cm) plate maintained the link between the crankshaft and the gearbox.

The front suspension was a product of Heynes' genius: each wheel had independent suspension through two wishbones and a long torsion-bar to provide guaranteed reliability, minimal maintenance and the bonus of being able to adjust the trim to within a millimetre; it was also astonishingly economical in its manufacture.

Now Jaguar had the modern, robust skeleton ready. All they had to do was to create a breathtaking body for their 'Super Sports'.

The quickest, easiest, and tried and tested method was to build an ash frame, then cover it with hand-shaped aluminium panels. Aluminium is ideal for producing a body in a hurry because of its flexibility, providing that you do not weaken it by altering the shape too often. At that time it was also one of the raw materials still free from quota restrictions.

Lyons was a very talented man, but he was not at all adept at designing a car on paper. His unique design methods left out the drawing-board stage completely.

Despite this blind spot, he was a born stylist and he relied on just two things: his eye and his instinct.

The first step in designing the XK 120 body was, therefore, the construction of an ash frame so that he could judge the visual balance and then, by making successive alterations to this full-size mock-up, Lyons eventually arrived at the line which he had visualised in his mind's eye. Once this outline had been fixed, he had the aluminium panelling produced in-house and then dealt with the finishing touches himself; the siting of accessories such as the radiator shell, lights and bumpers.

To get a more accurate idea of the car's appearance, Lyons took the precaution of having the mock-up put outside in the open air, to highlight any flaws. One of his creative quirks was to have these prototypes installed as a rule in front of his home, Wappenbury Hall, so that he could see his new child in a 'fitting' setting. He always consulted those who were in his confidence, such as his wife and friends, to find out what they thought of the design. When he looked at a new car in its natural environment, Lyons had a fiendishly accurate eye. He had a fixed idea of

A concour d'élégance *organised by the tourist office of the French town of Arcachon in 1951 included this open two-seater XK 120. 'Personalised' number-plates were all the rage, even in those days; the 120 went into production in 1948. The lack of footwell ventilators in the wings, separately housed sidelights and curved windscreen mounting are features which combine to suggest a production date of 1950.*

The XK 120 open two-seater American-style: white-walled tyres and cutaway spats to make room for the eared cap. This cutaway style was quite popular in the United States since it meant that you could have the best of both worlds — spats and wire wheels. Property of Philip Volosov.

the car in his mind and wanted results in record time. His loyal team of bodymakers and carpenters were used to his ways, and somehow or other managed to interpret his implied orders, half-finished sentences and muttered jargon. They had to grasp his meaning quickly and translate his vague directions into concrete results at top speed. 'A little longer there... make it a bit more elegant... more rounded, look out for the contour... it shouldn't dip so much... a trace more... There, that's better! But that wing should be more aggressive...'

The small team of men who helped Lyons turn his dreams into reality was intensely loyal and, as far as wages went, these men formed a sort of aristocracy at Browns Lane. There are some who would say that they earned every penny!

Within a matter of days William Lyons had his perfected prototype body sitting proudly outside Wappenbury Hall. The great man was satisfied and gave the go-ahead for a few test bodies to be built on the shortened Mark V chassis and for some chrome accessories to be added.

So, the production of the car took only six weeks from start to finish, two of the six being devoted to the body and accessories (radiator shell, bumpers, windscreen mounting, seats, dash, etc).

The aluminium panels were produced by H.H.Cooke & Sons of Nottingham and were assembled in the production shop at Foleshill. The only parts for which steel was used, for rigidity, were the dash, fire-wall, boot interior and wing infrastructure.

Everything had been done at such a pace that the XK 120 was ready in plenty of time for the Motor Show and Lyons even had the luxury of being able to road-test this marvellous machine. It was at this point that, much to everyone's delight, the Browns Lane team discovered that their new car went like a bomb!

The main reason for this was, of course, that no way was this magnificent new body going to make do with the Mark V's old 3½-litre engine. Indeed, it had been intended from the start as the home for the brand-new 3.4-litre twin overhead cam engine. The XK engine, therefore, took pride of place underneath the bonnet, its polished aluminium camcovers glistening brilliantly.

When, on 27 October 1948, the huge doors of Earls Court were opened to admit the first visitors to that year's Motor Show — they had been queuing for more than two hours — people stopped open-mouthed in front of the Jaguar stand. William Lyons had to struggle to hide a smile of triumph — the XK 120 was a winner! However, before long even some experts were saying that the car was too goodlooking, too fast and too cheap to be honest. Even its name — XK 120 — could that really mean 120 mph? Surely not!

And this was the beginning of the great debate which took place in the two British car magazines, *The Motor* and *The Autocar* — 120 or not?

But back at Earls Court everything was rosy. The 120 was the centre of attention and, even during the show, Jaguar's management had to wrestle with the problem of how they

Below: Top-flight racing drivers soon realised the 120's competition potential. In 1950, Stirling Moss won the Tourist Trophy at Dundrod behind the wheel of a 120.

Of all the rallying XK 120s, NUB 120 was probably the best known. It was in this car that Ian Appleyard and his wife Pat (William Lyons' daughter) had many wins in the demanding Alpine Rally.

ULSTER T.T.
1950.

Stripped virtually bare for circuit racing, these XK 120s were reduced to a tiny aero-screen and a faired-in rear-view mirror to minimise wind resistance.

were going to mass-produce a car which had been planned for only small-scale production. A solution had to be found, for the company could not afford to miss such a money-spinning opportunity.

The production techniques were not modified for the first 120s, with the same hand-building methods using composite materials — in other words aluminium panelling on an ash frame. Jaguar kept to this system until March 1950, by which time the waiting list was so long that they really had to do something positive to reduce it. You could reasonably expect to wait two years for delivery in those days, which is hardly surprising given the fact that in the 15 months up to the end of 1949 only 73 XK 120s were built.

Between 1948 and 1949 244 were produced using aluminium and these time-consuming methods, but they did not all pre-date the steel-bodied version, for aluminium-bodied 120s were still being made after the introduction of the steel model. This means, therefore, that you cannot date an XK 120 simply by referring to the metal used in its construction. The same applies to the straight windscreen mounts, crank-handle socket in the radiator, and cam covers which are not secured at the front.

While we are on the subject of aluminium bodies, we should put an end, once and for all, to the widely held belief that these were lighter than all-steel bodies. This is patently untrue, since the two weighed the same, give or take a few pounds.

The '120 or not' controversy started in May 1949. William Lyons chartered a Douglas DC9 and took off with a posse of motoring journalists. They were heading for that celebrated section of motorway at Jabbeke, in Belgium, where a works-prepared XK 120 achieved a straight-line 132 mph (211 km/h). The grinning driver, Ron 'Soapy' Sutton, then enjoyed himself by driving at 5 mph (8 km/h) in top gear past the astounded journalists. The 120 in question bore a registration number which was to become world famous — HKV 500. It was the second of the left-hand-drive models to be built, with a chassis number of 670002.

One of the few modifications on this car was the replacement of the ENV 3.64:1 axle by one with a higher ratio (3.27:1) to give optimum results on that long straight.

On the first run, with the hood and sidescreens up, HKV managed 126.8 mph (203 km/h). Less than an hour later the windscreen and hood had been removed, substituted by a tiny aero-screen and an aluminium tonneau cover over the passenger seat, and on this run the Tissot electronic timing came up with the mind-blowing figure of 132 mph. The standing start mile was covered at an average speed of 86.4 mph (139 km/h).

Following these dramatic figures achieved by Ron Sutton (Jaguar's chief test-driver), the next landmark in the controversy involved *The Motor*. One year to the day after its début at Earls Court, a production 120 was taken to the Linas-Montlhéry aerodrome in France where, in the expert hands of Harold Hastings, it just about reached 118 mph (190 km/h). This was very disappointing, since a prestige motoring magazine's test report always carries a lot of weight.

Although Harold Hastings was still sceptical about the 120's potential, he was a fair-minded man and agreed to return to Belgium, this time to the magic motorway at Jabbeke, to see whether the car could do better. And better it did, much to everyone's relief: the officially recorded speed on this occasion was 124.6 mph (200 km/h). An important point to note is that the car had all the standard accessories: windscreen, sidescreens and hood, just like any other production model. One other impressive result recorded at Jabbeke was a 0-60 mph acceleration time of 10 seconds.

Despite all these extraordinary timings, the XK 120 had to fight to be accepted as a true sports car, since its stylishness, comfort and luxury belied such a description.

At the end of the 1940s everyone, including the Americans, still thought of sports cars as being spartan, uncomfortable and delightfully unpredictable, especially when driving one through the muddy English countryside in a rally or trial.

There were many of these typically British sporty cars: M.G. TC, Riley, Lynx, Singer Le Mans, Morgan 4/4, HRG 1500, Aston Martin Ulster, Triumph, E.R.A. Invicta, Frazer-Nash, Squire, to name but a few.

For decades these models stood for *the* sports car in all its splendour, with its lack of refinements being the *sine qua non* of virile, open-air motoring.

Who cared if the sceptics turned up their noses at the XK 120 and refused to recognise it as a true sports car? Who cared about Laurence Pomeroy's hard-hitting articles in *The Motor?* Competition results soon proved the critics wrong and, in any case, Jaguar was not too worried about the British press at that stage since, with only ten per cent of its production being allowed to remain in Britain, it was overseas sales that counted. You will remember Lyons' commitment to importing hard US currency...

The Americans lost no time in falling hook, line and sinker for this new British import, which is not surprising if you take a look at the limited choice they had on the domestic market in such cars. With the XK 120 they found a machine that was fast, powerful and blessed with driving characteristics and roadholding which were completely unknown on their side of the Atlantic. Surrounded by chunky Cadillacs, fleshy Chevrolet Fleetlines, chubby Chrysler Imperials, bulging Buick Centuries and voluminous Ford Victorias, any poor American who was after a bit of spice in his motoring life could find nothing but chrome cathedrals dripping with accessories, plastered with ailerons and other protruberances.

These moving Christmas trees had trouble moving at all. Their 4- or 5-litre engines struggled to produce an unimpressive 100 bhp and wilted almost visibly at the sight of the 2 to 2½ tons of body which they were meant to shift. Some Americans were heartily sick of this oversized, overweight parade, and dreamed nostalgically of those incredible little M.G. TCs with not one spare ounce of flesh on their bodies and which, even with their tiny 1100 cc engines, could give you enough excitement in one drive to last a lifetime.

Come to that, the United States of America did not exactly lead the world in engine development. Just at random (cross my heart), take the Chevrolet Powerglide with 3,547 cc and 94 paltry bhp, or half that of the XK 120; or the Cadillac with its V8 engine and 4.3 litres capacity which could only summon up 129 bhp. It's not wildly impressive, is it? But then, the side-valve engine still reigned supreme in the America of the 1950s.

While we are on the criterion of power/capacity, France could not be called a world leader either. The booby prize went to the Delahaye 135 M with 26 bhp per litre. Next in line was the Salmson E72 with 32 bhp per litre, followed by the Talbot Lago-Record with 38 bhp per litre and, best of the bunch, the Panhard Dyna 110 with 46 bhp per litre.

The XK 120 in its standard production guise started out at 47.5 bhp per litre and finished up, four years later, with 61 bhp per litre.

Just looking at the specification/price, bhp/capacity and power per ton displaced ratios was enough to give the most hardened catalogue browser palpitations... all that performance, and luxury too, for the modest price of £998!

The Lawrie/Walker team finished an honourable 11th at the 1951 Le Mans 24-Hours race. It was also the year that Walker and Whitehead gave Jaguar its first Le Mans win.

The Coupes du Salon, 8 October 1951. This event was restricted to privately entered Series 2 cars and included a generous helping of XK 120s — four in all — as well as Delahayes, A.C.s and Talbots. It was staged at the Mont-lhéry circuit.

William Lyons had no trouble in living up to the promise he had made several months earlier. The American press welcomed the XK 120 with open arms, and dollar customers were falling over themselves to get their hands on the new Jaguar. In France, by contrast, customers were noticeable by their absence. The first coverage did not appear in the specialist press until 1950, and the French had to wait until 1951 to see the respected magazine L'Automobile award the 120 full-colour front-page treatment. The explanation for this apparent lack of enthusiasm is very simple. France had been devastated by the war and was concentrating on getting back on its feet. As far as getting back on four wheels was concerned, car ownership was increasing mainly through the 4 CV. The country was not rolling in money and the Treasury had better fish to fry than letting francs leave the country for such a luxury item. Those who were determined to have a 120 would find the dollars somehow, in any case.

The XK 120 was introduced to the French public at the Paris Motor Show of October 1949, a year after its British début. The President of the Republic, Vincent Auriol, opened the show, but then he opened anything which was capable of being opened — one might have been forgiven for thinking that this was the only function which the French constitution allowed its head of state to perform! But to get back to the Paris Motor Show. An inscrutable Vincent Auriol made his way past the Jaguar stand, looked, arranged his face into the traditional expression of restrained admiration, and that was that!

The French motoring world of the late 1940s was fiercely chauvinistic and protectionist. If you look at one of their motoring magazines from that era, you will find nothing but French cars: Delahayes, Talbots or Salmsons at the prestige end of the market, and 4 CVs, 203s and 2CVs at the bottom end. The French were absorbed in one thing: improving their engine performance with the help of Martin, Constantin Nardi or Autobleu, among others, so that the 203 could be upped from 42 to 47 bhp, and the 4CV from 18 to 21. As you can see, the XK 120's 162 bhp must have been beyond their comprehension.

However, in the space of just one year, between 1950 and 1951, Jaguar and the 120 began to make a reputation for themselves as race winners, and the 1950 Motor Show at the Grand Palais marked the real start of the XK's career in France. Those fashion-conscious customers who could get their hands on black-market dollars knew where to spend them, since owning an XK 120 gave you the touch of class which no other car could. The first French buyers were not your ordinary motorists: Francoise Sagan, Maurice Mességué, Shahpur Bakhtiar, Cinzano, the Duke of Talleyrand, His Majesty Bao-Din, Fernand Nathan, the Aga Khan, Danielle Darrieux, Boussac (three within three years), Fernand Pouillon, the late Princess Grace of Monaco, Bernheim, Michelin, Prince Halim Omar, Prince Sass ibn Abdul, Baron Bich, Berger, Metro Goldwyn Mayer, the star of Holiday on Ice.

All in all, 240 XK 120s were officially imported into France through the exclusive Jaguar distributor Ch.-F. Delecroix of the Royal Elysées company, based in the Rue de Berry, Paris. This figure was a drop in the ocean compared with the 12,055 120s produced — 1.99 per cent, to be precise. The first French 120 customer did not, in fact, take

Scenes from the record-breaking week at Montlhéry. For seven nights and seven days the XK 120 relentlessly lapped the circuit, with world records falling left, right and centre. Stirling Moss, Leslie Johnson, Jack Fairman and Herbert Hardley tirelessly took their turns at the wheel between 4 and 11 August 1952.
The French Jaguar importer, Ch. Delecroix is at the far right in the top photograph.

CETTE
JAGUAR
a battu
4 RECORDS MONDIAUX
et
5 RECORDS INTERNATIONAUX
à
MONTLHÉRY
DU 5 AU 11 AOÛT 1952

10.000 kilomètres	à 170 km	Record International
3 Jours	à 160 km	Record Mondial
5 Jours	à 160 km	Record Mondial
15.000 kilomètres	à 160 km	Record International
15.000 kilomètres	à 160 km	Record International
4 Jours	à 160 km	Record Mondial
4 Jours	à 160 km	Record International
10.000 Miles	à 170 km	Record Mondial
10.000 Miles	à 170 km	Record International

The 1952 Paris Motor Show. This birds-eye view shows the quick-release petrol filler cap on the triumphant Montlhéry XK 120, and the roof aerial which kept the drivers and back-up team in touch during that long, crazy week.

Philippe Renault won many classic car races at the wheel of this super-light and super-tuned XK 120 open two-seater which was prepared especially for high-level competition.

delivery of his car until 10 April 1951. His name was Monsieur Felber, and the chassis number 660051. The last French-imported XK 120 was delivered to a Doctor Vincent on 30 June 1954 (chassis No 681479).

Many other XK 120s arrived in France through less conventional routes however, and notably with the help of the US forces of SHAPE (Supreme Headquarters Allied Powers Europe) stationed in France. Some of the official imports were also ordered by these soldiers, whose wages were paid in dollars more often than not. These Americans were usually acting as middlemen and they would resell the 120s straight away to their French clients — at a handsome profit, of course! This was a satisfactory arrangement for all sides: the Frenchman had the longed-for XK 120, the American some extra cash and Jaguar another sale.

In these soldiers' home country, film stars flocked to buy the 120: from Elizabeth Taylor to Errol Flynn, they rushed to see who would be first to have their photograph taken

sitting at the wheel of this dynamic automobile. Humphrey Bogart, Robert Montgomery, Dick Powell, Clark Gable, Juan Manuel Fangio, and the Maharajah of Jaipur were just some of the personalities who succumbed to this Jaguar euphoria. The list of 120-owners read like a 'Who's Who' of the jet set, of people who thrived on excitement and who were determined to get themselves noticed. As for this last, the XK 120 guaranteed success for, in 1950 or today, all heads turn when this magnificent beast is on the streets.

Jaguar's achievement with the XK 120 soon had speed lovers wondering about its racing potential, and one particular event immediately sprang to mind — Le Mans! There was no question of the works entering 120s under its own banner in 1950, so the initiative had to come from individuals with their virtually standard production cars, although Jaguar did go as far as providing spares for those 120s entered in the race. This was better than nothing and did at least prove, if proof were needed, that Lyons was looking

The Berthommiés' XK 120 fixed-head coupé, which they entered in the 1952 Tour de France. The positioning of the flashers underneath the headlights anticipated Jaguar's lighting layout for the 140 — which appeared three years later.

An XK 120 open two-seater on the Nîmes speed-circuit, with Pivereau at the wheel. 20 March 1953.

An XK 120 open two-seater flat out round a bend on the
Montlhéry track during the 1953 United States Cups, run
on 12 April. The car is fitted with the five-nut fixing wire
wheels, to avoid having to replace the hubs.

Francine Cognet with her husband's XK 120 fixed-head
coupé. This car (chassis No 679655) was first put on the
road in 1952 and is an example of the model's durability
for, by 1959, it had travelled the equivalent of seven times
around the world with all its principal original components.
The car was subsequently overhauled... for its next gar-
gantuan journey!

to the future. Bill Heynes and 'Lofty' England, Racing Manager, flew in on the morning of the race to keep a close eye on the cars' performance.

The following three teams were entered: Heynes/Clark, Whitehead/Marshall and Johnson/Hadley.

Shortly after the start, Clark and Marshall had clutch and brake problems and had to settle for a disappointing 12th and 15th place respectively. Johnson and Hadley kept the Jaguar party's hopes alive throughout the night: they were still in fourth place at dawn on the Sunday and three hours from the finish they had moved up a place. It was not to be however, for a broken clutch plate put an end to the 120's first Le Mans. The day was sure to come... Just for the record, the eventual winner was a Talbot-Lago. At least the XK 120 had profited from the outing by gauging the opposition and finding out the car's weak spots.

After they had returned to Coventry on the Dunlop plane, Heynes and England began to play around with the idea of a works racing career for the 120. The car may well have been put together with indecent haste, but there was no doubt that it had competition potential. There was no time like the present, so the works decided to give the project all they had. Jaguar's sporting image, which had been so strong before the war, was now in the doldrums and the only way of re-establishing the marque's competition prestige was by winning, and by winning well.

Lyons and Heynes worked out their strategy. First, the aerodynamics had to be looked at, secondly the weight had to be reduced by at least one third, then the engine had to be worked on, the infrastructure be made more rigid and,

finally, there was room for improvement on the rear suspension. You might be forgiven for thinking that they would have done better to start again from scratch with a new car.

When it came to the aerodynamics, Coventry called on the services of Malcolm Sayer, who had once worked for the Bristol Aviation Corporation. The team knew that if Sayer could not come up with the goods, no one else could.

The first works-prepared competition 120 was ready the same year. It was designated XK 120C, the 'C' standing for competition. The 'XK 120' was soon dropped from this designation to give the better remembered name, C-type.

After the abortive, but nevertheless worthwhile XK 120 sortie in the 1950 Le Mans, the car's first real success came through William Lyons' son-in-law, Ian Appleyard. The event was the 1950 Alpine Rally and Appleyard had as his navigator his wife, Pat — Lyons' daughter. The car was painted white with a registration number which soon became well known in motoring circles: NUB 120. Appleyard drove brilliantly throughout the rally and returned home with the coveted Coupe des Alpes.

One is forced to admit that those theoretical 160 bhp did not seem to be all there, and the works itself admitted that because of the poor petrol quality the test-bed dynamometer had never shown more than 152 bhp.

This slight shortfall persuaded Jaguar to develop a more powerful version of the XK which would match up to competition drivers' expectations. The result was an instant improvement in results, with the 1950 International Trophy meeting at Silverstone providing one of the highlights.

1953 Tour de France. This was a classifying event seen at the finish line in Nice. All the famous names in the motoring world were present.

An XK 120 open two-seater in snow-covered France (Lyons-Charbonnières).

XK 120 fixed-head coupé number 6 surrounded by its competitors during the 1953 Tour de France.

Three of the five Jaguars dominated the proceedings and finished by taking the top three places, with Peter Walker in first.

It was at about this time that the name of a shy, young and very talented driver began to be associated with Jaguar — Stirling Moss. His links with the Coventry marque lasted for several years and he was to make an enormous contribution to Jaguar's competition success.

Until 1951, only one type of body was available to the XK 120 purchaser: the spartan roadster. The term 'roadster' is somewhat anachronistic as it is an American expression which was not used by Jaguar until the E-type came out some ten years later. Jaguar's own description of the XK 120 was 'open two-seater' usually abbreviated to OTS. It was in this version that 7,612 XK 120s left Browns Lane, and it is in this version that the car is best known.

On 14 March 1951, the second XK 120 body was revealed to the public: that of the fixed-head coupé.

For the most part, of course, it adopted the OTS' line, but in addition it had a small rounded fixed head which looked very attractive, as well as improving the car aerodynamically. Many commentators saw in the coupé echoes of the only one Jaguar ever produced on an SS 100 chassis. Some more contrary critics said it resembled the Bugatti 57 Atlantic which, with its once revolutionary styling, was ten years old by 1951. The XK 120 FHC was always to be steel-bodied, although the bonnet, boot and doors used aluminium.

The bulbous cockpit top protected a luxurious interior which had that unmistakable and inimitable British flavour. Leather was used as lavishly as ever, although now it was even more supple, taken from cattle which the reputable firm of Connolly reared and slaughtered, processing the top-quality skins to produce this 'Vaumol' hide.

There was an abundance of walnut veneer — the dash, window mountings and door cappings were all given the wood treatment. Wool carpeting was the finishing touch to this opulent, comfortable cockpit which was more like a luxurious drawing-room in its fitments than the driving compartment of a fast car.

Proper side windows protected the occupants from the elements, and a heater (what a luxury!) completed the overall effect of aristocratic ease which had been missing in the open two-seater. One aspect of the OTS' interior was repeated, with good reason, in the FHC: the dials on the dashboard revealed all the information anyone could want. There was a rev counter, speedometer, fuel gauge (combined with an oil level gauge which was unique in those days and very rare even today), oil pressure gauge, ammeter, water temperature gauge, battery discharge warning light, windscreen washer and wiper switches, dashboard lighting rheostat, heating control, light switches for the cockpit and dashboard... what more could you want? There was also, of course, a cigar lighter and a tiny ashtray. In short, the fixed-head coupé's interior was handsome, spacious, welcoming and warm, just what was needed if it was to win customers from the more 'sedate' end of the market, as well as the faithful speed enthusiasts.

Although the new coupé was startlingly good-looking, it had unfortunately put on a lot of weight; some one and a half hundredweight! The mechanical recipe was more or less the same, with that theoretical 160 hp and a Moss box. The only real difference was that the Salisbury axle had by now virtually taken over from the ENV, of which Jaguar stocks were gradually run down.

In April 1951, *The Autocar* took a standard 120 and subjected it to a series of gruelling tests with some very disappointing results, since this sample's top speed was only 115 mph (185 km/h), and acceleration from 0-60 mph took a shameful 12 seconds! So what had happened to the fabulous figures which *The Motor's* test driver had produced? The 120-or-not controversy started up again when *The Autocar* published its findings, so the Jaguar works decided to put an end to all the fuss by reworking the XK engine which had occasionally struggled to produce 150 bhp. The result of Browns Lane's endeavours was to be a '120 M', copying most of the C engine's characteristics, which would be offered in a 180 bhp version, with a compression ratio of 8:1, or a 190 bhp option (9:1 ratio). That should keep the critics quiet!

With this press criticism ringing in its ears, Jaguar was not about to rest on its uncertain laurels. It was determined to keep the initiative by producing race wins and speed records.

As far as competition success was concerned, there were no problems. The C-type proved its worth in 1951 by winning at Le Mans, although this result was cancelled out to some extent in 1952, when it failed to finish because of overheating. True to form, the Browns Lane brigade bounced back in fine fettle, set on wiping out the memory of this ignominious defeat by using speed tests to prove that the production 120 was unbeatable. The usual team flew to France with a thoroughly prepared standard 120 drophead

XK 120 number 8 stops for repairs in Nice during the 1953 Tour de France.

The motoring Tour de France in 1953. The number 6 XK 120 fixed-head coupé is seen between Colmar and Gerardmer.

coupé. Their destination was the renowned Montlhéry autodrome which had an honourable tradition of speed records. Leslie Johnson and his co-driver tore round the track for seven days and nights, averaging 100 mph (161 km/h), obliterating eight world records in the process, and thereby proving to the 120's detractors that their snide comments were based on journalistic half-truths and sheer cussedness.

The figures speak for themselves: during those crazy 168 hours they covered more than 16,850 miles (27,000 kms). They smashed the 48-hour record (5,298 miles — 8,517 kms), the 10,000 kilometre record (57 hours 54 minutes), the 72-hour record (7,600 miles — 12,230 kms), the 96-hour (9,713 miles — 15,631 kms), the 120-hour, the 144-hour and the 168-hour records.

This crop of new records had a considerable effect in France, for records were very fashionable in those post-war years, and many magazines led with the story, which helped to give the XK 120 a much wider appeal in that country.

This car introduced the special equipment which customers could now find in their Jaguar catalogue under the designation '120 M'. As far as modifications for improved performance were concerned, these had already been avail-

able for a year or so in the form of the C-type, and any knowledgeable amateur mechanic who wanted an extra 20 or 30 bhp could have performed them himself. But they were now offered as a run-of-the-mill option along with ten other, more conventional ones: a badge bar, chrome-plated luggage rack on the boot, bucket seats, aero-screens and cowled rear-view mirror, a special undershield, exterior spare-wheel rack, reserve petrol tank instead of the spare wheel, radio and anti-fog lamps.

The engine modifications (the 'M' in 120 M) were eight in number:

1) A redesigned camshaft which gave an increased valve lift (3/8″ instead of 5/16″);

2) domed pistons giving either an 8:1 or 9:1 compression ratio;

3) the C-type head with its straight ports and, as a complementary option, two large 2″ SU H8 carburettors;

4) a dual exhaust system to make the best of the modified engine;

5) a dynamically super-balanced crankshaft;

6) a lightened flywheel to allow very fast engine speed changes;

7) a heavy-duty clutch;

8) a modified distributor to give optimum advance through modification of the spark curve.

The man responsible for all the work on the head was Harry Weslake, who was still as stubbornly freelance as ever. Uprating the 120s had at last given them the muscle they deserved and made up for the weight problem the cars had had right from the start.

In April 1953 the third and last XK 120 version appeared — the drophead coupé. It was a genuine convertible with a mohair hood which was fully lined to hide the hood frame. This handsome model meant that one could combine the joys of open-air motoring with the luxury of saloon driving in poor weather.

There were several differences between the drophead and the roadster: the windscreen frame was built into the body; the doors were in a straight-line rather than a cutaway style; and there were proper wind-up windows and outside door handles. In contrast, there were few changes from the fixed-head, other than the roof itself of course; the interior, with its wealth of wood, leather and carpeting, was identical.

The XK 120 drophead coupé, which was the ideal compromise between the open two-seater and the fixed-head coupé, had a short production life of only 18 months, during which 1,765 were made. It is therefore the rarest member of the 120 family and the one which is at the root of many disputes concerning whether a real sports car should have such decadent features as real wind-up windows! One thing is for certain — the drophead coupé was a hit with the section of the motoring public who felt that driving a sports car should not automatically lead to a bout of pneumonia.

One special feature of the drophead coupé's hood was that the rear window could be unzipped.

Partly because of the lateness of its introduction, and partly because so few were produced, the XK 120 drophead coupé led an uneventful life with no real pep-up equipment being offered as an option — no twin exhaust, no special camshaft, no big valves. Similarly, very few DHCs were fitted with wire wheels, almost all being delivered with those well-known spats which hid the rear wheels almost completely and gave the model that individual, slightly old-fashioned, but nevertheless upper crust appearance.

The 1955 Monte Carlo Rally. Delling and his XK 120 fixed-head coupé at the Munich start. They were out of time on the Hamburg stage.

In France, the XK 120 achieved pleasing results in rallies and hill-climb events. Babolat in the 1950 Touraine Rally.

Many private entrants had confidence in the XK 120. Here R.Mansbridge is taking part in the 1954 Coupe des Alpes.

All the standard DHCs were given the 3.54:1 Salisbury axle, replacing the ENV 3.64:1 version.

In May 1954 John Bolster, *Auto Sport*'s road tester, tried out a strictly standard DHC and obtained a top speed of 119.5 mph (192.5 km/h). In his report he tried to communicate the thrill which driving the DHC had given him:

"A long run in this car is a pleasure that is difficult to put into words. Whether it is its complete indifference to all kinds of road surface, its silence and smoothness, or the feeling of always having more power in reserve, I know not."

Most DHCs went straight to the United States, as did the majority of FHCs and OTSs.

One American motoring magazine, *Popular Mechanics,* had a system of canvassing owners' opinions and publishing the results of these surveys in its columns. Despite the rather erratic after-sales service and the time it took for delivery of spare parts, overall satisfaction with the 120 in the States was high. Some criticisms did come to light, however, of the lack of room, the slimline bumpers and the fact that there was no automatic gearbox option.

William Lyons, who was counting on success in the American market, was of course paying close attention to their reaction, and responded in double-quick time to any adverse criticism. It goes without saying, therefore, that almost all the modifications to the 120 range were dictated by the all-powerful American customers.

I could go so far as to say that, if you were to study the conclusions drawn from the United States tests, you could predict the next Jaguar model with a fair degree of accuracy!

This works prototype shows a pre-series C-type stripped down to its essentials. Everything is here, apart from such accessories as radiator shell and lamps. The C-type's clean line made it one of the most widely admired racing cars of its day.

THE C-TYPE

JUNE 1951—AUGUST 1953

THE NO-HOLDS-BARRED SPORTS CAR

The encouraging results of the three XK 120s entered in the 1950 Le Mans 24-Hours event led, almost instantly, to the creation of a 'competition' version. There were several very good reasons for this decision, for a rallying or circuit-racing victory was worth all the paid publicity in the world when you were trying to sell a sports car. In addition, the spin-off from racing wins had a pleasing reaction on saloon car sales figures, as the saloons were powered by the same unit, in the shape of that magnificent 3.4-litre twin overhead camshaft engine which was now fitted throughout the Jaguar range, replacing the 1.7-, 2½- and 3½-litre units. This across-the-board use of the XK made for much more efficient production and assembly methods, and any diversification was therefore out of the question.

Paradoxically, the XK 120C, abbreviated to C-type, bore scarcely any relation to the car on which it was based; the 'C' might have stood for 'chuck-it-all-away-and-start-again! Indeed, in many ways it was a completely original car.

To start with, there was the infrastructure. Gone was the massive heavy chassis with its huge side-members which, despite its apparently sturdy configuration, had a tendency towards twisting out of true. In its place there was a comparatively delicate network of welded tubes, looking slightly spider-like, which was extremely rigid in spite of its rather fragile appearance.

This very unusual tubular chassis, a welding *tour de force,* was in effect a cradle designed to carry the engine-gearbox-axle assembly. It was a handsome and complex piece of engineering, but also a stroke of genius in its design. The rear axle, for example, was not linked to leaf springs, but to transverse torsion-bars. This innovation was inspired to a great extent by the rear suspension on a front-wheel-drive Citroën dating from 1934, so proving that there is nothing new in this world! However, the advantage of this design change was that the rear suspension could be adjusted — a vital factor in high-level competition driving. The movement generated in the torsion-bars was damped by the classic Newton telescopic shock absorbers instead of the lever-arm system used on the original 120.

Moving forward to the front suspension, there was little if any change, for the same arrangement as in the 120 had been retained, with its double wishbones, torsion-bars and anti-roll bars. The only modification was the reinforcement of the wishbones and torsion-bars.

The first major difference in the front of the car was the steering, since the Burman box had been discarded to be replaced by a stylish and precise rack and pinion arrangement which was more direct and very light. The number of turns from lock to lock was now just 2¼.

The braking system had also been reworked to make it more efficient and less inclined to overheating, with the braking surface being increased 50 per cent.

Since the new car was intended for competition driving only, it was important that no superfluous items be included, with the result that hoods, spare wheels, windscreens, boots or comprehensive tool kits were out.

The tubular chassis supported an all-aluminium body, and the front section, including the wings, lifted up to give access to the engine. The bodyline was low, flowing and restrained in a pure, simplified boat style. Aerodynamically this gave very low wind resistance, although the drag factor could have been even better.

William Lyons gave in to strong pressure from Malcolm Sayer on the styling and made a slight concession to the then current Italian spider style, but this Jaguar was still very much a Jaguar, even though the only element retained from the XK 120 was the design of the radiator grille. The sober appearance of the C-type was evidence of its design aim: maximum performance. All that mattered was flat-out speed, acceleration, roadholding, aerodynamics and braking reliability.

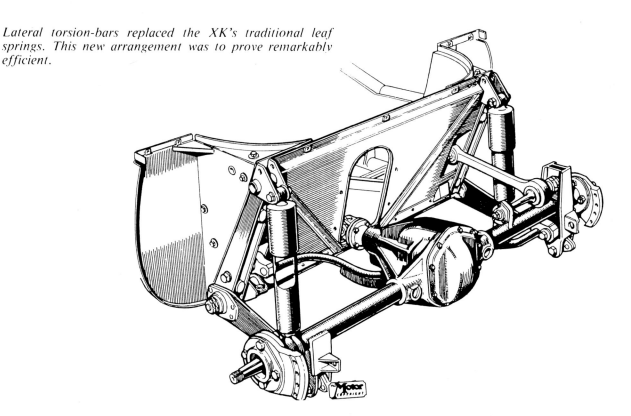

Lateral torsion-bars replaced the XK's traditional leaf springs. This new arrangement was to prove remarkably efficient.

The C-type produced 210 bhp and weighed some 660 pounds (300 kilos) less than the 120. If, with all these goodies riding on 600 x 16 front racing tryes and 650 x 15 rear racing tyres, the car could not come up with more than 150 mph (240 km/h), then it was not worthy of the Jaguar name.

As for the most important component — the engine — Heynes, Baily and Weslake used everything they knew on it. Without spoiling its inherent reliability, they soon managed to extract 45 bhp more than with the basic version, and most of these were accounted for by improved breathing.

There was no one better than Harry Weslake at producing a superbly designed cylinder head. This was the programme:

1) Increase the diameter of the exhaust valves by 3/16" to 1 5/8", and also the exhaust ports to 1 3/8" (3.5 cms).

2) Modify the valve springs to avoid bouncing at high speeds.

3) Use a high-lift camshaft because of the increased valve lift: 3/8" (9.5 mm) compared with 5/16" (7.9 mm) previously.

4) Fit two 1 3/4" H6 SU carburettors. Although these were used on the first heads, they were soon replaced by 2" H8 SU carburettors which were better suited to dealing with the large volumes of gas at engine speeds over 3,500 rpm. The change to these enormous H8s brought with it a special inlet manifold, with enlarged bores so that the gas flow from the carburettors would not be restricted.

These H8 carburettors showed great craftsmanship; unitary sand-casting gave them a rather rough finish and, because of their rarity, they are highly prized by modern collectors. This type of carburettor has no auxiliary starting mechanism, for the richness of the mixture is altered by the mechanical raising or lowering of the jet sleeve. A sort of open-topped box was fitted in front of the inlets, so that the two H8s received identical quantities of air.

5) The compression ratio will vary from 9:1 to 8.5:1 depending on the fuel octane rating and the engine tuning.

6) Use a different damper and bronze-indium thin-wall bearings in the bottom end of the engine, retaining the other components from the basic 120.

Once all these changes had been made and a satisfactory distributor had been fitted, Weslake could produce 205 bhp at 5,500 rpm without the slightest risk of any breakage.

The transmission was more or less the same. There was a lighter flywheel, a stronger Borg and Beck clutch, a gearbox which permitted easier changes, and a Salisbury axle (3.31:1 ratio) which would later be used on all models.

The brakes had been improved, too. This was the least one could expect with such a fast car. There was a larger braking surface and automatic adjustment for wear on the front brakes, through an ingenious Lockheed system. Owners of standard XK 120s would benefit from this innovation since, after proving its worth on the C-type, the Lockheed system was adopted for the production 120.

Finally, the light-alloy-rimmed wire wheels played a considerable part in cooling the drums, while also reducing the unsprung weight.

Many Jaguar enthusiasts see the C-type as the finest sports car that Browns Lane ever produced. The few who have been lucky enough to take one out on the road say that driving a C-type is nothing like being behind the wheel of a 120. This reaction is hardly surprising, for the C-type is not a hotted-up version of the XK 120 but a completely different kettle of fish. It was designed almost from scratch and its relationship to the 120 is similar to that of the 120

Top: This C-type is in a later stage of assembly and has its headlight fairings, 16-inch wire wheels and a nearside door. Still missing are the radiator shell, paint, and upholstery.

The Le Mans C-type assembly shop. This C-type still has the four side air vents, old-style bonnet louvres, and straps (1951). At this stage, of course, drum brakes were still being used on the C-type.

and the SS 100, in that it marked the birth of a new generation.

It is an accepted fact that progress in automobile technology always comes through racing development, and if any one constructor has done more in this field than the others it is Jaguar.

The C-type's racing career really began on 14 June 1951 in front of the stands at Le Mans. Jaguar entered three teams: Johnson/Biondetti, Moss/Fairman and Whitehead/Walker, all driving works C-types. There was also an XK 120 in the event, but it had been privately entered by Laurie and Walker.

Twenty minutes into the race the three C-types had already opened up such a lead that it looked as though the other marques had come along just to make up the numbers! This was a pretty impressive beginning when you consider that there were Talbots, Ferraris, Aston Martins and Cunninghams among the opposition, with such famous drivers as Gonzales/Marimon, Chaboud/Vincent, and Rosier/Fangio in a 4½-litre Lago Talbot.

By the end of the first lap Stirling Moss had been only four seconds behind the leading Talbot. On the third, Moss had passed Gonzales and taken the lead, looking unbeatable and smashing the track record on the 20th lap with an average lap speed of 105 mph (168 km/h).

The two other C-types followed in Moss' slipstream and, for some glorious time, it looked like being a one-two-three for the C-types.

At about 8.30 pm, when it looked as though it was a one-marque race, disaster struck when an oil pipe flange broke due to vibration and forced the Johnson/Biondetti C-type to retire. There was panic in the pits, for the three cars had exactly the same type of steel pipes and there was no chance of carrying out preventive work on the other two right in the middle of a 24-hour race.

The C-types seemed doomed when, not long after, Moss' car was taken out of the race by a broken con-rod, caused by lack of oil pressure as a result of... a defective oil pipe flange. At that stage Lofty England did not think his stable had a cat in hell's chance of providing a finisher, let alone a

winner. Whitehead and Walker were Jaguar's last hope and they had strict orders to take no chances. The opposition was also cursed with mechanical trouble and, against all expectations, the surviving team nursed their C-type to victory, having covered the respectable distance of 2,244 miles (3,612 kms) at an average speed of 93.49 mph (150 km/h). To say that the Jaguar team were over the moon is the understatement of the year — champagne flowed like water that Sunday evening!

Around the back stood three cars, covered by tarpaulins, which had been waiting disconsolately ever since the Coventry bandwagon's arrival. These cars were not needed in the race, but had been standing by just in case. Each one had a code-name: LT1, LT2 and LT3. They might have passed for common-or-garden XK 120s, but this was far from the truth. If you looked at them closely you could see that they were very, very special. They had magnesium alloy bodies; engine access through a mini-bonnet, since the bonnet itself was integral with the wings — C-type style; and a special super-light chassis.

These three cars had, in fact, been brought along as a back-up squadron.

Two of these LTs are still in existence today and represent probably the high point of special XK body development.

The 1951 Le Mans victory was a vital one for Jaguar and marked a turning point in the make's fortunes. It was also the almost inevitable result of William Lyons' intention to succeed at Le Mans: he was determined to win, and he concentrated so doggedly on achieving that one goal that it almost became an obsession.

A Le Mans 24-Hours victory has marvellous repercussions, both in Europe and the United States, for the event has an almost magical prestige and legendary importance which provide an irresistible challenge to anyone involved in motor racing. This 1951 success brought Jaguar more international fame than any other victory could have given them.

From 1951 onwards, Coventry's race development programme went full steam ahead, devouring hundreds of

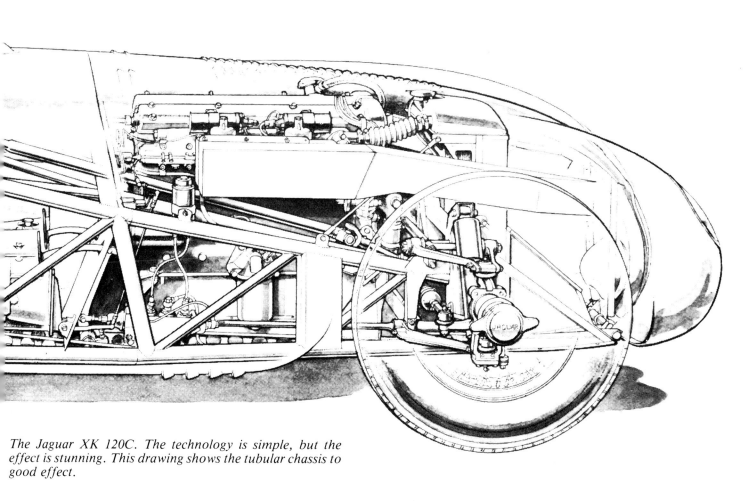

The Jaguar XK 120C. The technology is simple, but the effect is stunning. This drawing shows the tubular chassis to good effect.

The entire front section of the C-type hinged forward to give easy access for servicing and repairs. The famous 3.4-litre XK engine shown here has three Weber 40 DCO3 carburettors which draw in air from a purpose-made box.

The cam covers were fitted with the traditional 'breathers' to aid lubrication of the top end of the engine and recycling of gas under the covers.

Since maintenance would have to be carried out on the C-type during the night, lighting was provided under the bonnet. In the background you can see the quick-release oil filler cap which was a common feature on competition engines.

thousands of pounds in the process since, although one might think that competition success brings 'free' publicity for a marque, in reality it is a horrendously expensive business. The XK 120C, which had originally been conceived solely as a racing car which would make headlines in the press and on radio, was so successful that Lyons decided to put it in their brochures and to offer it to the public from August at the final price of £1,495. At the same time, anyone who wanted to improve the performance of his production 120 could buy the C-type special equipment, which included the twin exhaust, fuel tank with quick-release cap, solid-centre clutch, 9:1 pistons, high-lift cam, 1½ inch reinforced torsion-bars, and high-efficiency brakes.

The Le Mans victory also highlighted any flaws in the mechanics, and the oil-pipe flange weakness was immediately analysed and rectified to avoid any repetition of this failure.

The C-type's win was really rather cheeky when you think that this had been its first major outing and that Jaguar, as a relative novice in the event, had pitted itself against Briggs Cunningham's impressive armada, Talbot's solid experience and Ferrari's highly developed technology.

The 1951 Le Mans also brought overnight stardom to Stirling Moss, at the tender age of 20, who had won his driving stripes as well as his boss's respect, despite his enforced retirement from the race.

The C-type also proved two things to the world at large: it was the fastest and the most reliable car on the circuits. This was all it took for the 120, now three years old, to become the centre of flattering attention once again. British magazines were full of the Jaguar exploit, which extended to the other Browns Lane products. All this marvellous publicity was aimed more at the Americans, as the XK 120C was an unattainable luxury for most Britons, not because of its price but because so few were available on the home market. If you could not pay in dollars, then hard luck!

More valuable publicity came two months later with the RAC Tourist Trophy, which was held on the Dundrod circuit. There, Stirling Moss outclassed all the other drivers to win one of the greatest victories in all his Jaguar career.

1951 was turning out to be an epic year, and it finished

with William Lyons and his loyal team of men feeling on top of the world. They were never content to sit back and gloat, and already the works was deeply involved in a new, more efficient and more durable braking system — the disc. Development was carried out jointly by Dunlop and Jaguar and, by early 1952, the system was ready and had already been given a thorough workout by Norman Dewis, the works' chief tester.

In the Mille Miglia — that incredibly demanding event held in southern Italy — Moss did not finish due to a driving error, but at least he had the opportunity of putting the brand new brake system, which had been fitted to his C-type, through its paces. Ferrari and Mercedes took the top places and the race was chiefly memorable for the emergence of Mercedes' new rising star — the 300 SL.

Stirling Moss had his revenge in May, during the International Trophy Meeting at Silverstone, when he drove a C-type to victory, as well as a Mark VII in the touring car race.

Jaguar looked more closely at the reasons for their failures than at the factors which contributed to race wins, for the Coventry management wanted Le Mans to be the pinnacle of their 1952 sporting season. The opposition was looking ominous, with Mercedes bringing out the big guns with the 300 SL. Moss, who had been very impressed by the car's showing in the Mille Miglia, put the wind up Lyons by telling him how easily the 300 SL had overtaken him on the straight. Alarm bells started ringing in Lyons' head, for if there was one thing which he feared and respected it was the striking efficiency and determination of the Germans. This new challenge preyed on his mind, since he had it on reliable authority that Mercedes was determined to win Le Mans at any price.

With less than two months to go before the 24-Hours race, Lyons therefore took it into his head to make some changes to the C-type, with the aim of getting more speed on the long Hunaudières straight. How were they going to extract that vital little bit extra out of the car to cook the Mercedes' goose? Jaguar's solution was to play around with the drag coefficient and redesign the front of the car. The XK 120C was therefore given a longer, more dipping nose and a smaller radiator grille; the rear was also altered slightly to reduce drag. At the end of the day, the three works C-types were almost unrecognisable, and the new body format gave a theoretical bonus of about 3 mph (5 km/h) on the interminable Mulsanne straight. It was hoped that Stirling Moss would no longer have to say, as he did after the Mille Miglia, that it felt as though his car was not moving at all when the 300 SL zoomed past him!

Right from the start of the practice sessions for the 1952 24-Hours race it was obvious that all was not well. The cars were so obviously unready that Bill Heynes even advised his boss to throw in the sponge there and then and go back home. The new frontal design was causing serious cooling problems and, despite a last-minute modification on the air intake, the engines were having to work at a constant temperature of between 95 and 100°C.

Two hours after the start the three C-types were overheating so badly that they had to trundle ignominiously back to the pits — the race was over as far as they were concerned. The Jaguar brigade had a hard time trying to hide their shame at such a public humiliation. The three teams of Rolt/Hamilton, Whitehead/Stewart and Moss/Walker had to watch glumly as the Mercedes 300 SLs profited from the C-types' failure. The worst of it was that the Mercedes were not anything like as fast as they were made out to be!

The 1951 Le Mans 24-Hours. If ever a marque deserved to win, Jaguar did. Peter Whitehead and Peter Walker's car passed the finish soon after this photograph was taken. Their victory resulted in vastly increased sales over the following years.

Another remarkable feature of the race was that Levegh, driving a Talbot, insisted on taking the car round on his own for the whole of the 24 hours, without the slightest respite. Just one hour from the end, haggard, exhausted and hardly knowing where he was, Levegh was put out of the race by a broken crankshaft, so that the notorious 300 SLs had victory dished up to them on a plate despite their disappointing showing and their play-safe approach to the race. As proof of the fact that the Mercedes' speed had been over-estimated, a privately entered standard C-type easily exceeded the German cars' total distance in the following year's Le Mans.

The post-mortem on that 1952 event went on, and on, and on... theories and excuses were bandied about endlessly. If only someone or other had thought to enter a production C-type... If only the weather had been cooler... If only the three C-types had been fitted with a separate header tank, instead of that old-fangled radiator which had meant cobbling together that ghastly hump on the bonnets of two of the cars... But 'if onlys' have never changed history, so we shall leave the matter there.

The arguments about what really caused the overheating have, in fact, never been fully resolved, for it is very probably that the small air intake was not the only reason. The cooling system itself was not, perhaps, equal to the task. Immediately after the race the cooling system was revised and the header tank was separated, once and for all, from the radiator by placing it behind the engine and connecting the two with long pipes.

Coventry decided to prove that the nose shape had nothing to do with the overheating, by running one of the Le Mans C-types on the MIRA circuit near Nuneaton. The only modifications were a redesigned water-pump impeller and enlarged piping. Result: even after several hours' flat-out driving, there was no sign of overheating.

Nevertheless, the plunging bonnet style on these 'droop snoots', as they were called, was scrapped, not because of any concern about cooling efficiency but because of the problem of weight distribution which led to a certain degree of instability at high speed. The 'droop snoot' was therefore given an honourable discharge: the production C-type was now on general sale and Jaguar did not want to involve its customers in the teething troubles of a new body design, so risk-taking was not on the cards. Everything had to be rugged, reliable, tried and tested to the Nth degree. It was even considered too premature to fit the production C-type with disc brakes, since Lyons preferred to have every single snag ironed out before letting the general public loose on the new braking system.

Lyons' target customer was a peculiar breed of motorist: he would be a motor-racing fan, a skilled driver and one who did not give a hoot for home comforts. If this imaginary customer lusted after a spartan car, his dream was realised in the C-type. There was no heating, no hood, no boot, no windscreen; nothing that was not strictly necessary for driving hard and fast. If it rained, you just groped for the plastic mac and made the best of it. Experienced C-type drivers say that the only way to avoid a soaking when there is a real downpour is to put your foot down so that the tiny 'Brooklands' aeroscreens will deflect the rain over your head.

The first comprehensive test drive undertaken for *The*

Sometimes you can try too hard. In an attempt to improve the C-type's aerodynamics and so gain a few extra miles per along the Hunaudières straight, Jaguar gave their 1952 C-types a completely new profile. Unfortunately the new design produced cooling problems, and the 1951 victory was not to be repeated in 1952. The number 18 car of Rolt and Hamilton was forced to retire after three hours due to a blown gasket.

Motor notes the C-type's outstanding qualities and describes the car as being the fastest one they had ever road-tested. Here is their report:

"An extremely fast and docile car intended for advanced competition work.

"The road test of the Jaguar 120C presented several problems. This model was first introduced in 1951 and immediately received international prominence as a result of an outstanding victory at Le Mans. It was, however, made absolutely clear at the time by the Jaguar Company that, unlike the well-established 120 model, the 'C' version represented a car designed entirely for competition motoring and was not in any sense to be confused with the touring version which had already shown itself capable of more than 124 mph in our hands.

"By late summer of 1952 the Jaguar 120C model began to emerge from the Coventry factory in sufficient quantities to merit the description 'steady production' and it therefore seemed desirable that steps should be taken to carry out a normal road test of this interesting machine.

"Safe and comfortable transportation for two people must form an essential part of any sports car however spartan, so it was decided to combine a maximum speed run on a closed motor road in Belgium with a drive to the Nürburgring in Germany and a subsequent passage over some of the major Autobahnen in Europe.

"The weather was most unfavourable during the preliminary trials. The conditions under which the maximum speed tests were performed made it wiser to time the car electrically, with only the driver aboard rather than the two-passenger method normally adopted by this journal. Dry spells fortunately intervened for long enough to make the acceleration figures thoroughly representative. When the crew assembled in Brussels to drive the car to Germany they did so with the satisfying knowledge that the Jaguar had averaged a mean speed of over 143 mph and in so doing had established certain Belgian sports car records.

"The problem of the crew's luggage stowage at first appeared to be an insurmountable one. The 40-gallon petrol tank occupies the whole of the tail, and the two cockpit seats have no appreciable space behind them. The body sides, which constitute the driver's door and the passenger's elbow room, proved so commodious that all the impedimenta of a prolonged trans-Continental journey could be housed therein, leaving additional room for a quantity of waterproof clothing (rendered necessary by the absence of hood and normal windscreen).

"The many thousands of enthusiastic motorists who have watched the 120C in numerous races may have considered the vehicle far removed from the comforts of civilization but, in fact, bearing in mind the necessity for maximum possible performance from such a car, the amen-ities are attractive and well-planned. The driver and passenger sit well inside the Jaguar and, despite pouring rain, very little road dirt penetrates even when the car is driven fast. There is a certain snugness in the cockpit and the engine provides just sufficient warmth to give an impression of well-being, which is greatly amplified as soon as the wheels start to turn.

"Let there be no mistake. The Jaguar 120C justifies absolutely the overworked term of thoroughbred. A stranger, taking over the car for the first time at the height of the Brussels rush hour, finds a docile and tractable machine completely without temperament, ready to trickle through the traffic and proceed along slippery *pavé* and wet tramlines with most of the silence and comfort of the modern touring car. The astonishing flexibility of the 120C is best appreciated by a study of the performance data. It is sufficient, here, to say that second and third gears cope with any situation from walking speed to 100 mph and, within a very few hours of first acquaintance, the experienced driver feels well able to travel at speeds in excess of 120 mph, whenever the road and traffic conditions render such motoring prudent.

"The highest praise must be given to the steering charac-

Following the C-type's phenomenal 1951 racing successes, unsponsored drivers soon started entering their own 'C's. In the 1953 Moroccan Grand Prix at Agadir, Berthommié drove his C-type home in third place.

The 1953 version, complete with disc brakes. Three Weber carburettors played a key role in winning another Le Mans 24-Hours race for Jaguar. The winning C-type was an impressively handsome and clean-cut car. On the bonnet you can see the vent for the air intake.

teristics of the Jaguar. This rack and pinion mechanism is not only light and responsive but sufficiently high-geared for the driver to change direction more by wrist action than by arm movement. Additionally the car must be one of the truest 'straight-line runners' the world has yet seen.

"We have stressed that the 120C is basically a racing car and, accordingly, the equipment is planned to meet the exacting needs of international contest. The accessibility of the entire engine, when the front end of the body is raised, could hardly be better. Incidentally, when this is done, under-bonnet lights come into action in case they are needed and there is no part of the power unit which cannot be tackled in the minimum of time.

"The bonnet is secured by two straps and three fastening levers. The position of the side handles calls for some criticism because their quick operation will almost certainly remove a large area of skin from the fingers. Another matter for some comment is the cup-like guide tube for the sump dip-stick, because this is in the slipstream of any road dirt and soon attracts more grit around the orifice than is desirable.

"Instruments are confined to essentials. The large matched dials of the rev counter and speedometer are placed where they can be seen in a split-second glance.

Other instruments comprise an ammeter, oil pressure gauge, fuel gauge and water temperature recorder. A very desirable attachment to the car under test was an additional switch on the right-hand side of the body which brought the car's horn into action until reset, thus leaving the driver free to deal with other matters when overtaking at very high speeds. This switch is supplemented by a normal horn button, placed so that either the driver or the passenger can reach it quickly, and on the left-hand side of the scuttle there is a group of separate lighting switches. The headlight dipping control is mounted on top of the gearbox cover and a large anti-dazzle driving mirror gives a good rearward view from its cowled position amidships.

"The car has an ingenious, permanently-attached, zip-fastened tonneau cover which shrouds the passenger's side of the cockpit when this is not in use. In addition to the aero-screen available for the driver, a similar model can be mounted on the left-had side of the car for the passenger. Both bucket seats look alike but are somewhat different in construction. That of the driver is extremely luxurious and, although a little narrow across the hips, gives excellent support in the right places and is high enough from the floor of the car to overcome the unpleasing impression of sitting with legs stretched straight out in front. The

Briggs Cunningham looks intently at the brand-new disc brakes on this C-type (XKC 053).

passenger seat covers a large tool box, wherein lies all the necessary equipment for wheel changing and other deeds, but this makes the cushion very shallow and considerably less comfortable than the driver's version. The passenger also sits a little higher than the driver and so needs goggles at any speed in excess of 50 mph. It is noteworthy that the driver can achieve double this figure without having to protect his eyes in this manner.

"The 40-gallon tank does not appear materially to affect the handling of the car, whether it is full or nearly empty and, at the end of 500 miles' extremely hard driving, a check showed that the Jaguar had consumed no appreciable amount of oil or water. A noteworthy example of the attention to detail is the provision of drilled extremities on the petrol and oil filler caps, so that these may be sealed whenever race regulations require. The car ran on first-grade pump fuel of Belgian as well as German quality and did so without audible protest. There was no tendency to 'run-on', even when heavy traffic of a large industrial town raised the coolant temperature some 15 degrees above its normal 55°C. Despite the small-capacity battery, the engine

never failed to start at the first touch of the button — the car being left in the open each night.

"The really excellent road-holding qualities of the Jaguar were exercised during some fast runs on the Nürburgring. Only on the one significant straight could top gear be used for any distance, and the demands made upon the brakes, particularly on the downhill section, were deliberately rendered excessive. Although the pedal pressure was high, brake fade was practically non-existent and at no time did the engine, despite its severe thrashing, show the least loss of tune. Apart from a curiously rasping exhaust note which could be heard only momentarily at a little above 2,000 rpm, the 120C is a very quiet car, and workmen patching the road surface on the German racing circuit were in some danger of being caught unawares, particularly where their viewpoint was thought to be sufficiently good to obviate the customary warning signal indicating road maintenance. After the long climb towards the Karussell the circuit is shaded by fir trees, and here a damp surface retained from overnight rain gave ample indication that the 120C is a very stable car in the wet.

"Subsequently the test of the Jaguar was transferred to a famous motor road and it was here that its remarkable ability to cruise in the neighbourhood of 120 mph with sharp bursts of acceleration up to 135 mph, demonstrated the great ease with which the car can be directed when running fast. The steering is neither light nor heavy but so instantly obedient to wrist movement that a piece of timber which had fallen from a lorry was avoided at near maxi-

XKC 052 during a refuelling pit stop at Le Mans in 1953. The Moss/Walker pairing finished second. Those pictured include Lofty England, Stirling Moss and, on the far left, William Lyons.

Tony Rolt in the C-type which won the 1953 Le Mans 24-Hours. The C-type was beginning to earn a reputation for being invincible.

mum with so little effort that the incident passed unnoticed to the passenger. As the speed climbs beyond the 130 mark, the car does tend to feel a little light, but a curious sense of becoming faintly airborne is offset by no loss whatever in directional control. At such speeds there is no shake or even tremble in the body, nor is there anything to indicate that much higher speeds would not feel equally safe to the occupants of the car.

"The driving of the Jaguar XK 120C on the motor roads of Europe is in fact a great and memorable experience, and tribute must be paid to the designers and executives who have made possible such a fine contribution to British automobile engineering."

Coventry's top priority was to wipe out all memory of their disastrous failue in the 1952 Le Mans, and this was why they immediately sent a production 120 out to Montlhéry to beat some records. The final tally was eight new world records achieved during seven days and nights of hell-for-leather driving round that celebrated circuit.

This bunch of records may not have been as useful as an historic racing victory, but at least it proved that the standard 120s could boast more than just a pretty face.

Stirling Moss made up for Le Mans in the Rheims 12 Hours. This race takes place just a month after the Sarthe event, and winning it is to some extent a consolation prize for drivers or cars which have made a poor showing at Le Mans. For the 1952 Rheims Moss drove a traditionally bodied C-type which showed the opposition the way home and proved the efficiency of the disc brakes.

From this point onwards, other manufacturers began to realise that you needed discs to win races and the C-type just kept on winning with monotonous regularity: the Jersey International Sports Car race in July, Ian Stewart driving; the West Essex CC organised by the *Daily Mail* in August, Stirling Moss driving; the Goodwood 9-Hours in the same month, with Moss driving again; the SSCC Turnberry meeting — Moss again; the Shelsley Walsh Hill Climb in September, Walker driving; the Wakefield Trophy with Stewart; the Prescott Hill Climb with Walker; the Elkhart Lake Hill Climb in the USA, Phill Hill driving; the September Goodwood meeting where Tony Rolt was the winning driver, and a drum-braked C-type was pitted against a disc-braked model for five laps; the Seneca Cup race at Watkins Glen in America, John Fitch driving; the Bristol MC and LCC with Stewart driving.

And that is just the C-type's major successes in 1952. If I had listed the meetings where it gained a second or third place, this book would be even thicker!

Towards the end of 1952 some changes were made in the body design, bearing mainly on the side air intakes and the arrangement of the louvres on the top of the bonnet. These alterations, together with a modification of the tail design, make it easier to identify the year in which a certain C-type was produced. The C-type was given a thorough workover, however, in preparation for the 1953 Le Mans. The main purpose of the exercise was to get rid of some surplus

The winning Rolt/Hamilton pairing at the 1953 Le Mans in XKC 051. They covered 2,540 miles (4,088 kms) in the 24 hours. The real winner of this event was the new disc brake system which was soon fitted to the majority of racing cars.

weight, so that anything which could be spared or slimmed down was attacked with gusto. Just take a look at what they did: the gauge of the chassis tubing was reduced; one single 12-volt, 37 amp-hour battery was used, instead of the two 6-volt ones which had a capacity of 64 amp hours; since the starter motor would not get much use during the 24-Hours, and then only when the engine was still warm, a smaller one was adopted with a lightweight aluminium cover; the copper electrical cable was replaced by aluminium cable; a tiny control box was used; the original heavy dynamo was substituted by a lighter low-capacity model; very lightweight headlamps were specially commissioned from Lucas which still gave maximum illumination.

The weight loss achieved by these measures was as follows: 6 lbs (2.7 kgs) from the dynamo; 5 lbs (2.3 kgs) from the starter; 40 lbs (18 kgs) by dispensing with one of the batteries; 4 oz (113 grams) on the control box (every little bit counts!); 1 lb (453 grams) shaved off the headlamps; 11 oz (310 grams) with the switch to aluminium cable. It may not look like much if you take each item individually, but the total weight saving was getting on for 53 pounds (24 kilos).

The guiding principle was reliability, for Lyons and Jaguar did not want to see a repeat of the 1952 Le Mans fiasco.

Bearing in mind that the lights would be needed for only eight hours and that the battery did not need much juice for starting the car, they selected a dynamo pulley with a smaller diameter, which meant that it would turn more slowly and therefore be more likely to last out.

Two HT coils were fitted so that, if one packed up, there was another in reserve.

Since the C-types would be going flat out for 24 hours with the throttle wide open, they could get rid of the vacuum advance device and fix the spark timing in the distributor to maximum advance. This explains, in addition, why there was no threading on the large 2-inch H8 carburettors for the vacuum advance tube inlet.

They used special 'Dykes' top piston rings to avoid detonation in the bottom end of the engine through the fuel leakage past the more normal piston rings. The classic Dykes rings are surprisingly elastic and hardwearing, and will withstand high pressure despite their apparent fragility. They are marketed by the Bricovmo company.

Jaguar had learned its lesson from the split petrol tanks of the previous year, and they drew on aviation technology for the new design: a flexible tank with an astonishing 50-gallon (225-litre) capacity. Its two main advantages were that it was very light and was virtually guaranteed not to split.

In addition to this programme aimed at weight reduction, ensuring reliability and safety, Heynes gave the XK unit some extra punch. The first major revision concerned the carburettors and, for the first time, Jaguar sacrificed its patriotic instincts by doing away with the large 2-inch Skinner Union H8s and opting for the Italian Webers, which were much more suited to high-level competition. Three 40 DCOE twin-choke (indicated by 'DC') were therefore used, which would deliver bumper quantities of fuel to the combustion chambers, giving better efficiency at top revs — especially between 4,000 and 5,000 rpm, where the two H8s had been distinctly uncomfortable.

There were few other changes to the Le Mans C-type, apart from the introduction of a steel damper for the crankshaft.

The C-type was now some 110 pounds (50 kilos) lighter and had about 10 bhp extra under the bonnet, so it was now straining at the bit to take its revenge on the Le Mans circuit. There was one further modification which was rather surprising, in that the cooling system had reverted to its original form: the separate header tank system had been given the push, and it was back to the good old one-piece radiator. The shape of the water-pump vanes did, however, follow the late-1952 design, as this was the result of some intensive research into preventing the formation of steam pockets which cut off water circulation between the radiator and the engine block.

In the transmission the single-plate Bork and Beck clutch, which was unable to match up to the increasingly rigorous demands of competition driving, was abandoned in favour of a slightly more complicated, but very much more resilient and positive, arrangement. This was the triple-plate Borg and Beck with a 7¼-inch (18.5-cm) diameter which motorcyclists will know well. As for the rear axle, which was still fixed, it was was given a Panhard rod to help keep the wheel tracking accurate on bends.

Last, but most definitely not least, the car was fitted with disc brakes. These had now proved their effectiveness and Lyons felt they were a major plus-factor in the company's attack on Le Mans. This Girling-Dunlop-Jaguar researched system had no servo assistance in its original version, and they had had to get round the pedal pressure difficulty by a very long piston stroke in the master cylinder.

All the big guns were lined up for the 1953 24-Hours, jostling elbows with the three official Jaguar teams of Moss/Walker, Whitehead/Stewart and Rolt/Hamilton. There were to be challenges from Ferrari with its 4.1- and 4.5-litre brigade, Allard-Cadillac, Alfa Romeo's 'flying saucer' (disco volante), a supercharged Lancia, the Aston Martin DB3S, Gordini's 2.3-litre, the Cunningham and a 4.5-litre Talbot. Even though the Pegaso Z 102 was not there to make matters worse, it promised to be a titanic struggle for victory.

You have probably noticed that Mercedes was another absentee. It had decided to rest on its 1952 laurels, or maybe just did not fancy its chances against such strong opposition. Ferrari, in particular, were annoyed by Mercedes' decision, for they had been robbed of the chance of a rematch with the Germans whose non-participation was not a very sportsman-like gesture. Lofty England, with typical British phlegm, let it be known to all and sundry that the rather 'flukey' victory of 1952 would not be repeated.

He could not have put it more plainly. Mercedes' brief announcement of their intention not to enter the 1953 Le Mans had a touch of paranoia about it: 'Since we have established our undisputable superiority, we no longer feel it necessary to run the 300.'

Jaguar did not, however, start as hot favourites as far as the press was concerned, due to their abysmal failure the preceding year and, before the race had settled down, it looked as though the motoring journals were to be proved right. Were the Coventry team to be jinxed for the second year running? Moss was having fuel feed problems and had to return to the pits. Meanwhile Tony Tolt was having better luck, gaining the upper hand on the Ascari/Villoresi Ferrari. Despite his setback, Moss came back on the track and slowly but surely moved up through the field. The disc brakes were working like magic, for although the C-types could not equal the Ferraris on the straights, they put the brakes on later than any other car, while the Ferraris were still cautiously decelerating behind them. Hamilton's was the fastest C-type, clocking up 148.2 mph (238.5 km/h) on the Hunaudières, with the Alfa Romeo 'flying saucer' registering 150 mph (241.5 km/h), the 5.4-litre Cunningham-Chrysler 149.75 mph (241 km/h) and the 4.5-litre Ferrari 149 mph (240 km/h).

Moss was making steady progress and had even caught up with Whitehead's C-type. In the early hours of the morning the discs were showing their superiority and the Rolt/Hamilton pairing had a comfortable lead over the Ferrari. Sadly, as the first light of day broke, one of the Ferraris crashed at the Maison Blanche, killing its driver, Tom Cole. By the end of the morning racing manager Lofty England knew that, barring accidents, Jaguar was going to win. Moss was having such a blinder that he pulled up to third place, and then moved into second when the leading Ferrari retired with a broken clutch. In fourth place, behind the Cunningham, came Whitehead/Stewart's C-type, and so it was that, at 4 pm, with only the Cunningham splitting them, the three C-types took the flag at the end of the 1953 Le Mans. It was the record to break all records. The Coventry team was shouting with triumph, crying with joy, giving bear hugs all round. The psychological barrier of a mean 100 mph had been breached — and how! — with 105.9

The Rheims circuit consists basically of four sections of main roads, and is therefore very fast. The Scott Douglas/Sanderson C-type made its first long-distance outing for the Écurie Écosse stable in this 1953 Rheims 12-Hours race. XKC 046 had been travelling at more than 133 mph (215 km/h) before slowing for this 90-degree bend.

mph. Without doubt it was the greatest performance ever by one model on the Sarthe circuit. A privately entered C-type even managed to snatch ninth place and, in so doing, exceeded the distance covered by the winning Mercedes 300 SL in 1952. To add to the magnitude of this achievement it should be pointed out that the car ran with the now old-fashioned drum brakes!

As a postscript to this momentous 1953 Le Mans, here is the text of the telegram which William Lyons sent to Buckingham Palace:

"The Jaguar team humbly present their loyal duty to Her Majesty and wish to advise her that in her coronation year they have won for Britain the world's greatest international car race at Le Mans, France, yesterday."

The C-type enjoyed many other historic victories in Great Britain, France, Italy and America. Moss once more took his revenge in the Rheims 12-Hours and, with every race, the supremacy of the disc-braked cars became so patently obvious that, within the space of a few months, all the constructors were changing to the new braking system. Had they not done so they would have had to settle for their cars being perpetually distant specks in the Jaguars' rear-view mirrors.

However, Jaguar knew only too well that it still had to be on its mettle as far as technological progress was concerned for, if Ferrari and the rest were going to climb on the disc-brake bandwagon, the C-types would have their work cut out coping with a 12-cylinder 4-litre-plus rival. Coventry therefore had to keep their research and development men

Hamilton in a disc-braked C-type for the 1954 Coupes de Paris. It is hard to think who could have beaten him, despite the redoubtable opposition which included Ferraris, Lancias, Gordinis and Aston Martins.

on their toes if the marque was to keep its number one position in motor racing. It was because of this constant need for innovation that the C-type was destined for the scrapyard even before it crossed its first finish line.

Only 54 C-types (if you include the Le Mans works cars) were produced during the model's short career. Between 1951 and 1953 it was an extremely popular racing car, and the very reasonable asking price added to its attraction for private drivers. Seventeen C-types were exported to the United States.

Three examples were sold through official channels to French customers by Delecroix:

XKC 016, engine number E1016.8 to Monsieur Glans, via Peignaux of Lyons; XKC 025, to Monsieur A.Roboly; XKC 035, engine number E. 1037.8 to Monsieur Heurtaux.

Today the C-type is a venerated, respected, idolised, cosseted and, most importantly, a much-copied classic car. This last is the highest mark of respect that one can pay to any model. And the price you can pay, even for a replica, is high too. Several coachbuilders will supply you with one, providing you can supply them with £20,000 in addition to an E-type which they use as the base for the replica. Some of these specialist companies are such experts in working with aluminium that they can produce quasi 'C-types' which are virtually indistinguishable from the real thing; there is a great temptation to 'borrow' chassis numbers from cars whose actual fate still remains a mystery!

Pared down and beautiful: OVC 919 in the capable hands of Duncan Hamilton.

This line drawing of the XK 140 open two-seater brings out the aggressive lines provided by the design of the front wings, low-cut doors and sweeping rear end.

XK 140

OCTOBER 1954 — FEBRUARY 1957

REFINED POWER-HOUSE

Jaguar's XKs featured frequently in the 1950s' gossip columns, along with their equally glamorous owners. Of course, the Coventry cars were now referred to as 'Jags' by the fashionable set, in the same breath as 'Rolls' or 'Mercs'. For a long time Jaguar had a slightly snob image alongside its sporting one, on both sides of the Channel and the Atlantic. This is in part due to the aesthetic appeal and luxurious fittings of these great cars, but also due to the stars who have rushed to buy them, such as the French author Françoise Sagan who used to be a regular crowd-stopper as she drove through the fashionable streets of Paris in her 120 OTS.

The date for the opening of the 1954 London Motor Show was October 15, and it was to be the public's first sight of the XK 120's successor: the XK 140. Why wasn't there an XK 130? Heaven knows!

The XK 120 had been the infant prodigy of 1948 but, since it was produced in such a rush, it had some flaws which prevented it being a great, and increasing, international success. If I were a schoolteacher writing a report on the 120, I would probably be tempted to say: 'A very talented pupil, although his work is a little slap-dash. Could do much better.'

Although the 120's major flaws were absent from the 140, some of the charm had gone too. There was one particular reason for the reduced visual appeal: the North American market.

This combination of advanced technology and slightly dated appearance gave the XK 140 a distinctive personality.

William Lyons had had to bow to the requirements and criticisms of his American importers and, if you read the very last road-test report for the 120 drophead coupé published in the American journal *Popular Mechanics* during 1954, you will find comments on all the aspects which were to differentiate the 140 from the 120: bumpers, radiator grille, steering, comfort and power.

Some of the body design changes struck you at first glance. To start with there were very large, heavy bumpers which harked back to the Mark VII with its imposing front and rear fenders. These somewhat oversized hunks of metal were the logical product of the Americans' standards for town driving. Another peculiarity of the bumpers was that the mounting was not integral with the wings, as it had been on the 120, but was now just bolted into the chassis. The result was that there was little likelihood of the wings being dented in a minor collision. Despite this advantage, it must

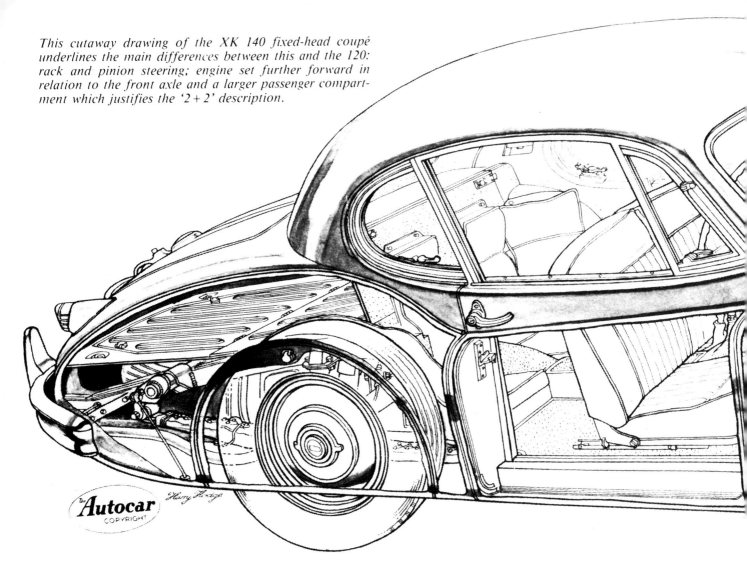

This cutaway drawing of the XK 140 fixed-head coupé underlines the main differences between this and the 120: rack and pinion steering; engine set further forward in relation to the front axle and a larger passenger compartment which justifies the '2 + 2' description.

An immaculate XK 140 engine compartment. The C-type head has enormous hand-made 2-inch (5-cm) H8 carburettors which were originally fitted to give the racing C-type more punch.

be said that Jaguar had gone from one extreme to the other; from the purely decorative bumpers on the 120 to the generously proportioned (to put it mildly) examples on the 140.

The radiator grille was also redesigned to make it both sturdier and cheaper to manufacture. It was made from chrome-plated Zamac with seven slats; the inverted V-shape at the top extended into a long chrome strip which ran the length of the bonnet mid-line.

The boot lid was transformed by the bumper and the positioning of the number-plate. A chrome strip, identical to the one on the bonnet, divided the boot lid vertically and, in addition, there was an enamelled medallion showing Jaguar's Le Mans wins.

As you walked round the 140 you noticed other details: the 120's tripod headlights had been replaced with 'J' headlights, so called because they had the letter 'J' on the central anti-dazzle part; there were stop lights on the rear, and flashing indicators set low on the front wings.

All these obvious body changes gave one the first impression that this was an American-style facelift and not a brand new model. But one should not judge a book by its cover and, true to this saw, the real innovations were hidden away under the bonnet and in the passenger compartment.

The engine made a dramatic contribution to the public's quest for performance, for the standard 140 was fitted with the most powerful of the 120's range, which had previously only been available as an option. It produced a genuine 190 bhp and, alongside this 'standard' version, customers who wanted to stand out from the crowd could specify a high-power cylinder head on their Special Equipment XK 140s. This was the C-type head which was easily identifiable by a cast badge with a red background on each camshaft cover; and, so that you could be absolutely sure that you had the improved head in your car, the letter 'C' was cast into the aluminium cylinder block, near to the spark plugs.

There were four features of the C-type head which made it so special: the inlet valve diameter stayed at 1¾ inches (44.5 mm) but the diameter of the inlet porting was increased from 1 7/16 inches (34.5 mm) to 1 5/8 inches (41.2 mm); a different valve seat angle; high-lift camshafts and dual exhaust.

With all these appetising ingredients, the C-type head could be counted on to give 210 bhp at 5,740 rpm.

Staying with the engine, it was noticeable that the power unit had been shifted forwards three inches (7.5 cms). Two benefits accrued from this repositioning. First, weight distribution was improved and with it roadholding, so that

the car developed a more pronounced understeering characteristic. Secondly, those precious three inches could be used to give the driver a little more room in the cockpit.

There was a revised internal layout, so that anyone taller than 5 feet 9 inches (1.75 metres) could at last drive in a normal relaxed manner, without having to wriggle his way in and find his own secret method of fitting himself in between the seat, steering wheel and gear lever.

For those used to driving the 120, the 140 was as different as chalk from cheese. There was no more of that traditional but hideously uncomfortable driving position where you sat bolt upright, arms close to your chest, and ribs almost touching the wheel. You could now begin to believe that you were at the wheel of a truly modern car.

The position of the steering wheel played an important part in this new interior design revolution, and it was also the clue to one of the other major new introductions: the steering itself. The ancient recirculating-ball Burman box had been replaced by the Alford and Alder rack and pinion system inherited from the C-type, which was accurate, flexible and responsive; and the column connecting it with the steering wheel was no longer in one straight piece, but consisted of two half-shafts articulated by universal joints.

There was a very satisfactory reduction ratio (2¾ turns

111

The XK 140 fixed-head coupé was always available in a 2 + 2 version (with two rear occasional seats), unlike the XK 120 range which had offered no 2 + 2 option. Even the elongated roof could not spoil the car's visual balance.

Spoked wire wheels prevented the XK 140 from looking too heavy and drew your attention away from the enlarged cockpit.

from lock to lock) which meant that even the most delicate female wrists had no trouble in turning the wheel at slow speeds, or even with the car stationary. As the rack and pinion steering was connected to the chassis through a flexible mounting, any kicks produced by uneven road surfaces were effectively absorbed.

If you lifted up the bonnet you found a radically different radiator. It was much more efficient, and the surface area in contact with the air had been increased by 20 per cent by setting the radiator at an angle. This inclined position had been dictated, to some extent, by the repositioning of the engine. Behind the radiator was a brand-new eight-blade fan which gave improved cooling in town driving and when the engine was idling.

Beneath the engine, the massive cast aluminium sump had been replaced by a smaller pressed steel version which had a slightly smaller capacity.

A peculiarly British feature, which was first introduced on the Mark VII saloon and which was offered as an option on the 140, was an overdrive supplied by Laycock de Normanville. This ingenious, but costly, device enables you to drive at high road speeds but with the engine turning 1,000 rpm less than you would need in fourth gear for the

same result. Since the engine turns more slowly it is therefore less noisy, uses less petrol, and wear is reduced. The overdrive 140s were all fitted with the 4.09:1 Salisbury axle.

This complicated arrangement, which is very popular in Britain and which in effect provides a fifth gear, consists of a sort of auxiliary gearbox with epicyclic train and two gears.

To use the term 'fifth gear' is obviously incorrect, since one can only engage overdrive from fourth.

The overdrive unit is fitted to the end of the gearbox, occupying quite a large space — to the extent that it makes a hump inside the car itself.

An attractive small faceted switch glowed brightly when overdrive was brought into action; this facia-mounted switch activated a solenoid which, in turn, controlled the locking system for the main pinion of this epicyclic train. You can therefore pass casually into overdrive, without even having to depress the clutch pedal and, when you want to change back to normal gearing, you merely have to switch off the overdrive and there you are, back in fourth.

Still on the subject of transmission, there was later to be an innovation which was typically American (as opposed to the typically European overdrive). This was the introduction of the celebrated Borg and Warner automatic box with torque convertor, which was supplied as an alternative to manual gears from October 1956. Despite the many advantages which your run-of-the-mill driver might see in this system, few XK 140s were supplied with this option, since the sports car enthusiasts who purchased the XK 140 did not like the idea of this converter using up about 40 bhp of its operation, when they wanted all the bhp they could get to shift the car at top speed! This American equipment was limited to the fixed-head and drophead coupés, as was the overdrive.

The C-type was used as a model for the 140's suspension, with the 1½-inch (38-mm) torsion-bars. At the back of the car there was a departure from what was essentially a 120 arrangement, with the replacement of the hydraulic shock absorbers by telescopic Girlings which required a minor modification for the location of the upper support brackets.

The three body styles of the 120 had appeared at intervals over a five-year period, but the XK 140 was available right from the start in fixed-head, drophead and OTS versions. One of the truly new features incorporated into the drophead and fixed-head coupé design was the provision of two occasional seats in the back which, although more suitable for children than adults, were fairly roomy if the front seats were moved fully forwards. Some of the space for these seats was provided by the relocation of the two 6-volt batteries to a position in the front wings, just behind the wheels.

This 'two-plus-two' concept was fairly revolutionary in British sports cars, though not in touring cars, and the new passenger accommodation was yet another result of the demands of the North American market.

This was also true, of course, of the massive bumpers which looked out of all proportion to the car in contemporary British eyes. Lyons, however, was determined that his cars should not be rejected by the US Federal Commission with its draconian regulations, so he chose to fall in with American requirements by fitting such large bumpers that there was no chance of administrative foul-ups with American sales. At least the XK 140's bumpers did their job, unlike those on the 120, and if they added to the car's weight, well, that was just too bad! An interesting design point concerning the rear bumpers is that they were originally made in one piece to protect the whole of the tail on the prototype version, but on the production model this single

An XK 140 open two-seater in an English rural setting makes an attractive picture. Cars sold on the domestic market more often than not had spoked wheels painted to match the body. Chrome-plated wire wheels tended to be *reserved for export models. There was very little difference between the XK 120 fixed-head coupé and its 140 counterpart, except for the radiator grille, headlights, bumpers, and a few chrome details.*

bumper was halved, with the number plate in between the two 'bananas'. This design modification helped to make the car look less heavy from the back view.

If you lifted up the boot lid there was no spare wheel in sight; instead, the luggage area was luxuriously carpeted and, if you wanted to get at the spare, you had to remove the base panel. This meant (as it still does with many other cars today) that when you had a puncture you had to remove all the luggage from the boot and put it on the ground in order to take out the spare wheel.

There was a nifty hinged bulkhead which provided access to the inside of the car from the boot. All you had to do was to open two locks with a square key, which did double duty for undoing the spats on the rear wheels. This feature meant that, with the bulkhead lowered, you could transport long objects such as golf clubs or fishing rods. It was these extra touches which so impressed Jaguar's clientèle.

The increased space inside the car, both at the front and at the back to make room for the occasional seats, meant of course that the overall outline was very different from previous XKs. This was especially true of the fixed-head coupé. It had a slightly shorter bonnet; the passenger compartment roof sloped more gently at the back and was 6¾ inches (17 cms) longer; there was a little less room in the boot; the windscreen was more vertical, and the glazed surface area was considerably greater than on the fixed-head 120.

Any rear-seat passengers had to be able to get into the back easily and, even with the front seat backs pushed down, it was still necessary to make the doors 5½ inches (14 cms) wider to avoid any poor adult rear passenger having to risk grievous bodily harm when trying to get into the 140 fixed-head coupé. The door-opening mechanism on this model was in the form of a push-button handle, similar to that used on the boot lid. This doorhandle design was restricted to the fixed-head, with the drophead keeping the old lever type and the OTS, of course, having no outside handles at all. On the first hundred or so of the fixed-head the doors were in aluminium, but for some reason the works changed them to steel in 1955, despite the increased weight which this entailed. This additional weight also gave problems with the door hinges, which were not really hefty enough to carry the steel version, so that before long you had to start lifting the door up to close it. This abnormally rapid hinge wear poses some tricky problems for modern fixed-head restorers.

Apart from the occasional seats, there were no outstanding changes inside the car. Two tiny ashtrays replaced the single central one which the 120 had boasted; the rear-view mirror had been modified; the four-spoke steering wheel had been retained, but at last it had lost its sharply protruding boss which the authorities, with reason, had pronounced dangerous; the indicator switch was now mounted on the centre of the dashboard, instead of on the steering wheel as previously. This change had been dictated by the adoption of a two-section universally-jointed steering column. The horn, however, was still on the steering wheel boss, with its famous jaguar head decoration.

The XK 140 fixed-head coupé could have been a complete styling disaster when you consider the dangers of trying to make a 2 + 2 out of what is basically a two-seater car, but the opposite was fortunately the case. It was a

A works photograph of the XK 140 drophead coupé shows the workmanship used in the production of Jaguar's hoods. All three body styles (open two-seater, drophead coupé and fixed-head coupé), were available on 15 October 1954 — the day of the XK 140's launch.

The open two-seater was the raciest member of the XK 140 family. Its lighter weight and powerful engine made speeds of over 125 mph (200 km/h) perfectly feasible. It was the only model in the 140 range not to have two occasional rear seats. In all, 3,354 open two-seaters were built, of which only 73 had right-hand drive. The lightweight hood folded away out of sight behind the seats and the side screens could be stowed in the boot to give a streamlined, ultra-sporty look.

beautifully balanced design and, even if it lacked the almost ethereal beauty of the XK 120 fixed-head, it still stands out as a wonderful example of classic, attractive styling. As with the 120, the 140's wire wheel option meant that spats could not be fitted to cover the rear wheels. Nevertheless, for comfort, appearance and braking, many owners chose 54-spoke Dunlops for their fixed-heads in place of the standard disc wheels. Chrome-plated wire wheels were optional on export models.

Because of its sterling qualities, its comfort, roominess and performance, the fixed-head coupé was a great success throughout its production life.

The drophead coupé was not, strangely enough, a fixed-head with the roof cut off to be replaced by a folding hood — as had been the case with the XK 120. There were scarcely any body panels on the fixed-head which were

interchangeable with the drophead, and certainly not the bonnet, wings or doors. Despite this, the drophead was still a 2 + 2, although the interior layout was different. The front bulkhead was moved forward only three inches (7.5 cms) — in other words, it followed precisely the forward re-location of the engine. The batteries were taken out of the back of the car to make room for the two occasional seats, but in the drophead coupé version alone, a single 12-volt battery was fitted in one of the front wings, as opposed to the two 6-volt batteries in the fixed-head. The removal of these batteries was not enough in itself to provide space for the two mini rear seats, so the depth of the boot was reduced.

All the same, if you compare the drophead XK 140 with its 120 equivalent, the hood line looked remarkably similar, despite the difference in passenger accommodation. The same holds good with the doors, deflectors and side-windows, which were also identical to the 120's.

In contrast, interior finish followed the same pattern as the 140 fixed-head as regards the abundance of wood and luxurious upholstery, whereas the hood mechanism, lining and interior lighting were modelled on the 120 drophead. In an effort to improve rear visibility and safety, the tiny rear window of the 120 was replaced by a larger one in transparent plastic.

As for the OTS, it was so like its 120 older brother that, apart from details I have already mentioned such as the bumpers, radiator grille, indicators and various chrome accessories, one had to look very closely to find the minor differences between the two, which included the new dashboard angle. That said, it was a genuine 140, with adjustable seats, room for your legs under the steering wheel, and many of the other innovations which the 140 family shared. It differed from its siblings in having aluminium doors, since weight was an important consideration in this true sports car model. The OTS options available, which underlined its racy character, were bucket seats to give better support on cornering; a Brooklands-type aero-screen, instead of the windscreen; and an uprated 220 bhp C-type engine. There was one non-option, in a manner of speaking, for the OTS had no overdrive facility.

The driving characteristics of the 140 range varied enormously, depending on whether you were in a fixed-head or an OTS, whether overdrive was fitted, whether you had the standard 'M' or 'MC' version, which axle ratio was used, etc.

The optional extras available on the 140 were as follows: anti-fog lamps, exterior luggage-rack, chrome wheel trim, Dunlop racing tyres, chromed wheels with chrome-plated spokes, and windscreen washer. I have already listed the purely mechanical options.

In France, only a limited number of XK 140s was imported — for the same reasons that applied to the XK 120 — 168 in all being sold through the Royal Elysées company. This was a very small proportion of the 9,051 which were built, and sales averaged 40 or so annually. The customers included many famous names in the worlds of sport, commerce and the arts: Raymond Loewy, who was to order a new body from Boano; Martell (brandy); Ricard (liqueurs); Berger (pastis); Robert Lamoureux; the Duke of Talleyrand; Ferdinand Beghin; Balkany; Annie Soisbault; Parsy; Françoise Sagan; Bernard Consten, etc.

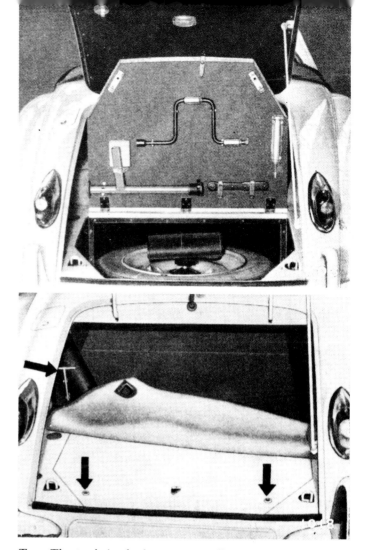

Top: The tools in the boot were well organised. When you lifted up the boot floor, concealing the spare wheel, you found the jack, wheel spanner, jack handle and grease gun fixed underneath; a comprehensive tool kit fitted snugly on top of the spare wheel.

Above: There was a hinged bulkhead at the back of the boot, giving access to the car's interior, which enabled long items to be transported. The key on the left released both the bulkhead locks and the boot floor panel.

A works drawing of the XK 140 fixed-head coupé fitted with disc wheels. Spats were supplied with disc wheels alone, since the eared nut on the wire wheels stood out proud of the body sides.

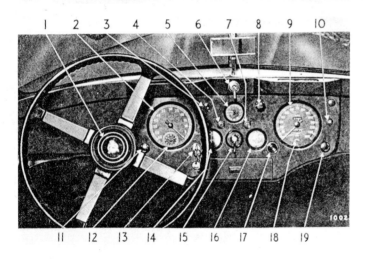

The XK 140's comprehensive instrumentation. Polished walnut was still featured on this model's facia, but was absent from the XK 150.

1. Horn
2. Rev counter
3. Starter button
4. Ignition warning light
5. Oil pressure and water temperature
6. Indicator
7. Flashing indicator warning light
8. Screen wiper switch
9. Speedometer
10. Screen washer button
11. Panel light switch
12. Clock
13. Ignition switch
14. Ammeter
15. Sidelights/fog lamps switch
16. Petrol gauge
17. Cigar lighter
18. Headlamp warning light
19. Heating control

Many illustrious coachbuilders tried their hands at re-bodying the 140 for the major motor shows in Geneva, Paris, Turin, London and New York. They included Vanden Plas, Ghia, Michelotti, Loewy-Boano, Zagato, Martial Oblin of Brussels, Bertone and Frua. Most of them produced bizarre and unusual cars using the 140 base and very few achieved the clean line and balance of the Jaguar works design.

The XK 140 was far less well-known in France than it was in America. The French motoring enthusiasts raved over the new model, but few people outside the automobile world knew of its existence. There was no authoritative or comprehensive road test carried out on the 140 in France, either. This was not the case in Great Britain, of course, for the respected motoring journal, *The Autocar*, published a detailed report in December 1955. Its tester concluded that the 140 happily lacked many of the 120's faults and that it was civilized, well-balanced, relaxing to drive and powerful. But you can read his conclusions on the fixed-head coupé for yourself:

"In October, 1952, the Jaguar XK 120 special-equipment coupé was road tested by *The Autocar;* at that time it was not for sale in Great Britain, which must have been extremely tantalizing for enthusiasts who had the purchase price ready. After a time, of course, the XK 120 was available on the home market and the model became very popular, especially among those who like to travel fast and far.

"At the 1954 London Motor Show the XK 120 was succeeded by the XK 140, and events have proved that the title 'Fiercer Jaguars' given to *The Autocar* description of the new models in the issue of 15 October of that year was indeed apt. The trend these days is for more bhp per litre, and Jaguars have never lagged behind in this field. The present standard version of the well-known six-cylinder, twin overhead camshaft engine develops 190 bhp as compared with 160 of the XK 120 engine, and when it is fitted with the high lift camshafts and 8:1 compression ratio of the special-equipment model, the power output is increased to 210 bhp at 5,750 rpm.

"In addition to increased power output from the engine, the chassis has benefited from lessons learnt on the racing circuits of Europe. Road holding, steering, brakes and suspension have been improved, and have helped to make the XK 140 a car in which it is possible to average very high speeds indeed over long distances with greater ease than in its predecessor.

"The weight distribution of the Jaguar XK 140 coupé is now 50.3 per cent at the front, and 49.7 per cent at the rear, as compared with 47.5 per cent and 52.5 per cent of the XK 120 coupé as tested by *The Autocar* in 1953. This has been achieved by moving the engine further forward and placing the battery, previously located behind the seat, in the engine compartment. This extra weight on the front wheels is the most decisive factor in the improved cornering ability. It results in a controlled degree of drift such as was achieved on racing cars of the past, when small-section tyres were fitted to the front wheels to achieve the same purpose by sliding, without the science of the action being fully understood. The car is fitted with rack and pinion steering, and the front torsion-bars have been increased in diameter.

"The extra power output has resulted, not unnaturally, in an increase in maximum speed, and the special equipment model — in this case including racing tyres — is capable of 130 mph in overdrive top gear. At this speed the engine was turning over at 4,900 rpm, with overdrive engaged. When the car is fitted with an overdrive, the axle ratio is 4.09:1, which gives an overall transmission ratio of 3.19:1.

"It is probable that by dispensing with the overdrive and having the optional axle ratio of 3.31:1, the maximum speed might be increased slightly. But for all normal road use in Great Britain, and fast touring on the Continent, the combination as provided on the test car proved adequate and delightful. In conditions where fast cruising is limited by traffic congestion and inadequate roads, the lower ratios provided by the 4.09:1 axle give superlative acceleration and enable very high average speeds to be maintained. The readiness with which 100 mph can be reached, rather than the absolute maximum, is the car's outstanding attribute.

"It is on such roads as the Routes Nationales of France that the car comes into its own. Heading south from the Belgian motor road where the maximum speed figures had been taken, the Jaguar seemed naturally to be turned in the direction of Le Mans, where the marque has achieved such fame. It was the return journey against the clock that made the greatest impression. Maximum speed was used in the intermediate gears, with the change from top to overdrive being made at 5,500 rpm. Le Mans was left at 10.20 am and the Jaguar was at Le Touquet airport at 2.28 pm. Two short stops were included in this time, and the last 90 of the 220 miles journey were on wet roads.

"In overdrive the car seemed to don the proverbial seven-league boots, and the tall poplar trees lining the long straight stretches of road appeared like a giant fence rushing by. Despite such sustained hard work, the oil pressure

Seen from this unusual angle, the XK 140's body line is a marvel of breeding and balance.

was steady at all times and there was never any sign of overheating.

"One very noticeable feature of the Jaguar coupé is its comparative silence at speed. The car cruises very happily with the speedometer needle hovering between the 100 and 110 mph marks, and the crew is able to converse in normal tones, despite an audible intake roar in the higher-engine-speed range. There is a complete lack of exhaust boom. However much this might please the out-and-out enthusiast, it can become overpowering in confined quarters. Wind noise also is at a very low level, and the car is restful to travel in.

"The major part of the road test was carried out with the car using racing tyres, and the high-pitched whine over smooth tarmac associated with this type of cover was noticed because of the general noise level. Road Speed tyres are standard equipment for the XK 140, and the difference in rolling radius of this tyre and the racing type makes a considerable difference to the speedometer reading. In the data panel the corrections given are for racing tyres, which give 20.3 mph in top gear per 1,000 engine rpm and 25.9 mph in overdrive. When rechecked with Road Speed tyres the speedometer corrections were as follows:

Car speedometer	10	20	30	40	50	60	70	80	90	100	110	120
True speed	12	20	27	36	45	55	65	75	85	95	105	115

"Another remarkable point about the XK 140 is its docility and flexibility in traffic or when travelling slowly. It is quite possible to accelerate from 10 mph in top gear without protest from the power unit. Not many years ago a twin overhead camshaft engine with an 8:1 compression ratio would have been a temperamental beast. Difficult to start, it would have oiled up plugs at low speeds and stalled at inconvenient times.

"Not so the Jaguar — it has an automatic starting carburettor, and after the car has stood in the open overnight one merely switches on the ignition, waits a second or two for the float chambers to fill, then presses the starter button. It was never necessary to press the button a second time, and after a few minutes' running the starting carburettor would cut out automatically as the engine reached operating temperature.

"During the road test, when a great number of miles were covered at high speed, no attention was needed apart from maintaining the oil level and no water was added to the radiator.

"The car would trickle gently along with other traffic in crowded city streets, drawing attention only because of its attractive appearance. Its hill climbing abilities would appear to be limited only by the need for maintaining adhesion of the 600 x 16 tyres. If the driver changes down on a main road gradient it is only because he has been baulked by other traffic or because he wishes to indulge his *joie de vivre*.

"In two hours on the Continent, the car covered 123 miles, and on occasions such as those the overall fuel consumption of 21.7 mpg was helped to a great extent by con-

tinuous use of the Laycock de Normanville overdrive. Operating only in top gear, the overdrive is brought into action by moving a small switch, illuminated in the 'on' position, fitted on the extreme right side of the facia panel. On a number of occasions the overdrive was engaged at maximum revs — 6,000 rpm — and the unit came into action with a barely noticeable pause and no sign of clutch slip.

"There is little difference between the times taken during the performance tests and those recorded with the XK 120, for increased power output has to deal with an increase in weight of one hundredweight. What should be borne in mind is that the extra weight has meant more room and comfort for the occupants of the car, with a higher maximum speed and improved fuel consumption. The wheelbase remains the same, but the XK 140 is three inches longer, one and a half inches higher, and two and a half inches wider than its predecessor.

"The suspension is a happy combination — there is comfort at low speeds with none of the teeth-chattering effect which in the past was associated with a sports car, even over cobbled roads, and with the tyres inflated to the pressures recommended for high speeds, the ride is still comfortable. Indeed it is possible to write a legible hand at over 110 mph. There is no sway or heeling over on fast corners, and the driver knows that there is reserve to allow for any of his own shortcomings. Restraint is required with the throttle pedal on wet surfaces, for when carrying out the standing-start acceleration tests it was found easy to spin the rear wheels on a dry road.

"The improved weight distribution, achieved mainly by repositioning the engine, has eliminated the oversteer noticeable in the earlier XK 120, and the suspension is firm without being harsh. The steering is light yet very positive. Road shocks are felt to some extent through the steering wheel and the best control is achieved by allowing the wheel to 'float' in the driver's hands.

"The driving seat is tailored to the car's performance. It has a more than adequate fore and aft adjustment, and this, combined with the telescopic steering column, enables drivers of vastly different proportions to achieve a comfortable position. A tall driver does not find he has to peer under the top rail of the windscreen, and one very quickly becomes accustomed to the divided windscreen glass. More room for the right elbow would be appreciated.

"The brakes proved entirely adequate for the high speeds involved. Under extreme conditions they did not fade or grab, but each application was accompanied by a rather annoying squeal from the front drums. The brakes call for heavier pedal pressure than usual when an emergency stop is required and some might prefer a measure of servo assistance. The brake pedal is well placed in relation to the accelerator, so that heel and toe gear changes can be made when approaching a corner. The hand brake lever is placed close to the gear lever on the passenger side of the propellor shaft cover.

"The clutch transmits 210 bhp to the rear wheels without protest in the form of slip or judder. It is necessary to depress the pedal completely to achieve a noiseless gear change, and the pedal travel is very long without achieving a light operating load. The gear change is satisfactory, but with a long movement of the lever from first to second. The

President René Coty, accompanied by Charles-F. Delecroix (Jaguar's French distributor and Managing Director of Royal-Elysées), opens the 1956 Paris Motor Show. On the right is B.Masson, director of Jaguar's overseas sales. This was the first appearance of the famous compact monocoque saloon, the Mark I. An XK 140 drop-head coupé was also on the Jaguar stand.

box itself could be improved if the ratios between first and second were slightly closer. First gear is desirable for starting from rest.

"Long-distance touring in the grand manner can be enjoyed only if the car is comfortable, and in this respect the Jaguar is ideal for two persons. There is an ample seat adjustment and the passenger is able to stretch his or her legs out. The back rests are not adjustable, but the angle is well chosen for comfort and control. It is possible for one adult to ride behind the driver or passenger with some discomfort on long journeys, or as an alternative there is room for two children. The comfort was impaired on some occasions by a draught around the ankles which came through the body trim below the facia when the window was slightly opened. A recirculation-type heater is part of the standard equipment and this functions well as a windscreen demister, although the fan is very noisy, and quite disturbing at low road speeds.

"Lighting is in general good. Yellow bulbs were fitted in the headlamps for Continental use and these were not entirely adequate at high speeds, but experience of other cars with the same type of headlamp using normal bulbs has shown that they permit full use to be made of the car's speed after dark. The twin fog lamps on the test car form part of the special equipment. The interior of the car can be illuminated by lights set in the roof lining and controlled by

An XK 140 open two-seater at the 1956 Arcachon concours d'élégance. A detail worth remembering is that wire wheels could be supplied painted to match the bodywork.

a switch on the facia; it was felt that they might be brighter. The instrument illumination can be dimmed by rheostat. There is a light built into the luggage compartment lid.

"By lowering the hinged flap in the front of the boot, the capacity can be greatly enlarged, but this prevents use of the rear seat. The floor of the boot is hinged, and beneath it are stowed the spare wheel and tools. The quality of the tool kit is in keeping with the car. The one-piece bonnet is released by pulling a catch beneath the facia, and some slight knack is required to find the safety catch on the front of the radiator grille. The supporting stay for the bonnet is clipped in a rather awkward position, especially for a short person.

"The number of cars capable of reaching 100 mph has increased in the past few years. There are very few which can reach this figure in under 30 seconds, as the XK 140 does with ease. More important, it can be held in overdrive to become a comfortable cruising speed with very low throttle openings and to record a fuel consumption of near enough 22 mpg. That these figures can be achieved in a car whose comfort and safety are superlative implies the highest praise for the team responsible for its creation. When these qualities are related to its price, there is no other car which can approach it in the high performance sphere, and it is a fine advertisement for the British automobile industry."

What a glowing reference! Even one of Jaguar's own dazzling advertising campaigns could only have had half the effect of this impressive editorial report in *The Autocar*. It was almost *too* good!

However, despite its exceptional qualities, the 140 was never a great success as a racing car, and there are two possibilities for its dearth of placings in major events — either the XK 140 fell short of the 120, or the 140 just could not match the opposition between 1955 and 1957. Although the 140 did have its moments, as in the 1956 Le Mans, such occasional triumphs did not make up for the overall lack of racing laurels.

Some carping critics said that the 140 had lost its sporting character in favour of a GT image, placing the accent on comfort and luxury, but the real reason was that all over the world, and most of all in Europe, other powerful, fast and handsome cars were appearing on the starting grids. So the XK 140 did not have a limited competition reputation because it was an inferior car to the 120, but because its contemporaries were so much better than their predecessors.

The vogue for sports cars was taking off world-wide, including Great Britain, where some companies were producing high-performance, stylish and sometimes relatively expensive models. Take the Triumph TR3, for example, which was approaching 115 mph (180 km/h) with a 2-litre 100 bhp engine; the Morgan Plus-Four, which borrowed its standard mechanical unit; the MGA, which was visually a fantastic car, even if it could not quite break the sound barrier; the Austin Healey 100, which was also verging on 115 mph with 112 bhp up its sleeve; the Lotus XI which could boast a genuine 112 mph from its diminutive 1,098 cc engine; and finally the Aston Martin DB2 4, which charged along happily at 125 mph (200 km/h) with its twin overhead cams, 3-litre power unit and 140 bhp.

Italy was not being left behind either. It could boast Alfa Romeos, Lancias, Maseratis and, of course, the fearsome Ferraris which had, in the space of five or six years, developed an impressive range of high-performance cars thanks to their extraordinary V12s with four overhead camshafts. By 1956 no Ferrari was doing less than 155 mph (250 km/h), whether it was the 500 Mondial Testa Rossa, the 250 Gran Turismo, the 750 Monza, the 410 Super America, or the Competition which notched up more than 175 mph (280 km/h).

France was in the running also, with the 2.5-litre 120 bhp Talbot Lago, whose four-cylinder engine powered the sports car to 118 mph (190 km/h), and even the United States had the Corvette and its deadly rival, the Thunderbird. In short, Jaguar had long lost its overall supremacy, and William Lyons — who had never rested on his laurels (even if they were decorated by *The Autocar*) — began to put his mind to the XK 140's successor.

The 1956 Le Mans 24-Hours. Bolton and Walshaw's PWT 846 was the only XK 140 which ever participated in this endurance event, and it by no means discredited the Jaguar marque.

An XK 140 fixed-head coupé at the finish of the 1956 Tour de France in Nice. Although the 140 could never do better than a placing in road events, it was known for its excellent reliability.

They had got there in the end! The final prototype was ready. This front view of the first D-type, taken in May 1954, shows the model's clean lines which were mainly a result of aerodynamic tests. This fascinating photograph includes Malcolm Sayer (extreme left) who worked on the aerodynamics; P.Weaver (second from left) chassis development; Bob Knight (third from left) engine development; and Norman Dewis, Jaguar's chief test driver, shaking the hand of F.R.W.England, racing manager.

D-TYPE

JUNE 1954—AUGUST 1956

A BORN WINNER

The D-type was not conceived as a car which would give a respectable performance at Le Mans; on the contrary, it was designed to win Le Mans. William Lyons was not the sort of man who would embark on such an ambitious and ruinously expensive development programme with the aim of keeping up with the Le Mans crowd. Nothing but the best was good enough for him. The D-type's success exceeded even Jaguar's expectations, which only goes to prove that there is some mysterious alchemy at work when it comes to car development for, even though companies other than Jaguar had exceptional engineering talent in their armoury, none of them could produce the uniquely superb D-type.

Having to follow the example set by the XK 120C and its marvellous performance in the 1953 Le Mans 24-Hours, the new car had to be even faster and cover even more ground than its predecessor. With the wealth of Jaguar's technological heritage at its back, the D type was to go so fast that its rivals were knocked for six and spent years waiting for the D-type to fade away and lose its domination in competition motoring.

As with the C-type, the 'D' in D-type came from the abbreviation XK D but, despite the alphabetical sequence, the D-type was not a logical progression from the C. In many ways, including their construction, they were two totally different cars.

The D-type was created in the top-secret section of the Browns Lane works, and an élite group of people were invited to try out Jaguar's latest stroke of genius. The 1953 Le Mans winners, Rolt and Hamilton, were just two of the privileged guests. Their job was to get the last ounce of speed out of the prototype.

The highly qualified men, who had to go through a very rigorous selection procedure before they were allowed to work in the closely guarded development department, were themselves responsible for giving the new car its nickname of 'D-type'. This nickname was, of course, chosen by the Jaguar management as its official name when the time came to baptise their latest creation. There was no particular reason for the choice of the letter 'D'. 'C', of course, had stood for competition, but 'D'? Well, it certainly cannot have stood for disc, as many people have suggested, for the C-type already had disc brakes way back in 1952. But, perhaps it did stand for disc; this explanation is no less credible than some of the opinions expressed about the SS initials in the 1930s and '40s!

Between the C-type and the D-type there was a machine which is traditionally and apocryphally called the 'proto C-D'. This prototype formed a perfect bridge between the two cars, as it was 50 per cent C-type and 50 per cent D-type. It had the tubular chassis of the C-type and the D-type's body contouring, which has since become a classic

of its kind. This C-D prototype was only used for full-size aerodynamic studies which were orchestrated by Malcolm Sayer, so we can really look on this transition model as a rebodied C-type.

Tony Rolt was the first to take out the D-type and put it through its paces on the Motor Industry Research Association's track outside Nuneaton, only a short distance from Coventry. There were all kinds of hiccups on this first outing which postponed all thoughts of any proper testing but it was obvious, nevertheless, that the new car was a real goer. The test sessions were continued on the circuit for which the car was designed: Le Mans. Tony Rolt was in the team again, after his frustrating time on the MIRA track, and he was more determined than ever, in March 1954, to drive the prototype to its limits. His instructions for this first session were very precise, and Rolt was itching to push the car harder. Succumbing to temptation, ignoring all the safety regulations and thumbing his nose at the track officials, he decided to do just one more lap with his foot hard down. Afterwards he admitted that he had been a naughty boy, but the result of his transgression was simply phenomenal. The D-type quite simply smashed the old record (held by Ascari) to smithereens. In that one illicit lap Tony Rolt knocked more than four seconds off the track record.

The Jaguar team, which had come for the tests, could not get over the figures. No one had seriously thought that the car could be ready by June, only three months distant, but now that they had seen the Le Mans track record taken apart it was 'all systems go', and a madcap race against time started in an attempt to have the works D-types ready for the 24-Hours. They were carried along by an absolute

certainty that victory was theirs for the taking.

The prototype which had had an abortive outing on the MIRA track bore little resemblance to the D-type as the public saw it at Le Mans in June. The final model was like a dream — a masterpiece of streamlining created by Malcolm Sayer, who still had some tricks up his sleeve, as we shall see later! The problem which faced Malcolm Sayer is easy to put into words, but hellishly difficult to solve: if you want to travel above certain speeds, say 125 mph (200 km/h), you find that you have an invisible but powerful obstacle to get through — air. At lower speeds you hardly notice any wind resistance, but at high speed air becomes a solid and impenetrable wall which, try as you may, you just cannot break through. You charge at it and it pushes you back; you try again and it seems to have you in a vice, you are swimming through treacle and it swallows up all those precious horsepower which the engineers struggled so hard to produce.

To tackle this unseen enemy you forget about any increase in horsepower for the time being, and spend a few years studying aerodynamics, just as though you were going to design a plane. Your reference books are full of strange new terms like coefficient of penetration, drag factor, frontal surface, air flow, Cx trap, wind tunnel, etc....

If you find all this too heavy going, you call in a specialist in aerodynamics — the best one available, of course. Jaguar's choice was, naturally, Malcolm Sayer. He had served time with the Bristol Aircraft Corporation and if anyone knows about wind resistance it is an aircraft boffin. Sayer had a passion for fast cars, and his two greatest achievements were to be the D- and E-types.

How did he set about producing the streamlined D-type?

142

Well, he began by lowering the centre of gravity and reducing the frontal surface area. He then roughed out a design and tried out various small-scale variations in the wind tunnel. Next he asked the engineers to set the engine at an angle so that the bonnet line could be lowered; he streamlined anything which could create air turbulence; gave the car more straight-line stability by extending the line of the head-rest back and down to the tail, to steer the car at speeds of over 175 mph (280 km/h) on the long Le Mans straights; and then laid great emphasis on the little-understood importance of reducing drag at the rear. A bonus of all this hard work was that the car he came up with was incredibly beautiful.

Vertical stabilisers became all the rage; over the next few months all the constructors adopted these aerodynamic 'rudders' in the conviction that it was the remedy for high-speed instability and that it enabled their drivers to relax for a few seconds on the straights. Lotus, Mercedes, Aston Martin, and even Chaparal climbed on the bandwagon.

But I must not jump the gun, for the first 1954 Le Mans D-types did not yet have those famous fins projecting out of the headfairing. THEY DID SEE PAGE 425

If there is one thing which goes to show above all that the D-type was not a progression from the C-type it is the construction methods which were used on the two cars. The C-type had a chassis, but the D-type did not. It brought in the age of the monocoque car.

In the case of the D-type there was a central structure in very light alloy, consisting of a network of elliptical section tubes which were welded together, and on to which the aluminium panels were riveted. This shell was strengthened by cross-members which went the whole length of the car, making up the central part and incorporating the two seats and the driving controls.

The D-type comprised three sections: the central structure was extended on either side by two-substructures; the rear section, which was bolted on to the main section, catered for the fuel tanks and the spare wheel; the forward substructure, consisting of a cradle of interconnecting tubes which were welded to each other and to the main section, carried the power unit and suspension.

The front tubular part, which housed the engine, was soon found to be a nuisance if it suffered even the slightest frontal impact. For this reason, less than a year later, this section was bolted on to the load-bearing structure, instead of being welded, so that it could be easily removed if repairs were needed.

The front bulkhead, which served a dual role as a firewall, played a vital part in the car's rigidity as it was extremely strong. Its design also enabled the driver to stretch out his legs, and that was a much-appreciated luxury! Moving back to the rear bulkhead, the opening for the transmission shaft was calculated to within a millimetre to ensure that the overall structure would not be weakened.

As for the front suspension, there were no surprises in store for anyone who was acquainted with that of the XK which was repeated in the C-type. There were the two long-based wishbones and torsion-bars which did their usual highly efficient job. The anchorage points for the torsion-bars had obviously to be thought out carefully, since you cannot just place them anywhere on a monocoque car. An unusual little touch was that a precision scale adjuster was fitted to this torsion-bar anchorage point, so that the car's trim could be regulated to within a millimetre. However,

The all-aluminium D-type moves for the first time, with William Heynes, Jaguar's chief engineer, at the wheel. Created as a Le Mans winner, the D-type proved to be the most fabulous racing car of all time. It left such a mark on its time that all later sports cars owed something to the D-type and bore some resemblance to it. It was the archetypal sports car. A works photograph dated 12 May 1954.

A cutaway drawing of the short-nose D-type, by Vic Berris.

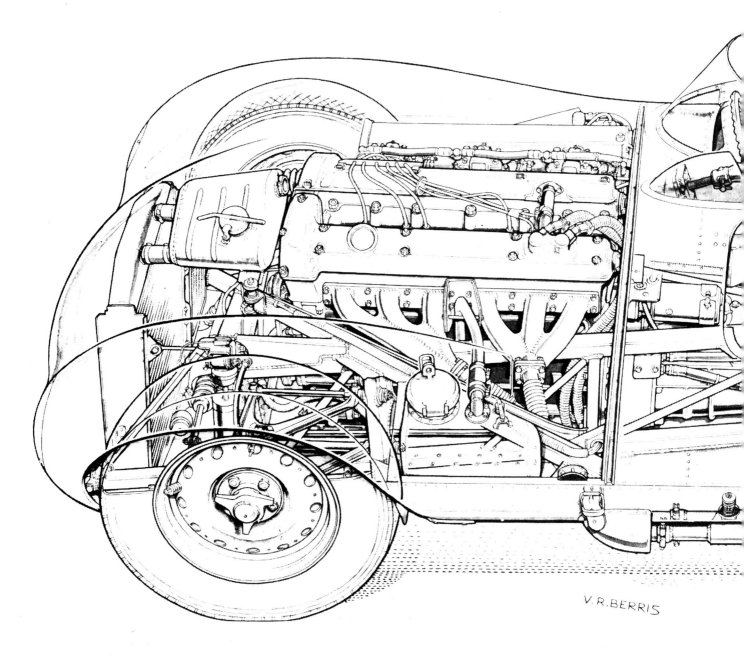

V.R.BERRIS

when you realise the difficulties inherent in torsion-bar adjustment, you might wonder whether this scale adjuster was of any real use.

There was no difference in the steering mechanism, either. The Alford rack and pinion had been used on the C-type and then extended to the 140 range, so there was no reason for Jaguar to look further than this well-tried system. Its general characteristics were precision and responsiveness, with the added bonus that it needed only 1¾ turns of the wheel from lock to lock.

Moving backwards to the rear suspension, it was slightly different from the C-type's, although it used the same basic principles. The transverse torsion-bars were connected to a

pivot anchored to the rear bulkhead. The linkage of the axle end with the bar was effected by a thick steel plate which was perfectly rigid. These two linking arms were repeated on the other side of the axle, but unsprung, thus forming a sort of parallelogram, intended to improve the performance of the axle which was still, unfortunately, the fixed Salisbury variety. It was an interesting arrangement which behaved rather like a double wishbone suspension. Wheel movements were damped by telescopic Newton absorbers fitted with stops: enough said!

Dunlop disc brakes, as on the second-generation C-types, were employed. The disc brake system was by now gremlin-free, although it had developed into a pretty complex set-

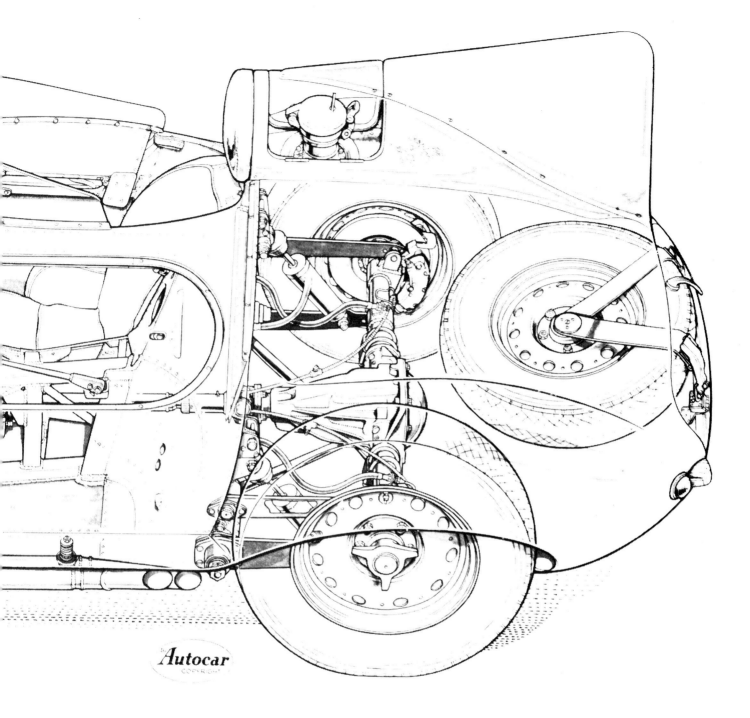

Autocar

up, with no less than six pistons and six quick-change pads working in unison on each disc. Multiply that by two and you will have an idea of the complexity of the perfected system!

It was, of course, these disc brakes which had been such a help in taking Jaguar to the top in motor sport, but every car component was always under review to make sure that Coventry was keeping up in the technological race. This was why Jaguar and Dunlop kept plugging away at disc brakes, seeing how they could improve them even further.

Front-brake cooling depended uniquely on the air-flow directed to them.

The amount of pressure required on the brake pedal was

substantially reduced, thanks to a hydraulic servo which used energy provided by a Plessy pump driven by the prop shaft at the back of the gearbox.

For the first few months the D-type's major brake problem was that the 12¾-inch (32.5-cm) diameter discs overheated badly. Ventilation was inadequate and the high temperatures led to the brake fluid boiling away happily for all it was worth.

One of Jaguar's trademarks — wire wheels — was missing on the D-type, though the C-type had been sporting them only a few weeks before. They had been replaced by much lighter magnesium alloy wheels which retained the eared centre-lock. These new Dunlop wheels stuck to the

The driving seat of a D-type as seen by the Jaguar Le Mans drivers when they climbed into the cockpit. As on many Jaguars, the rev counter seems to be graduated back to front. This did not stop the engine turning over at 8,000 rpm! The speedometer is graduated up to 180 mph (290 km/h). This spartan but very efficiently laid out cockpit is a model of its type. An aluminium panel closed off the passenger compartment when it was not needed. All that protected the driver from the elements was a small sheet of perspex.

familiar 16-inch (42-cm) diameter, but the width had been increased to 5½-inches (14-cms) in the interests of improved roadholding. Fifteen large and 15 small holes were alternated around the edge of the wheel to assist cooling and to lighten the car's unsprung load even more. In effect, the new Dunlops were the most beautiful wheels in the world... or so many Jaguar enthusiasts say.

The dominant feature in the driving position was an incredibly handsome three-spoke steering wheel made from super-light alloy.

There is hardly any need to say that the instrumentation was comprehensive and well designed, since this is the least one can expect in a Jaguar! It even boasted non-reflective glass, which is a definite plus for drivers who sit glued to the wheel for hours on end. I might as well run through the instruments, nevertheless, just in case you are thinking of buying a D-type. There was a rev counter, marked up to 8,500 rpm and complete with 'tell-tale' needle, oil pressure gauge, ammeter, petrol gauge and a water temperature gauge.

The bucket seat took up a large proportion of the cockpit, with more space being allotted to the driver than to any possible passenger. In fact during a race an aluminium panel closed off the right-hand side of the cockpit (on left-

This was the first time that Jaguar D-types were seen at Le Mans: in 1954. The works came within a hair's breadth of victory but had to settle for second place. The whole team is out to push the cars to the start.
No 12 (OKV2) was driven by S.Moss and P.Walker.
No 14 (OKV1), which finished second, was entrusted to A.Rolt and D.Hamilton.
P.Whitehead and K.Wharton drove No 15 (OKV3).

Although he did not make it to the end of the 1954 Rheims 12-Hours, Stirling Moss, driving a D-type in partnership with P.Walker, beat the lap record. Behind Moss, wearing glasses, is W.Heynes, who was at the root of Jaguar's technological progress, both in racing and production cars. Leaning against the stands, in the background, is Gérard Levecque, who worked for the French importers and helped Jaguar in organising their Continental movements of people and cars.

hand drive models, of course) to avoid the creation of turbulence, and this also made it clear that the D-type was principally intended to be a single-seater racing car with the driver's seat offset, rather than a two-seater sports car.

A plexiglass wrap-round windscreen protected the cockpit, starting level with the front of the head rest and going round to the same point on the other side. It was hinged at the door so that the two could open together. The word 'door' might be thought a slight exaggeration when you look at the tiny hinged section through which the driver entered the car!

Jaguar kept some of the C-type's best features, such as the one-piece bonnet which hinged forward to give easy access to the power unit. The front view was totally unlike that of the C-type however. There was no radiator grille whatsoever, merely an oval air intake, rather like a mouth, on the end of the bonnet. This open mouth shape was to become one of the constant features of Jaguar sports cars; it was almost as much of a trademark as the traditional shape of the radiator grille on the 120, 140, 150, Mark I and Mark II.

The back end of the car was dominated by the headrest, which sported a stabilising fin from late 1954 onwards. There were three stages in the evolution of the final tail design. The first was a headfairing without a fin, the second a fin which was fastened securely to the headfairing, and the third a completely integral fin which merged smoothly with the headfairing and the tail.

The back of the car, which was bolted on to the central section, was taken up almost entirely by a 36½-gallon (167-litre) tank, divided into two independent compartments. The quick-release filler cap was revealed by lifting up a hinged section of the headfairing.

The D-type was both smaller and lighter than the C-type. The wheelbase measured 7 feet 6 inches (2.28 metres), front track 4 feet 2 inches (1.27 metres), rear 4 feet (1.22 metres) and the car's weight, including petrol, oil and water, was approximately 18 cwt (900 kgs).

By fitting the engine at an angle of 8 degrees the Jaguar team was able to reduce the bonnet height by two inches (5-cms) and, with it, the frontal area which was the part of the car which had the hardest battle with wind resistance. When you are dealing with such high-level design, the least pound of weight and the tiniest fraction of an inch can make all the difference between success and failure. When Malcolm Sayer developed the 1/10th scale model in the wind tunnel, he knew to within the odd mile per hour what the car's ultimate top speed would be.

I have left the most important until last: the engine, gearbox and rear axle.

Why have I done so? Perhaps because they did not differ radically from those on the C-type, or perhaps because the speed merchants who knew their racing engines had expected to see a new, dynamic racing engine instead of a pepped-up series one. It still had its six cylinders, for it was the grand old XK engine which had already reached the limits of its potential. They had been trying everything they knew for several months, but nothing worked... the most advanced and highly developed cylinder head; wider and straighter inlet ports; oversize inlet valves with a 1 7/8-inch (4.76-cm) diameter; a sleek camshaft, which allowed maximum valve cross-flow at top engine speeds; the breather

Rheims 1954. Jaguar was hell-bent on taking its revenge
after its defeat at Le Mans a few weeks previously. Peter
Whitehead came up trumps by being first at the finish after
12 hours of hard racing. He and his co-pilot, Ken Wharton,
gave the D-type its first victory. This particular car (chassis
number XKC 404) still exists today and has retained its
original OKV 3 registration number.

Victory at last! One month after the 1954 Le Mans 24-Hours, P.Whitehead and K.Wharton drove their D-type, OKV 3, into first place in the Rheims 12-Hours, with another D-type driven by A.Rolt and D.Hamilton coming home second.

system on the cam covers; a new casting design for the exhaust manifold, giving a more horizontal result to avoid slowing up the exhaust gases; three DCO3 45 Webers... nothing seemed to be able to ginger it up. There was no way that the XK was going to give more than 250 bhp without a serious risk of it cracking up, and Bill Heynes and Harry Weslake were only too well aware of the fact.

The lubrication arrangement was the only true innovation. They decided to try the dry-sump system. I will just run through it in case you don't know how this works. Instead of keeping a few gallons of oil in the bottom end of the engine, which meant fitting a large sump there which would make it impossible to drop the engine down and bring the centre of gravity down to road-level, they employed a large separate sump fitted with a scavenge pump, radiator and oil filter, so that the sump below the engine could be dispensed with, and the engine unit could be lowered a good four inches (10-cms). The auxiliary oil reservoir could be as big as they liked, and they opted for one with a 36-pint (25-litre) capacity.

An added advantage of this system was that there was no longer any risk of the light alloy cooling fins breaking in the standard wet sump system. There was, however, one disadvantage for anyone wanting to make normal road use of a D-type in that, if you wanted to pop into town to pick up the morning paper, you would have to sit with the engine running for a good 20 minutes to warm up your 28 pints of oil before you could move off. But then, who uses a D-type to go to the newsagents?

Dry-sump lubrication was used on all the D-types, but was restricted to true racing cars. One of the dry sump's plus points in competition was that it helped keep the road wheels firmly on the ground at very high speeds, or when taking the crown of a hill. The phrase 'dry sump' is of course inappropriate, since there is just as much oil circulating and in the reservoir as in a wet sump system.

On the subject of cooling, you may be interested to know that the aluminium radiator came from Marston-Excelsior and that the header tank, which usually sat on top of the radiator, was, as with some of the C-types, detached from the radiator and moved out of the way in order to reduce the height of the car.

I cannot miss the opportunity of putting to rest an old wives' tale which is often repeated, even by motoring know-alls, and that is the myth that the change to the dry sump system had the happy side-effect of increasing the D-type's engine output. Absolute rubbish! It produced not a fraction of a horsepower extra, whether it were hp, bhp, DIN, or anything else.

The 3.4-litre XK power unit never exceeded 250 to 260 bhp or, at least, not safely. And this last was very important to Jaguar, for the marque had a reputation for reliability, and this was a key factor if you were going to try to win Le Mans, since it was no good trying to squeeze a few extra horsepower out of your engine if it meant that it would crack up at any minute.

So there was no question of embarking on the perilous adventures of boosting, special fuel mixtures, fitting three valves to a cylinder, desmodromic valves, or any other of the techniques which one might think of to increase an engine's performance. There is no point in taking the whip to a horse when he cannot go any faster!

The D-type's maximum 250 bhp was attained with the engine turning over at 5,750 rpm which, with a long-stroke engine, could have meant breaking point but for the fact that every part had been meticulously weighed, adjusted, polished and balanced to make sure that vibration was kept to a minimum.

The clutch was no surprise — a Borg & Beck with three 7½-inch (19-cm) plates, hydraulically operated. The gearbox, however, was a new design produced by Jaguar, with syncromesh on all gears, including first, since, as the box had been conceived with Le Mans in mind, it was thought that first would be needed for the hairpin bends.

An oddity in the layout was the siting of the starter motor on top of the gearbox, instead of underneath where one would have expected to find it.

A compact, low, menacing, fluid and short-nosed car with a breathtaking profile, the D-type was now ready to burst out on an unsuspecting world. All it needed was a top-rank circuit and opposition to match.

The circuit, need I say it, was Le Mans, and the grand occasion the 24-Hours race. Even during the practice sessions the D-type's performance had been astounding. The timers had shaken their stopwatches in amazement, convinced that they were not working properly. But no, the evidence was there in their hands. The lap record had been obliterated by Tony Rolt, who had averaged 110.75 mph (270 km/h) on the Mulsanne Straight at the bottom of the Hunaudières.

Jaguar produced three cars for the 1954 Le Mans 24-Hours, run as usual in June. The first D-type was given to Rolt and Hamilton (OKV 1); the second to Moss and Walker (OKV 2); and the third to Whitehead and Wharton (OKV 3).

Facing the three works D-types, Ferrari brought along its 340 bhp 4.9-litre and its 290 bhp 4.5-litre cars, Lagonda its Bentley V 2, Aston Martin the DB3 S, Gordini its cracking twin overhead cam models, Talbot entered its 4.5-litre hemispherical head car, Maserati a 3.5-litre, and Cunningham — the American at Le Mans — had called up the cavalry.

The 1954 Le Mans will be remembered for the rain, mechanical problems and Jaguar's run of bad luck. Despite its blistering bursts of speed on the Hunaudières, the D-type was not braking as well as they had hoped compared with the Ferrari, which was eating up the track with its superior acceleration and braking power. The Jaguars seemed to be having misfiring trouble which meant that the plugs were changed repeatedly, but to no avail. The mechanics then realised that the problem was probably nothing to do with ignition, but was perhaps due to a fuel supply fault and, sure enough, when they looked at the filters they found a very fine greyish deposit blocking them which had passed through the gauze filtering in the pit tanks. At that point they simply removed the filters, since they were proving a hindrance rather than a help, adjusted the carburettors, and the cars ran like a dream. All went well until Stirling Moss' brakes packed up, coming out of the Mulsanne Straight. How ironic that he should have been put out of the race by one of the features which had been the making of Jaguar's competition prowess — disc brakes! The next disaster came in the shape of serious gearbox trouble on OKV 3. Whitehead did all he could but he eventually had to throw in the sponge.

So there was now only one D-type left (OKV 1) to uphold Jaguar's reputation, which at this point looked like disappearing overnight. Hamilton and Rolt gave it all they had

OKV3, chassis No XKC 404 (and subsequently XKD 404).
This car has become a motor racing legend, and can still be
seen today in exhibitions of old racing cars.

The engine of the D-type which won the 1954 Rheims 12-Hours. It had the wide-angle cylinder head, Weber 45 DCOE carburettors, special breathers, straight ports, and developed 300 bhp.

Because of its second placing in the 24-Hours race, the No 14 D-type was given the place of honour on Jaguar's stand at the October 1954 Paris Motor Show. The show was officially opened by President René Coty, with the French Jaguar importer Ch.-F. Delecroix and his son.

A works photograph of 1954 showing what the 1955 production model was going to look like. This short-nose D-type had no fin. Tucked away behind their perspex visors were the Lucas headlamps and tiny flashing indicators.

and even managed to drive the D-type into a position less than a lap behind the best car in the field — Trintignant's Ferrari! Hamilton later revealed that he took some crazy risks with the engine.

But courage, talent, tenacity and daring were not enough. It was almost as if Jaguar was destined not to win Le Mans that year. Nevertheless, OKV 1 by no means disgraced itself with its second place result, although first place is the only one that has ever counted for Jaguar.

Bill Lyons and Bill Heynes, who had been following the race from the stands, had practically nothing to say afterwards.

Le Mans 1954 may have been a fiasco in Jaguar's eyes, but it was really a great achievement. The D-type had proved itself and, taking into account the unpredictable problems with the fuel-filter elements, it was obviously a star of the future. And it had taken first place in the Index of Performance, since the Ferrari's engine capacity was almost half as large again as that of the D-type. Small consolation, perhaps, but it was better than nothing.

There was another pleasant surprise in the placings for, although a Cunningham had taken third place, fourth had been snatched by a genuine series C-type.

The 1954 Le Mans had taught Jaguar a great deal, not

least the necessity of ruling out any possible mechanical foul-ups, especially the unpredictable ones! No matter what it cost, Jaguar had to win, for they had gone too far to give up now.

The next real chance for the D-type to shine came with the Rheims 12-Hours classic. Whitehead and Wharton showed a clean pair of heels to the rest of the field, which consisted of more or less the same cars which had been entered at Le Mans the month before. Stirling Moss registered the best lap time before, unfortunately, being forced to retire by a broken gearbox.

The 1954 racing season continued with some brilliant performances by C-types, which were far from being on the scrap-heap. Among the most striking C-type successes were Goodwood, where Cs took the first three places; the West Essex race; Oulton Park; the Dutch Sports Car Race at Zandvoort; the Wakefield Trophy; the International Charterhall Meeting; Watkins Glen; Brands Hatch, and others.

The 120 also made its mark at some prestige meetings, but the most striking development was the appearance of Jaguar-engined cars from various sources: HWM, Tojeiro, Jaguara, RGS/Atlanta and Cooper.

An attempt to run the D-type in the 3-litre class at the Tourist Trophy meeting in Ireland deserves a mention, since the factory saw this as an ideal opportunity to try out the short-stroke 2.4-litre engine which was to be put in the compact monocoque saloons that appeared a few months later. This saloon was to be Jaguar's most commercially rewarding line with the retrospectively named Mark I, followed by the Mark II.

So this series 2.4-litre (83 x 76.5 mm) engine was placed in the D-type and it was sent into action to see whether the 193 bhp which were produced by this oversquare engine at 6,000 rpm gave the results one would expect from a power unit which was going to drive the new saloons. In the TT 'action' there was one broken scavenge pump, and the engines fell apart as though they had been built with Meccano. Whitehead and Wharton managed to struggle home however, and took fifth place in their category.

Jaguar rushed to erase the memory of the oversquare's humiliation to avoid any discredit attaching itself to the new unit which, despite the TT fiasco, was a fine piece of engineering.

The honours for the 1954 motor-racing season, therefore, belonged mainly to the C-type and to non-works teams. Lofty England let slip one day that the factory and William Lyons might have soft-pedalled the D-type a bit to give C-type owners a better chance of winning a few pots. Whether this was an act of kindness or of enlightened self-interest on Lyons' part, it was certainly good marketing sense in so far as the cars were manufactured to be sold. However, now that the D-type was really up to the mark and C-type production had stopped, the works could start thinking about putting the D-type on sale to the public.

The first six D-types were snapped up instantly: Johnny Broadhead took OKV 2, John Goddard OKV 3 and the Ecurie Ecosse bought two others. Hamilton purchased OKV 1 for his own private use, but don't ask me how much it cost him, because I honestly don't know.

1955 saw the start of series D-type production. The most important change from the design used for the original six examples was at the front of the car. This was the stage at which the front tubular part of the structure was bolted rather than welded to the central section. There are no words to describe the sinking feeling you had in your stomach if you bumped the front end of one of the original D-types — however gently — into another solid object. Utter desolation is the nearest I can come to it. Jaguar, therefore, had to do something about the eminently dent-able aluminium alloy and they chose, instead, a much more robust and sensible solution: nickel-steel tubes. These were not as thick in cross-section as the aluminium ones, so there was no weight gain, and another detachable tubular frame-work was added to take the radiator and oil cooler.

1955 JAGUAR 'D' TYPE

A Jaguar drawing which put on record the amazing lines of the 1955 D-type. This long-nose version is a shining example of what can be achieved by a talented specialist in aerodynamics and an extraordinary team of engineers.

157

Jaguar men burning the midnight oil. Three D-types being fussed over as last-minute adjustments are made. In a few hours these cars will be lining up for the start of the 1955 Le Mans 24-Hours.

Le Mans 1955. I.Bueb and D.Hamilton are on their way to giving the Jaguar D-type its first victory on the Sarthe circuit. The long nose, all-enveloping windscreen, and fin extension from the headfairing were the visible characteristics of the works 1955 D-types.

The other major difference was again at the front of the car, which was extended by 7½-inches (19-cms) with the aim of improving air penetration. These new D-types were inevitably referred to as the 'long-nosed' Ds, while the 1954 Le Mans cars were, of course, the 'short-nose' model. The 'long-nose' cars were given two air scoops at the front to make brake cooling more efficient.

The perspex windscreen was made even more all-enveloping by being taken right back to the headrest, to stop side winds whistling across the back of the driver's neck. All the body modifications, including a slightly longer tail and a fin which formed a more fluid line with the back of the car, were carried out under Malcolm Sayer's instructions. He was determined that the '55 D-type' would be aerodynamically the best car the world had ever seen, or was ever likely to see. He was so meticulous that he even asked the mechanics to cover the body joints with wax to avoid the formation of 'air traps'.

At the same time as this streamlining was being worked on, the development workshop was putting the brakes under the microscope, reducing the servo action slightly, and improving cooling and the composition of the discs.

The engine could not, of course, be left out of this review programme, and the subject of scrutiny was the cylinder head. This was the stage at which the famous 'wide-angle' head was developed, and here is its story.

The noticeable absentee from the 1954 Le Mans had been Mercedes, but everyone knew that they had not given up the ghost as far as the 24-hour classic was concerned; in fact, it was an open secret that, somewhere deep in the Stuttgart factory, Mercedes was working on a fabulous new car which already had a name — the 300 SLR Desmo, after the fiendish new valve arrangement. It looked as though Mercedes was on to a winner since, theoretically at least, with the valves not being subject to bouncing at high speeds, there was no limit to how fast the engine could turn. Also, as Jaguar had discovered to its cost, since the D-type lagged behind the Ferraris in acceleration power, Browns Lane had to concentrate even harder on obtaining more horsepower if the D-types were to make any impression in 1955.

As usual, William Lyons called in Harry Weslake, who immediately set to work with Bill Heynes to cast a magic spell on the head for, at that high development level, the cylinder head is your only hope if you need more power. There were not that many options open to them. To start with, they increased the diameter of the inlet valves from 1 7/8-inches (463-mm) to 2-inches (508-mm) to satisfy the XK's huge appetite at high speeds; and, to evacuate the burnt gases more rapidly, they increased the exhaust valve diameter to 1 11/16-inches (430-mm). The only problem was that, with such large-diameter valves, they are quite likely to rattle against each other. The only solution to this is to increase the angle of the valve stems and, as a by-product, to widen the distance between the seats.

The angle of the exhaust valve was increased from 35 to 40 degrees, while that of the inlet valve remained at 35 degrees. The alteration in the exhaust inclination has led to this head being referred to as the '35/40' or, more familiarly, the 'wide-angle' head.

Having increased the valve diameters, they also widened the timing to gorge the combustion chambers with fuel.

Heynes and Weslake, therefore, decided to redesign the camshaft, increasing the lift from 3/8-inch to 7/16-inch; the difference of 1/16-inch (1.6-mm) may not sound much, but it has a dramatic effect on the gas flow if, at the same time, you have widened the valve timing.

These engines were handled and assembled by a rigorously selected group of specialists. All the component parts were meticulously weighed, ruthlessly X-rayed and invariably balanced. The piston-rod assemblies were re-weighed before being fitted. Crankshafts were balanced dynamically with the flywheel and damper, after having been balanced statically on their own by gradually gently filing away at the counterweight.

A scrupulous check was made on the valve clearances, in a room which was kept at a temperature of 20°C. Even the tiniest nut was secured by drilling and pinning after it had been screwed on to its opposite number.

Nothing was left to chance in this quest for perfection, with each man assuming responsibility for his own engine.

Once all the pieces had been put together, the test bed showed that the modifications had produced an additional 30 bhp, which must have brought a smile to Lyons' face. There had also been a shift in the torque, for the maximum 280 bhp was now produced at only 5,700 rpm.

We all know that what you gain on the swings you lose on the roundabouts, which in the case of the new engine meant that the car's sensational performance at high speeds would have to be paid for by a lack of the hitherto guaranteed flexibility at low speeds. Still, the engine had been designed for maximum power at 5,000 rpm plus, so who cared if it did not run so smoothly at 1,500 rpm?

Before downing tools, the competition management decided to dispense with the old Salisbury axle and to replace it with a robust ZF differential on the three works D-types which were to run in the 1955 Le Mans.

In the midst of all this frantic activity on the works racing cars, William Lyons reminded his loyal customers that the short-nose production cars were still available, as well as a civilised cylinder head option (35/35), for the very reasonable price of £2,700.

When you come down to the nitty gritty, the only difference between the two models was really that extra 30 bhp which had cost Jaguar a small fortune to obtain.

That year saw five 'long-nose' D-types produced for works use — in other words for Jaguar to enter at Le Mans. It is no secret that 67 D-types were built during 1955 and 1956. Forty two came on the market, of which the majority — 18 — went to America. Ten stayed in Great Britain, three were exported to Australia, two to France, and the rest were shared by Canada, Belgium, Cuba, New Zealand, Spain, Finland, El Salvador, The Congo and Mexico. Of the rest, nine cars were destroyed in the terrible Browns Lane fire in 1957 and 16 bodies were used on the road version which was given the denomination XK SS. These developments took place in 1957, so see later in the book for details!

June 1955: the Jaguar factory was working flat out for the main event of the year, the Le Mans 24-Hours race.

The great day had come. All the protagonists from 1954 were there, but the public's eyes were glued to the Mercedes 300 SLR. There were three of them, with their impressive metallic finishes, entrusted to Levegh/Simon, Fitch/Kling,

Sanderson executing one of many tricky manoeuvres at the Aintree National on 23 June 1956. The Écurie Écosse D-type (XKD 561) was fitted with a 3-litre Wilkinson engine.

and Moss/Fangio. With such an impressive team and such a car it seemed obvious that this was going to be a race to remember, and the spectators held their communal breath in expectation of an epic battle between the model which had just won the Mille Miglia (the 300 SLR), the one which had almost won the year before (the D-type) and the defending champion (the Ferrari).

To fill you in on the others, who had by no means come along just for a Sunday afternoon stroll, there were Aston Martin, Maserati, Cunningham... and the other old Le Mans faithfuls.

The three works D-types were to be driven by Hawthorn/Bueb, Hamilton/Rolt and Dewis/Don Beauman. A little further down the line there were two more D-types, though these were the short-nose version. One was entered by The Equipe Nationale Belge and the other by Cunningham.

Everyone expected a no-holds-barred contest, but no one could have anticipated the dreadful accident which was to cast a shadow of mourning over the 1955 Le Mans only two and a half hours after the start. It was one of the greatest tragedies in the history of automobile sport and those who still remember the carnage which occurred on that day, more than 28 years ago, probably cannot bear to think back to that scene of devastation and suffering.

For a reason which is still unclear, Levegh's metallic grey Mercedes bounced off Lance Macklin's Austin Healey, ploughed through the barrier, then exploded in the middle of the tightly packed crowd, killing 81 people and injuring more than a hundred. There was utter confusion: panic-stricken survivors tried to get away, over broken bodies littering the ground; the wounded were trampled underfoot; and those who had seen it all happen were, understandably, in a state of shock.

Some of the other drivers had not realised what had happened, for their concentration was so great that any off-track happenings just would not have registered. For a while it looked as though the race would be stopped, but the officials decided to let it go on. Some hours later, during the night, the managing director of Mercedes sent a cable to Le Mans with instructions for the other two Mercedes, which were still in the race, to retire. It was the least one could have expected.

We shall therefore never know whether Jaguar would still have won the race had the 300 SLRs driven on. Be that as it may, the somewhat hollow victory went to Hawthorn and Bueb. The mass slaughter at Le Mans was not the only tragedy associated with the race, for while he was on his way to watch the event Lyons' son Michael was killed in a road accident. The tragedy occurred some 20 miles from Cherbourg when Michael collided with a lorry. It is thought that, tired after the long Channel crossing, he dozed off at the wheel and, when the bright headlights of an oncoming lorry brought him round, he instinctively pulled hard over to the left instead of to the right.

This sad loss had a strange parallel in the identical fates which befell Jean, the son of Ettore Bugatti, and Dino, Enzo Ferrari's son.

The 1955 Le Mans was therefore to remain a painful memory for many people. The D-type had come out of the event with honour, taking first and third places, but the

The 1956 Rheims 12-Hours race. Fairman/Titterington's long-nose D-type went on to finish third.

Duncan Hamilton and Ivor Bueb celebrate their victory in the 1956 Rheims 12-Hours in XKD 605. The traditional beverage is on hand! Behind the two drivers, Lofty England and Charles Delecroix are getting ready for the customary 'family' snapshot.

doubt which attached itself to this achievement — because of the Mercedes — had to be dispelled as soon as possible, for William Lyons was set on proving the D-type's merit.

Mind you, there was one statistic which confirmed, without question, the D-type's superiority, for the winning car had covered 14 laps in the last hour of the race, while the 300 SLR's best effort had been 13.

Road and circuit victories during the rest of the 1955 motor racing season helped to boost the D-type's reputation. I won't say that the D's successes were countless, but the list was pretty impressive.

One of the experiments carried out on a guinea pig D-type was the fitting of a de Dion-style rear suspension, together with a rear anti-roll bar to mitigate the effect of the slight understeer which was a D-type characteristic.

After the Le Mans catastrophe a new and drastic regulation was brought into force which limited the capacity of petrol tanks. Some of the 1955 Le Mans cars carried up to 66 gallons (300 litres) of high-octane fuel which, as was seen in the accident, turned them into high-speed bombs. The limit was therefore fixed at 130 litres (28½ gallons), effectively cancelling the rest of the French 1955 endurance racing season (including the Rheims 12-Hours event, in which a Mercedes Jaguar rematch had been eagerly anticipated).

However, Mercedes showed the mettle of their cars in the Tourist Trophy at Dundrod, where the 300 SLRs came in first and second, ahead of Fangio's D-type.

The season ended with a sensational announcement by William Lyons: the 1956 Le Mans was to see Jaguar's last

official works entries. Coventry would, of course, carry on producing and preparing D-types for other stables and private customers, but the Jaguar works team was to be disbanded. It was quite reasonable for Lyons to hang up his racing hat at this stage. There was hardly anything left to prove, and the spin-off from Jaguar competition wins was already so great that the advertising and sales division had enough copy for the next ten years! Browns Lane was making a handsome profit from the Mark IX saloons, the XKs to a lesser extent, and from the brand-new 3.4-litre and 2.4-litre saloons which required some hefty capital investment in new tooling due to their radically different design. Lyons wanted to concentrate on this new generation of

Changing a plug on the number 4 D-type of the winning
Flockhart/Sanderson partnership during the 1956 Le Mans
24-Hours. You can see clearly the 'large-format' windscreen with which all cars had to be fitted to conform to the
new ACO ruling. A fascinating detail is that the stop lights
have been purloined from a Mark VII saloon and have then
been turned through 90 degrees.

Le Mans 1956. The number 3 D-type of Fairman and
Wharton gives cause for concern. Behind it is the number 5
of Swaters/Rousselle.

cars, which was proving a fast-selling one, without having to divert much-needed capital to the racing division. The sums involved in competition development were, it must be said, nothing short of colossal. Lofty England has quoted the figure of £700,000 swallowed up in six years, which was a small fortune in those days.

Two widely differing but equally noteworthy honours were gained early in 1956: a Mark VII won the Monte Carlo Rally and, in the same month, William Lyons was dubbed a knight. Mr Lyons is dead — long live Sir William! True, the knighthood was in recognition of the man himself, but it was also in recognition of the extent to which car exports had helped the United Kingdom's balance of payments.

Coventry brought out the flags when Her Majesty came to visit Browns Lane. One of the most memorable photographs from this occasion was one of the radiant queen and her new knight with, in the background, Prince Philip and Bill Heynes deep in conversation.

Six new long-nose D-types were planned for the 1956 Le Mans. There were certain obligatory modifications if the cars were to fit in with the new regulations. I have already touched on the smaller petrol tank capacity, but other enforced alterations included a full-width wrap-round windscreen, as opposed to one which protected only the driving position; the provision of a proper door on the passenger side; the replacement of the aluminium cover over the passenger compartment by a sheet of perspex; and the use of a single-speed screenwiper.

Voluntary modifications included a weight reduction of some 60 pounds (25 kilos) by changing to a smaller gauge of aluminium for the body panels; an increase of 1/8-inch (3-mm) in the diameter of the front anti-roll bar, and the incorporation of a rear anti-roll bar also.

An important innovation on some 1956 models was Lucas petrol injection. I say 'some' advisedly, since Sir William was not one to put all his eggs in one basket. He decided to equip just two D-types with this brand-new system for, although Jaguar always wanted to be in the van of technological progress, the Lucas injection had only been on trial for six months, and a collapse of the system at Jaguar's last Le Mans appearance would prove a disaster for the company if all the D-types were fitted with it.

The idea of fuel injection was not that new, however. Back in 1950 two engineers called Barrington and Downing had described their research in this field. The novelty of this Lucas version was that there was a radical separation between the pressure pump and the metering and distributor unit which delivered a metered charge through a shuttle-

Écurie Écosse was to provide the Jaguar marque with a spectacular victory in the 1956 Le Mans 24-Hours, courtesy of R.Flockhart and I.Bueb. Notice the difference between this and the 1955 D-type; the windscreen completely encircles the cockpit and is much deeper, due to the new regulations.

168

The winning Sanderson/Flockhart pairing in front of their number 4 D-type which covered 2,5017.16 miles (4,034.9 kms) in the 1956 Le Mans 24-Hours.
Stirling Moss had driven in different colours this time — those of Aston Martin — and had been beaten into second place.

valve very close to the inlet valves. The electric high-pressure pump was sited at the back of the car, sucking in fuel from two pipes placed below the fuel tank. The fuel was pumped at a pressure of 1 kg/cm² through two filters and was then metered and timed in the distributor unit.

Six injectors in the inlet manifold were brought into action by pressure on the accelerator pedal. This pressure brought a guillotine device into play which was activated by a rack and pinion and a quadrant. A D-type fitted with Lucas injection made triumphant appearances at Sebring (USA) and in the Rheims 12-Hours race which, unusually, took place before Le Mans that year.

There was one other modification before we move on to Le Mans, and that was a very efficient lock-out device on first gear to make sure that a driver could not inadvertently shift down into first from fourth. The incident which led to this device being fitted was the tragic death of Tony Dennis who changed down from fourth to first by mistake, melting the gearbox pinions and locking the road wheels of his car.

Now we can move on to Le Mans in July 1956. The factory had entered three teams: Fairman/Wharton, in a fuel-injection D (XKD 602); Hawthorn/Bueb, also with a fuel-injected unit (XKD 605); and Titterington/Frère in a D-type with the traditional carburettors (XKD 606). The Écurie Écosse also put in an appearance with a D-type (XKD 501), driven by Flockhart/Sanderson, while the Équipe Nationale Belge produced a D-type (XKD 573) for Laurent/Rousselle.

The race did not turn out at all as Lofty England had planned it. This was not so much due to the opposition — Aston Martin (DBR1), Gordini, Talbot, Maserati and the Ferrari Testa Rossa among others — but to the cars themselves. The two D-types of Titterington/Frère and Fairman/Wharton, which were probably the fastest cars at Le Mans that year, were put out of the running almost immediately by a multiple shunt on the famous Esses. The run of bad luck continued for, shortly afterwards, the only works survivors — Hawthorn and Bueb — had to endure a series of pit stops due to misfiring, which left them with no chance of winning. Luckily for Jaguar, the good old XKD 501 from the Écurie Écosse, devoid of wide-angle head and

169

The 1956 Coupes du Salon at Montlhéry. A D-type travelling flat out.

fuel injection but fitted with quick-change brake pads, made up ground on the Aston BB3S and saved the marque's reputation by showing the rest of the field the way home and finishing in first place. It was some kind of consolation for Sir William and his team — a Jaguar had won, even if Jaguar had not! Never mind; there was no point in crying over spilt milk and, despite the disappointing result, this was to be the final appearance of a works-entered racing car.

At all events, William Heynes stated shortly before the start of the race that, despite its fabulous performance, the D-type was already an outdated car. This seemed a strange thing to say, but I shall come to his reasons for saying it later.

Meanwhile, early in 1957, Sir William Lyons had another tragedy to contend with: fire. In mid-afternoon on February 12 a ferocious blaze destroyed some of the Browns Lane production lines and workshops — in particular the main assembly unit where the pre-launch stocks of 3.4-litre (Mark I), Mark VIII and XK SSs were stored. The catastrophe made national headlines but, as so often happens when disaster strikes, the workforce pulled together and it is a remarkable tribute to their loyalty that production started up again within 36 hours of the last flames being extinguished.

The casualty list was appalling: 270 cars were damaged almost, if not completely, beyond repair, among them two D-type chassis and nine complete D-types; and the special D-type tooling and jigs were also lost.

When the accountants added up the total cost of the fire, including damage to buildings and lost sales, it came to £4 million.

Less than a fortnight later — February 26 to be precise — the public relations department announced the launch of the compact 3.4-litre monocoque saloon (later called the Mark I). It was the first four-door series car capable of 125 mph (200 km/h).

The motoring press was simply astounded. How on earth had that amazing man managed to pull it off?

Duncan Hamilton in OKV 1 (chassis No XKC 402). The Montlhéry Coupes du Salon, 7 October 1956.

Below: Breathtakingly beautiful — lowslung, compact, aggressive — the XK SS was, in effect, a D-type minus headfairing and fin, and plus some accessories which would make it into a road car. Eighteen of these cars were assembled, and it is therefore the dream of most Jaguar enthusiasts to own one of this rare breed.

Bottom: The XK SS' 'road' features included a proper curved windscreen, fixed sidewindows, a hood, narrow bumpers — forerunners of the E-type's — a luggage rack and a smattering of chrome. The 16-inch magnesium Dunlop wheels, with their triple-eared centre-locking nuts, gave this amazing car a suitably 'racy' appearance.

THE XK SS

JANUARY 1957—FEBRUARY 1957

Who but Jaguar could have had the self-confidence to take a car which had just won Le Mans and offer it for sale to the general public? Their reason for doing so was that the Americans wanted to buy D-types, as long as they could drive the cars on the freeway as well as the race track!

So the XK SS was quite simply a road version of the competition short-nose D-type. It had the shortest production run of any Jaguar, and is consequently the most sought after model today. The XK SS was built for six weeks only, during January and February of 1957, and only 16 officially came off the assembly lines, with a further two being made up from D-types in 1958. So the total number of cars which could lay claim to the designation XK SS was 18, including one curious example: an XK SS which the factory itself reconverted into a D-type.

We know every last detail about each of these XK SSs; in fact, they have family trees which an aristocrat would envy! If ever an XK SS comes on to the market, the price reached at auction is truly astronomical.

There are very few features separating an XK SS from a D-type: the windscreen, hood and bumpers are the main ones. Apart from these, the XK SS is a D-type right down to its wheels. It was as fierce as ever, although some of its wildness had been tamed for American use so that the car could be entered in the production sports car racing category, complete with hood and all!

Since everything in the motor racing sport garden was not that lovely at the time, the XK SS was also a rather good way of using up unsold D-type chassis by adapting them for road use.

So, if you're talking about the XK SS, you are really talking about the D-type, with a little bit of 'add one, take one away' thrown in.

Taken away was the headrest and fin, since it would have been a very odd-looking hood that could cover those up; the division between the driver's and passenger's compartments; and a few obtrusive and excessively 'racy' rivets.

Added were the windscreen, which certain sniping critics thought could easily be confused with the back window of a 1956 Chrysler — implying that Jaguar were cutting production-cost corners; the delicate little chrome strips front and rear, which a reviewer of the time almost mistook for bumpers; a mohair hood with matching cover; transparent sidescreens fixed to the doors; and the leather interior trim to add a touch of luxury.

There were other little details which added to the XK SS' chic side: the slim chrome trim round the headlight fairing; the two indicator lights sited low down at the front; the chrome-plated brake-light supports; illuminated number-plate; and an attractive chrome-plated luggage rack in case

This three-quarter-rear view of the XK SS makes the car look just as ferocious; it was not an accident that the exhaust pipes were positioned at the side!
The spare wheel was stowed away in the tiny 'boot' which incorporated the central part of the rear bumper.

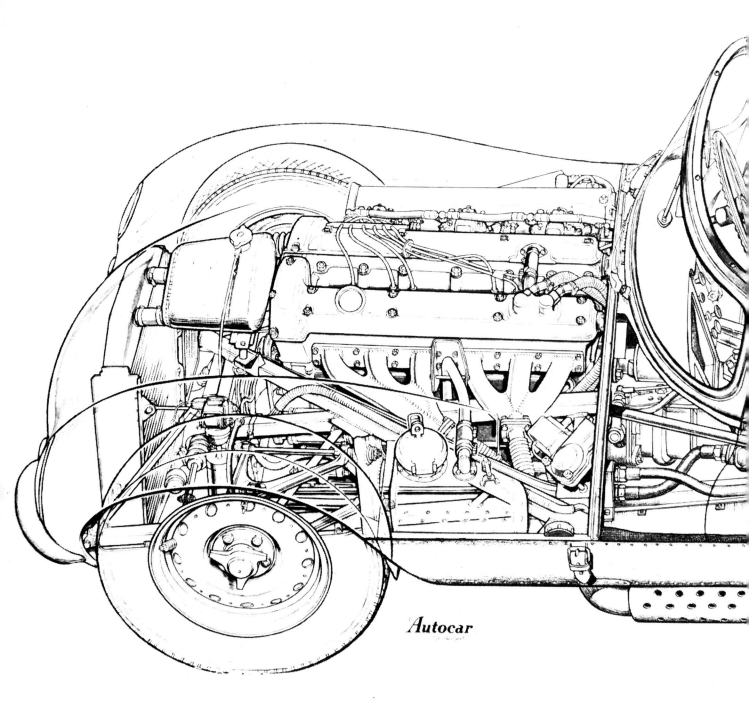

This cutaway view of the XK SS demonstrates that the car was virtually identical to the competition D-type. One should never judge a book by its cover!

A royal guest for Jaguar; William Lyons and William Heynes give Prince Philip a taste of the XK SS, basically a road version of the D-type and the model which, today, is lusted after by all sports car enthusiasts.

you wanted to take your high-performance racing car on a touring holiday!

There were some oddities on the XK SS which proved that it was basically a D-type, and that the hood was not really intended for use, *viz* the petrol filler cap. This was located inside the car, which meant that you had to take down the hood to get at it. If you had an aversion to the smell of petrol it was a good idea to choose a service station where the attendant had a reputation for never spilling a drop of petrol, otherwise you were in for a thumping head-ache from the fumes, and some dry cleaning problems.

Another pointer to its intrinsically D-type nature was that Malcolm Sayer was responsible for the body modifications, hood and windscreen.

The end result of all these alterations was as beautiful as a work of art — a piece of kinetic sculpture which was a knock-out from every angle.

Unfortunately, I have never had the chance of driving a genuine XK SS. If I had, I would probably be going into ecstasies about the tremendous thrill of sitting at the wheel of one of these rarely found classics.

There is only one XK SS in France and it belongs to the

Since the C-type it had become almost a tradition for the bonnets of Jaguar sports cars to hinge forward to reveal the engine. Dry-sump lubrication, 3.8-litre engine capacity, wide-angle head or not, these engines were frighteningly powerful and their performance figures could shake even the most blasé know-it-all.

XKD 533 a few days after it had been delivered.

1957. The start of the Le Mans 24-Hours. Jaguar was to scoop first, second, third, fourth and sixth places.

honorary president of the French Jaguar Drivers' Club, Dr Philippe Renault, who is one of the most enthusiastic Jaguar collectors under the sun. His car was originally a D-type (XKD 533) which was sold to Monsieur Moyonneur in 1957 and was then converted into an XK SS by Jaguar, on the request of Henri Peignaux, the Lyons Jaguar distributor. Consequently, a Frenchman rarely, if ever, gets the chance of driving an XK SS! Come to that, not many people in other parts of the world have had that privilege. One who did get the chance was *The Autocar*'s road tester, whose findings were published in the issue dated 3 May 1957:

"Handling impressions and performance — 0-100 mph in 14 seconds.

"Just over two years ago, colleague Michael Clayton had the opportunity to drive a C-type Jaguar, later to describe his experiences in print. His patient passenger that day, I eventually persuaded him to let me take over at the wheel, but by then it was almost dark, and raining hard. Memories of that night came back again recently when one evening I found myself in temporary possession of a later and even more potent product of the same factory, a Jaguar XK SS.

"Whatever the cars one has been fortunate enough to drive, anything of the nature of the XK SS never fails to produce a thrill. Delightful as the eager small cars can be, a big powerful engine has the advantage every time when one wants to taste the delights of real high-speed motoring. In this particular case, too, there was the added appeal that the car is, for the time being, unique, and to drive it is something of a privilege.

"Getting into the driving seat presents no particular problems. The diminutive door allows one to step over the sill; even if there were any difficulty in getting down behind this particular steering wheel, it is unlikely that any right-thinking person would complain. The deeply padded driving seat has a sharply curved backrest to hold the driver without any feeling of restriction. The seat cushion gives comfortable support beneath the thighs, and the door and sidescreen do not curtail arm movement. No seat adjustment is provided — such a car is better 'made to measure'.

"I have noticed before that with bodywork of this kind, where the seat and steering column are not adjustable for length, drivers of differing heights can still be comfortable. There are, of course, limits as far as the distance between the pedals and seat is concerned. The XK SS driving position, to my knowledge, seemed to suit three men of very different stature and the car was also driven by a woman who, however, preferred to have a cushion behind her.

"The well-curved screen is high enough to give ample protection, goggles being unnecessary. Instruments are kept to essentials — they consist of large diameter rev counter and speedometer on the left side of the column, with oil pressure gauge and coolant temperature gauge to the right. The direction indicator switch is also on the right, with a green warning light, and the horn button is by the door pillar where it can be conveniently pressed by one's knee. A small cubby hole with sufficient room for iron rations on a long drive (the tank holds 37 Imp. gallons) faces the passenger.

"Anybody fortunate enough to occupy the passenger seat must have short legs to be comfortable. The seat itself matches its opposite number for support, but leg-room is severely restricted. It is surprising how small an enthusiast can make himself when offered a ride in a car like this Jaguar!

"There is nothing tricky about starting up. A normal ignition switch with a key is fitted above the large diameter starter button. One push on the button and the car comes to life — alive with the throbbing of the exhaust from the twin pipes just in front of the left rear wheel; alive with the slight vibration — no more than a tickle — felt through the floor and the seat. There is a brief, harsh, mechanical signal and whine from under the bonnet, which smoothes out as soon as the revs increase. The needle of the chronometric rev counter stabs up towards the red caution line at 5,800 rpm, when the engine is blipped to check for hesitation.

"Clutch pedal movement is fairly short, and against more than average pressure, but the clutch had no vices. It is definitely either in or out, but there is no snatch or jerky take-off. On this particular occasion the clutch was not on its best behaviour and there was slight slip. It was not possible to spin the rear wheels on getaway on a dry surface, as could normally be done.

"In spite of this, it was possible to record a few highly impressive acceleration figures against the stop watch. The average time for the standing quarter mile was 14.3 sec, the speed reached being almost 100 mph. From rest to 70, 100 and 120 mph, the times were 7.5, 14.4, and 19.7 sec respectively. In top gear the time from 40 to 60 mph was 5.5 sec, 60 to 80 mph 6 sec, and 80 to 100 mph 5 sec. At about 4,000 rpm the power comes in so hard that a driver or passenger not accustomed to the car feels that he is perhaps in some rocket-propelled sledge.

"With the 3.54:1 axle fitted to this car, maximum speeds in first, second, third and top gears are estimated by the makers to be 66, 85, 109 and 144 mph at 6,000 rpm. This gives a figure of 24 mph per 1,000 rpm in top. Four other axle ratios are available: 2.93, 3.31, 3.92 and 4.09.

"The car's natural gait for steady driving is 20 to 30 mph higher than for fast cruising in a less ambitious sports car. On the open road, driving in comfort and without haste, 100 to 120 mph showed on the speedometer on each clear straight, and yet the braking power was such that the car nosed into successive bends at 60 to 70 mph without apparent braking effort after the bursts of speed. Just as impressive as the breathtaking acceleration is this smooth power of the brakes.

"Fuel consumption depends a great deal on how the car is driven, but the D-types, which are very near relations, managed approximately 12 mpg at Le Mans and the SS, driven normally on the roads, is capable of at least 18 mpg.

"The steering is very light and high geared, so that the tendency of the inexperienced is to be clumsy with it. At speeds of more than 100 mph on rough roads or cambered edges a contradictory 'grip lightly' technique is required, to give the requisite precise guidance without being heavy handed. Normal cornering as such seems to call for less delicacy of touch than driving straight on not-too-good surfaces. This quality, and the need to 'float' the steering, the XK SS shares with Grand Prix cars.

"The wind noise and the general effects of the engine and exhaust are not nearly so fierce as one might imagine or as they are remembered from earlier experience with the

In the 1957 Le Mans 24-Hours event, the French team of Lucas and 'Mary' finished a brilliant third, averaging 110.17 mph (177.298 km/h) and covering 2,644 miles (4,255 kms).

This D-type is unusual in that it has a headfairing but no fin. It is XKD 513, owned by Jean-Marie ('Mary') Brussin, who sadly was killed in this same car the next year, just past the Dunlop footbridge. The car was a virtual write-off but was rebuilt as a fixed-head coupé by Michelotti.

C-type, which had only a racing screen. When the XK SS gets really wound up, the occupants feel even more a part of the car, for a warm blanket of air wraps the cockpit and the cold slipstream rushes around the shapely contours, avoiding the interior like a static charge.

"Like most race-bred cars, the XK SS is superbly controllable and safe. These qualities were demonstrated during the latter part of the drive when it started to rain heavily. The wipers were switched on, and, like cut-throat razors, quickly swept the screen clear. The first experience with the car had been in the dark a few days previously; then the screen was covered with flies and the head lamps pointed skywards. This time a few drops of rain were not going to be allowed to interfere with my enjoyment, although caution was the word.

"Now, on the wet tarmac, the power readily spun the wheels, and pressing the throttle a little harder at an indicated 100 mph on the accurate speedometer would cause the back of the car to wag. The wooden-rimmed steering wheel was allowed to float lightly between my hands, and the car assumed an arrow-like course without lessening speed. To the chorus of wind and exhaust noise was added the whine of the Dunlop R.1 racing tyres which seemed to seal the car to the road.

"With so little weight — under 1 ton — and so much power available, there was no real necessity for constant gear changing. Because of the weather conditions, however, the box was used to slow the car more than might have been done had the roads been dry. The gear change was slightly stiff but the lever movements are precise and short between each ratio. First gear has synchromesh, like the rest.

"The speed of the car could almost be controlled by the gear box without resort to the Dunlop disc brakes — the most powerful set I have encountered. Triple pairs of pads

181

One of Jaguar's greatest successes: Le Mans 1957. Flockhart/Bueb's number 3 finished first, followed by Sanderson/Lawrence's number 15 in second place.

on the front and a double pair for the rear brakes produced tremendous fade-free stopping power. When applied at slow speeds with discs cold, there was a fair amount of squeal but this disappeared when they were applied hard. The pedal pressure is very light even for maximum effect, and the brakes could be applied firmly on wet surfaces with confidence.

"It is difficult not to run out of superlatives when describing such a car. The steering, light and extremely accurate as already mentioned, has understeer built into the design; slight kick-back can be felt from the road wheels. The suspension is firm without being harsh, and there is no sensation of roll on tight corners.

"Outstanding memories of my short experience of the car include the tremendous push in the back when accelerating hard; other traffic appears ahead, is overtaken and fades away in the mirror as if projected in the opposite direction. Also, the steering and roadholding qualities are such that they tend to take care of the shortcomings of a driver new to the car.

"The Jaguar XK SS is a true-blue sports car, in so much as it has racing characteristics with touring equipment. As such, it naturally has much more performance, safety and appeal than the run of sports cars — and in America it costs only $5,600."

One of the stranger aspects of this article is that it was written more than two months after the Browns Lane fire, at a time when the XK SS was just a memory, since the devastation caused by the blaze had put an end to all thoughts of producing any more of this model.

One of the greatest sports cars of all time was about to become a legend through its memorable achievement of winning Le Mans three times.

But, in spring 1957, no one knew that the D-type was going to notch up the third of these victories that June. Although Jaguar had called a halt to D-type production back in August 1956, this did not mean the end of the model's racing career.

That year saw the birth and development of a very simple idea: that of reboring the cylinders to 87 mm instead of the original 83 mm, to produce an engine capacity of 3.8 litres (3,781 cc, to be precise).

It is hard to be sure who was the first to come up with this scheme. Was it John Heath? Briggs Cunningham? Brian Lister? Bill Heynes? It seems likely that credit should go to John Heath who thought of it in 1952 but, whatever the truth of the matter, the technique spread like wildfire so that, by 1957, nearly all the D-types were blessed with the new bore/stroke ratio. Most of these conversions were carried out by Jaguar at the request of its sporting customers, who felt that this conversion gave a more reliable engine.

At Le Mans in 1957 nearly all the Jaguars that counted were lined up for the start, with 280-300 bhp under their bonnets, thanks to the 3.8-litre capacity, wide-angle heads and Lucas injection.

The Écurie Écosse brought along two long-nose D-types which had undergone superficial alterations to fit in with the new regulations. One of these was an 'old-fashioned'

An official photograph taken after the end of the 1957 Le Mans. Flockhart (left) and Bueb (right) are centre stage with, on Flockhart's left, Esso's competition manager, Bonin; the oil company sponsored the race.

3.4-litre version, driven by Sanderson and Lawrence, while the other was a 3.8 and the responsibility of Flockhart/Bueb.

An independent French racing team, called Los Amigos, had entered a D-type in which Lucas and 'Mary' (Jean-Marie Brassin) were trying their chances.

The Équipe Nationale Belge entrusted a D-type to two top-rank drivers: Frère and Rousselle.

Hamilton and Gregory were running a privately-entered carburettored 3.8-litre.

So there were five D-types lined up for the start, despite there being no works-entered models! The reliability of this superb racing car was amply proven by the fact that all five made it to the finish, which was no mean feat in itself. But even more surprising — and gratifying — was that the top

three places were taken by D-types, which was an unprecedented success. First were Flockhart/Bueg; second Sanderson/Lawrence; third Lucas/Mary.

And hold on to your hats, because the fourth finisher was also a D-type! It was the Équipe Nationale Belge's car driven by Frère/Rousselle.

It was not just a win, it was a walkover; the D-type did not just dominate the opposition, it wiped it out. It was, beyond question, the D-type's finest hour.

This was, effectively, the D's swansong — though 'operatic aria' might be more appropriate, with the Valkyrie in full flight! Although there was no Jaguar-entered car to share in the glory, it was, of course, Jaguar sales which reaped the benefit, and they did not have to lay out a penny in the process.

The XK 150 fixed-head coupé followed on from its XK 140 equivalent with the same basic line, but slightly updated. As with the XK 140, two occasional rear seats gave some measure of additional emergency passenger capacity without spoiling the undeniably 'sporty' nature of the new Coventry model.

XK 150

22 MAY 1957—OCTOBER 1961

POWER AND STYLE

The arrival of the XK 150 surprised most people and gave rise to some lively controversy. For some it was merely a transitional model with rather dated styling. For others it was a very attractive car and a success in its own right. Whom should one believe? Whether it was a dated or a classic car, one thing is certain: it was very much a link in the XK chain and, even if it was the last of the line, one could easily see that the 150 was a close relation of the 120. From the date of its official press launch, on 22 May 1957, the XK 150 critics were split into two camps — those who were unconditional supporters of the new car and those who would not give it garage room.

Supporters declared that it was beautiful, robust and up-to-date with all the good features of its aristocratic family. Opponents declared that the 150 was heavy, characterless, and that the XK qualities had been spoiled by the conflicting factors which had had to be taken into consideration during its design.

To some extent, the XK 150 was rather like the 140 in that, despite the obvious improvements on the preceding model, one could see signs of a gradual but steady movement away from the spartan thoroughbred which had started off the XK line.

The XK 150 was the result of an attempt to bring together Jaguar customers' contradictory requests in one car. They wanted a high-performance sports car, but with the comfort and civilised luxuries of a GT model; they wanted a small, racy car, but at the same time a bit more room for their shoulders would not go amiss; they wanted a two-seater, but it might be nice to have the kids along from time to time; they wanted brute strength, but a car which was happy to trundle along at lower speeds...

It is easy enough to see how, by trying to incorporate all these different factors in one new model, Jaguar was bound to come up with a controversial design which would impress some people and disappoint others.

However, the aspect of the new car which caused the greatest furore was its body design. Like much else in the XK 150, there was evidence of an attempt to take a middle line between two schools of thought, which led to an inability to dispense entirely with the long dipping bonnet and the enveloping wings, but at the same time a need to add a little of the 'pontoon' style which had made the Italians into the star designers of the age.

Because Jaguar had not had the courage of its convictions and opted for a distinctive, clear style, the body line

This works photograph of an XK 150 drophead coupé was used as press launch material. The major attraction of this model lay in its traditionally British and aristocratic good looks: 2,671 were built.
If you compare it with the XK 140 there are some obvious differences: the curved windscreen, flatter wing line, slightly wider body and enlarged radiator grille.

188

was less sleek, the wings more ponderous, the waistline a little too high and the superb flowing, curved line of the front wings was the baby which had been chucked out with the bath water. It was this magic wing line which had given the XKs their air of dynamism, of being ready to leap lithely forward, just like the leaping jaguar. But it seemed as though the big cat was getting old, lazy and fat — it was a sad sight.

The profile of the XK 150's front wings was almost horizontal, carried along to the back wing by the door design. There was a one-piece curved windscreen; the disappearance of the central divider made for better visibility and more efficient wiper action. The bottom rail, however, was 1½-inches (almost 4-cms) higher than on the 140's windscreen. The bonnet was 2¾-inches wider (7-cms) because the car itself was wider than the 140. The radiator grille had also been enlarged to provide better cooling. The rear number-plate had been moved up from its previous position between the two bumpers and was now square and positioned on the boot lid. This meant that the rear bumper was, as on the first pre-series 140s, back in one piece again.

So there was nothing really earth-shaking when you look at the design changes individually, but the overall effect was of a complete transformation. Somehow the car lacked Lyons' personal stamp, which had marked out all his previous creations. The old natural Jaguar elegance had disappeared, to be replaced by a car which had been dispassionately concocted by a development department more interested in pleasing all of the people all of the time than in coming up with a brand new creative design. Oh, for the good old Jaguar days!

The most striking aspect of the 150 was its close relationship to the 3.4-litre saloon of the time, which was retrospectively titled the Mark I. The 150 was clearly a two-door version of that handsome saloon which, despite changing features, was to remain as the archetypal sporty car for years. Once you are aware that the 150 was the two-door version of a Mark I, everything falls into place and you get a clearer idea of the car's true character. This marked resemblance is not altered by the fact that the 150 had a chassis and the Mark I did not.

Nonetheless, the 150 enjoyed a successful career and, although many still fondly remembered the 140's divided windscreen, the new car's qualities soon wiped out memories of the 140's charm, which was already beginning to seem rather outdated in 1957. As last in line of the XK generation, almost all its parents' faults had been eliminated, and it benefited from the technological developments which were being incorporated in the new Jaguar family during its highly secret conception in the Browns Lane R & D department.

To all intents and purposes the 150 inherited the 140's chassis, which itself was almost identical to that of the XK 120: two heavy, sturdy, box-section sidemembers with steel cross-members made it into a purposeful car which had no tendency to roll about on bad surfaces — but the other side of the coin was that the car was incredibly heavy.

The Coventry management knew that the days of the conventional chassis-based car were numbered with the arrival of monocoque construction methods which scored on both weight reduction and production economy.

Because of the disastrous fire of 12 February 1957 which

Those with an eye for detail will know that the XK 150 was the only XK which had the option of a leaping Jaguar mascot.

*Apart from the introduction of disc brakes, this XK 150
chassis is identical to that of the 140.*

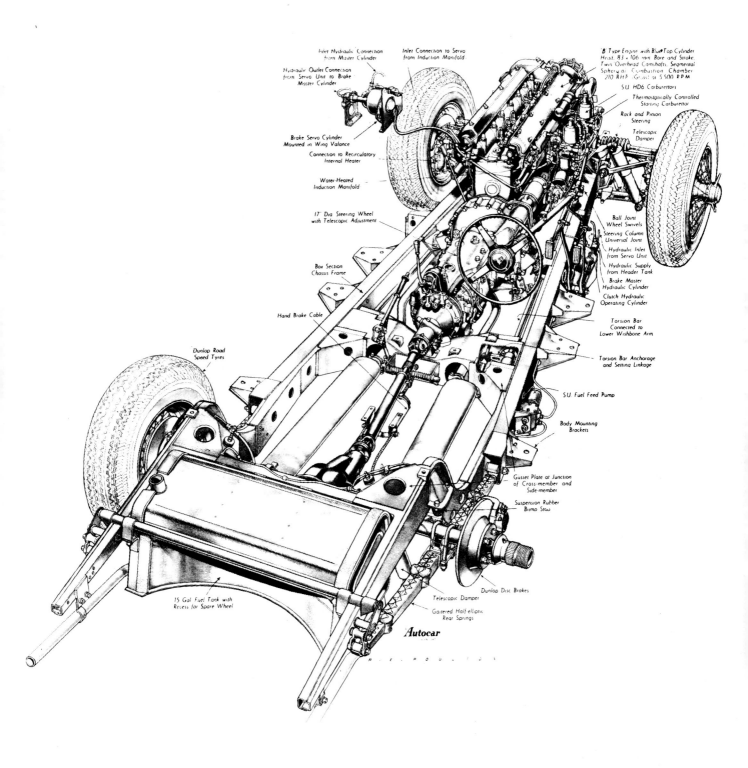

Inlet Hydraulic Connection
from Master Cylinder

Inlet Connection to Servo
from Induction Manifold

'B' Type Engine with Blue Top Cylinder
Head, 83 x 106 mm Bore and Stroke,
Twin Overhead Camshafts, Segmental
Spherical Combustion Chamber,
210 B.H.P. (Gross) at 5,500 R.P.M.

Hydraulic Outlet Connection
from Servo Unit to Brake
Master Cylinder

S.U. HD6 Carburettors

Thermostatically Controlled
Starting Carburettor

Rack and Pinion
Steering

Brake Servo Cylinder
Mounted in Wing Valance

Telescopic
Damper

Connection to Recirculatory
Internal Heater

Water-Heated
Induction Manifold

Ball Joint
Wheel Swivels

17" Dia Steering Wheel
with Telescopic Adjustment

Steering Column
Universal Joint

Hydraulic Inlet
from Servo Unit

Hydraulic Supply
from Header Tank

Box Section
Chassis Frame

Brake Master
Hydraulic Cylinder

Clutch Hydraulic
Operating Cylinder

Hand Brake Cable

Torsion Bar
Connected to
Lower Wishbone Arm

Torsion Bar Anchorage
and Setting Linkage

Dunlop Road
Speed Tyres

S.U. Fuel Feed Pump

Body Mounting
Brackets

Gusset Plate at Junction
of Cross-member and
Side-member

Suspension Rubber
Bump Stop

15 Gal Fuel Tank with
Recess for Spare Wheel

Telescopic Damper

Dunlop Disc Brakes

Gaitered Half-elliptic
Rear Springs

Autocar

*Queuing up for the trim shop. These drophead coupés are
still waiting for their hoods.*

had gutted part of the factory, only the fixed-head and drophead coupés were offered to start with, the OTS being held back until March of 1958.

So there were two new bodies to clothe the good old robust chassis although, as usual, the real changes lay underneath.

One of the major selling points, and the one on which Jaguar based its campaign, was the provision (only as an option to start with) of the new Dunlop disc brakes. These had more than proved their worth at Le Mans since the epic race of 1953 in which they had played a decisive part in Jaguar's victory by providing such short braking distances.

William Lyons chose this moment to introduce disc brakes to the general motoring public because he was by now absolutely convinced of the system's efficiency, reliability and resistance to overheating.

A product of joint development by Jaguar and Dunlop, the introduction of disc brakes marked a mini-revolution in series production cars. Only a few companies — Triumph (TR3), Austin Healey (100) and Jensen (Interceptor) — had beaten Jaguar to it, and that only a few months earlier, with the same type of disc brake, using a single pair of calipers and equipped with efficient servo assistance.

As a matter of fact, not one 150 was delivered with the XK 140's Lockheed drum brakes, although this was a catalogued option. Actually, it is mystifying how anyone could have thought of fitting the 150 with the Lockheeds — and Jaguar soon realised the truth of this and scrapped the drums — when the 150 was to be given a whole heap of extra horsepower which would have made mincemeat of any brake drums!

The servo assistance was by the vacuum method and provided considerably increased braking power with light pedal pressure. Servo assistance is, however, as the name implies, merely a driver's aid and is linked in direct propor-

tion to the amount of pressure on the brake pedal. Consequently, even if the servo fails, a driver can still stop the car, although he needs a lot more leg muscle to do it! An additional caliper on the rear discs was fitted for handbrake use, with the two being linked by a cable.

There were few significant changes compared with the 140 so far as the chassis and its attachments were concerned: there was the same rack and pinion steering, fitted to the chassis in an identical fashion; the double wishbone and torsion-bar suspension, with anti-roll bar at the front, was retained; and the rear suspension was equally conventional, with its eight half-elliptic leaf springs and telescopic shock absorbers. There was one slight sign of progress, however, in the shape of nylon interleaving between the main and second leaves.

The remaining chassis details were so much the same that, apart from the disc brakes, you would have had to look really hard to distinguish a 150 Owen chassis from its 140 relation without detailed inspection. But then Jaguar has never believed in change for change's sake.

Come to that, there was little difference in the engine — in its original version, at least. The standard basic model had those reliable 190 bhp under its bonnet, just like the 140, the only difference being that two HD6 SU carburettors replaced the old H6s. The 'D' in HD6 stands for 'diaphragm', as the jet was fitted to a rubber membrane instead of sliding up and down in a brass guide. Its two advantages were the elimination of fuel seepage and an easier richness adjustment.

The Special Equipment model was given a 20 bhp bonus. These 20 bhp were obtained, as usual and exclusively, by reworking the cylinder head. This new head was given the B-type title and managed to produce the same power as the C-type head, but at 200 rpm less, i.e., at 5,500 rpm instead of 5,700 rpm. Jaguar managed to obtain maximum torque

Layout of the instruments and controls on the XK 150 fixed-head coupé. Although their positioning had changed slightly since the XK 120 and 140, the instruments had not noticeably increased in number.

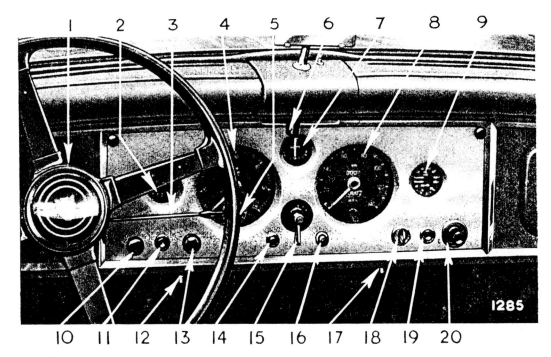

1. Horn
2. Petrol gauge
3. Indicators
4. Revolution counter
5. Electric clock
6. Heating control
7. Ammeter
8. Speedometer
9. Oil pressure and water temperature
10. Screen wiper switch
11. Panel light switch
12. Clock reset control
13. Heating rheostat
14. Screen washer
15. Dipped headlights
16. Interior light switch
17. Trip mileage reset control
18. Ignition switch
19. Starter button
20. Cigar lighter

A 1960 photograph of Jaguar's hood production methods. As can be seen, a great deal of detailed work was involved in this operation. A skilled worker is applying the layer of horsehair which formed an interlining between the water-proofed mohair and the lining material and which hid the ribs of the hood frame.

and BMEP at much lower engine speeds through increasing the exhaust valve diameter, through keeping the same inlet valve diameter, but altering the angle from 30 to 45 degrees, and through making the inlet valve faces slightly more curved to complete the hemispherical aspect of the combustion chamber. This superb B-type head consequently made less demands on the engine while obtaining a surprising amount of power for 1957, at comparatively modest engine speeds.

This new cylinder head was the only real innovation in the engine. The XK power unit had been going strong for ten years and there was no sign of it being put out to grass. As a basic design it had been so successful that there had been scope for uprating its output from 150 to 210 bhp simply by working on the camshaft, inlet porting and valves.

Anyone who had owned an XK 120, and had subsequently purchased an XK 140 and then the 150, was in for no surprises when he lifted up the bonnet. There was a sense of familiarity, even though some of the details might have changed: the two 1¾-inch carburettors; the provision of a separate water gallery for the inlet manifold (on the 140 this had been cast as an integral part of the manifold); a new radiator filler cap; and the windscreen water reservoir.

The remainder of the working parts were exactly the same: the clutch, gearbox, overdrive and rear axle. An XK 150 customer still had the option of a manual Moss box or automatic transmission with torque converter provided by the respected house of Borg & Warner, and there was the traditional choice of Salisbury axle ratios, depending on what use you were going to make of the car.

Wire wheels were still offered as an option, but in fact they proved so popular with Jaguar's customers that few 150s were delivered with disc wheels. It is worth reminding ourselves that, in addition to looking very sporty and seductive, wire spoked wheels also gave a better ride and improved brake cooling. Another factor was that, since wire wheels weighed about a quarter less than their disc equivalents, the weight of the car's unsprung masses was reduced by the same amount. As so few 150s were supplied with disc wheels, those that did have them have now become quite rare. One last thing about the wheels: when the 150 was delivered with disc wheels, it had spats at the rear which made the car look rather old-fashioned.

Even during the 140 era there had been some doubt as to the strength of a 54-spoke wire wheel, and this had been preying on Jaguar's mind for, when you are dealing with a car which is capable of more than 125 mph, you need to have complete confidence in your wheels.

This weakness in the spokes had become increasingly apparent at the time when they were available as a chrome-plated option. The chrome did a lot to improve the car's appearance, but it weakened the spokes by a good quarter.

In June 1958, Jaguar at last came to grips with the problem and increased the number of spokes from 54 to 60. The wheel rims still had a 16-inch diameter and they were fitted with the faithful 600 x 16 tyres.

Going back to the 150's overall dimensions, they were almost identical to those of the XK 140, as were the construction methods; there was an all-steel body, apart from the bonnet and boot which were still made from aluminium. Jaguar managed to convey the impression that the XK

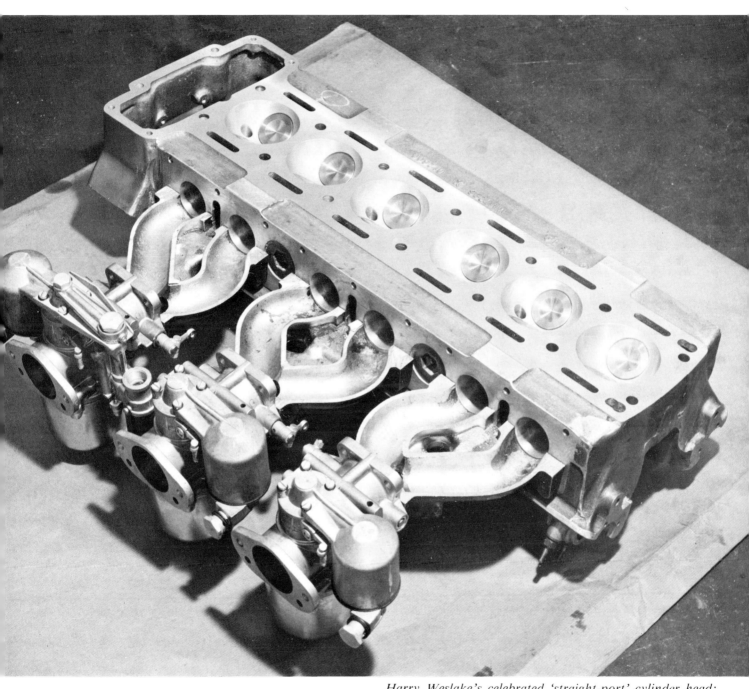

Harry Weslake's celebrated 'straight-port' cylinder head: each two-cylinder unit was fed by a large 2-inch (5-cm) HD8 carburettor through identical-length ports. Inside the head itself the 2-inch ports were as straight as possible, hence the 'straight port' nickname. The new cylinder head improved the XK unit's performance significantly, and this is why Jaguar fitted the little 'S' symbol to cars which had the benefit of the straight-port head.

Left: The small chrome 'S' crossed by a horizontal line attached to the top front corner of the door shows that this car's engine was fitted with the famous 'straight-port' cylinder head. There were 4,462 of this model produced, and it proved the most popular of the XK 150 range.

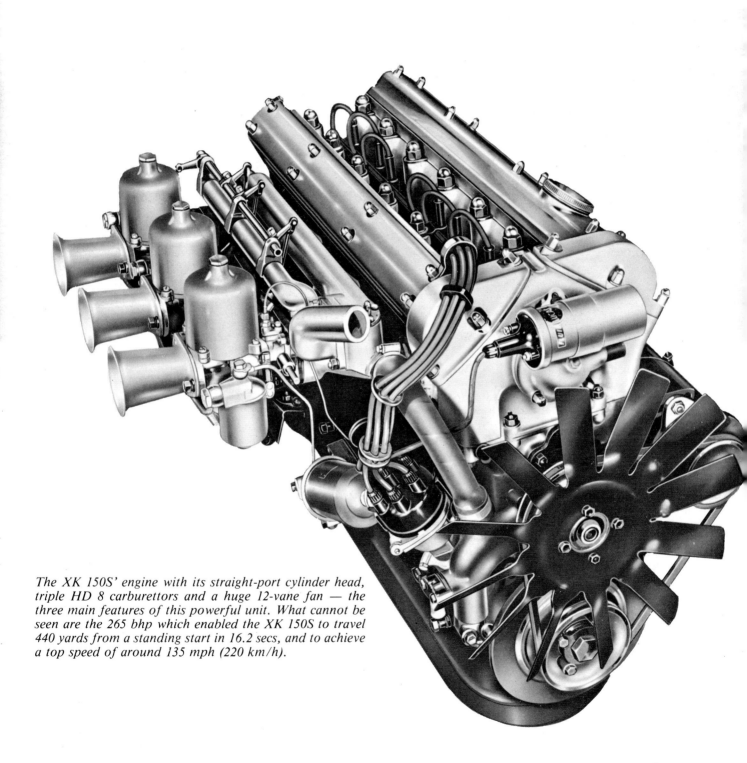

March 1958. The first XK 150 open two-seaters awaiting despatch at Browns Lane. Michel Cognet is seen leaning against an example which has been fitted with a hood.

The XK 150S' engine with its straight-port cylinder head, triple HD 8 carburettors and a huge 12-vane fan — the three main features of this powerful unit. What cannot be seen are the 265 bhp which enabled the XK 150S to travel 440 yards from a standing start in 16.2 secs, and to achieve a top speed of around 135 mph (220 km/h).

150 was a brand-new model, while at the same time limiting the tooling changes by a whole series of crafty technical tricks. For example, the bonnet was the same as the XK 140's, although it was widened by the simple device of incorporating a raised central strip which joined the two halves together, and the front end was cropped short to house the larger radiator grille. Simple, but brilliant! This sort of 'improvisation' enabled Jaguar to use the same bonnet tooling as for the 120 and 140, while making it look as though new ones had been produced.

One other important instance of the 150's production economies was that the new front wing profile was achieved simply by altering the tooling angle. This saving on investment in new matrices obviously allowed Jaguar to recoup its capital investment in the new model in double-quick time, and a detailed examination of the XK 150 reveals quite clearly the policy of using old wool for a new jumper — what the Americans would probably call a facelift. A few cosmetic touches enable one to identify, very accurately, the year in which any given model appeared.

Other modifications included a dip in the centre of the front bumper to follow the lower line of the radiator grille. This design feature was to be repeated on many Jaguars and was one of the trademarks of the Mark I and Mark II. The radiator grille was very reminiscent of the XK 120, in that it had its thin slats, although it was twice as wide as the earlier design. This same grille was used for the 3.4-litre saloon (the Mark I). The fact that the two cars shared the same grille contributed to the visual impression, which I

mentioned earlier, that the 150 was the two-door version of the 3.4-litre saloon.

For the first time a large Jaguar mascot appeared on the end of an XK bonnet. Collectors and restorers take note! If you are a stickler (and I trust that you are) for ex-works accuracy, this introduction date for the leaping jaguar is very important. So be sure to remember that it was current from 1956 to 1964 and that one notable difference from its predecessor, which lasted from 1937 to 1951, was that in the later version the rear legs were stretched out, not bent.

The first mascot had been designed by F.Gordon Crosby who had produced a jaguar, poised ready to spring, on a triangular base. It was at Lyons' own request that the sculptor straightened out the hind legs to give a greater impression of movement. The original mascots were all stamped (underneath) with a code which invariably began with the letters BD. These superb 7¾-inch (19.7-cm) long jaguars were made of zinc and were to be found on XKs, Mark VIIIs, Mark IXs, Mark Is and Mark IIs.

In its original version the 150 kept the 140's rear lights, and it was not until 1958 that the large Mark II-type tail lights appeared, with flashers in the lower orange section, and brake and parking lights in the upper red part.

Inside, too, there were a lot of changes — not all for the better according to some who felt that, by dispensing with the walnut veneering, Jaguar had thrown away part of the XK charm. The dashboard now boasted the same leather as the seats, and the doors were lined with the same and had integral armrests. The seats were a little wider, upholstered

with Connolly's sumptuous Vaumol hides and the usual two occasional seats were provided in the back. As always, there was a hinged section giving access to the boot from inside the car, so that long or bulky objects such as golf clubs could be transported.

Once you sat in the driving seat of a 150 you realised how much had been changed inside the car by the markedly increased comfort of the driving position and the improved internal lighting. You could tell that the car was wider, and those extra few inches made all the difference. From a rather cramped 140, the 150 changed the XK image into one of spaciousness and comfort.

As for the rest of the interior fittings, there were no important differences either in the instrument layout or in the door closing system. An XK enthusiast did not feel too out of place in the car, in spite of the initial impact of the extra space. He soon felt at home and those automatic driving movements came back. The new improved technical features would make him forget any critical first impressions.

The fixed-head coupé XK 150 weighed in at a respectable 28¾ hundredweight (1,461 kilos), or one hundredweight (51 kilos) more than the XK 140 FHC, which itself was a hundredweight heavier than the 120. The XK inflation rate,

with regard to weight, was becoming rather worrying! However, the prize for top weight went to the 150 OTS, which came out at half a hundredweight more than the FHC — an unenviable record! There is no getting away from the fact that the 150 was heavy — too heavy by half — and the extra horsepower which the engineers had worked so hard to achieve was absorbed straight away by the effort of shifting this monster. It was as though the fight for extra power was to be perpetually foiled by middle-age spread.

Since, along with its weight problems, the 150 had a larger frontal area due to the increased width, its drag coefficient was higher than the 140's and the car's top speed was thereby reduced overall, although it had more acceleration punch thanks to the B-type head.

One of the startling test findings was that the standard 150 FHC was slower than the monocoque 3.4-litre saloon, despite the fact that they shared the same power unit!

This was no laughing matter, as William Lyons well knew, for you could not, in all conscience, market a sports car which was slower than its saloon equivalent. Jaguar's immediate response was to cram in a hefty quantity of extra horsepower under the 150's bonnet. The date was February 1958 and, inevitably, William Heynes was given this tricky task. There were two solutions: he could either increase the engine capacity, or he could have yet another go at the cylinder head and distribution! This was the poser which led to the development of the S-type head that, as if by chance, coincided with the announcement of the OTS in May 1958.

To get a better understanding of the course of events, we have to go back a bit to the disastrous fire in the Jaguar factory which had forced Jaguar to restrict their 150 launch to the fixed-head and drophead coupés, whereas, in theory, the OTS should have appeared at the same time and in a pepped-up version. Since some of the vital equipment had been destroyed, Jaguar had to make do with what was left and so the OTS had to wait.

This 'S' version was to be the most powerful of all the XK series and was, once again, the product of Harry Weslake's mechanical genius. Weslake had stayed with the habit of studying turbulence and air flow, using full-size wooden models; a habit which had stood him in good stead, since he had already produced the original 120 cylinder head with Bill Heynes using this method. But what was to be the secret of this fantastic new head design which Jaguar was about to unveil? Nothing less than a marked improvement in the feeding of the combustion chambers, produced by a much straighter inlet port design.

The six cylinders were supplied in three pairs, each pair being completely independent of the other two, in contrast to the previous inlet manifold where the two groups of three were interconnected by a common chamber.

Weslake's new design produced a head which ensured that the fuel mixture travelled exactly the same distance to each cylinder. Simple but brilliant, yet again! This equality of distance, and the straightening of the ports, led to the head being called the 'straight port'.

As the cylinders were grouped in three blocks of two, three carburettors were of course needed, and rather than choose three 1¾-inch SUs, they decided to go for broke and fit three large 2-inch HD8 SUs.

So, one could at last feel that the engine had a breathing capacity equal to its rib cage. The straight-port cylinder head gave a radical transformation over 4,000 rpm, and provided an immediate increase of 40 bhp if 9:1 compression ratio pistons were used.

From a standing start, 60 mph (96.5 km/h) was reached in 7.8 seconds, an improvement of 0.7 seconds. The speedometer registered 100 mph (161 km/h) in 20.3 seconds, instead of 25.1 seconds, and top speed rose from 123.7 mph (199 km/h) to 132 mph (212 km/h). Just by looking at these

1958 Paris Motor Show. This was the début of the fastest of all the XK production range: the triple-carburettored, 3.8-litre XK 150 open two-seater. The small 'S' on the front upper corner of the door promised you 265 bhp.

The 1959 Paris Motor Show. The 150 drophead coupé is flanked on its right by the 3.4-litre Mark I which had just won the automobile Tour de France with Da Silva Romas, and the very first Mark II saloon, and on its left by the sumptuous Mark IX.

figures one can tell that the XK 150S 3.4-litre had been given some powerful medicine.

Following the rule that good things, like bad, never come singly, the OTS was announced at the same time — a handsome, subdued car which was some 90 pounds (40 kilos) lighter than the coupé to help its performance match up to its sporty appearance. It was a strict two-seater, with a very basic vinyl hood, but with genuine wind-up windows. Its customers discovered that an OTS need not necessarily be a wind trap and can even be as comfortable as a drophead coupé. The XK 150 OTS saw the end of detachable side screens and windscreens. Some thought it too civilised, especially those who hankered after the old-style, raunchy

open two-seaters. Apart from the mohair-lined hood, quarter-lights and occasional seats, there was little to differentiate the drophead from the OTS. The latter even lacked the distinctive cutaway doors of earlier OTSs.

With the OTS came an option of a Laycock de Normanville overdrive, which produced a final-drive ratio of 3.19:1 with the 4.09:1 axle, and there is no doubt that the whole package had been designed with the American market in mind, as proof of which only 92 right-hand-drive versions were produced. This is an astonishingly low figure when one realises that many of the 92 were destined for Commonwealth countries where people still drove on the left.

French sales figures were about average. 189 XK 150s of all body types were imported and some of them went to famous names: Bernard Borderie, the film producer; Karl Lagersfeld, the dress designer and perfume magnate; George Thil, the operatic tenor; film stars Mylène Demongeot and Martine Carol, etc.

Since the total 150 production tally amounted to 9,398, the French quota was fairly insignificant, especially compared with the 7,000 exported to the United States. Jaguar's

General de Gaulle at the opening of the 1960 Paris Motor Show. Bernard Consten's Mark II is the star attraction on the Jaguar stand. The XK 150 had only a few months' production life left and, with her, the XK name became extinct.

Looking at this photograph and at the two people who feature in it you can be sure that, despite the beautiful view, they will not be able to resist returning to their XK 150S open two-seater for long, since they will be able combine the joys of the countryside with the joys of their car!

fame and prestige in France were out of all proportion to the sales figures, but the marque had become a legend since the appearance of the XK 120 and, even if a Frenchman could not afford to buy a Jaguar, there was no law against him dreaming of owning one. Le Mans had also done a great deal to popularise the marque's name throughout the world, to the extent that the cars were purchased almost on their name alone.

In October 1959 came yet another Jaguar master stroke: the Mark IX's 3.8-litre engine was at last available as an option on the 150. The 3.8-litre engine was an open book to knowledgeable Jaguar enthusiasts, despite the fact that it had been put into production as recently as October 1958 with the aim of giving the heavy Mark IX saloon a little more zip. The recipe used to increase the engine capacity was the usual but effective one of increasing the bore (in this case from 83 to 87 mm), thereby increasing the capacity from 3,441 cc to 3,781 cc.

This had two logical consequences as far as power and torque were concerned: there was a 25 bhp increase, giving 265 bhp in the 'S' version, and the torque rose from 240 ft/lbs (32 m/kgs) to 260 ft/lbs (36 m/kgs) at the lower engine speed of 4,000 rpm as compared with the previous 4,500 rpm.

So, with increased torque at lower revs and a boost in power output, what more could anyone ask for?

The 3.8-litre model was available as an 'S' (with straight-port head and three HD8 carburettors) or in the standard version (with B-type head and two HD6s).

There was a supplementary piston option providing a choice between two compression ratio types:

3.8-litre S: compression ratio 9:1; 265 bhp output;
3.8-litre standard: compression ratio 9:1; 220 bhp output;
3.8-litre standard: compression ratio 8:1. 210 bhp output.

If you add to all these options the ones available for the 3.4-litre engine, which could also be supplied in 'S' and standard versions with two compression ratios, even the most demanding customer was spoilt for choice!

The 3.8-litre 150S was, of course, the most coveted of the 150 family, and many owners of the original standard model beefed up their cars with all the options which were available separately. Jaguar owners with more cheek than cash settled for buying a pair of chrome 'S's and sticking them on the doors of their standard cars.

Some 3.4-litre 150 owners tried having the cylinders re-bored to give the 3.8-litre capacity, but they then had the nasty surprise of finding cracks developing between the water jackets and the cylinders, due to the thinness of the dividing walls. It was with this fragility in mind that Jaguar opted for dry liners and barrel chroming to give greater resistance to cracking.

It was largely thanks to that little 'S' that the 150 earned its own gripping chapter in the XK saga and, when one thinks that the engine was having to drag along one and a half tons of dead weight, the car's performance figures are quite staggering! There is no knowing what they might have been if some six hundredweight (300 kilos) could have been shaved off its mass.

As a transition model, it hid its real nature pretty well, and the specialist motoring press gave it rave reviews for its engine, brakes and comfort rating. Without exception the specialist magazines agreed that it was one of the all-time greats. There was, however, universal agreement on the archaism of its structure. Chassis-based cars were by then virtually a thing of the past, and almost all motor car manufacturers had changed to the monocoque format which was much more suited to modern construction methods.

This, of course, was no secret to the Browns Lane crew and, before long, it was common knowledge that a new car was on the cards and that the 150 was not only an end-of-the-range model, but also the last of its generation. Nevertheless, 150 production continued into 1960 simply because the new car was not yet ready. It had always been Jaguar policy to keep its customers on tenterhooks, waiting for the next new model. But it was also vital that the new model should be worth waiting for, so there was no question of announcing it before all the snags had been ironed out. This new project was the reason for Jaguar not wanting to invest too much money in the 150, which was destined for the scrapyard even as it was unveiled to the public in 1957. This launch had taken place outside the traditional Motor Show surroundings, simply so that the public would not attach too much unmerited importance to the 150 range. As the months passed and Jaguar's pet new project was taking longer than expected to come to the boil, the 3.8 and 3.8S versions were produced to put paid to criticism that the 150 was slower than its monocoque saloon counterpart. In fact, it was with a view to keeping the sporting Jaguar flame burning that Lyons fuelled it with the famous 3.8-litre 'S' version which he had hoped to keep under wraps for his new car. However, this overlapping of engines and models was nothing new at Jaguar — it had happened before and would happen again.

The new monocoque construction methods were already being employed on the Foleshill production lines, but only for saloons in the shape of the 2.4-litre and the 3.4-litre models, the latter now being known as the Mark I in relation to the Mark II which followed it and which made front page news in its time. The shape of things to come was already present in those welded, pressed-steel bodies, which were both light and rigid, simple and quick to mass produce and into which the power unit could easily be fitted. Monocoque construction was taken for granted everywhere else in the world but, British conservatism being what it is, the technique was still in its infancy in the United Kingdom.

It was not just the heavy, massive chassis that was looking its age; the transmission, particularly the gearbox, looked tired. It was stiff, noisy, as heavy as a lorry's, and free of such niceties as synchromesh on first and quick gear changes.

Why was it that Jaguar's engineers knew how to produce such superb cars, but that Moss kept churning out such old-fashioned gearboxes?

This lack of modern technical solutions was even more puzzling when, as far back as 1948, the 120 had been given such revolutionary equipment as independent front suspension and torsion-bars.

Happily, there were occasional improvements which helped to draw attention away from the 150's more archaic features. Soon after the disc brakes were first introduced, quick-change pads were made available — a racing by-product — instead of the old system which involved taking

5 July 1957. An XK 150 fixed-head coupé starring in a concours d'élégance at Ermonville, France. Jaguar had used the same recipe which had brought it racing success: disc brakes. The car's number plate bears the legend, freins à disque, *just in case anyone is still unaware of the fact!*

the calipers off each time one wanted to change the pads. Another modification was the use of a Thornton limited-slip differential, which helped to lessen wheelspin thanks to a device which worked rather like a multi-plate clutch. This system enables almost all the power to be directed to the gripping wheel, thereby giving much better roadholding in such situations as accelerating strongly out of bends. This system had long been common in top-of-the-range high-powered cars, and had become an absolute necessity on the pepped-up 3.8 150S.

There is no doubt that it was this increased power which distracted customers from the rather old-fashioned technology which had been used on the rest of the car, for it is very unlikely that the car would have been anything like as successful if it had had to make do with the 120's 160 bhp, or even its standard 3.4 version's 190 bhp.

A cursory examination of the 150's European rivals gives ample proof that its enviable position on the sports car league table was due mainly to its performance figures. At the same time one must admit that there were some cars which could go as fast, if not faster, than the 150 with only half its power output. But then, they did not have the 150's weight to contend with. If you were to compare fuel consumption at high speeds, you would soon see how important weight considerations are, not only economically but also in the public interest.

The following examples will illustrate the concept of the sports car as it was beginning to be seen back in 1960: there

was the 356 A Porsche, with four cylinders, a 1,587 cc capacity, 115 bhp, weighing 16¾ cwt (850 kgs), fitted with 15-inch tyres and capable of 125 mph; the BMW 507, with its box frame, 3,168 cc capacity and weighing 5 cwt (250 kgs) less than the 150, was capable of a good 135 mph (220 km/h); but top prize had to go to Colin Chapman's Lotus Elite, with its lightweight monocoque structure, 1,220 cc capacity and 10½ cwt (540 kgs), which could clock up almost 120 mph (190 km/h).

Despite these statistics, we must not lose sight of the fact that the XK 150, like all the XKs, was aimed at a market where the weight/power ratio was not going to be upper-most in the customer's mind when he signed the order form.

The XK 150's production life ended in October 1961. For the previous year, only one body style had been available — the fixed-head coupé in 3.4-litre, 3.8-litre and 'S' versions. The model died as it had been born — with the minimum of fuss. Jaguar's concentration was now centred round the miracle car which had been four years in the making, and which was about to be unleashed on an expectant world. The country of its launch was Switzerland, the city Geneva. Its time had almost come.

Although the XK 150 had not been designed as a competition car, its performance and handling were so impressive that some rally drivers chose to use it as such. Here the Legourd-Gallier team are competing in the 1959 Tour de France.

One of the XK 150's rare rally appearances: Barbier and Liagre in the Lyons-Charbonnières Rally, 9 March 1963.

The E-Type Generation

THE SERIES 1 E-TYPE

3.8 LITRES: 15 MARCH 1961—OCTOBER 1964

SUCH STUFF AS DREAMS ARE MADE OF

The secret had been well kept and any slips of the tongue had been glossed over deftly, so that when the car appeared it had twice the effect. When the Geneva Motor Show opened its doors at 10am on 15 March 1961, a wave of euphoria seemed to engulf those who rushed over to the Jaguar stand. No one could remember, in the history of the Swiss Motor Show, such burning curiosity about — and such enthusiasm for — any car.

It was the superstar at the show, the prima ballerina. It made all the other new models look ten years out of date! The press snatched it up at once and, during the next few days, both the specialist magazines and the daily newspapers waxed lyrical about the most fantastic grown-ups' toy that any motor show had ever seen — the E-type.

It was dissected, analysed, psychoanalysed, discussed in university seminars by sociology students; was the subject of a doctoral thesis; was compared to a rocket, a monster, a cigar, an explosive. There were plenty of symbols to be found which would confirm its aggressive character; no one could miss its sexual symbolism which explained its pull on customers of both sexes.

Everywhere you looked you read that the car of your dreams was in the shops now and at a price you could afford.

People rushed to the Jaguar stand to place their orders, not even bothering to find out how long they would have to wait for delivery. Those with more money than sense, perhaps, happily travelled thousands of miles to be among the first to own an E-type. Customers tried everything they knew to get their names moved up on the waiting list; hysteria seemed to grip the motoring public.

Why did Jaguar choose Geneva for this launch? Why not the traditional confines of the Earls Court Motor Show? Their decision marked an attempt to break away from the insular British tradition and a wish to underline the break by choosing a motor show with both a European and an international reputation. A more down-to-earth explanation might be that the E-type was not quite ready for the London or Paris Motor Shows!

The XK 150 was still in the catalogue and sat a few yards away from the E-type on the Geneva stand, but it might as well not have been there for all the attention that was paid to it, especially since, surprising though it may seem, the XK 150 cost £55 more than the new bombshell.

E-type mania spread to the French press, too. Just read what they thought of the wonder car:

In February, *L'Auto Journal* had given an early warning of what was to come with its headline: 'Jaguar takes another leap forward'.

The E-Type Series 1... a splendid motor car. This is the very first official release promoting the latest creation from Coventry. The protective covers over the bonnet opening latches testify to the early development stage of the model.

In *L'Aurore,* André Bloch compared the car to a monster, and headed his piece: 'The power of a rail-car designed with acceleration and speed in mind'.

L'Auto-Journal's André Costa thought that the body-work was 'impressive'. Coming from him that was high praise indeed!

Science et Vie gave the car an unconditional thumbs-up: 'The new E-type Jaguar: a candidate for Le Mans'.

L'Argus played about with statistics, and the E-type's 260 km/h (162.5 mph) and 265 bhp, which gave a kilometre an hour for every brake horsepower. It was great fun, even though it made no technical sense.

The front page of *L'Equipe* covered the competitive aspect: 'The new E-type Jaguar launched at the Geneva Motor Show: opposition for Ferrari and Aston Martin'.

Paris-Jour led with a picture of the open two-seater beneath which it announced: 'The new E-type Jaguar, a revolutionary blend of sports and GT cars, will travel at 270 km/h (168.75 mph) and must therefore be the fastest touring car in the world'.

Every newspaper without exception, from the tabloids to the serious press, went into such raptures over the E-type that Jaguar had no need of paid advertising to make sure that its production lines were kept busy for months to come.

This ecstatic reception was repeated all over the globe, in the American, English, German and Italian papers; you name it, and 'E' was the letter of the day!

In October, at the Paris Motor Show, there was an action replay of Geneva. General de Gaulle came along wearing his thick-lens glasses so that he could get a clear view of the car which had all Paris flocking to the 'Salon d'Auto'. He was faced with the impressive sight of the fixed-head E-type, lounging voluptuously on its white-wall tyres near the 3.8-litre Mark II of Bernard Costen and Jack Renel, in

The Series 1 E-type's public début on 18 April 1961 at the Metropole Hotel in Monte Carlo.
William Lyons was there in person to publicise the new dream Jaguar.

which they had won the Tour de France for the third consecutive time.

The launch, of course, was masterminded by William Lyons. The car itself was marvellously packaged, but the launch itself was no less a marvel of marketing talent.

This all took place, of course, at the beginning of the fabulous '60s. Cinema, music and society were about to be revolutionised by the new-wave French directors, the lads from Liverpool and Marshall Macluhan, with his 'the medium is the message'; change was the order of the day.

The E-type was just the right kind of car for its time; aggressive and liberated. It was perhaps the most beautiful symbol of the 1960s, a decade which, according to the economists and sociologists, ended in 1973, when the world was knocked sideways by the oil and raw materials crises.

The E-type drew all eyes, even when it was standing still; on the open road it was breathtakingly beautiful — low, racy, flowing, sensual, aristocratic, showy, obviously too long in the nose but at the same time wonderfully proportioned. It was such stuff as dreams are made of, and the product of a team of men whose criteria were beauty, speed and acceleration.

Once you had recovered from the initial shock of seeing an E-type for the first time, you might have been curious about how the car differed from the XK 150 which preceded it. Obviously the car was in no way related to the 150, but rather marked the birth of a new generation. The most easily discernible difference was that the E-type was a

Prince Rainier of Monaco was already a fervent Jaguar admirer, since he had just bought a Mark II saloon. The incredibly long bonnet was obviously working its magic on

the spectators. The late Princess Grace almost eclipsed the ravishing E-type with her beauty.

monocoque car; quite a revolutionary concept for a mass-produced British sports car of the time.

What other sports cars were available in 1961, irrespective of price? Well, the choice included the Aston Martin DB4, Alfa Romeo Giulietta, AC Ace, Alpine, Facel Vega, Ferrari 240 GT and 400 Super-America, Jensen 541S, Lancia Flavia, Lotus Elite, Maserati 3500 GT, Morgan Plus Four, M.G.A. 1600, Porsche 356 B/1600, Volvo 1800 coupé, Mercedes 190 SL, Triumph...

Unlike the XK SS, which was simply a road version of the D-type, the E-type gave the impression of being a very civilised and very comfortable sports car. There were echoes of the D-type, of course, but the 'E' was a completely different kettle of fish, despite keeping that agressive appearance. One could not go so far as to say that there were no common factors linking the 'D' and the 'E', for their styling was the work of the same man: Malcolm Sayer.

Gone were the days when a sports car owner had to put on a brave face and pretend that he did not care a hoot about being out in the wind and rain. Now, with the E-type, he could sit at the wheel in his Sunday best, enjoy the car's dynamic performance, and arrive at his destination without wondering whether he was in for a bout of 'flu or rheumatism!

The new car's target market was the more 'mature' sports car enthusiast, who was not prepared to risk either his neck or his carefully groomed hairstyle — the rising executive. This was the kind of man who could afford to buy an E-type for, although the car was surprisingly good value for its £2,098, it was still capable of making a big hole in the man-in-the-street's pay packet.

At just over £2,000 it was, nevertheless, two-fifths the price of a Ferrari 250 GT Pininfarina or an Aston Martin DB4 GT; half the price of a Mercedes 300 SL; a little less expensive than an Alfa Romeo 2000 Spider; and about the same as a Porsche 90 drophead coupé.

When the XK 120 had been announced, 12 years previously, people had wondered how Jaguar could do it for the money. The same applied to the E-type when it was announced.

Over in France, an E-type was seven times as expensive as a Citroën 4CV, so it remained an unattainable dream for most Frenchmen. More realistic objectives were the newly introduced Match Renault 4 and the Ami 6, although even purchasers of these models still had their eyes on an E-type for the day their ships came in. The E-type Jaguar was extremely effective in spreading the faith across the

The faithful twin-overhead-camshaft XK engine was a constant source of amazement, both in its design and its seemingly unlimited potential. With a straight-port head and three HD8 SU carburettors its output was 265 bhp (note the exterior bonnet opening which featured on the first E-types).

213

The E-type's very own 'Tour de France'. After Geneva and Monte Carlo, the E-type landed at Marseilles and went on to Lyons where it was exhibited outside the Charbonnières casino. Charley-Jean Delecroix, the Jaguar importer, explains the finer points to Henri Peignaux, the first and largest French Jaguar concessionnaire.

The E-type arrived at Paris' Grand Palais exhibition hall in October 1961 and immediately attracted a crowd. The scenes outside the Motor Show venue were repeated inside. This photograph was taken from an upstairs window of the Grand Palais and shows the E-type's wonderfully clean lines.

Rolling off the transporter at Marseilles, the new starlet continues its whistle-stop tour of France. The date was 20 April 1961.

channel. Schoolboys, undergraduates, not to mention the older working young men, yearned to own such a car.

Young men of all ages saw the E-type as a passport to success with the girls. They hoped that long low profile would have more effect on a susceptible young female's emotions than all the charm that 100 aspiring Valentinos could muster. The stories of the 1961 silly season were often about E-type owners; minor film-star scandals were always accompanied by the seductive throb of an E-type; if you wanted to be a pop star, an E-type was a must for your image; fashionable young men and Johnny-come-latelys could not afford to be without one. If you were in a position to visit a trendy nightclub dangling a Jaguar key-ring from your finger, you might find young ladies queuing up for the honour of a date with you!

But, although owning an E-type could be the ideal key to success with the opposite sex, this rather racy image tended to overshadow the car's deservedly high technological reputation. It was a star performer in its own right and, even 20 years after it first hit the world's roads, you still get the same giddy feeling and tightness in your stomach when those 265 bhp break free and take you a quarter of a mile in 15 seconds from a standing start. Its amazing acceleration pushed you back into your seat, and you felt as though you were a football being kicked by some giant aiming to score a goal.

Nowadays, we seem to need twice the number of cylinders to give the same sensational effect — just look at a modern Ferrari. The combination of powerful acceleration and very high speeds calls for a skilled and experienced driver. As André Bloch wrote in the columns of *L'Aurore*: 'This is the dream car for someone who can drive almost with his eyes shut, with nerves of steel and lightning reflexes', but he added meekly, 'I have often been scared witless driving this car! 0 to 100 km/h in 7 seconds, top speed of 240 km/h.'

He is quite right. When you're driving an E-type flat-out there is no time for consulting the Highway Code or your road atlas. Everything happens so quickly that, when you come to a hazard, you have to use instincts developed over years of driving. Do what feels right, and pray! That lorry way ahead of you may be doing 50 mph, but from where you are sitting it's coming backwards towards you like a rocket at 100 mph.

You can relax and enjoy yourself at speeds under, say, 110 mph (175 km/h), your elbow resting on the armrest and your fingers drumming on the steering wheel in time to the music on the radio. But go any faster and the whole picture changes, because the adrenalin starts flowing, you have to concentrate fiercely, both hands taking a firm hold of the wheel; the slightest mistake could cost you a nasty fright, if not your life.

This rear view reveals several features of the Series 1 fixed-head coupé E-type: bright aluminium facia, seat design and exhaust arrangement. The reversing light was attached rather hastily by the importer to meet homologation requirements.

October 1961. Charles de Gaulle, the French President, greets Charley Delecroix (Jaguar's importer) and looks with interest at the undisputed star of the 1961 Paris Motor Show. Dunlop had supplied this E-type's white-walled tyres especially for the show.

Some inexperienced young lads who have tried to impress their girlfriends by driving at 150 mph (240 km/h) are now escorting angels, for common-or-garden driving skills just will not do at these speeds.

But let's take time out to look at the genesis of this wonderful new Coventry car.

The E1A Prototype

The E-type first began to take shape on a sketch pad back in 1957. The concept emerged some time after the dramatic Browns Lane fire, when Jaguar were having to set new targets and evolve new designs in order to start up sports car production again and develop a new breed of cars to follow the XKs.

The rough specifications called for a car with something like a 3-litre capacity, a 285 bhp output, 150 mph (240 km/h) potential, and capable of doing 20 mph (35 km/h) in fourth without complaining. The new model also had to be reliable and comfortable, with production scheduled at about 100 per week.

Inevitably, William Heynes was given the job of masterminding the development and, before you could say Jack Robinson, a prototype was being evolved. As the new car was to follow in the sporting footsteps of the C- and D-types, it was bound to bear the letter 'E' in its codename, and the first prototype was named E1A. The month was November 1957, and within seven weeks a full-size mock-up of the car had been constructed. It was a monocoque structure, consisting of welded aluminium panels (hence the 'A' in E1A), and was smaller than the series E-type as we know it. In effect, E1A was a 9/10ths scale car which looked as though it had been designed with a pantograph to make it slightly shorter, lower and narrower.

A sub-assembly, consisting of a welded framework, was bolted on to the front bulkhead of the centre monocoque to carry the engine and front suspension; this arrangement was similar to that used on the D-type. The bonnet, too, was one piece, and made up the whole of the front of the car. As on the D- and C-types, it hinged forward to give easy access to the working parts.

The reinforcing structure, as such, was made up of box-section magnesium-alloy tubes, a perfectly workable solution but one which had to be scrapped as it was difficult to repair. In 1958 few garages, even specialist firms, had access to argon arc welding equipment, and this made the welded magnesium alloy framework impracticable.

In this, the first 'E' prototype, there were no headlights or bumpers on the front of the car, so that no bumps would create barriers to the smooth flow of air over the body. Under the bonnet lay the 2.4-litre short-stroke XK power unit from the contemporary saloons, since it was the only one which fitted.

This 2.4-litre was a genuine XK unit, but the stroke had been shortened to 76 mm, making it oversquare since the bore remained at 83 mm. In its standard saloon incarnation the 2.4 developed only 115 bhp, but in the E1A it produced 200, thanks to the traditional, but nevertheless effective, recipe of modifying the inlet and exhaust cylinder head departments.

As you can see from the illustrations, E1A was a spartan car; the doors were rudimentary, there were no interior fittings, no paintwork on the aluminium body, and a simple perspex sheet for the windscreen. It was a real no-frills prototype.

One of the most important innovations in the E1A's development was the long-overdue independent rear sus-

The 1961 Paris Motor Show. The two E-type bodies — roadster and fixed-head coupé — were on the stand. Once the doors were opened the Jaguar stand was surrounded within seconds, just as it had been at Geneva.

pension. Heynes realised that Jaguar had been a little laggardly in that sphere and that the time had come to do away with the old rigid rear axle.

The front suspension had acquired its independence way back in 1948, so it had taken ten years for the rear of the car to catch up.

The very first gesture towards independent rear suspension had been directed at the very last D-type (XHD 501) which had been fitted with a de Dion rear axle. This was a move in the right direction, but it did not give real independence to both wheels. Heynes was not satisfied with this solution, especially since all the 'specials' into which Jaguar had been asked to fit their own engines had, for many years, been blessed with independent rear suspension: HWM, Lister, Tojeiro, etc.

Bill Heynes therefore went back to his drawing board, determined to persevere until Jaguar could produce its own system, for he was a great believer in this arrangement. The result was a design with two swinging links connected to a differential and with coil-spring suspension; it was intended to be an easily detachable rear suspension.

In the first E1A version it was fixed directly to the monocoque through a reinforcing layer which doubled the thickness of the sheet steel, strengthening the fixing. Oddly enough, as a result, the differential was a permanent fixture and fitting! Even apart from the technical problems which

raised their ugly heads if you wanted to remove the suspension, this set-up was unbearably noisy and there was no way of bringing the noise level down to one which even the most long-suffering driver would tolerate. Several experiments were carried out in an attempt to insulate the differential, but they all proved fruitless.

Despite these noise problems the first road tests were more than promising, and the car's roadholding was a constant source of pleasure for the test drivers. The positive benefits of independent rear suspension had therefore been proved beyond question. However, one serious defect showed itself right from the start, and that was brake overheating.

The reason for this was that, in an attempt to reduce the unsprung weight, the engineers had lightened the ends of the axles by putting the calipers and discs right up against the differential. The result soon made itself felt; with insufficient ventilation, and jostling elbows with a hot spot, the discs heated up to such an extent that any braking power virtually disappeared.

Other companies had tackled this problem with varying degrees of success, but it is fairly surprising to learn that in the England of 1957 only two firms could boast an efficient independent rear suspension — Lagonda and A.C. So, it would not be strictly fair to say that Jaguar was lagging a long way behind the rest of the field in this department.

The E-type roadster stole the limelight on the Jaguar stand at the 1961 Paris Motor Show. Behind the E-type is the Mark II which B.Consten and C.Renel drove to win the automobile Tour de France for the second year running. In actual fact, Jaguar had achieved a hat-trick in this event, for Da Silva-Ramos had won in 1959 in a Mark I.

The little E1A was put through the mill for more than a year, to discover all its faults and rectify them as and when they appeared. Its handling and performance impressed all the test drivers, as is shown by this confidential report written by the editor of *The Motor,* who was lucky enough to be given the chance to give the E1A a lengthy road test.

This letter, which was published for the first time in Paul Skilleter's fine book *Jaguar Sports Cars,* was addressed to Richard Dangerfield, at the time a director of the Temple Press publishing concern, and was dated 14 May 1958.

"I spent the past weekend in a car of such sensational potential that I feel that you might wish to know about it. The car is a Jaguar, known at the moment as the E-type. This car has been developed from the Le Mans-winning D-type but incorporates numerous improvements. The rear suspension is independent and the disc brakes inboard. Aerodynamically it is superior to the D-type and therefore faster.

"Sir William Lyons asked me last year about my test run course between Brecon and Carmarthen. This route combines a few fast straights with numerous extremely fast bends and some very slow ones. It is seldom flat for more than a mile at a time and for comparative purposes I would mention that a good Ford Zephyr driven flat out can cover the 48½ miles between St Peter's Church, Carmarthen and the River Bridge at Brecon in 57 minutes. The fastest run until last Sunday was in David Brown's Aston Martin with Le Mans engine and experimental disc brakes. This covered the distance in 50 minutes. I would explain that on these runs reasonable respect is paid to the several built up areas encountered and cars are never driven in a manner hazardous to the public, but the time of day for fast cars is chosen with care to avoid lorries.

"Knowing this, Sir William said he had a proposition to make. It was that he would lend my wife and myself a prototype of an entirely new model and, having acclimatised ourselves to it, we should then make the run with a view to comparing it with the Aston Martin and other fast vehicles driven on that route. Six months later Mr Heynes advised me that the car was ready and we first set eyes on it a few days ago. It is a very beautiful machine and although ours was minus hood and headlamps these are most gracefully incorporated on the production prototype which I also inspected. Production is expected to begin in the autumn and the target is 100 of these formidable sports cars per week. With a 3-litre engine it will develop 286 bhp and I visualise a road test speed not very far short of 150 mph, which is going to make us think.

"On Sunday morning soon after 7 am in perfect conditions we made a 20-mile warming-up run and then 'had a go'. The result was almost fantastic. The first 20 miles from Carmarthen to Llandovery was covered at an average of just over 70 mph and Brecon was reached in 43 minutes, giving an overall average for the 48½ miles of 67.7 mph. The return journey was made at a fast touring speed by my wife but nevertheless equalled the Aston Martin record of 50 minutes. At no time did we exceed 120 mph. Subsequent test runs were equally astonishing, thus a 50-mile section between Carmarthen and Devil's Bridge showed an average of 50 mph despite considerable heavy traffic, and consistently winding roads.

"It will be seen therefore that the new Jaguar is a potential world beater and in a separate envelope I enclose a selection of pictures taken this weekend mostly outside my stables because we maintained maximum security and did not let the car come to rest in populated places."

This account gives food for thought if you remember that this prototype was fitted with a 2.5-litre engine, and especially if you have ever driven on Welsh roads!

The time was ripe then for the second prototype which would be devoid of the E1A's faults. The new version was the E1B and it was a full-scale car this time, instead of the E1A's 9/10ths scale. The nickname for this car was the 'Pop Rivet Special', which needs no explanation except to say that the body panels were no longer welded together and that they were made out of steel sheets.

You can tell, just by the time devoted to the E-type's development, that Sir William could no longer allow himself the luxury which he had enjoyed in the good old days of the XK 120, of locking himself away with his minute development team to conceive a new car and to launch their creation with hardly any preparation. He was now at the head of an industrial giant and any thought of improvisation had to be stifled. Seat-of-the-pants design had had to be replaced by a methodical research and development programme and by clearly defined demarkation of responsibilities, so that individual engineering teams tackled one specific problem which had been assigned to them.

Just one example of the new methodical and cautious approach to development is the evolution of the independent rear suspension which had given so many headaches to Bill Heynes. It was fitted on the 3.4-litre saloon (the Mark I) in place of the rigid axle, so that its characteristics could be studied during weeks of searching tests and modifications to the components: the diameter and height of the springs, dampers, joints, wheel clearance, braking, etc.

All this hard work was amply rewarded, for the rear suspension which it produced was beyond reproach and, once series production was under way, it never gave the slightest cause for concern.

E1B's creators were now very happy with their handiwork, and had been delighted to find that, as a full-size car, it was infinitely more handsome than the E1A. The rear suspension had now been developed into an autonomous unit which could be bolted in place in a matter of moments.

The 'Pop Rivet Special' was effectively a laboratory animal and never really had to cope with the realities of the open road.

For the next part of the story we shall have to go back in time a little, to see it in perspective.

Forerunner of the E-type and part of the linking chain between the D- and E-types, this prototype bore the E1A code-name. The 'A' stood for aluminium. Despite the lack of headlights, the prototype's styling is very similar to that of the production E-type. This rare photograph shows a call at the factory petrol pumps prior to test sessions. The registration number is merely temporary; it was used on many Jaguar test models.

E1A leaving for road tests on 14 November 1958. Seen from a three-quarter view, this 9/10ths scale prototype looks even more like the final series car.

The E2A prototype

Picture in your mind a tall, bulky American with a Hollywood smile and a Texan-sized wallet. He was to earn the nickname of 'The Le Mans American' and was a motor racing fanatic. His name was Briggs Cunningham and he had long shared one of William Lyons' most cherished ambitions — to win Le Mans. When an American is dead set on an objective, to the point where it rules his life, sparks are bound to fly.

1957 was Jaguar's year, the year when the D-type swept the board at Le Mans. The factory had withdrawn from active competition the year before, since Jaguar's works-entered cars had already won enough races to last a lifetime. The Jaguar racing division had been eating up more than its fair share of precious cash, and this money was needed elsewhere.

To cut a long story short, the Jaguar ball was in the private entrants' court now, although there is no doubt that few other marques had invested as much money in a works' racing programme between 1951 and 1956 as Jaguar.

Since he had reached his Le Mans objective and felt that there was nothing left for him to prove, Lyons decided to spend his time working on a new car with the aim of turning his Le Mans victories into hard cash through commercial sales.

Come to that, even if he had still wanted to take an active part in motor racing, it is doubtful whether the Jaguar board would have let Sir William have his way.

Although he had created the marque and had been given a knighthood in recognition of his services to the motoring industry, Sir William was now 60 years old and was starting to ease up slightly on his workload. In any case, since the business had been expanding steadily over the years, it had grown to the point where he could not hope to have a finger in every Jaguar pie. He was no longer the autocratic and all-powerful boss of 15 years earlier, who had made decisions and ruled over his company rather like a feudal lord with the help of his own flair, talent and nerve. He now had to explain himself to a host of knowledgeable and demanding shareholders, and to bow to the decisions of a board of directors which was more concerned about the company's financial health than about embarking on another risky enterprise.

The E-type was therefore to be one of the last projects for Lyons and his loyal team of stalwarts. For this reason, if no other, Lyons wanted the new baby to be his most memorable and successful one.

In 1960, the French Automobile Club de L'Ouest, organisers of the Le Mans 24-Hours race, had, together with the Commission Sportive Internationale (CSI), brought in an important change in the rules which put a limit on engine capacity, in the hopes of extending the range of potential winners beyond the few famous firms who had sufficient funds to develop large-capacity engines.

The new formula, described as 'International', therefore promised to make the 24-Hours more of an open race in which even rank outsiders stood a chance with the new 3-litre limit.

At the same time as the ACO introduced this new ruling, they also brought in a new regulation about windscreens, which thereafter had to measure 15 centimetres (6-inches) in

This cutaway drawing of the E2A prototype reveals its close resemblance to the E-type of the following year.

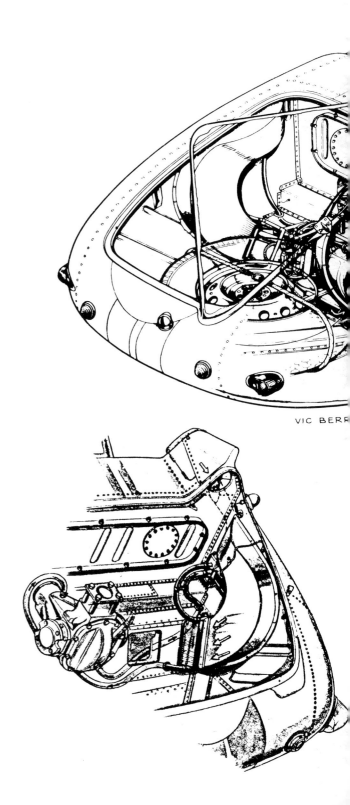

VIC BERR

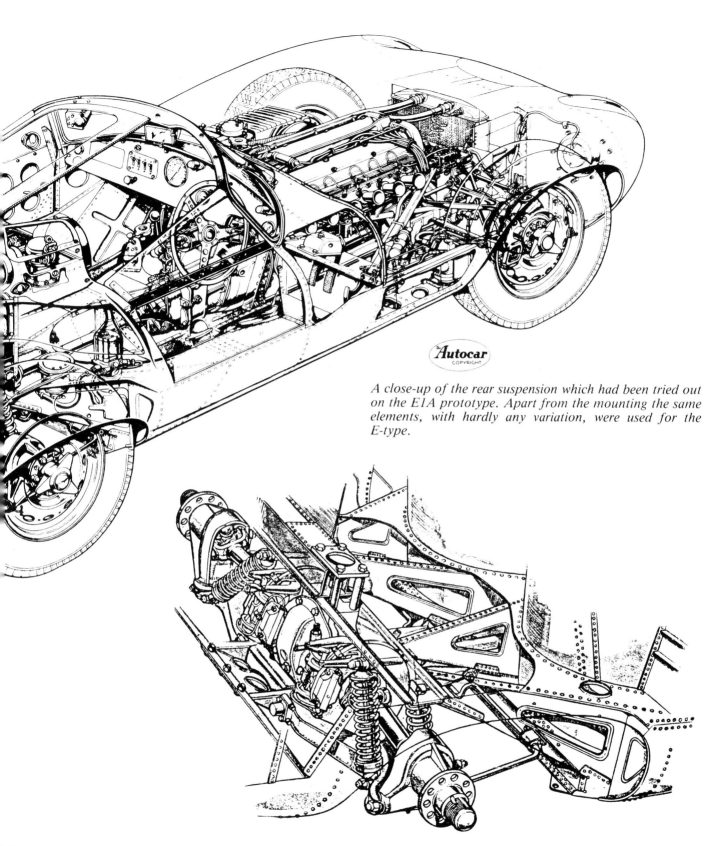

A close-up of the rear suspension which had been tried out on the E1A prototype. Apart from the mounting the same elements, with hardly any variation, were used for the E-type.

The driver could switch on an electric pump which circula-
ted oil from a separate cooler through the differential to
disperse any excessive heat produced by the inboard disc
brakes.

height. This put paid to the old symbolic perspex aero-screens; now all the cars had to have proper glass windscreens which were set at an angle to reduce wind resistance.

The new windscreens looked completely out of proportion on sports cars, and their large surface area posed a tricky problem: that of rain and screen wipers. Few had looked that far ahead, so there were likely to be some surprises among the future Le Mans cars.

Briggs Cunningham had a colourful racing history, and he had always wanted to use ever bigger and more powerful engines. He was such an enthusiastic character, with money to burn, that he managed to persuade Sir William to build him a special car for the 1960 Le Mans.

Faced with Cunningham's persuasive arguments, Lyons agreed to the American's request. Sir William probably did not need much persuading anyway, since this was an ideal opportunity for killing two birds with one stone, as Jaguar

was absorbed in E-type development. So it was that Cunningham found himself presented with E2A, the third pre series 'E' prototype.

As far as Jaguar was concerned, Cunningham could no have timed his approach better, for it helped with the finan cing of the new prototype which would have been buil whether or not the American had come on the scene.

Apart from the pop rivets, which give it a very 'racy' look Cunningham's E2A 3-litre prototype (seen here before i left the Jaguar works) gave a very good idea of what wa being developed in the workshops prior to its fanaticall successful launch some months later at the Geneva Moto Show.

3 April 1960. Le Mans test sessions with the 3-litre Cunningham prototype. You will notice that it had not yet been fitted with its tail fin.

The 3-litre prototype. Cunningham prepared the Jaguar — seen here at Browns Lane — for the 1960 Le Mans. It still has the D-type's headfairing with tail fin, and the magnesium alloy Dunlop wheels. In many ways it is typical of the kind of cars which were produced to conform to the new ACO regulations for the 3-litre class.

The short-stroke, fuel-injected, 3-litre engine in Briggs Cunningham's E2A prototype. Adjustments are being made to the car on the Sarthe circuit.

F.R.W. 'Lofty' England directing the 3-litre prototype's test sessions.

The 2.4-litre block had been rebored to bring it up to just under the 3-litre limit and the works coaxed it into producing 293 bhp at 6,750 rpm, thanks to Lucas injection. With its 85 mm bore the engine was now almost square, which was no bad thing in theory. As near as makes no difference it was the same engine which had been supplied for the preceding year to D-type owners who wanted to race their cars in the 3-litre category.

Unfortunately, although the engine looked ideal on paper, in practice it proved rather fragile. Nevertheless, it was a beautiful piece of work, made entirely in aluminium, which knocked pounds off the car's weight and lightened the front suspension. Apart from the use of light alloy, this was basically the 2,997 cc D-type power unit, with dry-sump lubrication, titanium rods, featherweight pistons with a 10:1 compression ratio, a 7/16-inch cam lift, very wide 53 mm diameter valves and slide-throttle Lucas fuel injection which was activated through a rack and pinion connected to the accelerator pedal. It was all good, well-tried stuff.

There was a more original development in the cylinder block, where the angles of the inlet and exhaust valves were very different: 35 degrees for the inlet and 40 degrees for the exhaust. You probably remember that the D-type's wide-angle head was a 35/40...

Lubrication followed that of the D-type; one high-pressure pump and two auxiliary ones provided for oil circulation between the sump and the block.

Nor were there any surprises in the transmission. A fully synchronised four-speed gearbox was linked to the engine through a triple-plate 7¼-inch (18.4-cm) diameter clutch. The 3.31:1 axle ratio was specially selected for the Le Mans circuit.

Clothing this predictable assembly was the body itself, with its monocoque structure of riveted aluminium panels, completely devoid of paint. A front framework was bolted on to the bulkhead to house the power unit and front suspension. The independent rear suspension was the recently developed easily detachable assembly. One of the bonuses of the E2A's development for Le Mans was that this new suspension would be given a very thorough workout over the gruelling 24-hour race.

This suspension centred round the differential from which protruded the half-shafts carrying the disc brakes, and the lower links supported the combined spring-damper units of which there were four — two on either side of the differential.

One of the nasty snags which the works had to deal with was the overheating of the disc brake system, which was sited right up against the differential. During long-distance running, this reached such intolerably high temperatures that the engineers had to devise the maximum air circulation to keep the whole assembly down to a reasonable temperature, and they also insulated the differential via a protective plate.

Brakes are, it is true, intended to transform kinetic energy into calorific energy, but there are limits! The discs had soared to 1,000°C and the differential oil to 300°C with the latter leaking out all over the place. At 1,000°C the discs started cracking up, and any braking contact vanished into thin air.

Consequently, Jaguar provided a special cooler for the differential oil, with electrically pumped circulation. It was as easy as that. As for the disc brakes, air vents were drilled through to the front of the car wherever possible.

The steering and front suspension were identical to the tried and tested D-type's.

In many ways, then, the E2A was virtually a D-derived model, with the headfairing and fin making the comparison inevitable. But in other ways it bore many E-type features, although this was of course impossible to deduce at that stage.

It was a superb car, even though the oversized windscreen looked a bit incongruous. It was also a promising car, even though it weighed some 70 pounds (30 kilos) more than the D-type.

The April Le Mans practice sessions looked good, especially after last-minute snags had been ironed out.

Walter Hansgen, whom Cunningham had signed up together with Dan Gurney, lapped at an average speed of 121.42 mph (195.4 km/h), which made E2A second fastest after Phil Hill's Ferrari which had notched up 124.76 mph (200.78 km/h). Cunningham was happy enough, for there were still two months to go before the curtain went up and he was confident of success once the final tuning adjustments were made. The only significant modification to the car was the installation of the D-type's fin to give greater straight-line stability on the endless Mulsanne straight, the fastest stretch on the circuit.

When the cars lined up in the rain on 25 June 1960, Hansgen and Gurney were very optimistic, in spite of the impressive competition which included Maserati, Ferrari, Corvette and... Jaguar. Yes, another Jaguar — a privately entered D-type — was there too.

Unluckily for Cunningham and his car, a very minor

Cunningham's 3-litre passed into Guy Griffith's hands. It has lost its fin and has gained a bulge in the bonnet to accommodate the 3.8-litre engine and Weber carburettors.

collision with a Ferrari put paid to his hopes. The fuel-injection pump and a pipe had been damaged and, although the patch-up job which was carried out on them held for some hours, it eventually cracked up. The pump consequently was working below par, leading to overheating of the head and the number two piston, with the result that a gasket blew.

By the middle of the night it was all over, and the 3-litre Cunningham returned disconsolately to the pits. All the same, the outing had not been a complete disaster since E2A had shown its potential.

Briggs Cunningham was naturally disappointed, but his stubbornness and determination to succeed impressed the Jaguar works, which had followed the race very closely and was pleased with the car's performance, despite the fuel pipe breakage.

There were rumours that Jaguar might be coming back to racing, but... one wonders what E2A might have achieved if it had not been for that breakdown; it *could* have won.

It was with this tantalising possibility in mind that Jaguar returned to the grindstone, and the preparation of the E-type for its launch. Despite the feverish activity, the new car was not quite ready when the October London Motor Show came around. It was not the end of the world, for there was always Geneva!

Come to that, the Jaguar management was quite sold on the idea of a continental launch, thinking that this might give the car a more cosmopolitan image.

They were still ruled by the principle of 12 years before — export or bust.

Before Cunningham took E2A back with him to America, the car was given a 3.8-litre engine with triple Weber carbs and dry-sump lubrication. Because the 3.8 was

that much taller than the 3-litre unit, the works had to fashion a hump in the bonnet to accommodate it: a sign of things to come in the series E-types!

This prototype is now owned by Jaguar enthusiast Guy Griffith and you can see it, minus its fin and windscreen, in the Cotswolds Museum.

The French motoring press buzzed with conjecture about the E-type's styling for weeks before the Geneva launch. They had some idea of what the car would look like, thanks to a few small leaks. *L'Auto Journal* published a drawing by a journalist who was obviously trying to make his name, with the claim that this was a scoop revelation of the E-type. Unfortunately for the magazine, and luckily for us since we can enjoy the sketch with hindsight, the journalist's vision bore no resemblance whatsoever to the real thing!

Cunningham's 3-litre prototype in the 1960 Le Mans practice sessions. Because of the new ACO regulations, the car was fitted with the short-stroke power unit. It was driven by the Gurney/Hansgen team.

The E-type
Series 1, 3.8-litre
March 1961—October 1964

It was the most beautiful and honest car for a long time; some people said 'of all time', but that might have been a slight exaggeration.

This first production E-type was closer to the XK SS than the 'D', with a similar, but less dumpy, body than the former; with a similar profile but with the curves flattened out somewhat; with some identical features, such as the bumpers. It was, however, even more flowing, subtler and sleeker; a gleaming beauty on which endless care had been lavished. It was the car of everyone's dreams.

Incidentally, it was also the E2A, but with a more sensual outline and a better-proportioned windscreen!

The first few cars were known as 'flat floor'. This was a reference to the floor design which made it very difficult for tall people to get in behind the wheel and drive in any comfort. This flaw was soon dealt with, as only those cars produced between March 1961 and January 1962 were cursed with it. The factory made a modification which put an end to the agonies of a six-foot plus driver.

The E-type followed on logically from the D-type in many ways. It used a steel central monocoque which stretched from the back end of the boot to the scuttle at the front. This central section included the windscreen and the passenger compartment.

A front sub-assembly, consisting of a framework of Reynolds 541 box-section steel tubing, was bolted on to the monocoque, just as it had been on the D-type and E2A. This framework housed the engine, steering and suspension of course.

The same kind of independent sub-assembly on the rear of the car took the suspension, transmission and rear brakes, and was fixed to the central monocoque in a re-markably rudimentary fashion: it was bolted on through six connecting positions after the brake system had been disconnected.

The bonnet was a marvellous piece of work, which opened in the now-traditional manner. It consisted of 12 parts and hinged forward to reveal all the mechanical bits and pieces and the front suspension. It may have been a coachbuilder's nightmare, but it was a mechanic's dream. Body repairers may not have been so impressed, since even a minor bump resulted in a repair job — though it was all good business! However, adjusting a new bonnet to fit a car such as the E-type needed a high level of skill to achieve a perfect alignment.

On the first few E-types the bonnet louvres were pressed out of a separate sheet of steel which was let into the bonnet whereas, a few months later, these openings were pressed straight into the upper steel bonnet panel. The exterior

The E-type's début at Geneva in March 1961. Sir William Lyons himself did the honours at the launch and presented the right-hand-drive 9600 HP-registered E-type which was to symbolise for years the epitome of sports car design. The absence of a horizontal bar across the radiator is typical of pre-series E-types.

The presentation E-type registered 9600 HP was used for most of the British tests. Test-drive reports in the press mostly referred to this particular car, since it was the one loaned to motoring journalists for testing.

the cam covers and the bonnet which prevented the paintwork discolouring or blistering through the intense heat which was being generated underneath.

The E1A and — at first — the E2A prototypes had not sported this hump, since they had been equipped with the short-stroke power unit which was that much smaller.

Although Jaguar was to some extent forced to use the bonnet-hump solution, it in fact proved to be a design asset, since it relieved the large-area gentle curve of the nose without breaking up the line too much.

Two sub-contractors shared the manufacture of the E-type bodies: Abbey Panels supplied the nose section and outer body panels, while Pressed Steel Fisher were contracted for the infrastructure.

bonnet-locking device was soon replaced by a latch operated from inside the car.

The sumptuous E-type bonnet was like a poem to the glories of speed, and made a very important contribution to the car's aesthetic appeal. At the time, people said that the E-type was all nose; indeed, it was so amazingly long and low that it was almost a mystery how Jaguar had been able to fit the famous, bulky XK engine, together with its large oil sump, under the bonnet without setting the engine at an angle. In actual fact, it was only through fashioning the longitudinal hump into the bonnet that Jaguar had been able to fit in all the necessary parts and still be able to shut the bonnet. The hump also provided an air cushion between

Sub-contractors were needed for body production, since no single company could think of investing the huge sums required for the enormous hydraulic presses and for producing the matrices for series car production on a large scale... except Jaguar, perhaps!

The massive amounts of investment capital required for body production meant that, at that stage, two industrial giants supplied most British car manufacturers. Pressed Steel had a virtual monopoly as sole supplier for Austin, Hillman, Morris, M.G., Riley, Rolls-Royce, Rover, Singer, Standard, Sunbeam and Wolseley.

Although the E-type bodies arrived, sometimes by the

Jacques Charrier, a film star of the 1960s, was one of the first Frenchmen to own an E-type. To achieve this aim, he asked Royal Elysées if he could buy their demonstration model, the one which had been used for test drives and for ratification for the import licence. 'Jaguar fever' was beginning to take a hold in France.

trainload, from outside, the cars themselves were of course assembled at the Jaguar works.

Building a self-supporting monocoque structure is not an easy business; to make sure that the car is as rigid as possible, you have to incorporate an awful lot of reinforcing sections, cross-members, longitudinal members, tunnels and the like. An identical monocoque design was used for the fixed-head coupé and the open two-seater, since the factory felt that it had built enough rigidity into the design to make any further reinforcements superfluous on the open two-seater. Despite this confidence, the fixed head certainly made the coupé much more rigid, and this model clearly had less give in its structure than the roadster. When the roadster E-type appeared in 1961, a lot of attention was focused on the way the frame seemed to twist on bad road surfaces.

There was, indeed, some movement with the open cars, but it was rather exaggerated by the roadster's critics who felt that the car was too goodlooking to be flawless. Isn't it strange how, as with 'dumb' blondes, so many people cannot accept that a motor car can be beautiful *and* reliable!

So, despite these carping criticisms, the roadster's construction was hardly less rigid than the fixed-head's.

The roadster — an American term for an open two-seater first used by Jaguar to describe the E-type — and the fixed-head coupé were essentially the same car, as the roadster could be supplied with the optional extra of a hard top. This was an interesting development, since it was the first time that the marque had officially offered such an accessory. The interesting roadster/hard top combination was made possible by virtue of the fact that the soft hood sank almost completely into the car when it was folded back.

The roadster had a beautifully balanced line: the windscreen mounting was so delicate that you hardly noticed it, and the bumpers had never been so non-functional (the latter were discreet curved chromed strips with dainty vertical impact absorbers both front and rear); the car's waistline was accented by a chromed band, level with the door tops; the handsome faired-in headlights helped to make the car rather rocket-like in appearance, with scarcely any protruberances breaking up the smooth line.

The boot was symbolic rather than practical, but you could still squeeze an average suitcase into it. The delightful rounded windscreen was supported on only three sides, since the upper mounting was merely there for cosmetic reasons to cover the rear-view mirror mounting. Windscreen visibility was assured by three wipers, a rather unusual number which was just one of the novel features which gave the E-type its mystique.

The three-spoke steering wheel took up a fair proportion

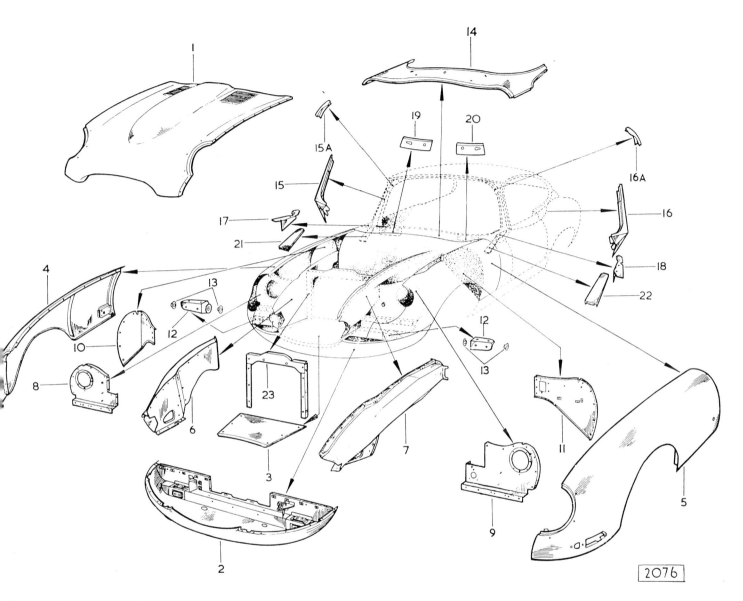

The constituent parts of an E-type bonnet. When you look at an assembled car you have difficulty in believing that they are so numerous. But then the coachbuilder's art consists of disguising such facts!

2076

Perspective line drawing of the E-type's front tubular framework. This assembly could easily be detached from the central monocoque section, and housed the engine and front suspension. You can easily distinguish the bonnet opening axis on the left.

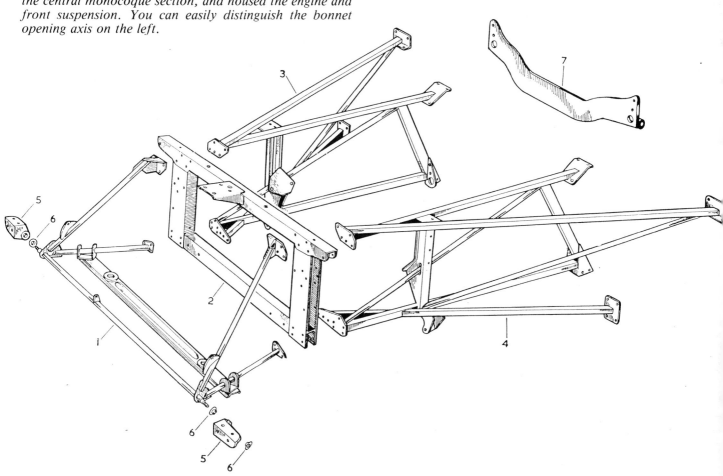

Jaguars move along the line in the trim shop. They are waiting for their finishing touches, such as headlamp fairings, number-plate mountings, etc. The Series 1 E-type is followed by several Mark IIs (1962).

of the driving position and the typically Jaguar dashboard told the driver all he needed to know about the health of his car. There was a large rev counter, and the speedometer shared the same dimensions. Also in evidence were an ammeter, petrol gauge, clock, water temperature and oil pressure gauges. There was also a group of aligned switches which controlled mechanical operations such as lighting, heating, etc. Beneath them Jaguar had provided a plastic strip which labelled each switch, making things even easier for the driver. It is hard to think of anything more the designers could have provided to improve driving comfort and to keep the driver better informed.

The seats gave adequate support, although they were not quite as comfortable as one might have hoped. Needless to say, they featured Connolly's Vaumol leather upholstery.

The unlined cloth hood, which was manufactured in the works' own trim shops, could be raised and lowered with one hand, which was an advantage, although its ability to let in the rain was a distinct disadvantage — it was not

unknown for owners of these early E-types to have to bail out the passenger compartment!

The actual length of the car was very surprising. It seemed to go on for ever, with its long nose stretching out into the distance but, if you were to take a tape measure to it, you would find that it was actually shorter than an XK 150. On the other hand it looked so sleek and missile-like that it was a shock to learn that it was actually wider than the 150!

The interior was light and efficient-looking. The driving position was quite well thought out, even though one had to have an adolescent's suppleness to wriggle into the seat. If there is one thing you must never do, it is to make yourself look ridiculous by struggling into a fixed-head E-type! You must make a clean, flowing entrance, showing supreme confidence and no hesitation when it comes to the various phases of this complicated procedure. The best thing for the mature driver is to practice in the privacy of his own garage

THE E-TYPE JA

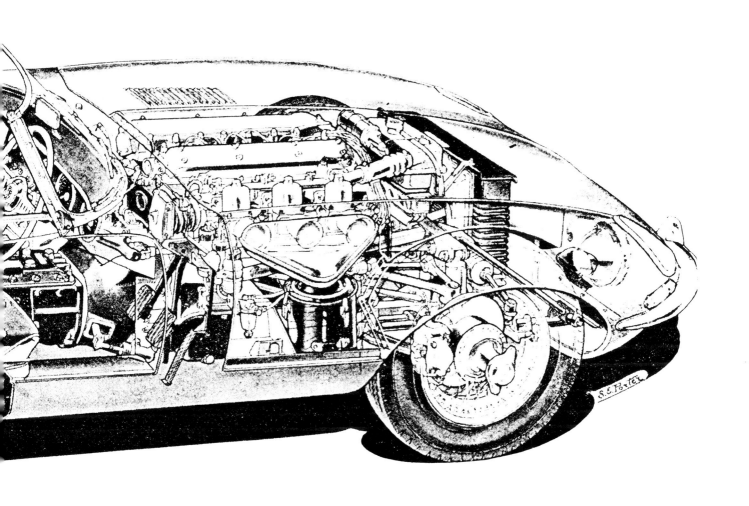

AR ROADSTER

lly appeared in The
E-type's construction.

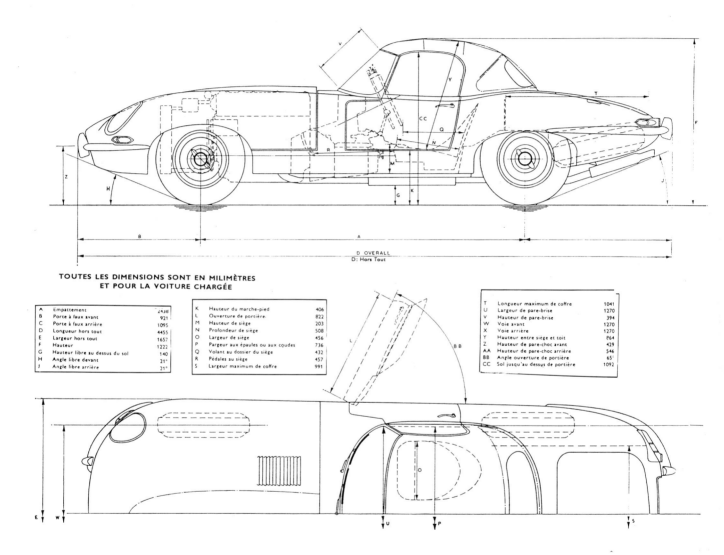

TOUTES LES DIMENSIONS SONT EN MILIMÈTRES
ET POUR LA VOITURE CHARGÉE

A	Empattement	2438	
B	Porte à faux avant	921	
C	Porte à faux arrière	1095	
D	Longueur hors tout	4455	
E	Largeur hors tout	1657	
F	Hauteur	1222	
G	Hauteur libre au dessus du sol	140	
H	Angle libre devant	21°	
J	Angle libre arrière	21°	

K	Hauteur du marche-pied	406
L	Ouverture de portière.	822
M	Hauteur de siège	203
N	Profondeur de siège	508
O	Largeur de siège	456
P	Largeur aux épaules ou aux coudes	736
Q	Volant au dossier du siège	432
R	Pédales au siège	457
S	Largeur maximum de coffre	991

T	Longueur maximum de coffre	1041
U	Largeur de pare-brise	1270
V	Hauteur de pare-brise	394
W	Voie avant	1270
X	Voie arrière	1270
Y	Hauteur entre siège et toit	864
Z	Hauteur de pare-choc avant	429
AA	Hauteur de pare-choc arrière	546
BB	Angle ouverture de portière	65°
CC	Sol jusqu'au dessus de portière	1092

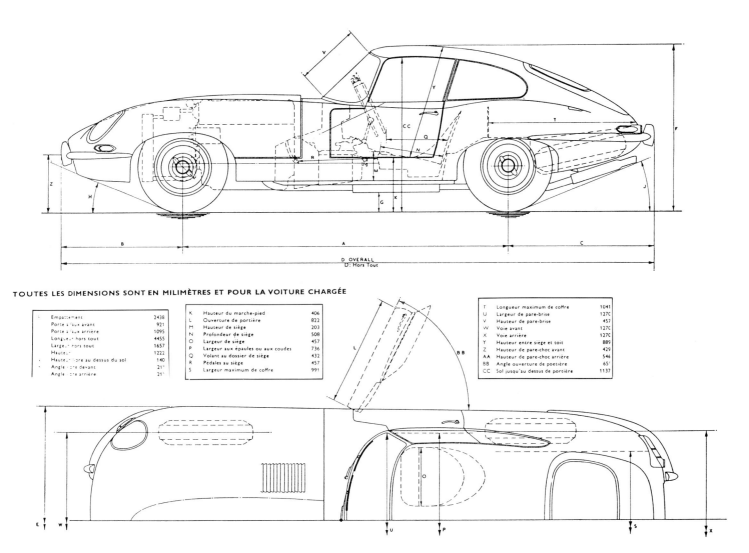

TOUTES LES DIMENSIONS SONT EN MILIMÈTRES ET POUR LA VOITURE CHARGÉE

Empattement	2438
Porte à faux avant	921
Porte à faux arrière	1095
Longueur hors tout	4455
Largeur hors tout	1657
Hauteur	1222
Hauteur libre au dessus du sol	140
Angle ... devant	21°
Angle ... arrière	21°

K	Hauteur du marche-pied	406
L	Ouverture de portière	822
M	Hauteur de siège	203
N	Profondeur de siège	508
O	Largeur de siège	457
P	Largeur aux épaules ou aux coudes	736
Q	Volant au dossier de siège	432
R	Pédales au siège	457
S	Largeur maximum de coffre	991

T	Longueur maximum de coffre	1041
U	Largeur de pare-brise	1270
V	Hauteur de pare-brise	457
W	Voie avant	1270
X	Voie arrière	1270
Y	Hauteur entre siège et toit	889
Z	Hauteur de pare-choc avant	429
AA	Hauteur de pare-choc arrière	546
BB	Angle ouverture de poetière	65°
CC	Sol jusqu'au dessus de portière	1137

*Diagram and dimensions of the roadster and fixed-head
coupé E-types, issued in French by Jaguar.*

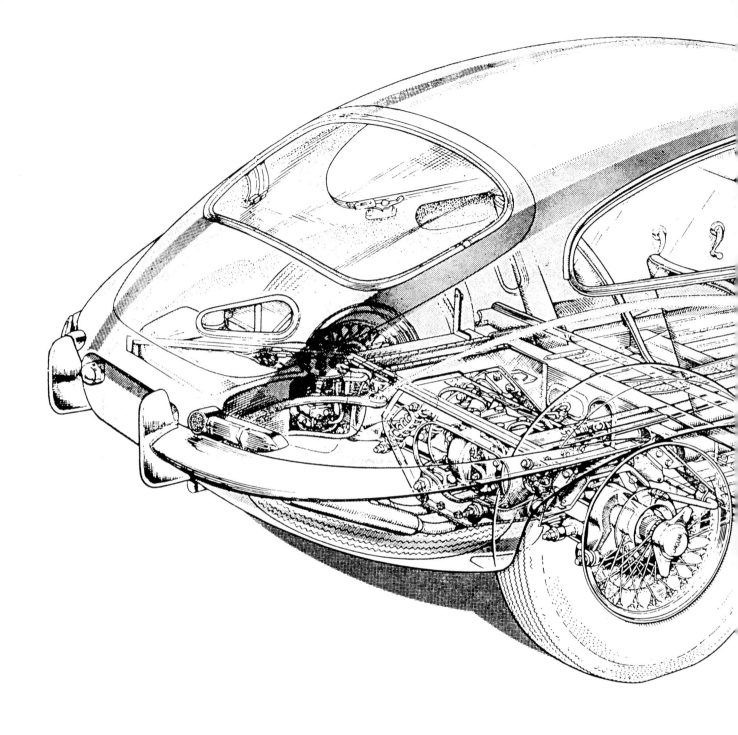

THE E-TYPE JAGUAR

This 'cutaway' of the fixed-head
the most important structural de

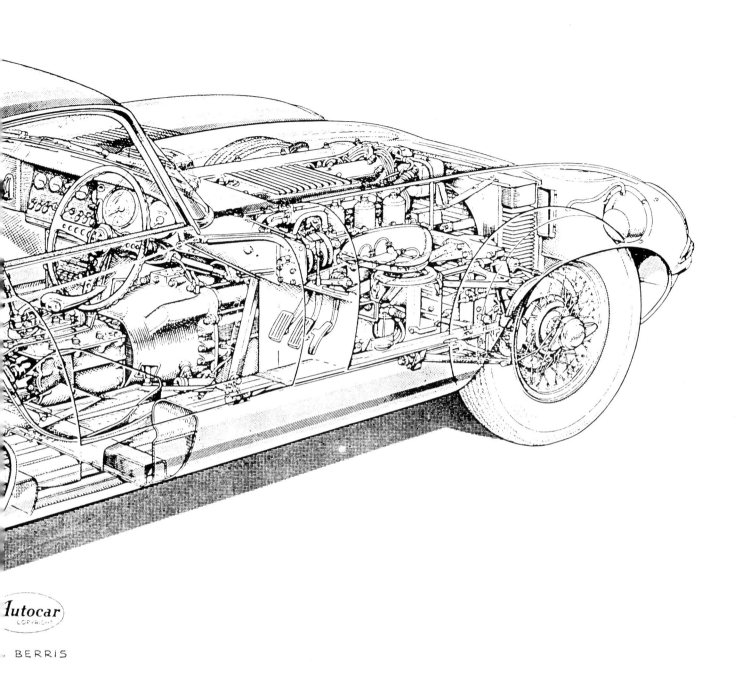

BERRIS

FIXED-HEAD COUPÉ

inted from The Autocar, *shows
model.*

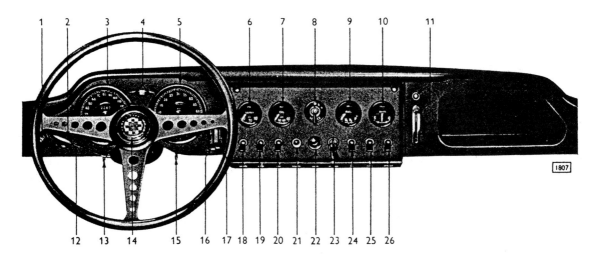

Instruments and controls — left-hand drive

1. Full beam/dip control
2. Brake fluid warning light
3. Speedometer
4. Indicator warning light
5. Rev counter
6. Water temperature
7. Oil pressure gauge
8. Lighting switch
9. Petrol gauge
10. Ammeter
11. Starter switch and warning light
12. On/off switch for indicators and lights
13. Trip mileage reset control
14. Horn
15. Clock reset control
16. Heater — air control
17. Heater — heat control
18. Screen washer
19. Screen wiper
20. Map-light
21. Starter button
22. Cigar lighter
23. Ignition
24. Heating fan
25. Dashboard light
26. Interior light

(extract from owner's handbook).

The flat floor and bright aluminium central console were the main distinguishing characteristics of the interiors of the very first 3.8-litre E-types.

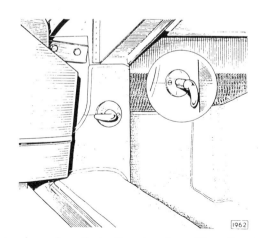

Bonnet release handle in the closed position (inset, open).

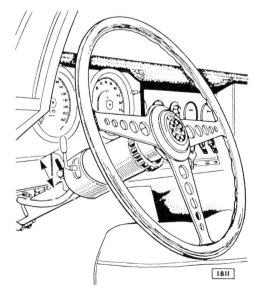

Adjustment play for the steering column angle.

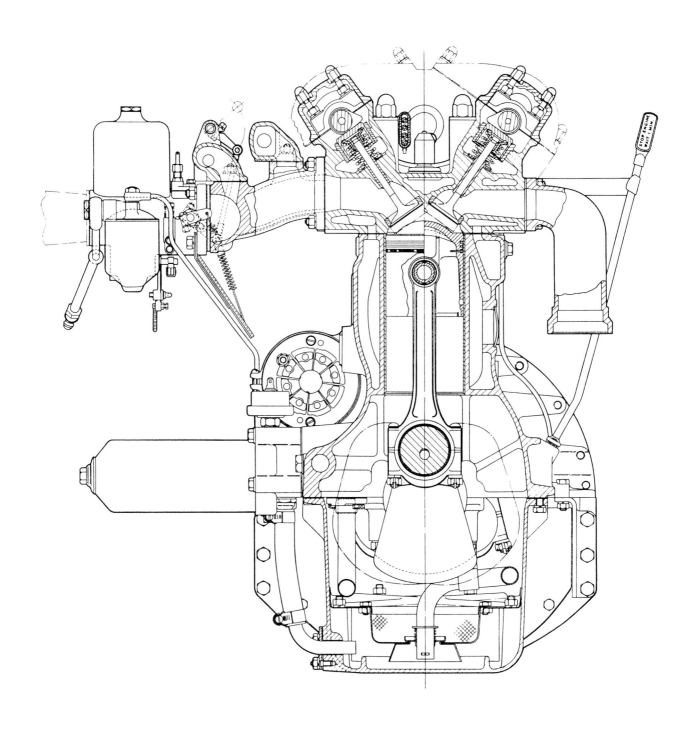

Cross-section of the 3.8-litre E-type engine.

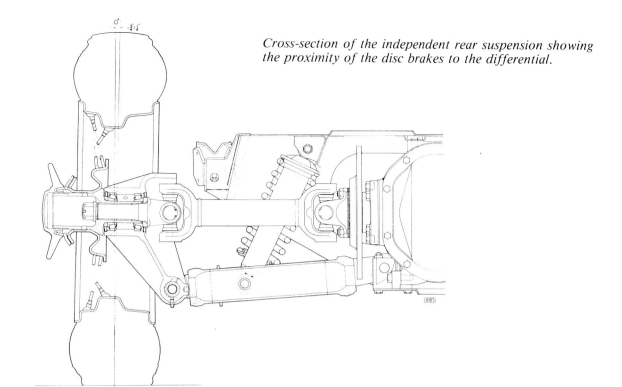

Cross-section of the independent rear suspension showing the proximity of the disc brakes to the differential.

Front suspension, rack and pinion steering, and front brake assembly, also showing the torsion-bar adjuster (inset).

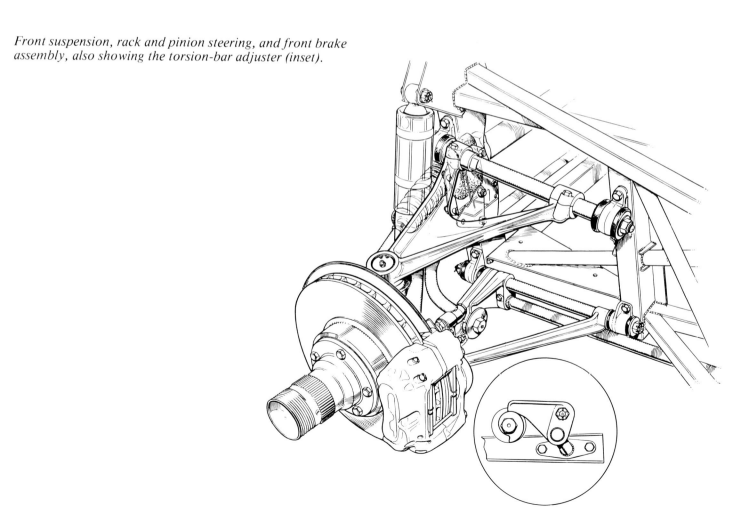

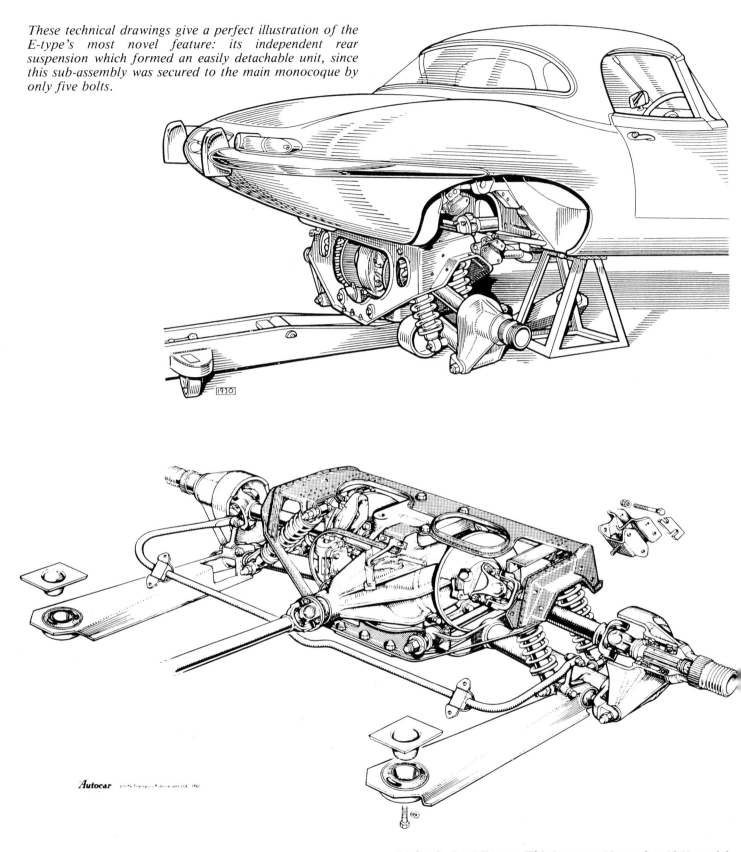

These technical drawings give a perfect illustration of the E-type's most novel feature: its independent rear suspension which formed an easily detachable unit, since this sub-assembly was secured to the main monocoque by only five bolts.

Autocar c H Ps Transport Publications Ltd 1961

Right: Series 1 E-type. This is a post-November 1961 model as can be seen from the seat backs and the absence of an exterior bonnet lock.

every night for two weeks, until he can do it with his eyes closed.

The optional glass-fibre hard top for the roadster fitted precisely, so that you could use your car in any weather and for almost any purpose.

The tool kit was, as always with Jaguar, comprehensive and, as in many of the marque's cars, the spare wheel was stowed away under the boot floor.

In contrast to the 120, 140 and 150 (where the roadsters were simply fixed-head coupés with the roof being replaced by a soft top), the fixed-head E-type had its own special profile, thanks to the redesigned rear. The line flowed away in a 'fastback' style and this gave the car a very dynamic and purposeful air. Fixed-head enthusiasts never approved of the roadster's supporters, with each group warily keeping itself to itself.

Large, hinged quarter-lights carried the side windows further to the back, while a rear door (opening from inside and hinged from left to right) included a glass window. This design gave a large boot capacity and improved interior illumination.

Despite the sloping tail on the fixed-head coupé, the curved wing top was retained although it merged into the tail at the rear of the car.

The back of the fixed-head's interior was naturally different from that of the roadster. A comparatively large floor area separated the seat backs from the rear window.

There were no other differences between the fixed-head coupé and the roadster.

If you lifted the bonnet you would discover that the car was powered by more or less the same engine as that in the 3.8-litre XK 150S. The basic long-stroke unit had, by then, been powering road and racing Jaguars for as long as 13 years.

The cast block was topped with the straight-port cylinder head, together with its three 2-inch HD8 SU carburettors. Maximum power output was still 265 bhp at the remarkable engine speed of 5,500 rpm. Engine revs were in any case limited with this power unit, because of its long-stroke design.

The long- versus short-stroke controversy filled the columns of the motoring press and, wherever you looked, you could find brilliantly propounded theories on the evolution of the oversquare solution. The 87 x 106 mm engine was attacked from all sides — just fancy using an engine with a 5,500 rpm limit when the opposition was roaring away at 7,700 revs!

No matter what revs an engine can produce, the XK unit produced some very effective ones in spite of the fact that all the contemporary theorists seemed to want to consign it to the scrapyard. On paper their arguments seemed irrefutable: a 'square' or 'oversquare' engine had obvious advantages if one compared the inertia forces, since the piston's stroke affects the square as a factor in the piston's weight, whereas the bore affects the cube...

The long-stroke's real problem lies in the inclination of the moving rods and from the fact that the crankshaft has

Scotland 1962. Series 1 3.8-litre roadster E-type. Many people think that this was the finest car of all time.

pins which are more overhung, and therefore more susceptible to torsional vibration.

In this regard, the short-stroke design enables the engineers to use a very compact and robust crankshaft with a greater overlap between pins and journals with, as a by-product, much easier balancing.

As for the volumetric efficiency of the two, well that too was a matter for dispute. Engineers gaily ignored anyone who did not share their views; some swore that you could only have optimum volumetric efficiency with a long stroke, while others felt that it was the bore which determined an engine's breathing power.

Since the XK 150, Jaguar seemed to be moving a little in the direction of a squarer geometry through an increased bore, whereas back in 1950 it had been an ardent supporter of the long stroke, since it enabled them to achieve good torque at moderate engine speeds.

The only difference between the power units of the XK 150 and the E-type lay in the cooling system, as the E-type had a separate header tank so that the low bonnet height could be achieved.

Another novelty was the installation of an electrically driven two-vane fan, which was activated when the temperature reached 85°C. Once the coolant temperature had been reduced to the desired level, the fan cut out and so saved on precious horsepower. The saving might have seemed only marginal, but every little bit counts!

One thing which was universally criticised in the 1961 motoring press was the excess weight of the cast-iron block.

At the same time, they approved of the good qualities of this tried and tested unit: its phenomenal resistance to wear; exceptional reliability; fuel economy; and twin overhead camshaft, which made it ideal for high-speed travel.

Since the tooling costs for this unit had been absorbed a long time before, Jaguar was in no hurry to change the engine model which, after all, had proved its value. What is more, this decision by Jaguar's management helped to keep the price of this fabulous car down to realistic levels.

While we are on the subject of amortised components, I suppose I shall have to mention the gearbox, though I would rather gloss over it for, in this respect, the E-type was far from being up to the mark. Customers wondered how much longer they would have to put up with the old Moss box before stocks had been completely exhausted. There is no doubt that it came as a disappointment to the more lively drivers, with its sluggish, noisy temperament, and its lack of synchromesh in first gear. If one looks at the rest of the car in comparison, Jaguar's reliance on the Moss gearbox can only be explained by the firm's long-standing commercial relations with Moss Ltd and by overstocking of these slow-moving components which had the not inconsiderable advantage of being cheap!

Overdrive was not available, even as an option, and neither was automatic transmission. The Borg & Beck clutch was perfectly adequate, providing one did not push it too hard by confusing the production E-type with a circuit-racing car.

The problems of placing the discs near the differential — which permitted a significant reduction in the unsprung weight — had at last been mastered by the use of silicone-based seals. There was accurately directed forced ventilation, so that heat was dispersed pretty efficiently.

The front brakes will come as no surprise to anyone who has read the chapter on the XK 150. As a brief reminder, each caliper had two pistons which activated Mintex quick-change pads to bring them into contact with 11-inch (28-cm) diameter discs at the front, and 10-inch (25-cm) diameter ones at the rear.

As with the XK 150, the handbrake was connected to the rear discs via a cable and two extra calipers, one for each disc.

The hydraulic system was doubled — witness the two master cylinders and two reservoirs — to give added safety. Braking was assisted through a Kelsey Hayes servo unit which made use of the vacuum produced in the inlet manifold when the engine was running.

Any E-type enthusiast worthy of the name should know the principle of 'suspended vacuum'. I suppose it may seem rather complex, but what modern technology isn't? In a suspended vacuum system there are two separate compartments, with a piston in each sealed with a rubber diaphragm. When you are not using the brake pedal these two pistons are in a state of suspension, which means that there is a vacuum on either side of the diaphragm and the pistons are held up against the end of the cylinders by calibrated springs.

When pressure is applied to the brake pedal, on the other hand, the pressure created in the master cylinder moves a hydraulic piston in the servo valve, which makes the servo assistance. What could be simpler? The vacuum power is stored in a reservoir and can be supplied for three or four pumps on the brake after the ignition has been switched off.

The principle behind this kind of assistance enables mechanical brake pressure on its own to actuate the cylinder calipers, should one of the components fail.

Despite all this high technology, the E-type's brakes are now considered mediocre, for what passed muster on the relatively uncrowded 1961 roads is found wanting in the Picadilly Circus conditions of 1984.

The 3.31:1 final drive unit was of the standard limited slip variety and came from Salisbury. It was the classic hypoid bevel type which provided scope for a significant lowering of the transmission shaft. As I have already explained when describing the E2A prototype, the differential housing was connected to a framework which supported the rear suspension assembly.

This suspension consisted of two pairs of coil springs integral with hydraulic telescopic shock absorbers. This twin-pair layout was interesting for a couple of reasons:

each spring was only half the size it would have needed to be had it been working on its own, so bulk was reduced; each half-shaft enabled the many different shocks to be dealt with more efficiently.

At last, the E-type brought in the use of 15-inch diameter wheels, with 72 strong spokes. The car, and with it the centre of gravity, was thereby dropped considerably.

It was the first time that Jaguar had rejected the old 600 x 16 wheels in favour of the 640 x 15 variety on a sports car. The E-type benefited greatly from this innovation and gave drivers remarkably efficient roadholding. The ride was in fact so comfortable that sports car afficionados still doubted how this could be achieved without interfering with the car's roadholding capacity. Doubting Thomases!

One of the first French-registered E-types. This 1962 example had an exclusively French feature: the chrome 'bumper' across the nose to help minimise the effect of minor head-on shunts. This optional extra was offered by the French importers.

The E-type had its French rallying fans. Here, Cardi competes in the 12th Tour de France.

27 May 1962. Lumsden/Sargent's lightened E-type in the ADAC 1,000-kilometres, on the Nürburgring.

*9 March 1963. A good showing by the Pointet/Mosnier
3.8-litre E-type which went on to take eighth place in this
Lyons-Charbonnières rally.*

Steering was very direct, and therefore very precise — 2.6 turns of the wheel from lock to lock. It returned with ease to dead centre and was very light, as long as the car was moving. This subtle criticism is intended, for in town traffic or at a standstill you needed a fairly hefty physique!

The turning circle could quite easily have been improved without too many changes to the front suspension.

The driving position was relaxing, rather than designed with efficient sports-style driving in mind. The height of the wheel could be adjusted, but it was still rather low for a tall driver. I'll pass over the first few E-types with their dreaded flat floor — if you are over six feet tall you will know why! Heel and toe operation of the pedals was pretty well out of the question. You had to settle for the achievement of actually wriggling into the driving seat and somehow making room for your limbs; you couldn't expect to have jam on it as well, by being able to drive the car with any degree of comfort!

One of the fixed-head coupé's drawbacks soon showed itself when it was being driven in town traffic or in hot weather, and that was the lack of ventilation. It quickly became very muggy inside the passenger compartment, and the proximity of such hot spots as the engine and gearbox did not make things any better.

The air vents underneath the dashboard were just not up to the job of maintaining a fresh air supply inside the car. However, you could always bomb along with the side windows and quarter-lights wide open, providing the weather was fine.

Visibility was up to scratch — even to the rear, despite the rather shallow rear window — and the general feeling of driving an E-type is one of riding a fast and responsive animal.

The car draws away from a standstill with no apparent effort at all; you can accelerate to 40 mph (60 km/h) in first, and second will take you smoothly up to 75 mph (120 km/h) without batting an eyelid. Within a few seconds you are gliding along in third at 110 mph (175 km/h); change up into top and the excitement really begins!

If you are doing 125 mph (200 km/h) — as long as it is on a wide, straight, well-surfaced and empty stretch of road — you would hardly believe that you are travelling so fast, and it takes a couple of glances at the speedo to convince yourself. The floating sensation carries on up to 150 mph (240 km/h), providing that your road is even wider, straighter, better surfaced, and emptier than before. But you have to be on your toes at this speed for, if there is the slightest suspicion of a side wind, or if you are overtaking a juggernaut, you soon sober up and your heart starts thumping against your rib-cage. Between 125 mph (200 km/h) and 150 mph (240 km/h) the difference is not so much one of road speed as of speed of reflexes. Somehow the miles per hour above 125 are of a completely different character from those below that figure. It is almost as though each mile is about 440 yards shorter!

Travelling at more than 125 mph sorts out the skilled drivers from the run-of-the-mill motorists, and the wheat of the genuine speed-lover from the chaff of the more orthodox breeds.

Before you can push the car to its limits, you find yourself resisting the temptation, easing off to 125 mph and taking some deep breaths in an attempt to relax your forearms and the back of your neck.

19 May 1963. The first of the 3 litres-plus GT E-types, this Therstappen/Ruthardt 3.8 went on to finish 16th in this ADAC 1,000 kilometres (Nürburgring).

16 March 1963. Start of the Rallye de l'Ouest for the Cardi/Klukaszewski pairing. Third in the GT class was to be their reward.

Guy Verrier before the start of the Picardy Rally, 5 May 1963. He was forced to retire after three hours.

Cardi/Klukaszewski's 3.8-litre at Spa-Francorchamps during the 1963 Tour de France.

At 150 mph the tension can be horrendous, for the slightest lapse in concentration or relaxation of your grip on the wheel produces a corresponding deviation in the car's trajectory which transforms the most generously wide motorway into a single-track country road. It is also worth bearing in mind that you cannot put too much store by the brakes when you are travelling at those speeds!

Although the E-type could not really be described as a noisy car, it was not that quiet either, especially at high speeds. Perhaps this was due to its monocoque construction which increased resonance, or to the lack of efficient insulation, but one must remember that the E-type's price was incredibly low for such a sophisticated sports car, and that any extra attention to the noise problem would inevitably have brought an increase in that price. Also the car was already heavy enough, without any addition of sound-proofing materials, since the fixed-head coupé weighed 24.1 hundredweight (1,224 kilos) and the roadster 24 hundredweight (1,219 kilos). Compared with the Ferrari's 19.3 hundredweight (980 kilos), the E-type was a cumbersome model and, where sports cars are concerned, you might as well double any pounds in weight over the ton mark.

Even though E-type owners of 1961 were not overly concerned about petrol consumption, the French press was continually stressing the new car's economy. *L'Auto-Journal*'s tests showed 12.6 litres per 100 kilometres at 90 km/h, and 17.8 litres over the whole of their road test during which speed peaks of 190 km/h were reached. The E-type's modest appetite for petrol stemmed, to a great extent, from its aerodynamic profile. It might not be considered an ideal aerodynamic design today, but in 1961 it was pretty impressive.

The E-type was priced at 30,000 francs in France, and was in great demand. Ch. Delecroix, the Jaguar concessionaire, had a hard time fending off requests from his friends and best customers to be the first Frenchman to own an 'E'.

The very first E-type imported into France — chassis number 885006 — was a metallic grey fixed-head coupé which was used as a demonstration model and for roadtests. It was also handed over to the French weights and measures authority so that they could supply a licence for the model's import. The actor Jacques Charrier, who was determined to acquire an E-type by fair means or foul, almost took root outside the Royal Elysées premises and succeeded in reserving the very first car, which was supplied to him as soon as the import licence had been approved. This fixed-head E-type is now in the possession of an enthusiastic Jaguar collector, François Bergès, who is restoring the coupé with a view to racing it.

It was in this very car that Michel Cognet, head of after-sales service at Royal Elysées, caused an almighty traffic jam by bringing the car to a halt outside the Hôtel Crillon on the Place de la Concorde at six o'clock one evening. There were so many drivers following his every move that he had to resort to getting up at dawn when the Paris streets were virtually deserted in order to put the car through its paces.

Looking back on those days, Monsieur Cognet recalls the lengths to which his compatriots went to find out more about this demonstration car. Some people even confronted him when he stopped at a red light and demanded that he open the bonnet so that they could take a look at what was underneath!

Gast's unsuccessful E-type run in the Rallye de l'Ouest, 22 March 1964.

The 3.8-litre power unit. Three fat 2-inch (5-cm) SU HD8 carburettors each take responsibility for one pair of cylinders.

A Belgian entry at Antwerp, 6 May 1952. The 3.8-litre E-type is seen here at the start of the flying kilometre stage.

17 May 1964. Spa Grand Prix. A 3.8-litre E-type caught by the camera as it comes out of a tight bend.

The second production E-type sold in Britain (chassis number 850005). It was to finish second in the Spa Grand Prix in the hands of Michael Parkes, following its victory at Goodwood, when Graham Hill had been its driver.

THE LIGHTWEIGHT E-TYPE

1962—1964

AN E-TYPE WITH A SUMMER FROCK

Less than a year after the E-type's Geneva launch, Jaguar decided to produce a competition version. As had been the case when the C-type was developed from the XK 150, the Browns Lane management knew that the first priority was to lose some of the production car's weight. The E-type would not make much of an impression on the race track if it had to shift the standard model's 24.1 hundredweight (1,224 kilos).

So the number one objective was to reduce the E-type's weight by a quarter. Jaguar had never embarked on such a project unprepared, and their competition experience over the ten preceding years was going to stand them in good stead.

The development of a lightweight model was in part caused by pressure from private entrants who wanted to race the new car. In 1961 many drivers wanted to pit their wits, and their machines, against the might of Aston Martin, Ferrari and Lotus, to name but a few who were sweeping the board at prestige meetings in Britain and Eire.

Beginner's luck was already paying off for some private entrants of virtually unmodified E-types, with victories at Oulton Park in April, Crystal Palace in May, and a handful of placings at other venues. It gave food for thought.

During the second quarter of 1961 John Coombs' specialist factory modified an E-type which was due to be raced by Roy Salvadori with the aim of seeing what the new model was capable of. The car's chassis number was 850006, and its registration number — BUY 1 — soon became famous. It was the third series E-type sold on the domestic market, the first one having gone by right to Lofty England (850004) and the second to a Mr Sopwith (850005); it was this car which won at Goodwood that April, in the hands of Graham Hill. BUY 1 (later to become 4 WPD) was to be the first, pre-Jaguar, lightweight E-type. Coombs' work was extremely useful to Jaguar, as the Coventry firm could take a look at the Coombs-prepared car and perhaps draw some lessons from it for their own lightweight production.

There were several interesting features on Coombs' lightweight racing 'E': he knocked more than 150 pounds (70 kilos) off the weight, by using aluminium wherever possible; he modified the engine so that it yielded an extra 30 bhp; and substituted a five-speed ZF gearbox and a special rear axle.

This was, of course, just a little experiment in the lightweight field, for the Jaguar version went much further than Coombs' one. The ball was now in Browns Lane's court, as 1962 was drawing to a close.

Before we look at the 12 works lightweights in detail, it is worth mentioning that each had its own individual peculiar-

ities, which is why all 12 are identified either by their chassis numbers or their owners' names. Nevertheless, they all share several features.

To begin with, the 12 can be broken down into two separate sub-categories — the 'semi-lightweights' and the 'full lightweights' — depending on whether or not they were fitted with a light alloy engine block.

Let us begin with the body. Jaguar's first move was to change to riveted and welded aluminium panels; next came the construction of a framework of narrow-gauge welded steel tubing; and finally an aluminium hard top was made integral with the central monocoque section which supported the welded-tube front framework.

Although at first glance the suspension components looked identical to those on the series cars, closer examination revealed many specially produced parts, including the torsion-bars and wishbones.

At the back of the car the Mark X's framework had been adopted almost intact because of its generous size. The only difference lay in the coil springs and dampers, as the Mark X's would have been too tall for such a low car.

The hub carriers, too, were a Mark X bequest although, as with many other parts of the car, Jaguar drilled through, or incorporated cavities in, any piece of metal which was not part of the car's stress-bearing structure.

The differential housing still bore the Salisbury signature, but inside there was no connection with the glorious marque which had been fitted to Jaguars since 1952. The internal organs came either from ZF or Thornton.

The brake system was virtually identical to that used on the production E-types, except that there was an extra air vent to help cooling... it is a shame that it could not improve the brakes' performance!

Externally, the 'lightweight' was very different from the production car: the body had been stripped down to essentials; there were extra air vents, plus a huge petrol filler cap which disfigured the boot panel; and 15-inch magnesium alloy D-type wheels — but it was more than just a superficially modified standard car.

With all these modifications and a cast-iron engine block, the result was a 'semi-lightweight' and, despite the equivocal 'semi', there was already a significant improvement in performance thanks to the weight loss and the high state of tunc of the engine.

The next step, in other words the use of an aluminium engine, only applied to some of the lightweight E-types, since doubts about the aluminium unit put some people off using it. You will understand their reasoning when you have read what follows.

The main problem with the aluminium block stemmed from the fact that it was put into short-run production without sufficient research. It was not a brand-new design, but was simply cast from the same moulds as its iron predecessor.

May 1952. The Nürburgring 1,000 kilometres. The Lumsden/Sargent team drove this lightweight E-type (chassis number 850663) with the registration number 898 BYR.

Top left: Graham Hill at Silverstone in May 1963. He is driving a works-prepared lightweight (chassis number 850658).

Centre left: Lightweight fixed-head coupé E-type entered in the 1962 Le Mans 24-Hours. Briggs Cunningham and Roy Salvadori were to finish fourth (chassis number 850659).

Bottom left: 1963 Le Mans 24-Hours. Part of the Cunningham attack force.

Grossman's number 15 met a sticky, but happily not fatal end in the 1963 Le Mans event.

Not surprisingly, at the slightest hint of overheating or excessive engine speeds, the aluminium block began to distort. Equally unsurprisingly, therefore, you can count the number of aluminium blocks which survived intact on the fingers of one hand. Some people reckon that the only reason for some of these units having come through is that they were never given any hard racing work to do.

Be that as it may, the aluminium engine is a feast for sore eyes, and looked very promising on paper. The special D-type wide-angle (so called because of the 35/40 valve engine) cylinder head was used; as near as makes no difference it was the same one which the XK SS and the most extravagant version of the D-type had employed. The inlet valve diameter was 1 11/16 inches (53 mm) and that of the exhaust valves 2 1/8 inches (43 mm). The cam lift was very high at 11/16 inches (1.2 cm). Lubrication was by the dry-sump method, but differed from the previous Jaguar system in some respects: oil was supplied from a separate reservoir by an aluminium high-pressure pump combined with a cleaning filter controlled by a pinion on the end of the crankshaft, and another aluminium scavenge pump was driven by a pinion on the number four main bearing. There was Lucas fuel injection.

The crankshaft itself was not the same as the production E-type's, in that it was longer and slightly wider at the front. Pistons and con-rods were within a whisker of the D-type's, and the compression ratio never fell below 10:1.

Perhaps I glossed over the injection system. To fill you in on the details, it used a short 3-inch (7.6 cm) inlet manifold with the mixture being delivered through nozzles to each cylinder individually.

Apart from the larger capacity, the engine was identical to that which had powered Briggs Cunningham's E2A.

The great advantage of the aluminium unit was, of course, its light weight — it tipped the scales at some 150 pounds (70 kilos) less than its cast-iron counterpart.

By the time the development engineers had finished with it, this unit could produce a guaranteed 300 bhp. One bold and determined American even managed to wring 340 bhp and a tiny bit more out of it in the eighth of the lightweight series, chassis number 850664. As you have probably guessed, this American was none other than Briggs Cunningham, who also acquired two other lightweights: number two and number seven. As you can see, since only 12 lightweights were assembled, Briggs snapped up a quarter of the total production!

A lightweight E-type, chassis number 890193. This fixed-head coupé was a one-off produced by the works for its original owner, P.Bardinon. Its unique aspect is that it is a left-hand drive model. The bonnet air vents were added by its current owner, Philippe Renault.

Aluminium block and Lucas petrol injection are the main differences between this and the standard version. This engine, number RA1356-95, is fitted in the car shown top left.

P.Sutcliffe's lightweight E (chassis number 850666). It came ninth in the sequence of 12 or 13 which can claim the title of Jaguar lightweight E-type.

Peter Lindner out in front early in the Nürburgring 1,000 kilometres, 1 May 1964. It didn't last long, sad to say!

Number 16 eats up the Le Mans track during the unforgettable 1964 24-Hours (chassis number 850662). Lindner/Nocker's superb lightweight fixed-head coupé was forced to retire in the 15th hour because of a blown gasket.

A back view of Peter Lindner's 'low-drag' E which ran in the 1964 Le Mans 24-Hours. The series E-type and the lightweight version had little in common, except for their profile. This is the most sought after of all the E-type models.

As one might have expected, Briggs Cunningham entered all three in the 1963 Le Mans. Although the cars did not disgrace themselves only one finished, taking ninth place after some lengthy pit repairs for a damaged nose — the result of a collision.

The last time Jaguars were seen on the Sarthe circuit was 1964.

Over a period of time the teutonic ZF five-speed box was taken out of a fair few of the lightweight 'E's, despite its many qualities. It had two important drawbacks: one was its very heavy cast-iron sump; the other was that its operation used up 23 bhp all on its own! To put this in perspective, the good old close-ratio Moss box with its unsynchronised first gear consumed only 15 horsepower.

To complete this already gloomy picture, the steel ZF casting had a different coefficient of expansion from the alloy engine block, and the back of the latter tended to crack when the under-bonnet temperature peaked.

Owners of the lightweight E-types with aluminium engines reverted to the old cast-iron block, almost without exception. It was virtually the only way they could race their cars to their full potential.

Nine of the lightweights were roadsters fitted with an integral hard-top roof. Three others were given the famous low-drag fastback roof which had resulted from some wind-tunnel experiments. This top was a little reminiscent

of the fixed-head coupé's roof, and was designed to reduce drag at the back of the car. Inevitably, these three E-types were referred to as the 'low-drag' coupés.

All three are now in the United States: the first is the Cohen/Lumsden/Sargent car; the second Dick Protheroe/Walter Hill; and the third Lindner/Nocker.

The lightweight 'E' never really made its mark on motor racing history; Ferrari 250 GTO drivers certainly did not lose any sleep over it. If only that aluminium engine had had some kind of reinforcement built into it, to prevent distortion... If only...'

It *should* have had the better of the Ferrari, since it weighed 100 pounds less, which counts for a great deal when you are dealing with weights of between 2,000 and 2,100 pounds (900 and 950 kilos).

No one ever won a race with 'if onlys', so we shall have to settle for admitting that, from 1961 to 1963, the 250 GTO Ferraris were invincible on the international racing circuits — rather as the Jaguar C- and D-types had been between 1953 and 1957.

Although it had an abortive racing career, the lightweight E-type is a fascinating car. If you are lucky enough to see one of these cars on a circuit one day you will see what I mean.

These clay-footed angels are now coveted cars; they are rarer than the C- and D-types and even than the XK SS. All

12 are still in existence and their stories are known down to the last detail. Should one ever change hands the news would travel faster than by jungle telegraph.

Had the 'lightweight' not been cursed with such fundamental flaws it might have been to the series 'E' what, ten years earlier, the C-type had been to the production XK 120.

As had happened with the 250 GTO, the lightweight's homologation in the GT category was obtained by the cunning device of including the series E-type in the 100 cars which had to be produced for a car to be accepted. The series E-type became the 'special', while the lightweight version was officially declared a series model. Red tape is there for the cutting, after all! But, going back to the Ferrari, the 'O' in 250 GTO stands for *Omologato,* and you do not have to be a linguist to translate that word!

In any case, the lightweight 'E' was successfully homologated in the GT class, which gave it much more racing scope.

You may think, from my earlier comments, that this could not have been much of a trump card for a car which did not live up to its racing potential, but there *were* some lightweight victories. Most of them came in America, for American drivers seemed to have more faith in the car than their European counterparts.

The life stories of these beautiful but fragile cars are very

eventful. They were subjected to continual body and mechanical modifications so that, in 1984, there is only one which is still in an ex-works state. This obviously is the only one which was never raced. It is a left-hand-drive, fixed-head coupé model which was built specially for M. Pierre Bardinon, following a request from Michel Cognet to Lofty England. The car has all the 'lightweight' attributes, and it is the only real fixed-head produced with left-hand drive. In fact the factory had to produce some special components for the car, due to the position of the steering column.

This unique car is now one of the showpieces in the amazing range of Jaguars which have been collected by Dr Philippe Renault, founder-president of the French Jaguar Drivers' Club.

Pierre Bardinon owned many Jaguars, including some Tour de France Mark II-derived specials, an SS 100, some XK 120s, a 2.8-litre E-type and a D-type — XKD 606.

Bardinon's lightweight was, in fact, the 13th built, despite the fact that, traditionally, only 12 were produced.

Not long ago a 14th lightweight E-type turned up, with a somewhat dubious pedigree. It was 100 per cent a lightweight, asembled with authentic lightweight parts; the only snag was that it was not built at the right time. It cannot be called a replica, since all the parts are originals. So is it a genuine lightweight, then? Well, it is hard to say because it was built 20 years too late. The story of its creation is quite

Another E-type lightweight seen during the Rheims 12-Hours event; it was the ninth of the 'series' (chassis number 850666) driven by P. Sutcliffe and Bradley. The team had to settle for a 12th placing.

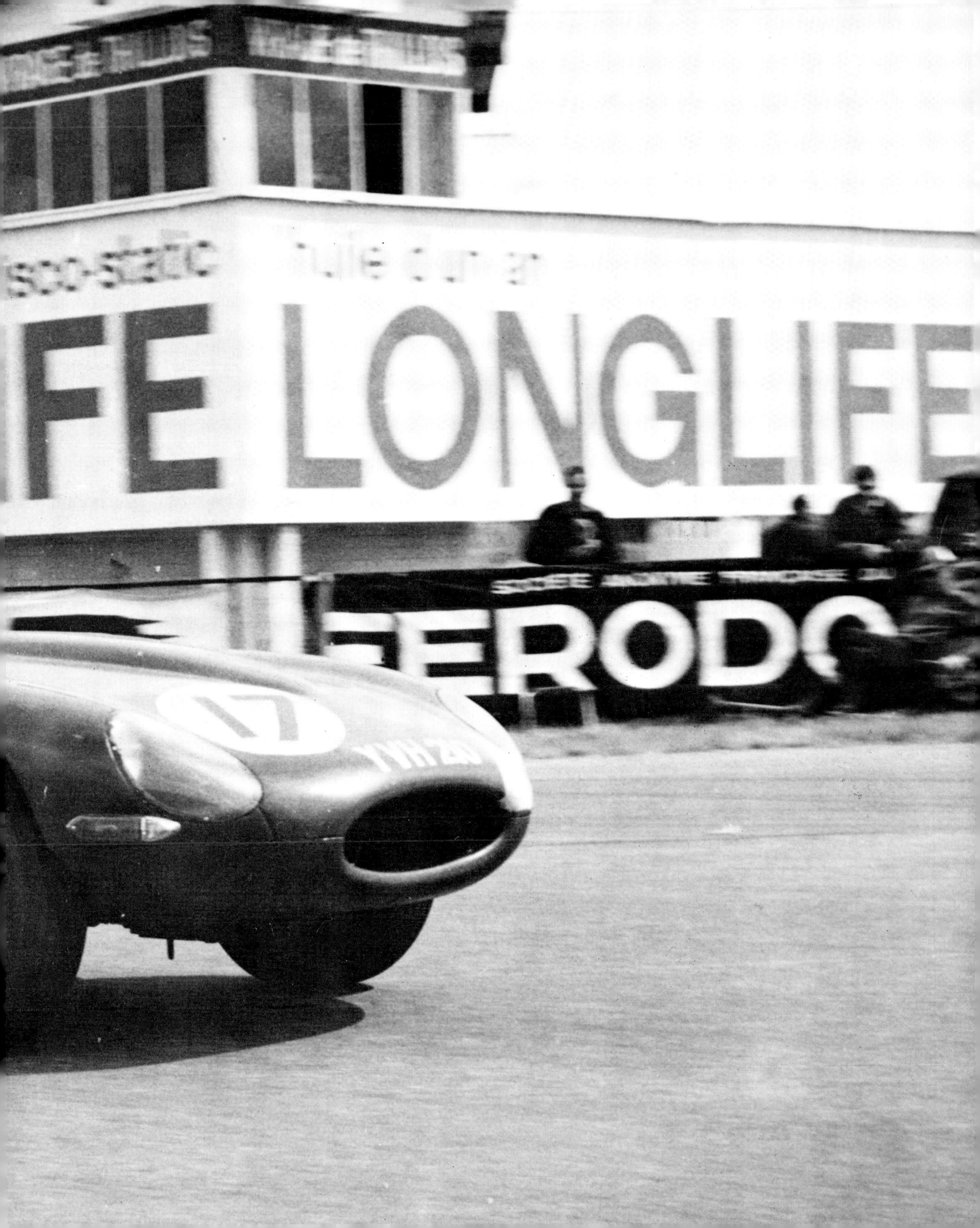
LONGLIFE
17

interesting. Anthony Bamford's famous company JCB (best known for fork-lift trucks) had owned a load of lightweight parts for quite a time: notably, two complete bodies which the firm had acquired when Jaguar stopped its production of 'specials'. As JCB was just letting the parts gather dust, Lynx Engineering — a firm specialising in Jaguars and unusual conversions — bought them up. At this point I should mention that Lynx had the advantage of having, in its works, the Lindner/Nockner lightweight which had been the fastest E-type in the world until its dramatic accident at Montlhéry in 1964.

Lynx' idea was, therefore, to kill two birds with one stone by rebuilding the Peter Lindner lightweight while producing an extra one from the 'spare' parts. Obviously there must have been enough parts for the job, since the new 'lightweight' appeared, as large as life and a perfect replica. Lynx' attention to detail was such that the car was even given a registration number of the period, taken from a wrecked E-type roadster of 1963.

This 14th 'lightweight' had a contemporary registration: 5081 WK. It goes like a dream (0-100 mph in 10 seconds) and is almost breathtakingly beautiful. If you are interested, you can buy it for a mere £30,000. For the facts on the others, read on:

850006: an E-type converted by John Coombs, which anticipated the official Jaguar lightweights in certain aspects. Its BUY 1 registration was later changed to 4 WPD. It was not, of course, one of the 12 — or 13 — genuine lightweigh 'E's.

850658: a lightweight conversion produced jointly by the works and John Coombs from his 850006.

850659: the first of Briggs Cunningham's three lightweights (alloy-engined).

850660: the third lightweight built. Aluminium engine. Kjell Qvale's car.

850661: the fourth lightweight. Aluminium engine. Property of C.T.Atkins. This car was to win several races in the United States, driven by Roy Salvadori.

EC 1001: a works semi-lightweight. It was the first one to be given the special low-drag top which made it reminiscent of the series fastback fixed-head coupé. It belongs to Dick Protheroe.

850662: the aluminium-engined car of Peter Lindner, the Jaguar concession-holder for West Germany. It proved to be the fastest of all the lightweight E-types, and was converted into a works low-drag model in 1964.

850663: the alloy-engined car of the famous P.Lumsden and P.Sargent duo. It, too, was converted into a fastback, but not by the works.

850664: the second Briggs Cunningham lightweight.

850665: the third lightweight to be bought by Briggs Cunningham.

850666: an alloy-engined car, owned by P.Sutcliffe.

850667: an alloy-engined car, owned by R.Jane of Australia.

850668: the property of R.Wilkins; aluminium-engined.

850670: car with alloy engine, owned by Phil Scragg.

Yet another E type lightweight. Dick Protheroe at the wheel (Coundley was his team-mate) in the 1964 Rheims 12-Hours (chassis number EC1001). This famous CUT 7 met with a nasty accident some time later. It has now been rebuilt and runs in classic car races with Roger Mac.

The Goodwood Easter Meeting, 20 March 1964. Lumsden's 'low-drag' lightweight fixed-head E-type (chassis number 850663) 49 FXN.

An action shot of a 4.2-litre E-type. With its hood lowered, the car has a beautifully fluid line.

THE SERIES 1 E-TYPE

4.2 LITRES: 9 OCTOBER 1964 — SEPTEMBER 1968

SOME FINISHING TOUCHES

Jaguar's saloons were becoming heavier and heavier. The sports models were going to need even more power and torque due to a new project which was called the '2 + 2'. The factory therefore decided to give the XK unit a thorough going over — everything short of designing a new engine — resulting in the first major revision of the power unit since its conception 16 years before.

It was a simple enough plan at the outset: Jaguar was looking for improved torque through a bore increase of about 5 mm; the same procedure as had been adopted when through a 4 mm increase, engine capacity had been upped from 3.4 to 3.8 litres back in October 1958.

By this stage, despite the cylinder liners, there was just no more room for an increase in bore — even a fraction of a millimetre extra — in the engine as it stood.

So the solution to this problem was bound to involve some drastic surgery. The cylinders would have to be re-spaced less evenly and, in consequence, a new crankshaft would have to be designed.

The result was that cylinders number 1 and 6 were moved outwards; numbers 3 and 4 were brought closer to the centre; and numbers 2 and 5 stayed put.

The new crankshaft was a brilliant piece of work and it formed a solid backbone for the power unit. It was made of high-tensile steel, with seven main bearings as before; was

even more rigid; had modified crank-pins to reduce the stress on the bearings; and a new torsional vibration damper was fitted on the front.

In other words, Jaguar really got its teeth into the XK unit. With the new bore of 92.07 mm and the faithful old 106 mm stroke, engine capacity had been upped to 4,235 cc; power output rose by between 22 and 24 bhp; and maximum torque increased from 260 to 283 lb ft (38.6 to 42 m/kg) at 4,000 rpm.

This ten per cent increase in torque had no effect on the car's top speed or acceleration, but it made for greater flexibility through the extension of the engine torque's practical range. To put it more simply even in fourth gear at 600 rpm, the engine responded without protest.

The acceleration, far from being improved, according to some people, had deteriorated for the reason that the final drive ratio was now 3.07:1 instead of 3.31:1. Acceleration tests from 0 to 60 mph (96 km/h) had yielded a time of 6.9 seconds for the 3.8-litre fixed-head coupé, but only 7 seconds for the 4.2-litre. This comparison may, however, be invidious for if the final drive ratio had been the same on both cars the 4.2's acceleration might have been better than the 3.8's.

As for the 0 to 100 mph (160 km/h) figures, the 3.8-litre achieved this in 16.2 seconds, whereas the 4.2 could only

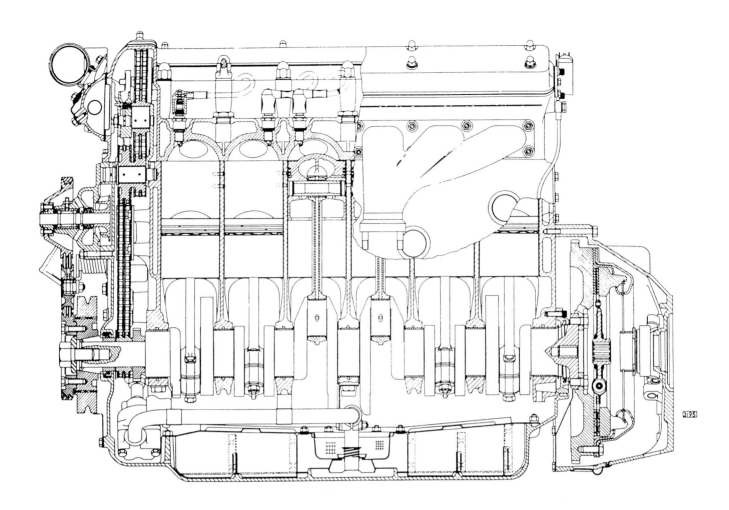

If you look closely you will see that the combustion chambers for cylinders 1, 3, 4 and 6 are not perfectly aligned with the head.

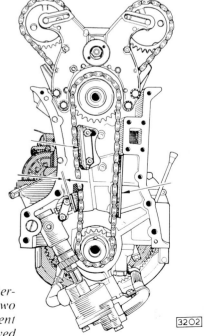

Chain drive of the 4.2; the bottom chain drives an intermediary sprocket which, in turn, connects with the two camshaft sprockets through a top chain. This arrangement has the advantage that the cylinder head can be removed without affecting the timing.

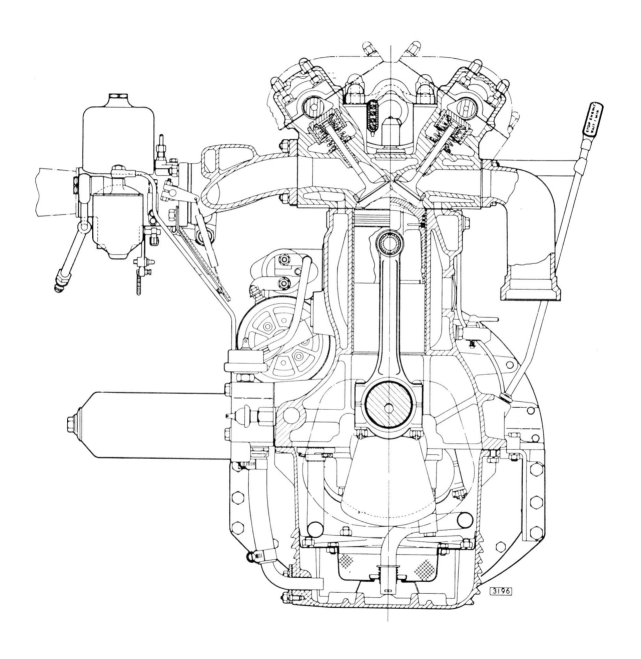

3196

Horizontal cross-section of the new 4.2-litre engine which took over from the 3.8 in October 1964. The new cylinder arrangement made room for an increase in bore and improved water cooling.

Assembling engines at Browns Lane in 1966. On the left you can see the test beds which were used to measure output. The large dial is a revolution counter marked off up to 6,000 rpm. Final adjustments and tuning are made at this stage.

manage 17.2 seconds. Allowance should be made again for the change in axle ratio.

On the plus side, there seemed to be a reduction in petrol consumption, but not enough to make it worth while. Allowance should be made again...

If you were to look at a dismantled 4.2 XK engine, you would notice immediately that the new cylinder arrangement had enabled an improved water jacket design.

The new cooling design gave markedly improved water circulation and thereby superior heat exchange.

A thermostatically controlled fan automatically cut in at 80°C, and cut out at 72°C when its job had been done. The water cooling system was pressurised and benefited by the addition of a high-level cross-flow water pipe, with the circulation being thermostatically controlled.

Efficient engine-cooling, linked with new pistons and new rings, helped to bring down oil consumption to an acceptable level. This was the least that could be expected, since 3.8-owners were rightly disgusted by having to keep two cans of oil in the boot at all times to feed their greedy engines.

Inspection of the cylinder head did not reveal any startling changes. In fact, the only real surprise lay in the fact that the combustion chambers had hardly altered their positions at all, despite the change in cylinder positioning. This strange disparity was to prove a perennial talking point for owners with a mechanical bent.

From the outside, too, the engine appeared vitually unchanged, except for the redesigned inlet manifold with its integrally cast water manifold. Three 2-inch HD8 SU carburettors stood proudly on the right-hand side of the engine and fed the cylinders through some very straight porting — even straighter than on the 3.8-litre straight-port head. There was an interesting innovation in this induction manifold, in that a balance pipe was included to ensure that the three groups of two cylinders should receive as equal as possible a charge from the carburettors, even if one of them should be out of use through a blocked slide or perhaps simply not be giving a rich enough mixture.

In spite of all these modifications, the 4.2-litre engine looked a bit improvised, with a cost-cutting flavour about it with those combustion chambers which were not even aligned with the cylinders.

The 3.8-litre E-type had introduced the submerged fuel pump... well that had bitten the dust! The 4.2-litre returned to the traditional twin pumps, which seemed to give better results in all circumstances.

There was a revolution in British car manufacturing prac-

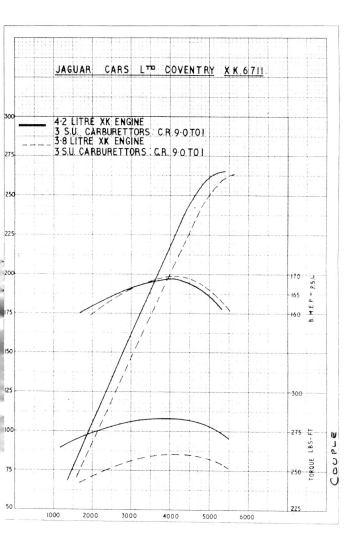

JAGUAR CARS L^{TD} COVENTRY X.K.6711.

4·2 LITRE XK ENGINE
3 S.U. CARBURETTORS. C.R. 9·0 TO1
3·8 LITRE XK ENGINE
3 S.U. CARBURETTORS. C.R. 9·0 TO1

A graph showing the comparative power and torque curves of the 3.8- and 4.2-litre engines. Although the power increase was minimal, the torque value had been improved significantly, and was better placed in the rev band.

Late 1964. At last Jaguar had introduced a gearbox which measured up to the car's performance. It was a works design, with synchronised first and everything the old Moss box had lacked. It was fast, quiet and flexible.

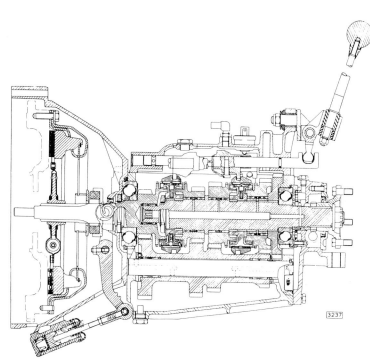

tice in that the battery connections followed international norms so that the negative terminal was earthed. It took the widespread adoption of car radios and alternators to put an end to this insular stubbornness, which shows itself by Great Britain doing exactly the opposite to the rest of the world.

In the case of the 4.2, a Lucas alternator replaced the outdated dynamo to provide a very high rate of battery charge, even with the engine at idling speed and all the electrics going full blast.

Another innovation — Jaguar was having a field day — was the pre-engaged starter motor which had taken the place of the rather weird set-up in which a sliding gear, mounted on a spiral nozzle, moved through centrifugal force and collided with the flywheel teeth with that distinctive click. Apparently, Jaguar owners in Greenland, Siberia and Alaska had been having a little difficulty in starting their cars in the morning because of the gear freezing solid to its shaft so that it couldn't engage properly. At least the Eskimos now had one less thing to worry about!

From the outside it was hard to tell a 4.2 E-type from the old 3.8, except by the discreet badge on the boot panel. But underneath hardly anything had escaped unchanged.

Let us start with the gearbox, which at last looked worthy

of a Jaguar. Happily, the works had finally used up its stocks of the old Moss box with its unsynchronised first gear — and about time, too! The 4.2 was therefore blessed with an all-synchromesh well-spaced four-speed box, with powerful lubrication supplied through a pump at the back of the box. Drivers no longer had to cross their fingers and stifle curses as they attempted a quick change down from third to second; now they could enjoy quick, quiet and positive changes which would satisfy the most demanding customer. Despite the new box's marked superiority over the Moss unit, the 'never happy' brigade complained that the passage from neutral into first was too stiff. The best solution to this problem was to engage second gear, from which position slipping into first was a piece of cake. If you were used to an even better gearbox than the 4.2's you might have found that the car was very noisy in second and third. This might have been caused by the gear angles.

A flexible and durable Laycock diaphragm-spring clutch connected the engine with the gears through a 10-inch (25-cm) plate. For contract reasons, the Laycock system was replaced with one from Borg & Beck in 1966.

Another cause for celebration was the adoption of more efficient brakes. New M59 Mintex pads gave a much more effective result, and a dual hydraulic circuit separated the front and rear brake systems once and for all. This dual circuit was controlled by a master-cylinder connected to the brake pedal.

The M59 pads had been developed specially for the E-type by Mintex. Jaguar had been at the end of its tether, trying to halt the decline in braking efficiency which was due to the overheating of the rear inboard discs — a problem which still remained to be solved. The new miracle material used by Mintex was much less heat-sensitive than other substances and, according to the manufacturers, had a much higher friction coefficient. Another of its qualities, apart from its resistance to overheating, was its very direct action, even at low speeds. The only slight drawback was that the pads squealed, but even in stop-start town driving the noise was not too infuriating.

Servo assistance was courtesy of the Lockheed system already described. Judged by 1984 standards, despite considerable improvements, the 4.2's brakes seem a little light for a 150-mph (240 km/h) car.

The remainder of the working parts escaped the new-broom treatment. The same limited-slip differential was retained; same steering; same front and rear suspension, bar a few teflon rings here and there in place of bronze ones, and slightly stiffer rear springs to prevent the exhaust pipes taking a hammering every time the car met a man-hole.

Impossible though it may be to distinguish a 4.2 E-type from a 3.8 just by looking at the body, the difference is immediately apparent if you take a look inside the car. For once, the redesigned interior met with almost unanimous approval. Take the seats, for example: they were deep and plush, giving good support to both back and thighs. Compared with the old-style bucket seats, these ergonomic masterpieces were more reminiscent of a luxurious lounge armchair than of a spartan sports-car seat. The enthusiasts who disapproved of the combination of comfort and sports cars just had to put up with it.

Another casualty in the revamping was the Bugatti- and Delage-style polished aluminium facia. This may have been

March 1966. The Series 1 4.2-litre fixed-head coupé introduced two occasional rear seats; the model was known as the 2 + 2. Longer doors, a deeper windscreen and a redesigned passenger compartment distinguished this model from the strict two-seater.

scrapped simply because it looked too functional, and might have been a deterrent to customers who preferred the Gran Turismo plushness to pared-down essentials. A padded glove-box snuggled between the two seats and did double duty as an armrest.

There were many other new features which would have stood out for anyone who knew the 3.8; there were detail changes to the dash instruments, the floor behind the seats, and in the boot.

It would be an exaggeration to say that the 4.2-litre E-type was a completely new car, but comparison with the 3.8 revealed a vast number of changes. This 'new' aspect is underlined by the fact that, apart from the body panels and windows, no 4.2 spare part was interchangeable with a 3.8 one.

In March 1966 came an announcement which was to split Jaguar enthusiasts into two opposing camps: the introduction of the 2+2. It was as plain as a pikestaff that the Americans were responsible for the model's appearance! Every time Jaguar added two occasional seats to its sports models, you could be sure that the tyrannical North American market was behind it. When you think about it, it is surprising that Lyons did not plan for this earlier when the two-seater E-type was on the drawing board, for it was inevitable that, sooner or later, some kind of back seats would have to be added.

It is worth remembering that 75 per cent of E-type production was earmarked for export to America; in fact, the United States had been the target market right from the start of E-type development. There was no way that Jaguar could hope to make much of an impact there with this model unless they gave it occasional seats, so one should not be offended by the decision or write off the 2+2's creators as lacking in taste! That being said, how was the modification achieved? The wheel-base was extended by 9-inches (23-cms) and given an extra 3½-inches (9-cms) in height so that, if necessary, a tall passenger could ride in the back. This same modification had been carried out on the 140 with some success, and the 2+2 E-type turned out to be a good-looking car, despite some people's reservations.

Inevitably, when the 2+2 first appeared, a few faces fell at the sight of this 'mutant' and there was a degree of breast-beating. However, it did not last long, for the 2+2 had its own individual character and many Jaguar enthusiasts are, even now, beginning to appreciate the charms of the long-wheelbased 'E'.

The factory had to do some clever things with the glassed area of the car — particularly the windscreen — in an attempt to disguise the added length and height of the 2+2. The doors looked enormous alongside the shallow ones which one could climb over on the roadster, and the increased area of glass helped to alter the front and side views of the basic E-type quite drastically.

A chrome strip ran along the top part of the doors, which helped to make them look less heavy.

Bearing in mind the problems with which Jaguar was faced when it put two extra seats in the E-type, you cannot deny that they came up with a pretty stylish car. But, on the way, they built and scrapped plenty of full-scale mock-ups. Men who worked with Lyons on the project can tell you that he flew into a rage when he first set eyes on the original

mock-ups because they were so ugly. Some were too tall, others too long...

Once the delicate balance between the depth of the windscreen and the length of the passenger compartment had been reached, all that remained was to start production.

As a postscript to the debate about the 2+2's aesthetic value, I will add that the majority of Jaguar enthusiasts are staunch defenders of the 2+2 faith, and go so far as to claim that this model was the most beautiful of all the E-types.

Getting into the car you were greeted by an almost vulgar profusion of padded leather; even the occasional seats were so welcoming that they deserved a more flattering descrip-

tion. They were still not large enough for two adults, but were adequate for two children, or one large adult passenger, providing he did not mind sitting sideways. In fact, the concensus of opinion was that the 2+2 was more like a luxurious mini-saloon than an extended sports car. The new model was, naturally, heavier than its predecessors and the factory fitted it with stiffer coil springs at the back to prevent the rear end 'bottoming' when the car had its full complement of passengers.

Another innovation which had been anticipated for some time, but which until then Jaguar had been unable to introduce due to the lack of space, was the option of automatic transmission with torque converter from Borg-

The first French-imported 2+2 4.2-litre E-type, seen here in the Bois de Boulogne, Paris.

Warner. Automatic transmission was very popular at that time in the United States, but had not really made its mark in Europe. The reason for this probably lies in the fact that America has those endless stretches of straight road along which you can drive non-stop for days without touching the steering wheel or the gear-lever.

The automatic option had already been available on the 140 and 150, so it is surprising that customers had to wait five years for it to appear on the E-type — better late than never, I suppose. As one reviewer put it: 'Messrs Borg-Warner change gear for you.'

Even the introduction of automatic transmission was enough to put some enthusiasts in a rage, as they felt that this was an act of sacrilege. I could have understood their attitude if the Borg-Warner transmission had been fitted as standard, but it was merely an option. After all, if you have £175 to burn, and you are not too worried about achieving record accleration figures, what the heck? There is no need to hurl abuse at anyone who prefers a surging Jaguar to a leaping one! Credit should also be given to the designers of the 2 + 2 for the many detail improvements which made the new model an extremely pleasant car to drive and to ride in. Air conditioning had at last brought an end to the sauna-like atmosphere of the past; accessories with built-in safety features abounded, notably the boot had become a protective barrier, thanks to the extra inches it had gained in depth; for extra storage there was plenty of space in the back of the car, if the occasional seats were folded down.

That year, 1962, was also notable for the merger of Jaguar with the mighty British Motor Corporation, in the formation of British Motor Holdings. The merger meant that Jaguar would thenceforth have to take extra care to preserve its marque image if it was not to be swallowed up in the corporate identity of this massive automobile conglomerate.

The United States Federal Safety authorities were becoming more and more demanding in their standards for imported cars. These standards seemed to alter from one month to the next, whether they applied to lighting, impact tests or whatever. It seemed as though every aspect of safety was a pretext for harassing the Browns Lane team and for keeping them from their beds at night. There were no two ways about it, Jaguar was counting on the American market and if the US authorities decreed that the E-type had to have bright pink bumpers, then bright pink bumpers it would have. If Jaguar had baulked at any of the American safety regulations, it would have resulted in whole convoys of E-types languishing on the docks of Newark, New Jersey, or even in them being sent straight back to Coventry without even having touched American soil.

As a consequence, several modifications were made to the E-type in 1967 and many observers deduced — rightly — that the car was being Americanised.

Even then, some drivers' clubs, led by the tempestuous Ralph Nader, declared that the drop-head coupé of the time was a moving insult to the god of safety. Unfortunately, they were to be proved right.

In the meantime, fault was found with nearly every aspect of the E-type, starting with the headlight fairings which were unacceptable to the American authorities.

Jaguar tried to steer a course through the minefield of safety regulations, all the time trying not to lose too much of the E-type's appeal — its clean, flowing line.

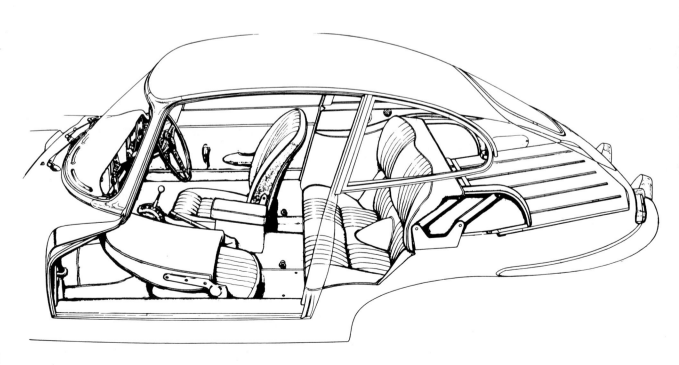

The luxurious, comfortable seating area of the Series 1 2 + 2 made for relaxing long-distance driving. The occasional rear seats received the same de luxe treatment as the front seats.

E-TYPE
Series 1½ 4.2-litre
October 1964-September 1968

The miniscule chrome strip which had previously joined the headlight fairing to the bumper had been given its marching orders.

Three body styles were available: the two-seater fixed-head coupé, identical to that on the Series 1 3.8-litre coupé; the 2 + 2 fixed-head with optional Borg-Warner three-speed automatic transmission; and the roadster, or open two-seater, which (in contrast to the 140 and 150) was not available in a 2 + 2 format.

One strange aspect of the even stranger Series 1½ E-type is that nobody knows for certain how many of these cars, with their five key features, were assembled.

Between the Series 1 and Series 2 E-types came a transitional model which has been given the rather odd name of the Series 1½ to show its place in E-type evolution. It is by no means an official label, however. I defy anyone to find mention of a Series 1½ E-type on any official Jaguar document.

This hybrid model was, at heart, a Series 1 car, though it had some features which remind one of the Series 2.

Since this E-type is now commonly referred to as the Series 1½, and since the name does indeed show that the model was basically a Series 1 with touches of the Series 2, I shall stick to it.

There were no drastic changes on the transitional E-type, merely a few detail modifications: the hood was now made of vinyl instead of wool; the glass panel in the headlight fairings had disappeared — this was a logical consequence of American safety legislation, which prohibited the fitting of glass on top of a glass headlamp (Ferrari and Mercedes had to make similar modifications); and the lever switches on the dash had been replaced by rocker switches. All these alterations had been dictated by the increasingly stringent safety requirements.

So, taken overall, these changes were far from earth-shaking, but at the same time the removal of the glass headlight fairings gave the E-type a completely different look. The headlamps had been moved forward slightly to give better illumination, and Jaguar had topped them with some rather odd chrome 'eyebrows'. Critics felt that this looked very messy and that Jaguar should have altered the bonnet panels to accommodate the headlamps' forward shift. It is easy enough to say such things, but Jaguar would have faced a hefty bill if they had ordered new tooling and matrices for a new bonnet design.

What the new headlight arrangement lacked in aesthetic appeal it more than made up for in efficiency. The lights made a much better job of showing you the road ahead than they had on the previous model, especially when the car was doing 75 mph in the dead of night.

There were two more changes. One was hiding away under the bonnet in the cooling system: two electric fans replaced the previous single two-blade fan, and there was the addition of a cross-flow device with expansion tank to improve the cooling system.

The last, and probably the least, alteration was so tiny that you would have had to search for it with a microscope.

1966. Paraffining E-types bound for foreign lands, to protect the paint. This is a 'Series 1½' E-type destined for the United States.

Bearing the strange 'Series 1½' designation, this 4.2-litre fixed-head coupé has signs of the Series 1 (indicator light positioning, bumper height, etc) and of the Series 2 which was to follow it: absence of glass headlamp fairing, headlights brought forward, etc. This works photograph shows that the Series 1½ designation was perfectly apt.

This works photograph sets out to prove that the Series 1½ 4.2-litre 2 + 2 fixed-head coupé can realistically be used as a family car.

Appearance of the Series 2 E-type in October 1968. The main exterior features which distinguish it from the Series 1 are the raised bumpers, flashing indicators located beneath the bumpers, protruding headlights, and absence of glass fairing on the latter.
The front and rear sidelights were exclusive to cars produced for the North American market.

This 1968 2 + 2 fixed-head coupé has been caught adding its own breed of aggressive elegance to a country byway.

THE SERIES 2 E-TYPE
18 OCTOBER 1968—SEPTEMBER 1970

NOT FAR SHORT OF PERFECTION

The Series 1½ E-type had given some small hint of what was to come, but the Series 2 proper made its very public début on 18 October 1968 at the London Motor Show. Jaguar had cut the launch very fine for, less than 48 hours before the show opened its doors, a special Jaguar team had been putting the finishing touches to the new E-type.

The Series 2 E-type was the product of an enthusiastic research and development department and of the never-stricter American safety regulations.

The car was still recognisably an E-type, but it had undergone a sea change in an attempt to adapt itself, despite the cost, to a changing world which seemed increasingly unsympathetic to thoroughbred sports cars. The devil-may-care 1960s were almost over and this Methuselah of a car had to change with the times or die. It had opted for change, but had fought tooth and nail to keep its original character.

The most obvious change at first glance was the much larger air intake in the nose, which transformed the car's appearance when viewed from the front. Why had Jaguar enlarged the 'mouth' by more than 50 per cent? It was not, as you might think, to improve engine cooling, but to make

the air conditioning more effective. Guess who had enough clout to bring this about... yes, you are right, it was the Americans! Air conditioning was virtually unknown in Europe, but it was a 'must' on all American series production cars, even the cheapest ones. For the E-type, therefore, air conditioning was a *sine qua non,* and Jaguar's big magic box could keep a young Texan cool in the middle of the desert — providing the windows were kept tightly closed, of course.

The supply of an efficient air-conditioning system had also been made indispensable by the new stringent American emission controls on carbon monoxide and dioxide. It was at about this time that people began to distinguish between 'American' and 'European' engines.

Jaguar's answer to this anti-pollution legislation was to fit two Stromberg CD Emission carburettors. It was a clever solution in which, at low engine speeds, the weak air-petrol mixture was reheated in a special manifold to make it more combustible. However, if you were travelling at high revs, a twin throttle opened to admit a full charge of the non-heated traditional mixture.

Unfortunately, as a result of fiddling around with the

4.2-litre engine to lower the pollution level, the car's performance suffered to the extent that it looked mediocre alongside that of the Italian V12s. and even compared with the American V8s which were beginning to look as though they meant business at last. Jaguar was all too well aware of the competition and the Browns Lane management scratched its collective head, wondering whether the time had come for exploring new avenues in engine development. If the E-type did not look to its laurels it would have to suffer the humiliation of watching Corvettes and Thunderbirds zoom past it as though it were a pick-up truck. This kind. of ignominy did not bear thinking about!

This was not a new talking point at Jaguar — way back in 1964 work had begun on a new engine project, the V12, but since this was still shrouded in secrecy we will stick with the 6-cylinder 4.2-litre unit for the time being.

Another visible engine modification, although really cosmetic, was the replacement of the polished aluminium cam cover by one which incorporated seven recessed black bands the length of the cover; this kept its looks far longer than the original burnished version.

Sir William Lyons had new projects up his sleeve, but he must also have had a load of worries on his mind. The commercial manoeuvring of BMC was just one example of what was happening in high finance and industry throughout Britain. It was the heyday of take-overs, mergers, liquidations and what have you.

Despite its merger with BMC, Jaguar was not on its last legs — far from it. Financially, William Lyons' division was disgustingly healthy. Expansion was continuing at a steady pace with surprisingly few hiccups, and Jaguar's economic base became stronger with every successful year, largely due to Sir William's genius. Somehow he had steered his company unerringly since 1935, helped by his accurate judgement of what the public wanted and by his ability to provide realistically priced luxury cars without succumbing to the temptation of making them too crammed with de-luxe accessories, which would have upped the cost considerably.

True, he did not pay his shareholders excessively generous dividends, but Jaguar shares rose so steadily on the stock market that they were rock-solid investments.

He had always followed bold, ambitious, expansionist policies which inevitably led to the occasional cash-flow problems, but the company always weathered the storm.

There are always risks attached to industrial management, but the way that every last drop was squeezed out of capital investment items (witness the good old XK power unit) more than compensated for losses incurred in speculative ventures. The originating costs for the XK engine had long been absorbed, so that raw materials and labour were the only costs which had to be borne in its production.

The 1960s saw many famous marques go to the wall or forced into mergers simply because they could not adapt to the changing times.

Rootes had absorbed Armstrong-Siddeley, Bristol and Singer. David Brown, of tractor fame, had taken over Aston Martin — with Lagonda thrown in — when the company was drowning in a financial crisis. In 1952 the Austin group had joined forces with the Nuffield organisation with Lord Stokes at its head to form the famous British Motor Corporation, which comprised Austin, Austin

Healey, Morris, M.G., Riley, Wolseley and Princess, while Leyland had acquired Standard-Triumph in 1962. Automobile construction was undergoing a radical change.

In 1964 the slightly tired Rootes group looked to Chrysler for support and, one year later, the venerable firm of Rover treated itself to a tasty morsel in the shape of Alvis, the red triangle marque.

Jaguar was by no means a wallflower in this industrial square dance and had even taken its own turn at calling the tune. Its first acquisition had been Daimler, which Lyons had long coveted because of its spacious, airy workshops, and because of its eminently respectable British marque image.

Sir William Lyons kept his eyes open for more bargains and bought out a few enterprises which were on the brink of collapse, such as Guy buses, Coventry Climax and Meadows.

Then, on the summer morning of 12 July 1966, people read at their breakfast tables that Jaguar and the British Motor Corporation were to be known as British Motor Holdings from that day. Once the initial shock had worn off, there was speculation as to whether this was a marriage or an act of cannibalism: who was eating whom?

Other questions that were being asked included: 'Has BMC merged with Jaguar to give it a more up-market image?' 'Despite its apparently solid financial footing, was

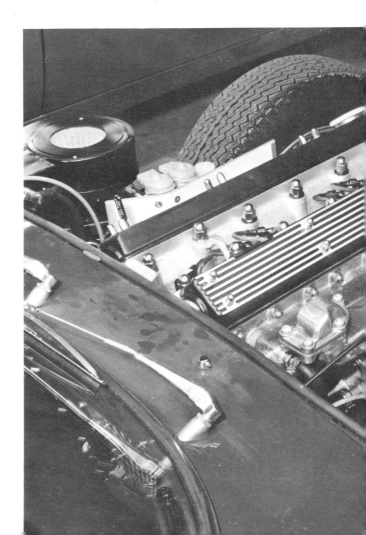

The Series 2 2+2 fixed-head coupé E-type photographed outside the Clères motor museum, near Rouen. The larger glassed area of the 2+2 made the passenger compartment seem very light and airy. The new windscreen design led to the Series 1's triple wipers being reduced to the more conventional pair.

The handsome triple SU carburettors have been given the push. Because of American emission regulations, our transatlantic friends had to make do with just two Strombergs.

Jaguar has always been known for its comprehensive tool kits. At 3, you can see the special tool for removing hub caps on wire wheels which did not have the knock-off winged caps, since the latter were banned in some countries.

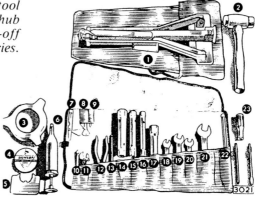

Trousse à outils

1. Jack
2. Hammer (copper and leather)
3. Hub cap remover
4. Bleed tube
5. Valve feeler gauge
6. Grease gun
7. Feeler gauge
8. Distributor contact-breaker points screwdriver
9. Tyre valve extractor
10. Tyre pressure gauge
11. Adjustable spanner
12. Pliers
13. Key (short)
14. Socket spanner (spark plugs and cylinder-head nuts)
15. Socket spanner (9/16-inch + 5/8-inch)
16. Socket spanner (7/16-inch + 1/2-inch)
17. Socket spanner (3/4-inch + 7/8-inch)
18. Open spanner (11/32-inch + 3/8-inch)
19. Open spanner (9/16-inch + 5/8-inch)
20. Open spanner (1/2-inch + 7/16-inch)
21. Open spanner (3/4-inch + 7/8-inch)
22. Key (long)
23. Universal screwdriver

Jaguar in trouble after that series of take-overs — had it bitten off more than it could chew?' 'Was the merger the result of a wrestling bout between Jaguar and BMC from which Jaguar emerged the loser after Pressed Steel Ltd came under BMC's corporate wing?' This last question is very interesting since, as you will remember, Pressed Steel had a virtual monopoly in the production of steel body panels... and Jaguar was one of its customers, so perhaps there was some truth in that rumour!

The news may have struck Britain like a thunderbolt, but it was more like a damp squib in France for all the media coverage it was given.

This industrial regrouping was to have a greater effect on Jaguar than seemed likely at the time of its announcement.

Sir William Lyons had not agreed unconditionally to the merger. His provisos were that Jaguar should retain its identity; that it should be autonomous; that its internal organisation should not be tampered with; and that all the management staff should keep their jobs. This was the price BMC had to pay before Sir William would agree to adding his signature to Lord Stokes' on the legal documents.

It is high time that we returned to the Series 2 4.2-litre E-type. There were many modifications which made it more comfortable, safer and more pleasant to drive.

Once again because of US Federal Safety Regulations, the bumpers had to be raised to the height of their American equivalents. This meant that there was no room for the flashers between the headlights and the bumper, so they were dropped down. There was a new regulation concern-

ing lighting area and the E-type's had to be doubled to conform.

The headlights were still not far enough forward for the federal officers' liking, since the E-type's prominent nose led to poor illumination in the centre of the car's path, so the offending lights were brought forward another 2-inches (5-cms). This made the car look even more frog-eyed than before and the factory had to manufacture deeper chrome trims, to camouflage the protruding top curves.

The same 'let there be light' rules applied to the rear of the car and the lamp clusters were doubled in size; if a job's worth doing... And as if that was not enough they added some more side lights.

The number plate mounting was square, to accommodate the Americans' square licence plates and, since this new mounting could not be combined with the old exhaust pipe position, the twin pipes were moved so that they lay either side of the plate-holder.

Viewed from the side, too, the 2 + 2 fixed-head coupé's profile had changed somewhat from the Series 1 version. On the latter, the windscreen was almost as vertical as a wall, presenting some wind-resistance problems at high speeds. Jaguar consequently set the Series 2's windscreen at a shallower angle to the vertical, with the bottom edge almost touching the rim of the bonnet opening. The actual change in angle from the vertical was 7 degrees — from 46 to 53 degrees.

One inevitable result of the more slanted windscreen was that its area was increased, so that more light penetrated

From 1968 onwards, for looks and ease of maintenance, the polished aluminium cam covers were given lengthwise black stripes. The 4.2-litre's cam covers are still like this today.

Diagram for adjusting the three SU carburettors, taken from the owners' handbook.

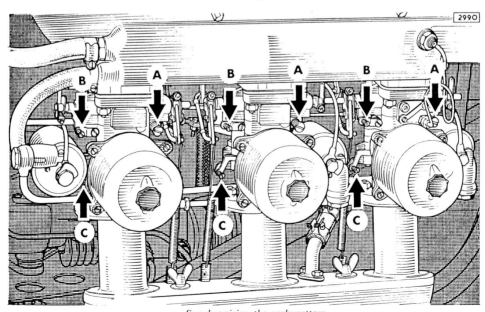

Synchronising the carburettors
A—Slow-running jet   B—Throttle adjustment screw
C—Mixture-control screw

into the passenger compartment. Understandably this modification met with widespread approval. One other consequence was that the triple wipers were replaced by the more conventional twin arrangement.

Despite the fact that the E-type's steering was already fairly light, Jaguar made driving even easier by offering power-assisted steering, which was supplied by Adwest in the form of a hydraulically assisted rack and pinion system. If you ask anyone who has tried this steering what they think of it, they will invariably reply, 'Fantastic!' There is no doubt that it makes driving a much more relaxing activity.

To comply with American impact safety regulations, the steering column was designed to telescope on impact.

The helix angle of the gear teeth in the manual box was changed with the aim of making the car quieter and gear-changing more positive. Some reviewers felt that there was no noticeable improvement; the previous box had been very efficient and quiet in third and fourth gears, with only a slight tendency to noisiness in first and second.

Moving on to the wheels, sports-flavour spoked wheels were still in evidence. Since the spokes were chrome-plated, Jaguar had to increase their number... yet again. They had started with 54 on the 120, and had then progressed steadily through 60 and 72 to the Series 2's 96 as the cars became heavier and more powerful. Indeed, this 96-spoke wheel was heavier than the disc variety! Strangely, bearing in mind its greater weight, the wire wheel was fitted as standard, with disc wheels available only as an option.

For once Jaguar broke with its recent tradition and chose

The Series 2 roadster was never offered in a 2 + 2 version. Nevertheless, the same large doors and long wheelbase were used. This is a European model, without the American flashing sidelights.

a Girling brake system instead of one from Lockheed. These were even more effective than before, with three pistons to each disc, each caliper having two pistons on one side and a larger one on the other.

As to the car's interior, the only noticeable differences were a slight change in seat design, recessed door handles, snap-off rear view mirror mounting, and dashboard details. If one looks at the three body styles offered on the Series 2 range — two seater fixed-head, 2 + 2 fixed-head, and roadster (with or without hard top) — one is struck by the fact that Jaguar did not include a 2 + 2 roadster, based on the fixed-head's wheelbase, which would surely have enjoyed a great success.

The reason for this omission is probably that a long-wheelbase roadster would have been too susceptible to deformation.

E-type production continued with no further modifications until 1970, since the works was concentrating its attention on yet another new model which, as usual, was taking rather longer to develop than anticipated. It looked almost as though Jaguar was keeping the public waiting until it had

used up all its E-type parts — the good old 'use up all the leftovers' policy!

The Americans fell hook, line and sinker for the Series 2 E-type, and in particular the 2 + 2. Be that as it may, the Americans were beginning to produce their own high-performance — higher-performance, in fact — cars, and Italy was leading the world in this field. In 1966 came the appearance of such legendary models as the Miura and the Marzal, to mention just two. Eat your heart out, Browns Lane!

With only a 3.4-litre engine, the Lamborghini 350 GT was developing 270 genuine bhp thanks to its V12 configuration. The Miura P 400 could boast an impressive 350 bhp from its 3.9 litres.

Whether you are talking about the Maserati Sebring or the Mistral (245 bhp with a 3.7-litre engine capacity), or any other model which was worthy of inclusion in the 'super-sports' élite, Jaguar seemed to be threatened from all directions on the horsepower front. The Corvette Stingray claimed 355 bhp with its 5.3-litre V8; the Ford Shelby GT 350 offered 306 bhp; the Oldsmobile Tornado gave a good 390 bhp with its 6.9-litre V8; even the Pontiac GTO boasted 340 bhp with a modest 6.3-litre V8; while Ford's Mercury Cougar produced 320 bhp to rival the Chevrolet Camaro and the Plymouth Barracuda. You will probably have noticed that I left out the A.C. Cobra with its diabolical 425 bhp obtained with a 7-litre engine!

V8s could definitely shift, even if most of these cars had inferior roadholding and braking, and were a great deal heavier than the traditional European sports cars.

This impressive list shows that the Americans were not about to let the grass grow under their feet, despite the fact that their technology lagged behind that of Ferrari, Lamborghini and Jaguar.

The crisis years in the automobile construction world were 1966 and 1967. Britain, which still clung to the 'Great' of its imperial past, was going through a disastrous period economically; Harold Wilson made his desperate attempt to save the value of the pound while the great car companies were rushing like lemmings into industrial conglomerates and hoping for a happier reincarnation, but finding that their death throes were merely being prolonged.

Jaguar came out of the crisis in good health, despite the fierce competition, mainly due to its low prices. Exports to America increased annually by a steady ten per cent; this happy export performance held up through to 1971, which was a record year for Jaguar both in gross production and in export figures.

The real threat came from cars which had bizarre names — the breathtaking and terrifying Lamborghini Miura, or the surreal Marzal — or impressive-sounding code names — Ferrari 275 GTB and 330 GT, or Aston Martin DB6 Volante.

It was only the high prices of these growling monsters which prevented them from poaching on Jaguar's market preserves.

William Lyons was not a man to hide his head in the sand and, although he was not the omnipotent figure of decades before, he was still looking to the future and the next Jaguar generations. The design possibilities were endless, since it was obvious that any new model would have to be completely different from the E-type which, because of its

original design characteristics, had had such difficulty in conforming to the ever-changing safety regulations.

The new engine, which had been under development for some time, had 12 cylinders in the now-obligatory V formation, and its capacity was 5.3 litres. By 1971 production had already begun but, sad to say, the new car for which it was destined was still a long way off completion. However, if the marque was to be given a boost, it was imperative that the V12 engine be offered to the customers, and the only solution was to pop it into the E-type body for the time being.

Jaguar enthusiasts were going to have to wait another two or three years for the new Jaguar sensation; it had to be a sensation, for nothing less would satisfy the Browns Lane team — just look back to the sensational arrival of the 1948 XK 120, and the equally stunning E-type which they had unveiled in 1961. As time was to show, Jaguar was still a past master at drawing the attention of the motoring world.

So, put a V12 into an updated Series 2 and there you have it: the Series 3 E-type.

The all-American Series 2 E-type: sidelights, Pirelli tyres with slim white bands and triple-eared knock-off hub caps.

A works photograph which was embargoed until Monday, 29 March 1971, the launch date for the Series 3 E-type. The differences between these and the Series 2 models are readily apparent: an even larger nose air intake, with radiator shell, headlights moved even further forward, and flared wheel arches to accommodate the extra-wide tyres, to name but a few.

THE SERIES 3 E-TYPE

29 MARCH 1971—FEBRUARY 1975

THE V12 WORKS ITS MAGIC

The XK 120 and 140 were not followed by the XK 160 and, similarly, there was never to be an F-type. Foreign Jaguar importers and UK distributors — such as Bert Henly — would have liked to see the Series 3 E-type come out as the F-type, but Sir William Lyons did not oblige.

The Jaguar V12 was not a new introduction, since it in fact dated back to 1967 and the XJ13.

If you want to produce a V12 and you already have a six-cylinder in-line engine at your disposal, your first reaction will probably be to join two 6s at an angle of 60 degrees and give them a common crankshaft.

This is such an obvious first thought that it did not escape the development engineers at Browns Lane, and when Baily began to sketch out the new unit he quite naturally played around with this configuration.

Many years before, in 1955, the idea of a V12 was taking shape at Jaguar. The D-type was at its peak and the engineers began to wonder whether they could give it a V12 to stretch its lead over the racing opposition, and if the resultant car could be exploited in a GT guise. However, Jaguar's colossal investment in racing development between 1951 and 1956, with Le Mans as its objective, put paid to any ideas of V12 development for quite a time. There was only so much money to go round, and racing was still being given top priority at that stage.

By 1957 the sporting image of Jaguar was well established and Lyons knew that, if he retired from racing right after the amazingly successful Le Mans victory that year, the firm would be able to live off its racing achievements for a long time to come. The Browns Lane management did not want to risk Jaguar's enviable reputation by going for another Le Mans clean sweep which, in any case, would not have been reflected quite so sensationally in sales figures as the 1957 win, so Lyons opted for spending the money elsewhere, on perfecting the 6-cylinder XK unit. Any plans for a V12 were still considered a trifle romantic.

The V12's time did come, eventually. The very first version was put together by hand, was seen to work, and was even fitted in a car, giving rise to over-optimistic rumours that Jaguar was about to make a racing comeback.

By mid-summer of 1964 the Browns Lane top-secret project was at last taking shape and the long-awaited V12 was being put through its paces on the test bed.

It consisted, as expected, of two 6-cylinder engines which shared the same block and the same crankshaft. The Jaguar trademark was obvious; even the aluminium cam covers shouted 'XK' at you.

As far as the cylinder heads were concerned, the only changes from the 6-cylinder design were slightly shallower

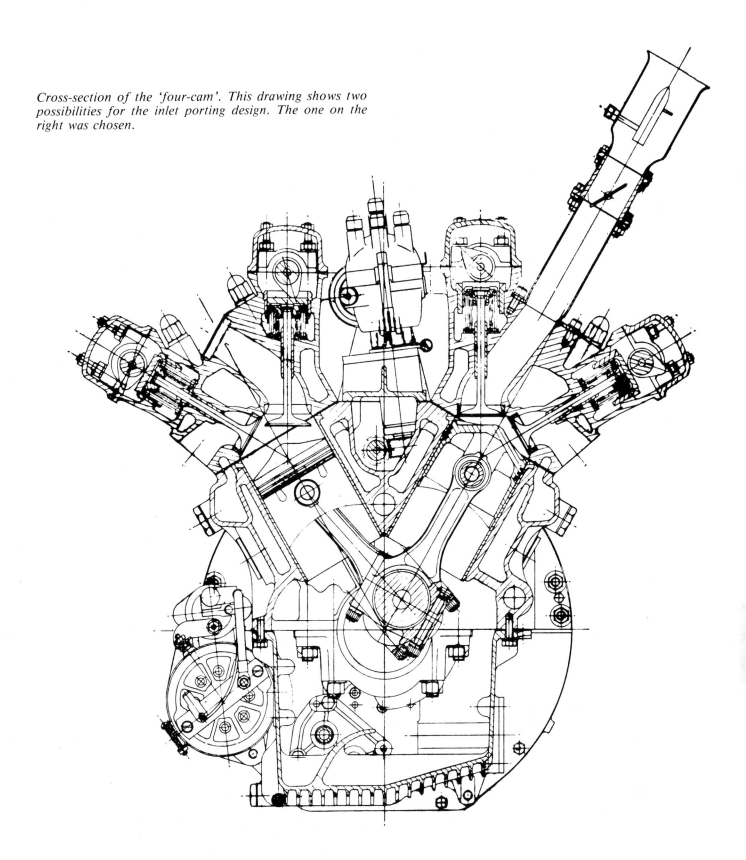

Cross-section of the 'four-cam'. This drawing shows two possibilities for the inlet porting design. The one on the right was chosen.

combustion chambers and a new inlet porting design which was dictated by the position of the carburettors.

With its 70 mm bore and 87 mm stroke, the engine capacity was close on 5 litres — 4,994 cc to be precise.

Two fuel-feed systems were planned: carburettors in the standard version and Lucas fuel injection in the super-powered model. The potential of the V12 was impressive: 502 bhp at the record speed of 7,500 rpm. These high revs were made possible by the almost square piston geometry. It looked as though the new engine was going to pack a hefty punch.

The prototype car, fitted with the V12 and a five-speed ZF gearbox, was tried out on the MIRA test track at Lindley, near Nuneaton — only a stone's throw from Coventry. Driven by David Hobbs, the car smashed the MIRA circuit record, clocking up a time of 1 minute 28.8 seconds which gave an average speed of 161.6 mph (260.07 km/h). It was a record which stood for a long time, which is

This is how a Jaguar series-production V12 with four cam-shafts would have looked. Of course, the twin-cam layout won the day. Induction is through 6 SU carburettors.

The V12's original configuration with four overhead camshafts. Effectively, it was two XK engines joined together but sharing a common crankshaft. Because of the high costs and complicated procedures involved in its manufacture, this design was rejected in favour of the much simpler twin overhead cam arrangement. The capacity of this ingenious piece of machinery was 4,991 cc, and its output 500 bhp at 8,000 rpm. It was fitted in the outstanding and unique XJ13.

not surprising considering the tight, demanding circuit with only a slight camber, if any, on the bends.

Until this first trial run, the car and its revolutionary engine had been covered in a thick cloak of secrecy, and only hand-picked men had been allowed to work on the project. Security was leakproof and the outside world had absolutely no idea of what was going on in the top-secret corner of the Browns Lane works. This car was intended to be a new Le Mans winner, but things did not turn out that way.

The prototype was in fact the nearest Jaguar came to producing an F-type. It might well have enjoyed the same memorable racing career as the D-type, but instead it ended up as a freak in the BL Heritage collection at Syon Park.

Its proper name was the XJ 13, and it was never taken any further. The body styling was remarkable and it was clear that the car was in a straight line of descent from the C- and D-types, despite its unique (for Jaguar) mid-engined layout.

The idea of a mid-engined car had been in the air since 1964, when Lola had produced a superb example. Jaguar planned to build a light-alloy monocoque, starting from the central engine principle. Inevitably, Malcolm Sayer was asked to design the body. Since aerodynamics were Sayer's speciality, the XJ13 turned out to be a working example of what could be achieved in this field. Various models were tried out in the wind tunnel, first at 1/30th scale, then at 1/20th scale and, finally, at 1/10th, while the engine was being perfected in another part of the factory.

Body and engine development were to take three years of hard, but also imaginative work for, despite Lola's mid-engined model, there was still a lot left to discover about this new layout.

So it was that in 1967 the first trials took place on the heavily guarded MIRA circuit. Security was so tight that David Hobbs was the only test driver present. The test sessions went on for weeks and produced increasingly conclusive results.

The car performed so well during these sessions that there was speculation about whether it would perhaps be worth starting small-scale production.

XJ13 was painted that precise shade of green referred to as 'British racing green' — BRG for short.

The most important component was, of course, the engine: the brainchild of Claude Baily and Harry Mundy. It was a magnificent beast with its two lines of six cylinders set

The one and only mid-engined Jaguar; the most sophisti-cated, most handsome and fastest of all the Jaguars, it never got beyond the prototype stage. This photograph was taken not long before the car's tragic demise.

Below: The XJ13 was an amazing car. It was hard to tell which was the back and which was the front. This beautiful beast was designed for speed and is seen here at the MIRA test circuit prior to test sessions before an invited audience of motoring journalists.

at an angle of 60 degrees; a massive seven-main-bearing crankshaft which transformed the linear motion of the 10.4:1 compression ratio pistons into a smooth rotating motion; and its twin-pump Lucas fuel injection.

The 386 lb/ft (57 m/kg) torque was achieved at 6,300 rpm, and at higher engine speeds increased power was produced without any increase in the torque figures.

The engine was not as heavy as one might have expected it to be, bearing in mind that it was almost like two 6-cylinder XKs stuck together. It tipped the scales at only 648 pounds (294 kilos), compared with the XK's 503 pounds (228 kilos). To keep the weight down, a light aluminium alloy was used where possible, and notably in the block itself in the form of an alloy labelled LM8. The list of such special alloys is endless: LM25WP; LM13P; EN40; EN16; EN52; 2KII... well, that will do to be going on with!

The V12 was a highly professional piece of work. Baily reckoned that it could produce 550 bhp if the revs were pushed to 8,500. Not bad.

The finished power unit was installed lengthwise bang in the middle of the monocoque structure, so that it sat just behind the driver's head. Needless to say, there was a very effective layer of insulation incorporated into the bulkhead between the cockpit and the engine.

Because of the engine's central position it is very hard to tell the back of the car from the front, as the shape is nearly symmetrical. But then, of course, the steering wheel gives the game away!

Wet-sump lubrication was used and 72 pints (41 litres) of oil were needed for this massive piece of machinery.

The other liquid capacities were on the same scale. Engine cooling was effected by 53 pints (30 litres) of the appropriate liquid, and there was a 40-gallon (185-litre) petrol tank to enable the car to do a few circuits of the MIRA track before it had to stop for a fill-up.

With all these extras the kerb weight of the XJ13 worked out at just over 22 hundredweight, which was rather excessive.

It was one hell of a car, all the same. Even though there is no point in daydreaming and trying to rewrite history with a succession of 'if only's, one is still tempted to wonder whether the Ferrari-Ford racing duels of 1963-66 might not have had more bite *if only* the XJ13 had been pitching in there with them.

The other parts surrounding the V12 engine were more conventional. There was independent front suspension, of course; double wishbone and coil springs, as one would expect from a monocoque car; Armstrong adjustable hydraulic shock absorbers; and independent rear suspension which, however, bore little outward resemblance to the E-type's in that one side of the wishbones was much longer than the other, giving the suspension geometry a Lotus-like appearance — not so surprising considering that it was designed by two Lotus men: Derek White and Mike Kimberley.

The rack and pinion steering was similar to the E-type's except that the turning circle was 16 feet (5 metres). Braking was originally provided by standard discs, but Girling ventilated discs were substituted in later development stages. As for wheels, the first prototype was fitted with the same 15-inch ones as the D-type, but later on wide Dunlops were used — 525 x 15 at the front and 600 x 15 at the rear.

Power was transmitted to the rear wheels through a 5DS/25 five-speed ZF gearbox with overdrive on fifth and integral final drive. The engine was linked to the gearbox through an 8½-inch diameter twin-plate clutch supplied by Borg & Beck. The engine/clutch/gearbox assembly was very compact and helped to even out the weight distribution.

The XJ13 showing its amazing turn of speed on the MIRA test track, just before the accident which wrote it off. There are, of course, few photographs of the original XJ13, which was rebuilt by the works some years later.

A view of the fuel-injected 12-cylinder XJ13's engine in situ. Its four camshafts are enough to drive the most hardened motoring enthusiast into frenzies of excitement!

Cutaway drawing of the XJ13 giving a clear view of the centrally positioned engine.

The team responsible for the reincarnation of the XJ13. On the far left, easily recognisable by his height, is F.R.W. 'Lofty' England. The engine is clearly visible for our delectation beneath its perspex cover.

William Heynes closely supervised the whole development and construction process.

The sophistication of the bodywork matched that of the XJ13's machinery. It was a monocoque structure, of course, but was very different from the D- and E-types. Working from Malcolm Sayer's blueprints, the Browns Lane engineering team produced a very original structure, which gave ample evidence of having an aircraft designer among its creators — the same aircraft designer who already had the D-type, Cunningham 3-litre and E-type to his credit.

Instead of a tubular chassis or central closed monocoque section, the XJ13 was given two box-section cross-members in aluminium which spanned the width of the car and connected with two longitudinal hollow sills which housed two of the three oil and petrol tanks. An aluminium floor section filled the middle.

Although the XJ13 was a very open car, the rigidity and lightness of this construction were never in any doubt.

At the front of the car, a diagonally reinforced cross-member carried the suspension, rack and pinion steering, radiator and header tank. Moving to the rear of the car, the two longitudinal sills stopped at the wheel arches to make room for the power unit and for a third, central fuel tank.

The anchorage points for the engine were chosen with a view to making the whole structure even more rigid. The drive unit, consisting of engine, gearbox and axle, could be removed in under 45 minutes.

One of the aircraft construction techniques used on the XJ13 was extensive riveting of the body panels. The 'boot' opened wide for easy engine maintenance, and this panel could even be removed entirely.

The cockpit was very similar to a D-type's. A proper windscreen and two small sidescreens protected the driver. On top of the engine there was a transparent panel, instead of an opaque one.

Other components included two 12-volt batteries, a Lucas alternator, 7-inch diameter 110-watt headlamps, a single-speed but very fast screen wiper, a Trico screen washer and cockpit heating.

The seats were covered with a combination of cloth and PVC. There were no seat belts, the floor was simply given a coat or two of paint and there was no jack, although there were two jacking points at each end of the car.

The windscreen glass was laminated, as one would expect of a modern racing car, although this was quite a novel feature in the 1960s.

If you love reading statistics, have a browse through this lot:

The XJ13 measured 15 feet 10 inches (4.83 metres) long and stood 3 feet and 5 inches (1.05 metres) tall. With full tanks it weighed a good 22 hundredweight (1,125 kilos) but, thanks to the V12, the power/weight ratio was impressive at 417 bhp per ton (424 bhp/tonne).

The performance figures were equally striking: at 7,600 rpm you could float smoothly up to 59 mph (94.5 km/h) in first gear, to 115 mph (185 km/h) in second, and in third you really started to shift at 142 mph (229 km/h), going up to 169 mph (272 km/h) in fourth. From there on, it was up to you; you did your best, put your foot down as far as it would go and started praying!

There are plenty more of these fascinating statistics.

A strange fate awaited the XJ13. On 20 January 1971 the XK13, which had been given a lead part in an advertising film for the launch of the V12 E-type, was brought out from under the dusty tarpaulins which had been shrouding it for the past three years. The prototype was to do a few laps for the benefit of the cameras.

A microphone and a camera were set up on one of the bends of the MIRA track to capture the action and the throaty roar of the V12 engine as the car sped past.

Everything went swimmingly to start with. The engine

XJ13 number 2. Should it be called a replica or an original? It is seen here in Jaguar's exhibition hall.

The XJ13's cockpit and dashboard. There are no frills or furbelows — everything is functional. Note the short gear lever on the right.

had been finely tuned and the car was going flat out. Disappointed at the prospect of having to trundle the car back under its wraps after such a short outing, Norman Dewis, the test driver, gave in to the temptation of taking the car round the track a few more times.

It might not have happened, but sadly it did: the old Dunlop tyres were just not up to the 160 mph (260 km/h) ordeal and the nearside front tyre blew out. The car literally flew up the banking, bounced off the safety rails and fell back on to the circuit, executing a series of impressive rollovers in the process.

The twisted wreckage lying smoking in the centre of the track was not a pretty sight. The film crew and the Jaguar team did not see how Norman Dewis could have survived such a crash, but happily he climbed out of the wreck in one piece — a credit to the XJ13's strength and rigidity. Unfortunately for horror fans the accident occurred out of range of the cameras and there is, consequently, no pictorial record of the prototype XJ13's sad end.

The remains of the car skulked in a corner of the Jaguar factory for months on end. And then one day the XJ13 was reborn, in a new, improved version. Construction began

The Paris Motor Show, October 1971. A decorated Series 3 V12 E-type in its roadster dress. It was on offer to the French for 55,300 francs, and to the British for £3,139.

three years after the accident and produced the second XJ13 prototype.

I could devote a chapter to the fascinating story of this reconstruction, but suffice it to say that several changes were made to the original design, including wider wheels and slightly flared wheel arches.

The XJ13 which is currently on show at Syon Park is therefore not the original prototype, but a Jaguar-built replica.

In one way — though it is not nice to have to say it — the accident solved a problem. Much to his disappointment, Sir William Lyons had already had to scrap any plans for XJ13 development, for the car could have overshadowed the E-type with its revolutionary construction methods.

It is not hard to imagine the customers being loath to spend their money on the E-type with its traditional transmission when, in the background, there was an ultra-modern mid-engined model in the pipeline.

The sales department was quick to see the danger and had strongly counselled Lyons not to go ahead with XJ13 production, even on a limited racing-car scale.

This is a common problem in the world of car marketing: a potential customer puts off buying a new car if he thinks that a new model is about to appear which will outdate the current range. The average Jaguar customer is fully briefed on the latest technological developments and is therefore even less likely to be fobbed off with an 'old' model than your average man in the street.

Naturally enough, Jaguar did not intend to put sales of their E-types at risk. But would the XJ13 have posed a threat to the E-type? Was it too far ahead of its time? Was there no way of producing a 2+2 XJ13? Or perhaps the engine was too expensive to manufacture? It is difficult to say whether the decision to shelve this project helped or harmed the marque, but looking back on it all it seems as though Lyons was wise to draw in his horns.

Experimental development of the V12 engine, with its four overhead camshafts, continued at Jaguar, but the unit lost its more sophisticated features.

Slowly but surely, a simpler — and therefore cheaper — version evolved until, eventually, the V12 was to become an economically feasible project.

There is no doubt that this early V12 presented several difficulties when it came to series production. At one stage there was even talk of producing a V8, but developing a V8 engine which would be destined mostly for export to the country which had made the V8 its own pet engine (the United States) would have been like taking coals to Newcastle.

The first main modification to the original design involved the replacement of the four camshafts by a technically simpler twin cam arrangement. This enabled the valves to be aligned, a flat-bottomed cylinder head to be used and the combustion chambers to be placed in the piston heads.

The second change was in the displacement, which was increased to 5,343 cc by a 3 mm enlargement of the bore.

Left: The 60th Paris Motor Show, October 1969. President Pompidou congratulates John Morgan, Jaguar's export manager, at the company's stand.

The 5.3-litre V12 with its Stromberg CD emission-type carburettors was the standard Series 3 production power unit. Four Series 3 E-types were supplied with the 4.2-litre XK engine, and the V12 was therefore almost exclusively the power preserve of the Series 3 cars.

A view of the V12 block which shows the removable liners and the camshaft drive chain.

A bottom view of the same engine revealing the crankshaft's main bearings.

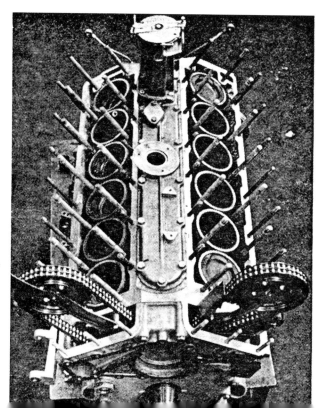

This V12 drawing reveals the complexity of the engine.

This was done with the aim of increasing the engine's torque to give better flexibility at low engine speeds.

With these modifications, plus a reduced compression ratio of 9:1 and breathing via carburettors, the V12's output was decreased to 315 bhp, but it had extraordinary torque through the whole gamut of engine speeds, and this more than made up for any loss of brute force.

Light alloys were used even more extensively than on the XJ13, with the result that the new engine weighed only about 73 pounds more than the old XK unit.

Following lengthy tests and several variations on the main theme, the definitive engine version appeared towards the end of 1970.

There was one slight hitch however, the new wonder car which was to follow on from the E-type was less than 'not quite ready'; Jaguar had not got any further than roughing out its outlines! This meant that the works was faced with the same old problem: should they put their latest technological masterpiece in a ten-year-old body at the risk of devaluing the new engine (you will remember that the same situation cropped up back in 1948, when Jaguar shied away from fitting the then brand-new XK twin cam engine in the obsolete Mark V's body, and instead produced the XK 120 in record time), or should they hang on and speed up body development so that they could have a sensational double baptism — a new car fitted with the revolutionary new V12?

William Lyons and his team scratched their heads, searched their souls and concluded that there was no chance of producing a new car within three or four years at the least.

That was that. The glorious V12, which had originally been conceived to boost Jaguar's reputation in the United States and to give a commensurate boost to the E-type's performance now that the XK unit was on its last legs, would have to settle for the E-type as its first home.

Working on the principle that it is not worth spoiling the ship for a hap'orth of tar, the E-type was given a new dress for the occasion.

This, therefore, was the story of the Series 3 E-type based on the new electronic-ignition V12 and the facelifted E-type body.

This time lag between new engines and new cars was, of course, nothing new for Jaguar — it had almost become an old friend among the many problems which arose during development.

When the XK unit was finalised there was no new car ready to take it . . . the result was the rushed XK 120. When the E-type was ready for launch a new engine was notable by its absence, so Jaguar had to settle for the XK 150's old 3.8-litre power unit. When the development engineers shouted 'Eureka' with their V12 under their figurative arms, they looked round in vain for a new car.

And when the XJS saw the light of day some time later, it would have to make do with the by then old-fashioned V1 unit.

Jaguar was counting on the novelty of their V12 to seduce the American market. Happily this optimism was not unfounded, for the United States responded with enthusiasm. Since the engine had been destined for transatlantic use right from the word go, it was built to US standards to avoid any tampering about with it at the last minute.

320

V12 cylinder blocks are passing through quality control after casting. One of the V12's great advantages was that the flat-head design, made possible by the adoption of one overhead camshaft per bank of cylinders, was very easy, and therefore inexpensive, to manufacture.

V12 assembly at Browns Lane. Here an engine with automatic transmission is being assembled, hence the torque converter.

The V12 seen from an unusual angle. Although the inlet valves are inside the 'V', the carburettors had to be placed outside to avoid the power unit being too tall to fit under the E-type's bonnet. This gives the inlet ports the appearance of tentacles and this resemblance has earned them the nickname of 'octopuses'.

The Series 3 E-types were to be supplied with two power options: the 5.3-litre V12 or the 4.2-litre 6-cylinder XK, the latter being restricted to the domestic market. A search of the works' records leads one to believe that only four 4.2-litre Series 3 E-types were assembled, only one of which was ever sold! Obviously, the V12 worked its magic spell on all and sundry, even on the conservative British. This two-engine option is reminiscent of the XK 100 engine which, in 1948 and '49, was offered alongside the 3.4-litre XK unit in the 120; and you will remember what became of the poor little 4-cylinder engine!

This lack of interest in the 4.2-litre option explains why the mention of 'Series 3' now automtically implies 'V12' when you are talking about E-types, and why no one ever thinks of adding 'V12' to the Series 3 description.

The V12 was designed to meet American emission controls and, with this in mind, Jaguar fitted it with four emission-type 175 CD SE Stromberg carburettors located in two pairs outside the 'V' of the two banks of cylinders.

To reach the cylinder head the mixture had to travel along an interminable length of tubing, but there was dramatically improved torque in the middle range of engine speeds, between 2,500 and 3,500 rpm. You are probably wondering why Jaguar had abandoned the Lucas petrol injection which had worked so well on the four-cam experimental V12. The reason is simple: if they had retained the

Lucas injection, they would not have been able to bring down the carbon monoxide and dioxide levels below the statutory US levels.

Jaguar had challenged Brico Ltd to produce an injection system which complied with American emission requirements, and the firm had responded in double-quick time with an ultra-sophisticated solution which used advanced electronic techniques to produce automatically controlled cold starting, a constantly optimum mixture in all conditions, low pollution and — to cap it all — an extra 30 or 40 horsepower.

Sadly, once this injection system had been perfected by Brico in collaboration with Jaguar, the firm decided not to go ahead with production; possibly because of the high unit cost, or doubts about reliability — who knows? Ironically, just after E-type production was finally halted the V12 acquired its precious fuel injection.

Injection on the Series 3 E-types was all-electronic — yet another revolution! Jaguar's choice was a Lucas system because of its astonishing performance record. This ignition was known as 'Opus', standing for 'Oscillating pick-up system', and used electro-magnetic impulses instead of the traditional mechanical device, which used contact breakers operated by a cam.

Elsewhere, Jaguar relied on tried and tested components, such as the two-row roller cam-chain drive, cast-iron cylin-

Body assembly shop at Browns Lane. The roadster is built on the same long wheelbase as the 2 + 2 fixed-head coupé. The strict two-seater fixed-head coupé was abandoned to rationalise the range. These photographs, taken in March 1971, show the bodies prior to being steeped in the degreasing baths.

der liners, Brico 305 valve seats, pumped lubrication with an additional oil cooler, and the conventional cooling system.

In the context of the unending 'power race', it is interesting to note that engine capacity had increased by 55 per cent, in a series of leaps and bounds, since the 3.4-litre XK's day. But then, we should remember that the dreaded phrase 'fuel crisis' had not yet hit the world's front pages.

With all its anti-pollution features, the 5.3-litre V12 unit could manage only 272 bhp at 5,850 rpm — not bad for a Jaguar engine, but less than one might hope for from a V12. One journalist went so far as to say: 'It is ten years since the 3.8-litre E-type appeared and, with twice as many cylinders and an increase of 1½ litres in engine capacity, this car's performance is slightly inferior both in acceleration power and top speed... it wasn't worth all that fuss and bother!'

True enough, the V12's power is feeble compared with its wonderful torque, but then the latter was its trump card as it made the engine so flexible. It was the V12's superior torque which made the Series 3 E-type so successful in the United States.

Jaguar could not afford to fail with its new engine, for the development and tooling-up costs were somewhere in the region of £3 million. They had had to install the latest in production lines, computerised automatic machinery, and had had to modernise the workshops in Radford, Coventry, which had previously been devoted solely to Daimler production.

As added evidence that this handsome 12-cylinder car had been intended for American consumption right from the day of its conception, the Series E-type made its début at the New York Motor Show in April 1971, where it was very favourably received by both press and public.

Comments included: 'The V12 has come to the people'; 'New wine in an old bottle'; 'Following in the footsteps of Ferrari and Lamborghini'; 'Middle-of-the-road Ferrari from BLMC'; 'How to surprise Americans'; 'A technological/commercial achievement: mass-production of a non-series car'; 'The most famous British sporting marque has gained its second wind' and many more.

As you can see, the press was pretty enthusiastic about the new car, and the new engine won an almost unanimous thumbs-up from the Americans. Jaguar had now become a member of one of the most exclusive clubs in the world — the V12 club, which now had three members, Ferrari, Lamborghini and Jaguar.

It was, moreover, a club with a diminishing membership, for only 36 years ago there were no less than 14 names on the roll: seven in the United States — Cadillac, Auburn, Franklin, Marmon, Packard, Lincoln and Pierce-Arrow; two in France — Hispano-Suiza and Voisin; two in Germany — Horch and Maybach; two in Britain — Rolls-Royce and Daimler; and one in Czechoslovakia — Tatra.

Flared wings, protruding headlamps and wide radiator shell, together with an additional air intake underneath, are the distinguishing marks of the Series 3 E-type seen from the front.

As well as the technological achievement of mass-producing the V12 engine, we should also recognise Jaguar's marketing achievement in making it possible to sell the sophisticated Series 3 V12 at such a ridiculously low price. It was the same old cry: 'How on earth do they manage it?'

The European motoring press followed in the Americans' footsteps, showering praise on the new Jaguar's head, with all the test drivers reaching the same conclusions. The majority was disappointed to see what was, at heart, a ten-year-old body on the brand-new engine. These reservations had little effect on the buying public, however, who bought the new car in their hundreds irrespective of the fact that it was not an 'F-type'.

This was the third and last E-type generation and, thanks to its V12 engine, it was to make its mark in Jaguar history.

To get down to basics, what were the differences between the Series 2 and Series 3 E-types?

Well, comparing their exteriors, the wheel arches had been flared to make room for the wide tyres, and to accommodate the wider track. The open 'mouth' had been covered with a grille to hide the innards, and there was an extra air intake underneath (one unkind journalist described the grille as 'a decorative birdcage').

Only one wheelbase was produced for the Series 3: the long one which had been used for the Series 2, 2 + 2. This wheelbase served both the fixed-head coupé and roadster, so the shorter wheelbase for two-seater models disappeared with the introduction of the Series 3.

Despite its longer wheelbase, the roadster was never supplied with occasional rear seats, the space being used instead for extra luggage capacity in what was now more worthy of the description 'boot' than had been the tiny area provided in the Series 1.

An optional hard top was still offered for the roadster, to make it a more civilised car in colder climes, and wire wheels had once more become optional rather than standard fitments, disc wheels being supplied as standard.

The new wider tyres were E70VR 15 Dunlops on six-inch rims. This significant increase gave the car a foundation suitable for its high performance. The wider base and flared arches added to the E-type's aggressive appearance, making it an even more attractive car in its Series 3 guise.

A rather nasty addition which had been dictated by American regulations was the fitting of Nordel rubber impact absorbers on the bumpers, capable of withstanding 5 mph collisions. Opinions on these little monstrosities differed widely!

So much for the outside of the Series 3 E-type. It may not sound much, but these few changes altered the E's appearance quite drastically. Between the first 1961 E-type and the 1971 model not many changes were made to the body: headlamps, radiator grille, wing lines, windscreen, and 2 + 2 variations; but taken together these alterations changed the E-type's character.

Structurally the car was more or less the same, except for the front framework which now had to house a V12 rather than a 6-cylinder unit. This framework was consequently reinforced to take the strain of the increased torque.

The front suspension was further improved by the adoption of an anti-dive geometry to offset the effects of intense braking.

There was still a choice between the three-speed automatic Borg-Warner box and the four-speed synchronised

A narrow Scottish country road overlooking a loch near Argyll. More importantly, this is a fine view of the back of a Series 3 'E', with the V12 badge telling the world of its sophisticated engine.

The Series 3 E-type roadster fitted with an optional hard top gave all the advantages of a fixed-head coupé in winter with the roadster's open-air advantages in summer.

Cutaway drawing of the Series 3 V12 E-type by Vic Berris. The long wheelbase alone was retained for use in the roadster.

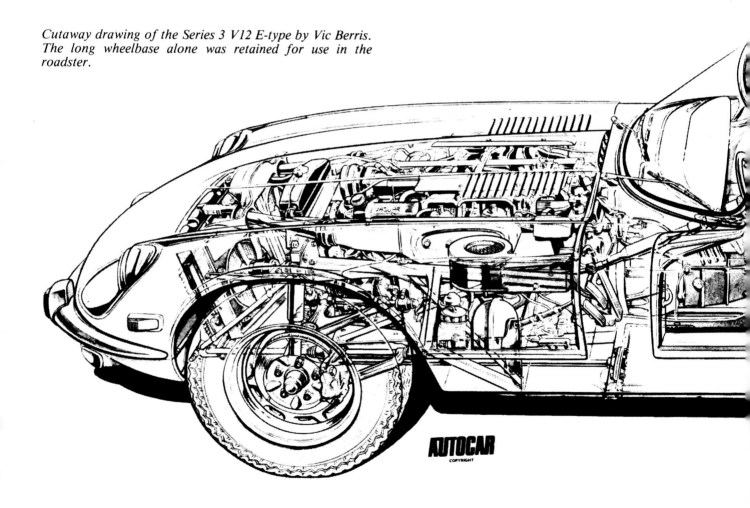

AUTOCAR
COPYRIGHT

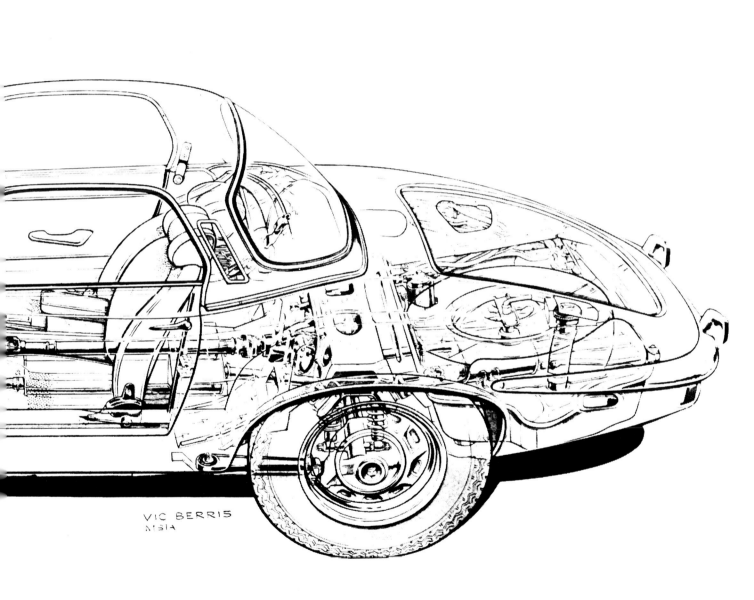

VIC BERRIS
MSIA

manual Jaguar gearbox which had been fitted to the 4.2-litre E-type. The only change in transmission was in the diameter of the clutch which had been increased to make it stronger.

The brakes, although not yet perfect, at least now had ventilation at the front, to match the rear arrangement. A limited-slip differential was still in evidence, and this was an increasingly vital feature in view of the ever more powerful engines.

The rack and pinion steering was repositioned, and benefited from the power assistance used on the XJ saloons.

Once you climbed into the driving seat, everything around you shouted 'Jaguar'. There is something special about Jaguar interiors — everything you need is at hand, the design is classic, the comfort exemplary, the concept functional.

There was a whole battery of switches and instruments, an embarassment of riches. But since one should not be lulled by such a wealth of instrumentation, let me hand Jaguar a few brickbats: the ashtray was a diminutive gesture; heating and ventilation rather feeble; the headlight dip control somewhat weedy; a rear-window demister sorely needed; leather seemed to be giving way to synthetics; and the horn was not mounted on the steering wheel boss.

The driving position deserved every bit of praise it received. The angle of the seat back could be adjusted, and the leather-bound steering wheel provided a comfortable grip. The diameter of the steering wheel had been reduced because of the new power steering. The height adjustment on the steering column was as welcome as ever.

Moving down to floor level, despite the passing years, any prospect of 'heel-toe' driving was out of the question. But then, you could not expect Sir William Lyons and his team to worry too much about such a relatively minor detail on their Series 3 E-type!

Now let me tell you what happens when you actually start

Fitted with a hard top, the Series 3 roadster offered all the advantages of the fixed-head E-type without taking away the joys of open-air motoring.

up a Series 3 V12 E-type. At the first request the 12 cylinders come to life with a soft purring noise, and warm up gently in the key of F-sharp until engine speed is about 1,000 rpm. When you have had enough of just sitting listening to this beautiful sound, you can press the accelerator pedal lightly a couple of times and you are rewarded by a leaping rev counter needle and a lovely throaty roar. It is not that nasty harsh noise that some V12s produce, but rather a muffled, pleasant rumble, as though coming from a soundproofed room. It is the noise of an engine which intends to give real performance and not just an impressively raunchy growl.

When you eventually get around to engaging first gear the car seems to take over, pulling you smoothly and decisively up to 50 mph (80 km/h). Next you pull the gear lever back and, before you know it, you are bowling along at 80 mph (130 km/h). Third takes you effortlessly to 105 mph (170 km/h), and from from there on it is up to you...

An illustration by Gordon Horner to celebrate the launch of the Series 3 E-types and the V12.

depress the accelerator gently and watch the speedometer needle climb inexorably round the dial: 120, 130, 140, 150...

Even before you reach 125 mph (200 km/h) you can hear the sound of the wind outside the car. Above that figure the noise is more that of a fighter aircraft's cockpit than of a plush saloon's luxurious interior. This is not a criticism of the car; on the contrary, you need to be reminded that you are travelling at a very high speed, otherwise you might think you are moving at a slower pace and this could lead to some dangerous errors of judgement.

As mentioned, thanks to the power steering Jaguar was able to reduce the diameter of the steering wheel, and the steering was also very responsive and direct: 3½ turns of the wheel took it from one lock to the other. Some sports car enthusiasts felt this was half a turn too much, but they made the mistake of believing that the Series 3 E-type had been designed for sports racing fanatics, and this just was not so!

The steering was agreeable, precise and predictable, not designed for the straight-arm brigade. Although Jaguar was renowned for its sports cars it no longer aimed its products exclusively at the sports market, but now included luxury-car connoisseurs and customers who wanted comfort and performance. The imaginary purchaser of a Series 3 E-type was a man who wanted to add a little excitement to his life while still enjoying the comfort and luxury of a large saloon; a man who wanted to turn people's heads, to take pleasure in driving an unbelievably handsome car, to have fun without taking any risks.

Come to that, every car in the E-type range was aimed at a totally different market from that of the Ferraris and Lamborghinis. Their performance was different, their prices were definitely not comparable, they had a different 'style', and their owners had different criteria when purchasing a car.

The Series 3 E-type weighed round about one and a half tons and, happily, this was no problem for the V12 engine. In a Series 3 E-type you often forget the power at your disposal — the engine is like a tamed wild cat — until you find yourself accelerating in top gear from ludicrously low speeds and you begin to realise what it is all about.

At cruising speed, around 105-110 mph (170-180 km/h), you can almost hear a pin drop inside the car, and the quietest passage from your favourite Mozart concerto can be savoured without intrusive noise.

The Series 3 was not such an aerodynamically successful car as the previous two models. This increased wind resistance goes a long way to explain why the E-type's top speed had not improved since 1961. But, yet again, I must underline the fact that the factory was not looking for a record-breaking 'rocket'.

Jaguar had been forced to make many compromises when they designed this car and the end result would never have made motor racing history in the classic events — it was never intended as a racing car, after all.

Although the laid-back Series 3 E-type did not join the racing fray, it had a heart of gold, being well behaved, responsive, and sticking to the road like glue. It did, however, give some cause for concern on very bumpy roads or in strong side winds.

To be more explicit: on bad road surfaces the car

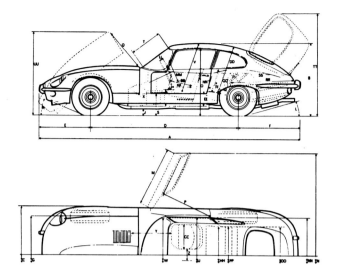

DIMENSIONS — FIXED HEAD COUPÉ

		Ins.	Cms.
A	Overall length	184.4	468.4
B	Overall height	51.4	130.6
C	Overall width	66.1	167.8
D	Wheelbase	105.0	266.7
E	Front overhang	36.3	92.0
F	Rear overhang	43.13	109.5
G	Front track	54.25	138.0
H	Rear track	53.25	135.3
J	Ground clearance—unladen	5.9	15.0
	—laden	5.4	13.7
K	Front clearance angle	21°	
L	Rear clearance angle	15°	
M	Door opening width	40.5	102.9
N	Overall width doors open	134.0	340.4
O	Ground to top of door	46.5	118.1
P	Door open aperture	35.0	88.9
Q	Bonnet aperture	33.7	85.7
R	Rear door aperture	28.0	71.1
S	Door step height	16.0	40.6
T	Windscreen depth	28.25	71.7
U	Shoulder room	49.0	124.5
V	Front headroom	35.5	90.2
W	Windscreen width (mean)	49.0	124.5
X	Pedals to cushion	19.75	50.2
Y	Front bulkhead to seat cushion	28.5	72.87
Z	Width between seats	9.0	22.9
AA	Front seat height	10.25	26.0
BB	Front seat depth	18.5	47.0
CC	Front seat width	17.8	45.3
DD	Rear headroom	33.0	83.8
EE	Rear seat height	10.0	25.4
FF	Rear seat depth	14.0	35.6
GG	Height of rear seat squab	17.0	43.2
HH	Width of rear seat squab (Min)	39.0	99.1
JJ	Steering wheel to cushion	8.6	21.9
KK	Steering wheel to seat squab	20	50.8
LL	Steering wheel reach adjustment	15	38.1
MM	Steering wheel diameter	2.75	5.7
NN	Rear knee room	7.5	19.1
OO	Maximum boot width	39.0	99.1
PP	Minimum boot width	36.0	91.4
QQ	Maximum boot length	52.5	133.4
RR	Minimum boot length	42.0	106.7
SS	Boot capacity	8-11 cu.ft.	0.22-0.31 cu.m.
TT	Maximum height boot open	72.5	184.1
UU	Maximum height bonnet open	58.3	148.0

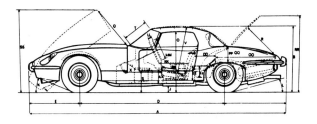

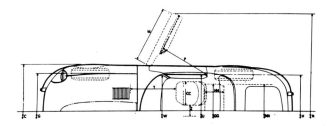

DIMENSIONS — ROADSTER

		Ins.	Cms.
A	Overall length	184.4	468.4
B	Overall height	48.4	122.6
C	Overall width	66.1	167.8
D	Wheelbase	105.0	266.7
E	Front overhang	36.3	92.0
F	Rear overhang	43.1	109.5
G	Front track	54.25	138.0
H	Rear track	53.25	135.3
J	Ground clearance — unladen	5.9	15.0
	— laden	5.4	13.7
K	Front clearance angle	21°	
L	Rear clearance angle	15°	
M	Door opening width	40.5	102.9
N	Overall width doors open	134.0	310.4
O	Ground to top of door	43.0	109.2
P	Door open aperture	35.0	88.9
Q	Bonnet open aperture	33.7	85.7
R	Boot open aperture	29	73.7
S	Door step height	16	40.6
T	Windscreen depth	19.2	48.8
U	Shoulder room	49.5	125.8
V	Headroom	33.0	83.8
W	Windscreen width (mean)	50.0	127.0
X	Pedals to cushion	22.3	56.5
Y	Front bulkhead to seat cushion	31.8	82.0
Z	Width between seats	9.0	22.9
AA	Seat height	11.0	27.9
BB	Seat depth	18.5	47.0
CC	Seat width	17.8	45.3
DD	Seat back to rear bulkhead	15.8	40.0
EE	Rear parcel box height	21.5	31.8
FF	Maximum rear parcel box depth	8	20.3
GG	Rear parcel box length	38.3	97.1
HH	Rear parcel box width	15.5	39.4
JJ	Steering wheel to seat cushion	8.6	21.9
KK	Steering wheel to seat squab	22.8	57.8
LL	Steering wheel reach adjustment	2.8	5.7
MM	Steering wheel diameter	15.0	38.1
NN	Maximum boot width	39.0	99.1
OO	Maximum boot length	41.0	104.1
PP	Maximum boot depth	10.3	25.0
QQ	Cubic capacity of boot	4.75	0.133
		cu.ft.	cu.m.
RR	Maximum height boot open	56.1	142.7
SS	Maximum height boot open	58.3	148.0

behaved rather oddly, wandering about a bit and floating up and down. This idiosyncracy was easy enough to cope with, but it did mean that you could not afford to relax your grip on the wheel, or let your mind wander either. On wet surfaces (as with any other car) you had to be a little more gentle and precise in wheel movements and braking.

Oh yes, the brakes. They still left room for improvement; after prolonged use the pedal travel would lengthen considerably and this was reflected in braking distances. Fortunately, provided you were given the occasional stretch of straight road and could let the brakes take a breather, they soon regained their usual efficiency.

With this proviso, only gentle pressure was needed on the pedal when the brakes were at full power, and as long as you treated them kindly they would never let you down.

However, you are probably still wondering why the Series 3 E-type was not raced more often. It may well have been because its large displacement put it in a category which was already overcrowded with purpose-built racing cars. That's as good a reason as any, I suppose.

Whatever the case, the Series 3 was the last of the E-type generation. It might even never have existed if the works had been ready with the F-type when V12 development had finished.

In the autumn of 1972, on 6 September, the Jaguar management breathed a sigh of relief at the ending of the longest strike in the company's history. It had been going on for 11 weeks, 6,500 cars (mostly earmarked for export to the United States) had been lost, and it even looked as though the last Jaguar car had been produced. The financial losses were catastrophic and Lord Stokes, the head of what was now British Leyland, went so far as to wonder whether it was worth bailing Jaguar out.

Engrossed in the launch of the new XJ12 saloons, Jaguar had too much on its hands to be bothered with the XJ-S. The preceding year, 1971, had been a boom year for the company, but the memory of it now left a bitter taste in the board's mouth, despite the 32,589 Jaguars and Daimlers which had been sold during those 12 months and which were serving as ambassadors of the British motoring industry in all four corners of the globe.

The 1972 strike was all the more devastating in that the year marked the 50th anniversary of the 'Swallow' company as well as the retirement of Sir William, who handed over the reins to F.R.W. 'Lofty' England.

In February 1975 the E-type was at last laid to rest, much to the disappointment of its many admirers. Nevertheless, the E-type would live on as one of the symbols of those crazy, swinging '60s.

It had been one of Lyons' favourite babies, but by 1975 it had become an outmoded, unaffordable luxury. The E-type's disappearance was inevitable, for between 1967 and 1975 there had been the war in the Sinai, embargoes on oil and petroleum products, the energy and raw material crises, stricter safety regulations, the rise of ecology as a 'today' science... those nine years might as well have been 900, for the social climate for such cars as the E-type had changed from sunny to ice-cold.

Every time you see an E-type you are probably reminded of that other world, a carefree, egotistical age when anything seemed possible, such was the industrial euphoria, and the sky was the limit in automobile development.

The dashboard of a Series 3 roadster with all the necessary specifications for the US market, including air conditioning, of course!

The E-type's demise was inevitable also because of its styling; what had looked like a dream-car in 1961 had become old hat in the 1970s. The time for sleek, rounded rockets was over, and the angular designs of the Italian school were in favour, with Bertone as its master... witness the Pirana.

The E-type was doomed also because it was so ill-suited to the new obsession among car manufacturers (apart from cost-effectiveness, that is) — that of safety, both active and passive. A really safe car is not made so by adding something here and taking something away there in piecemeal fashion. Safety must be incorporated right from the start, before so much as the smallest part of the structure has been produced.

And then again, the E-type could not have survived longer for, unless they kept up to date, the Jaguar team would soon lose its reputation for producing motoring sen-

sations. The XK range had lasted 13 years, and the E-type was now 14 years old, so it was high time that a replacement Jaguar was produced.

The final death-blow was delivered by the Americans. They, who so loved the E-type, killed it off with an overdose of regulations, as surely as if they had mined the assembly lines. So it was goodbye to the E-type, but goodbye also to the genuine open two-seater with nothing between you and the sky but your windblown hair. Picture, if you can, an E-type roadster complete with a Porsche Targa-type roll-bar... not a pretty sight!

The E-type had become a legend in its own time and, when the very last roadster rolled off the line at four o'clock on the afternoon of 12 February 1975, a heavy silence fell over the factory. Production of the fixed-head coupé had stopped in September 1973, and only the roadster remained in the catalogue. To lend added weight to the importance of this event, the last 50 E-types were painted black, with right-hand drive, chromed wire wheels and a little plaque on the dashboard signed 'W.Lyons'. Jaguar's marketing lads had turned up trumps again! There was one exception to this mourning attire: the great Jaguar collector

ge 337
1954 Series 1 4.2-litre E-type.
*lou, a '60s pop singer, with the very first 3.8-litre E-type
ench import (April 1961).

ges 338, 339
om left to right:
K 150 drop-head coupé.
type 3.8-litre fixed-head coupé.
K 140 fixed-head coupé.

ges 340, 341
1961 3.8-litre open two-seater E-type.
wner: Michel Cognet.

ges 342, 343
1963 3.8-litre E-type fixed-head coupé.
wner: Hubert Maechler.

ges 344, 345
e same car with, on the left, the bonnet open to reveal the
ecial-equipment Weber carburettors.

Pages 346, 347
A 1971 Series 3 E-type V12 2 + 2 fixed-head coupé.
Owner: Max Demagny.

Pages 348, 349
A 1971 Series 3 E-type V12 open two-seater with automatic
transmission.

Pages 350, 351
From left to right, and top to bottom:
A 1982 'E' version XJ-S (US model).
Back view of a very early 1975 XJ-S.
The XJ-S in its 'TWR' incarnation competing for the 1982
European production car championship.
An XJ-S dashboard.
The TWR XJ-S in action.
The V12 engine of the XJ-S HE.
The rebuilt XJ13.

140 KA 62

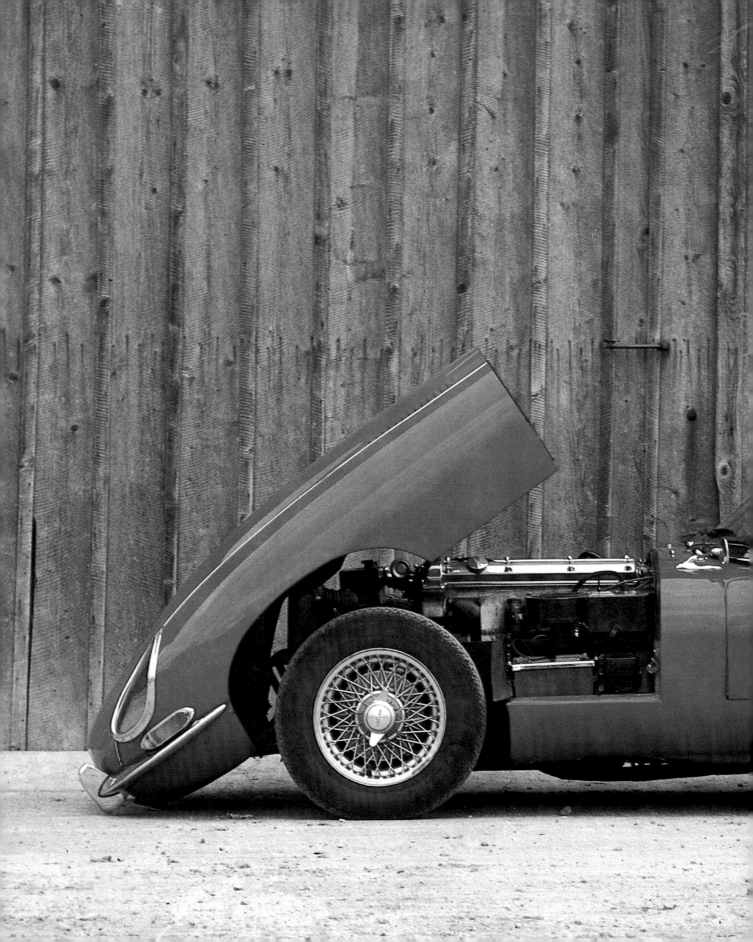

The V12 badge on the back is the envy of many Jaguar enthusiasts. Happily, the wrapping is as good as the powerful present inside!

Robert Danny rather unsportingly asked for his to be finished in dark green.

As for the very last E-type, it was to be preserved like a holy relic in the works' collection, where it still holds pride of place in the Browns Lane foyer, alongside a bright yellow Series 1½ E-type.

This last Series 3 E-type is probably the best conserved in the world, and it bears the famous chassis number IS 2872. Take note of that number, because you may come across some prettied-up examples which lay claim to higher chassis numbers than this!

Geoffrey Robinson, Jaguar's managing director, must have passed by this museum E-type countless times in 1975, but his thoughts were elsewhere. He was looking to the future not the past (however glorious that may have been) for, as a pragmatic businessman, he had had some say in extending the E-type's lifespan and delaying the appearance of its replacement — the XJ-S.

When Geoffrey Robinson took over the top executive job at Jaguar in 1973 he put aside all thoughts of a new model until he could be sure that Jaguar cars had regained their old reputation for reliability. This reputation had taken a few blows over the preceding few years, not because of poor Jaguar workmanship but because of flaws in the sub-contracted elements.

One of his first self-appointed tasks was to go over all the saloons with a magnifying glass, looking at every tiny accessory in order to reach objective conclusions about where the defects lay and to remedy them. This mammoth job took a very long time and it was due to this ruthless attention to detail that the XJ-S did not see the light of day until 1975.

A radical revision of pricing policies also dates from this time. British Leyland was determined to trade profitably and the new Jaguar therefore had to be sold at a realistic price. This was far from being the case with the Series 3 E-type for it had been scarcely more expensive than the Series 2 4.2-litre and, considering its V12 engine, it had been a genuine bargain!

Retailing at £3,139 the Series 3 V12 roadster had been a snip compared with the other sports car greats: Aston Martin's DBS V8 would have cost you more than double; a Maserati Ghibli could have paid for two E-types; and you could have bought two E-types less the odd bumper or two for the price of a Ferrari 365 GT84, a Lamborghini Miura or Jarama, or a Jensen Interceptor J. You might almost have thought your E-type had fallen off the back of a lorry!

But the Series 3 E-type was the last Jaguar bargain to be had, and when production stopped a new chapter started in Jaguar's history. Many aspects of factory life would never be the same again: production was cut back drastically; the world recession began to bite deep; the British automobile industry as a whole had fallen on bad times; BL dragged Jaguar into its internal problems and mass lay-offs and redundancies began to affect Browns Lane.

For a time it looked as though Jaguar's style of car had had its day. The general pessimism sapped executive energy, and Jaguar could not extricate itself from the problems of the group, however much it wanted to stay on the sidelines, both for the sake of the marque image and in an attempt to keep itself unsullied by what it saw as BL's rather decadent connotations.

Behind B. Tullius' Series 3 E-type is a black roadster with the option hard top: the very last E-type built has been kept by Jaguar (chassis number 2872).

Bottom left: Although the Series 3 E-type was rarely raced in Europe, it was a frequent sight in American events. Bob Tullius, the enthusiastic American who created the famous Group 44, achieved some remarkable wins in his very special Series 3 V12s on all the West Coast hill-climb courses. In the background are a Series 2 E-type, a short-nose D-type, and an XK 120 open two-seater.

Cockpit of B. Tullius' very special Series 3 V12.

The factory counted on the demand for XJ12 saloons to keep its production lines going, but also on the new model which it hoped would keep the leaping jaguar marque in the news — the XJ-S just *had* to be a winner, or else!

F.R.W. 'Lofty' England occupied the managing director's chair for just two years before opting for a well-earned retirement in 1974. Lord Stokes appointed Geoffrey Robinson as his successor, but the new managing director could stand the heat for only one year; he was basically a political animal and he soon returned to the political fold.

Meanwhile BL was making headlines in all the nationals, but not because of any sensational new cars. It was announced that British Leyland had been nationalised, and Lord Stokes was free to return to his beloved research.

All in all it was a glum time; the veterans of the glorious XK and E-type campaigns were growing old and most of them had retired already. You know them all by now: William Heynes, Claude Baily, Walter Hassan, Harry Mundy, 'Lofty' England and, of course, Sir William Lyons.

Their last joint effort had been the V12, and they had quietly left the stage.

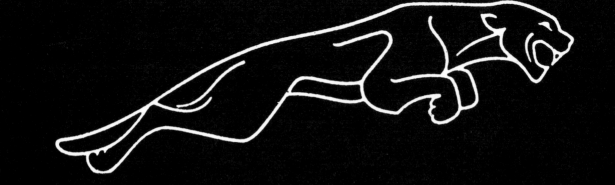

The XJ Generation

THE XJ-S

10 SEPTEMBER 1975—STILL IN PRODUCTION

INDISPUTABLY A JAGUAR

The Jaguar marque is still alive, it is even flourishing, despite the worldwide economic problems of the past few years. The XJ-S is also still alive and flourishing, and the fact that it is still in production means that it is on a par with the great E-types and the XKs. It differs from those two in that we can go out and buy a new one today — if we have the money — and judge it by modern standards.

When I read a full test report on the XK 150 I always have the feeling that I am reading about some memento of a bygone age and my judgement is therefore coloured by the indulgence with which we treat ancient inventions. The XJ-S is another kettle of fish. It will not get the rose-coloured-spectacles treatment, for it has no right to the automatic respect accorded to anything that is old and therefore treasured.

The XJ-S marked the beginning of a new era at Jaguar; it inaugurated the post-Lyons period, a time of cut-backs and of realistic pricing. In that respect the customers felt the effect, for the XJ-S is the most expensive car that Browns Lane has ever produced. When the new car was launched you would have searched the reviews in vain for that old headline: 'How on earth does that man manage to sell such a car at such a low price?' There were even some complaints that it was overpriced!

The XJ-S burst on to the motoring scene three years late, since it should have been launched at the same time as the V12 engine. The reason for this considerable delay is that

Jaguar had undergone a management transformation, and there were many top-level changes. Geoffrey Robinson had nailed his colours to the mast when he took over the top job: reliability and consolidation were to take preference over development and, before the engineers could have fun on the XJ 27 project, they first had to go over the fixed-head coupés and XJ saloons with a fine tooth-comb to eradicate any flaws and weaknesses. It was vital that Jaguar should keep its impressive reputation for reliability untarnished by those annoying little mechanical defects and break-downs.

Although the XJ-S was not announced until the autumn of 1975, its development had begun six years before, in the days when William Lyons was still running the show, and this is why his hallmark can be seen on many of the XJ-S' features. In most respects it is a Jaguar from road to roof, and the final link in the chain which had begun ten years before with the 2 + 2 E-type. Is the XJ-S a two-door fixed-head coupé version of the 5.3-litre XJ saloon, or is it a sports car — the long-awaited successor to the beloved E-type?

Anyone who expected a 5.3-litre XJ mutant dripping with luxury and comfort is probably still waiting, while the customer who was hoping for a super-E which would be king of the fast sports cars is still waiting patiently, too. So who was the XJ-S meant to please? What was the army of development engineers aiming at when they sat down at

There is no mistaking it for anything other than a Jaguar: the aggressive nose and aerodynamic line bear witness to the fact that Jaguar are the masters of the aristocratic British sports car.

their drawing boards to begin work on what was baptised the XJ 27 project? Was the XJ-S originally intended to be the F-type?

As usual, America was the target market for the new car, and the increasingly constricting safety regulations modified the original design beyond recognition within the space of a few months. Evolution of the final design was also influenced by the phenomenally successful XJ6 and XJ12 saloons, sales of which had made 1971 a record year for Jaguar Cars Ltd. Although Anglo-American relations were not quite as passionate as they had been in the immediate post-war years, more than 75 per cent of sales were still being made in the United States, so Browns Lane owed its transatlantic customers some consideration! That is probably putting it too mildly; the US Federal Safety Regulations were like a bible for Jaguar, and I should not

be surprised if every employee had to recite them by heart before he was allowed into the factory each morning!

Here is just one indication of the fact that the XJ-S had to be more than just a redesigned E-type: just try reversing an E-type into a concrete wall at 30 mph (48 km/h) without fracturing the petrol tank! That was just one of the exacting standards which the new car had to meet.

The press launch in France did not create much of a stir. The journalists found the XJ-S aristocratic, felt it looked sporty enough and that it had the old Jaguar magic, but they were not moved to the purple prose they had produced in 1961 when the E-type had made its début in Geneva. This comparative lack of enthusiasm may be explained by the switch away from dream cars to sensible cars, following the energy crisis. Anyway, the crowd of journalists who attended the launch frowned at the sight of the massive

The XJ-S is in remarkable contrast to the academic old-world background of an Oxford college. The Browns Lane publicity department knew what they were doing when they set up this shot!

bumpers, criticised the too high waistline, the too small windows, the poorly integrated front spoiler, the flat rear-window design, slightly outdated styling and, most of all, the lack of that spark of genius which had been present in most of Jaguar's past productions. They did not mince their words.

Once the journalists realised that safety had been the main criterion in the car's design, they began to understand the reason for some of its less appealing features and made allowances for them.

The XJ-S is so crammed with safety features that its specifications read like an accident-prevention handbook, or rather it is like an up-market showcase for some of the most sophisticated methods of passenger-protection. A few examples will suffice to show what I mean: extra-thickness doors with recessed levers; petrol tank sited between the boot and the seats, just above the rear wheels; an automatic cut-out which stops the electric fuel pump when a sensor registers an impact force higher than 3 gs — a fire prevention measure; telescopic rubber bumpers capable of withstanding 5 mph (8 km/h) collisions. This last is an extremely complex feature which, taken alone, shows the very advanced technology which was needed to satisfy the very demanding low-speed impact regulations. A Menasco strut works on a sort of telescopic shock absorber in which the 'fluid' consists of silicone wax. This wax is forced past the piston in the strut on impact. Silicone wax is used because of its miraculous properties, in that it can absorb kinetic energy and transform it into heat which, of course, softens the wax so that the shock can be absorbed. Within half an hour the wax has cooled and solidified, forcing the strut

(and therefore the bumper) back to its original position. Ah, the wonders of modern technology!

Of course, I have mentioned only the peripheral safety factors, for the rest were incorporated into the brakes, dashboard, steering wheel... you name it, it was as safe as houses!

If the XJ-S' outer covering did not exactly send reviewers into a state of ecstasy, what was underneath met with their heartfelt approval. It led Pierre-François Rousselot to head his piece in *L'Auto-Hebdo* 'More sporting than it looks'. The XJ-S kept its royal flush well hidden by its 33.1 hundredweight (1,700 kilos) and its automatic transmission. Why don't we take a closer look?

Very little had changed at the back of the car since the first E-type's day, bar a few detail improvements in the suspension. The broad outline of the suspension was the same, with identical springs, shock absorbers and the same drive shafts acting as upper links, but an anti-roll bar had been introduced. The final arrangement produced the most effective rear suspension any Jaguar had ever had.

Moving to the front of the car, the most important component was of course the V12 engine which had previously been fitted to the Series 3 E-type and the 5.3-litre XJ. It was the same V12 which had been universally acclaimed and which had turned the Mark X saloon (fitted experimentally with the V12 back in the 1960s) into a 150 mph (240 km/h) four-doored super-beast.

Jaguar's promotional material for the XJ-S announced it as one of the quietest cars in the world, and this was no exaggeration. The almost unearthly silence which reigns inside the car makes the rev counter indispensable, for otherwise you might be tempted to have a second go at starting the engine, without realising that it is already running!

The engine is so smooth at idling speed that you get not the slightest physical sign that anything at all is happening under the bonnet. There is no vibration whatsoever — you cannot even feel anything through your fingers if you rest them on the steering wheel; it is really quite eerie.

The only significant difference in the V12 was the engine's positioning. There was reason to expect that the XJ-S would be a mid-engine car, but no, the 12-cylindered unit was conventionally placed amidships in the front of the car. Truth to tell, Jaguar had never seriously thought of producing a mid-engined sports or GT car for road use. Any advantages in roadholding would have been more than offset by the lack of passenger space and noisiness of such an arrangement. A central engine may look attractively symmetrical on paper but it is not, surprisingly, of much help in improving weight distribution — odd though this may seem. There was a vogue for mid-engined cars from about 1968 to 1975, but it fizzled out and constructors returned to the more conventional front or rear locations.

The XJ-S was announced in fixed-head body style only, since at one stage in the car's development it had looked as though the Americans might introduce a ban on open cars, in the interests of safety. Even without the ban — which never materialised — the prospect of meeting all the safety requirements on a roadster looked likely to make a complete mess of any such version of the XJ-S.

With an overall length of 15 feet 4 inches (4.67 metres), the XJ-S' wheelbase was some 7 inches (18 cms) shorter than the short-wheelbase XJ6 saloon's; track was almost identical, and the general design of the monocoque structure was the same as on the earlier saloon. More important were the safety features incorporated in the design, including the thick doors and the petrol tank protection. The XJ-S' structure was extremely robust and its rigidity was never in doubt.

There had been some complaints about the steering on the Series 3 E-types and XJ saloons, namely that the steering was too light, felt woolly, and that this feeling of loss of

It is hardly credible that only 20 years separate these two Jaguars: the 1955 XK 140 and the 1975 XJ-S. The latter was the first of its kind imported into France.

The original series XJ-S; the design of the back end is to some extent a joint effort by Malcolm Sayer, who died in 1970 (he led the original aerodynamic research), and the Italian coachbuilder Vignale, who finished the task and produced this very original body.

contact could be dangerous at high speeds. The factory responded by firming up the power assistance with a reduction in the ratio. This produced the added bonuses of increased precision and a quicker response.

The XJ-S' front suspension copied the thoroughly tried and tested geometry of the Series 3 E-type and the saloons, with that ingenious anti-dive device to prevent the car's nose biting the dust during emergency stops. A stronger anti-roll bar than had been used on the E gave better stability.

The braking system on the front consisted of ventilated discs and four pistons fitted with the usual pads, and on the rear it was the traditional disc arrangement with twin pistons. It must be admitted that the brakes were still not as good as one had a right to expect from a 33-hundredweight car capable of at least 150 mph (240 km/h)... and with no engine braking capacity to speak of in the automatic transmission version. I shall not go on any longer on this touchy subject, except to say that the brakes could have been more durable.

Mix all these ingredients together and you have the most outstanding Jaguar sports car ever with regard to suspension, roadholding, weight distribution, handling and performance. If, as a garnish, you give it four Dunlop tyres which were produced specially for the car, you find yourself driving at 150 mph without the slightest qualm.

Then again, if you are very choosy, you could fit Michelin VR XWXs with even better results, and I swear that I am not saying that just because I am French!

Kent Alloy supplied the standard wheels — the ones which had previously been optional extras on the XJ 5.3-litre saloons. Wire wheel fans were not disappointed, however, as these were offered as an option. After all, some people feel that a Jaguar sports car does not deserve the name if it has not got wire wheels.

The inside of the car was handsome, restrained, welcoming, and had that traditional British luxury car feeling, though the 'luxury' aspect might have been toned down a bit since the old days; there was a marked shortage of wood veneer, a little less leather... and a bit too much plastic. Oh, for the good old days before synthetics were the exception rather than the rule!

The dashboard's appearance and contents were rather disappointing for a car of that class and, more especially, of that price. For example in 1975, when an XJ-S would have set you back £8,900, for the same price you could have bought a Mercedes 450 SLC; another £4,000 or £5,000 would have been enough for a Maserati Indy, Lamborghini Espada or Ferrari 365 GTB.

There is no doubt about it, the XJ-S' instrumentation was a real let-down. Nothing was missing, but it was all presented in such a tasteless fashion, topped by a sheet of transparent plastic which was unbreakable, non-reflective, and a nonentity come to that! It was really vulgar and unattractive. As far as the instruments were concerned, the speedometer was graduated up to 160 mph (260 km/h), the rev counter up to 7,000 with a red sector above 6,500 rpm. Between these two dials were vertical indicators for water temperature, petrol, oil pressure and battery condition, which gave the dashboard a rather plebeian look. They were more the sort of things you would buy from a discount catalogue. These indicators were controlled by variation in

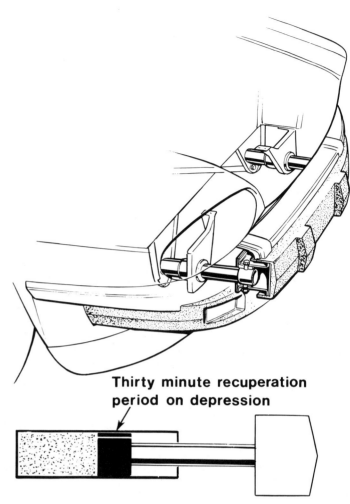

Thirty minute recuperation period on depression

The impact-absorbing bumpers which could take head-on blows at speeds of up to 5 mph (8 km/h). The detail drawing shows the wax-filled Menasco strut.

Top right: A mechanic's nightmare... this is the mind-boggling assembly which will confront him when he lifts up the bonnet. The fuel-injection V12 is a masterpiece of mechanical and electronic technology.

Drawing of a weird and wonderful V12, produced for research purposes only. The left half of the engine has carburettors (as on the E-type's V12) and the right has fuel injection, the eventual choice for the XJ-S.

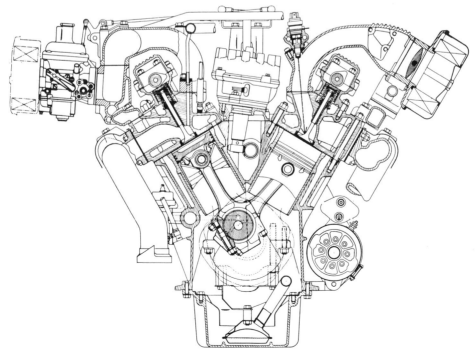

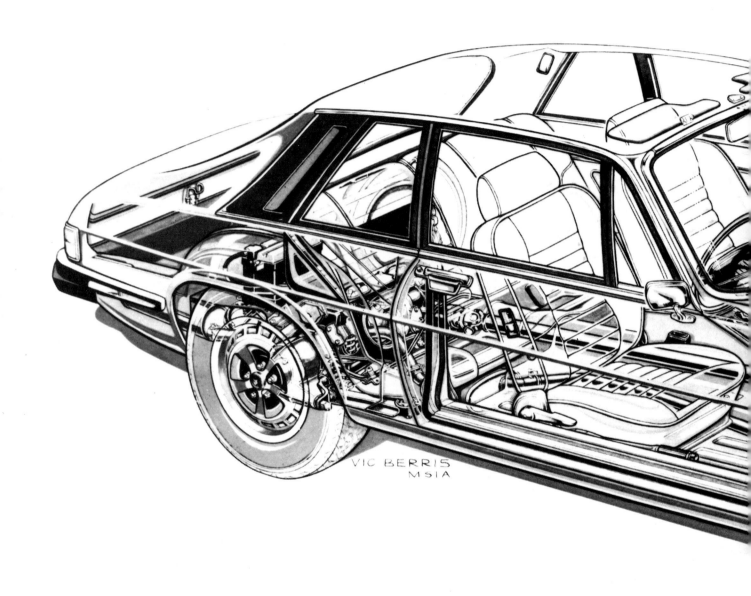

VIC BERRIS
MSIA

A Vic Berris drawing which commemorated the new
Coventry sports car: the XJ-S.

a magnetic field between two opposing coils, which made for an astonishing degree of accuracy.

There was an abundance of warning lights which kept the driver up to date with any malfunctions and the state of play under the bonnet and elsewhere in the car. There were 18 to be precise: red when there was a 'crisis', orange when there was cause for concern, and other bright colours to indicate different functions. These included hazard warning lights, headlights on, flasher indicators, gear selection, low oil pressure warning, alternator problems, low water level, low brake fluid, seat belt warning, low petrol, handbrake on, failure of a stop- or sidelight, rear window heater on, fog lamps on... you needed a map to find your way around, but at least they kept you company through long night drives!

There was nothing too revolutionary about the rest of the interior: inertia-reel seat belts; key-operated central door-locking system; electrically operated windows; heated rear window; superb air conditioning. The latter is especially impressive, as one would expect from a car aimed at the Americans! It is a Delanair system; you choose any temperature you wish between 18° and 30°C, keep the windows closed and within three minutes the car has been heated — or cooled — to the desired temperature, irrespective of the weather outside.

Of course, the nit-pickers managed to find some oversights: there was no oil level indicator, no lock on the petrol cap, no headlight wipers, and they felt the screen wiper

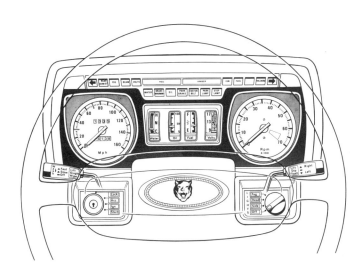

There is no manual gearbox option on the XJ-S. These works photographs show a beautifully designed passenger compartment including all the equipment a driver could possibly need.

speed was too slow. I am sure that the Jaguar development team, when they heard these criticisms, headed for the nearest short pier and took a long walk! There was so little to criticise that these complainants must have searched for hours to come up with this list! Somebody even grumbled about the fact that it took three or four turns to reset the trip-recorder.

One criticism which was valid was that of the seat design. Despite the thought that had obviously gone into them, the seats were not comfortable or supportive enough, and on long journeys one had to stop from time to time to massage the small of one's back. It is a great shame that such sumptuous seats, covered in perforated Connolly hides, should perform their function inadequately.

Before leaving this rather negative subject, I must add that the halogen Cibié headlights with their independent reflectors did not seem powerful enough for a car capable of more than 150 mph (240 km/h). The Americans, for some reason or other, vetoed these and had their own arrangement of two pairs of tungsten-bulb lights.

From the driver's seat there seemed to be some problems with visibility. The rear window was not particularly generous and there was a disturbingly large blind spot when looking over one's shoulder for overtaking vehicles or parking. The latter made town driving particularly hazardous unless one had a sound picture of the car's dimensions in one's mind. The restricted glass surface area also gave a distinct impression of gloom inside, especially when one was used to the airiness and light in other cars of the same-generation.

Noise suppression was one of Jaguar's main considerations and they used everything at their disposal to soundproof the XJ-S: carpeting, anti-vibration pads on the floor, thick insulation on the rear bulkhead; soundproofing materials incorporated here, there and everywhere; and no holes were drilled through the engine bulkhead for the dashboard wiring. The engine compartment itself was thoroughly insulated to prevent noise penetrating through to the passenger area; the silence was virtually complete. In this respect Jaguar had done a marvellous job and it was only at speeds in excess of about 110 mph (180 km/h) that any exterior sounds could be heard inside the car, and this was more through a slight deficiency in draughtproofing than through wind resistance. Surprisingly, despite the XJ-S' comparatively broad, angular nose, it had a more aerodynamic design than the E-type, so that its coefficient of air penetration was actually much lower.

The original wind tunnel tests were carried out by Malcolm Sayer, who had been responsible for the C-type, D-type and E-type bodies, but the final styling was the work of the famous coachbuilder Vignale, owing to Malcolm Sayer's death in 1970.

The XJ-S' body broke with the Jaguar tradition of provocative styling in favour of a more discreet and classy effect. It had gentle, rounded curves and the Jaguar trademark of a long bonnet, and that innate breeding which takes a while to appreciate. The XJ-S was meant for businessmen rather than flashy young men, as Jaguar themselves intended. They described the new car as one which everyone dreamed of owning, but which only a few could afford. There is no doubt that you had to be pretty well heeled to buy an XJ-S, for it cost more than three times as

much as the Series 1 E-type had in 1961 — and that is taking inflation into account. So the customer profile for the XJ-S was very different from the E-type's. The long and the short of it is that the XJ-S was not cast in a similar mould to the E-type and could not have been called the F-type without misleading potential customers.

If you are still sceptical, trot along to your nearest Jaguar dealer and sit in an XJ-S' rear seats; by no stretch of the imagination could they be called 'occasional'; a long trip in an XJ-S with its full complement of four passengers would never be the nightmare it was in one of the old 2 + 2s.

A choice of transmission was still available: either the three-speed automatic Borg-Warner or the manual Jaguar box. The latter was the same one which had been used ten years earlier on the 4.2-litre E-type. One wonders whether anyone ever specified the manual gearbox! In both cases, the final drive ratio of the good old Salisbury rear axle was the same 3.07:1. Manual transmission gave a slight advantage in top speed, whereas automatic provided better acceleration.

You have already met the V12 engine in the Series 3

E-type, so I shall merely provide a brief summary of its attributes: 5,343 cc, 12 cylinders in two banks of six set at an angle of 60 degrees to each other; seven-main-bearing crankshaft; one camshaft per cylinder; 90 mm bore, 70 mm stroke; 9:1 compression ratio; and — at last — electronic fuel injection. This was really the only possible supply system for such an engine and it had already served its time on the 5.3-litre XJ saloon with the same engine. The system chosen by Jaguar was originally patented by Bendix, developed further by Bosch, and had had its faults ironed out by Lucas for Jaguar. Why were carburettors unsuitable, you may ask? Well, it seems the answer is that fuel injection gives better fuel economy and flexibility. Only the electronic gadgetry of a fuel injection system can provide an accurately measured quantity of petrol in any given circumstance.

This fine V12 engine produced 285 bhp DIN at 5,500 rpm, with a phenomenal torque value of 294 lb/ft (41 m/kg) at 3,400 rpm. A power output comparison shows that the fuel-injection V12 produced 30 bhp more than the carburettored version used in the Series 3 E-type.

Jaguar's own petrol consumption figures indicated almost 13 mpg (16-18 litres per 100 kms). These figures were achievable, but you would have had to pootle along at 75 mph to do it, and life is too short and the XJ-S too fine a car for such half measures! If you drove the car hard, you would have been lucky to get 11 mpg (25 litres per 100 kms) out of it. So, you paid your money and...

The V12's torque is truly awesome. With so many ft/lb at your disposal you can virtually do what you like with this engine. Whether you are climbing into your XJ-S on a cold and frosty morning or have just been on a long drive through the Sahara desert, the engine starts up first time, smoothly and quietly. You let it warm up while you fasten your seat-belt, push the lever one notch backward so that the torque convertor is ready to go to work, then put your foot gently down on the accelerator pedal, sit back and wait for the car to take off.

And take off it does, in no uncertain fashion. The XJ-S is still an intoxicating car; it zooms you forward as if you are in a dream; the needles on the dials sweep round as if they could go on forever; the outside world drops away, any other cars on the road seem to be standing still. Within seven seconds you are doing 60 mph (97 km/h), the 100

Handsome, plush and welcoming, it seems a bit harsh to give these seats the rather dismissive epithet of 'occasional'.

The XJ-S has elongated Cibié headlights on European models. For the United States, these are replaced by twin headlamps with no fairings. This car exudes a striking aura of controlled power.

A stage in XJ-S assembly at the Castle Bromwich factory.

The trim shop (still at Browns Lane) has that indefinable 'haute couture' flavour, despite these computerised times. What is more, Jaguar still uses Connolly's top-quality hides as extravagantly as ever.

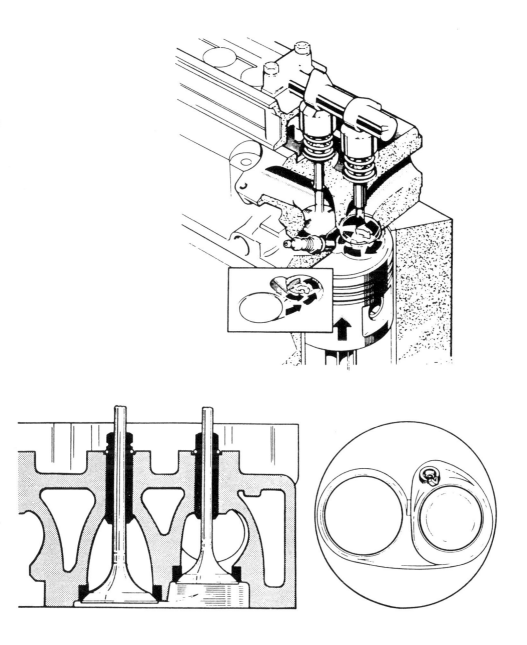

The HE cylinder head hinges on the new combustion chamber arrangement which gives improved combustion, thanks to the physical guidance of the mixture which produces much higher volumetric efficiency. The chamber consists of two zones: a small chamber under the inlet valve, which is connected by a narrow guidance channel with a larger chamber under the exhaust valve, where the spark plug is located. As the piston reaches the end of the compression stroke, the mixture is compressed in the hollow under the inlet valve and is then forced through the guidance channel, creating turbulence, into the real combustion chamber, at which point it is ignited by the spark. The high turbulence created by forcing the mixture from the small chamber into the larger one produces a much more homogenous mixture and, therefore, more uniform combustion. One of its principal advantages is that a weaker mixture can be used than would otherwise be the case.

mph (160 km/h) mark comes up less than ten seconds later and, while other drivers are still fumbling about for the gear lever to change up into second, you are bombing along at 125 mph (200 km/h), seemingly flying over the treetops, and wondering whether you can ever bear to come down to earth.

That is the V12 experience; the most fantastic grown-ups' toy that has ever been invented.

However, the XJ-S weighed in at 33.1 hundredweight (1,700 kilos) so it was a strictly earth-bound car, and it is difficult to think of it as a sports car in the true meaning of the words. Rather, it was a tamed wild animal wearing a luxurious but heavy coat, which could eat up the ground thanks to its amazing torque. In February 1976 the French journal *L'Auto-Hebdo* compared the XJ-S' torque with that of the most powerful contemporary Formula 1 racing cars; the XJ-S' torque value was more than 20 per cent higher! In second gear, with the engine turning over at only 1,000 rpm, the XJ-S could climb an 8-inch (20-cm) kerb-

The presence of the large 'HE' on the left of the boot shows that this car's engine is a real powerhouse. The famous 'Fireball' cylinder head entitled the XJ-S to its 'high efficiency' claim.

The brand-new wheel design and new bumpers enable one to identify an XJ-S HE at a glance. The other identifying features are hidden away inside.

stone without protest. Try that with your car some day, then you will realise the significance of a high torque value!

Roadholding was exemplary, behaviour eminently predictable, with either a slight understeer or a slight oversteer depending on the circumstances. These characteristics could easily be controlled, even at high speed on a tight, uncambered bend.

The XJ-S was such a good all-rounder that you always felt safe and secure at the wheel. There was no tendency to roll, and the ease and accuracy of the steering, together with such admirable roadholding, made it the king of the de-luxe grand touring cars.

All this praise must be tempered by one important criticism. With all that weight and hardly any engine braking in the automatic version, braking power — or the lack of it — reared its head once again in a Jaguar. There is no doubt that the XJ-S' Achilles heel was its brakes and their lack of staying power. I am tempted to say that Jaguar had a blind spot when it came to providing efficient brakes, despite the fact that it had been one of the first to introduce disc brakes

back in 1953. The evidence is there for all to see — just look at the E-type.

Pierre Rousselot, *Auto-Hebdo*'s road-tester, gave this account of his experiences at Montlhéry: "...The result was that, after one experimental lap (in other words I was travelling fairly slowly for about 9 kilometres (5.5 miles)) I had lost half my brakes and that, after one lap against the clock (in other words, a total of 18 kilometres (11 miles)), they still hadn't come back. From the safety angle this is rather worrying, because there are such things as 18-kilometre downhill roads and, even if the brakes did not give out completely there would inevitably be a large reduction in their efficiency. Jaguar's publicity department has repeated Aston Martin's claim of some years ago: the XJ-S can accelerate to 100 mph, then stop dead within 20 seconds. What they don't say is how many times the XJ-S can do this...''

Despite its few minor faults, and the one major defect, the XJ-S was a hit with the market at which it was aimed. That's what counts, after all. The lead time for delivery was

373

A new interior for the XJ-S HE. Jaguar felt that it was time to revive the tradition of using voluptuous wood dashboard and door casings. This step back in time gave a boost to the Jaguar tradition of aristocratic British sports cars.

frightening: Jaguar was turning out 60 XJ-Ss a week, but needed to produce 150 to meet the demand.

Although Lyons had planned a seven-year production lifespan for the XJ-S it is still in production today, so it is obvious that it is going to become a classic car. It is a much sought-after model, not as a second-hand working car but as a collector's item; it has what one might call its own 'fan club' which entitles it to the description 'superstar'.

As I write, I think back to the full-colour full-page advertisements which Jaguar inserted in the motoring magazines to publicise the XJ-S' launch. They showed a fiery red car with, below it, the simple words: '10 September 1975: a black day for Modena, Stuttgart and Turin.'

Five years later, in June 1981, there came a decisive step forward with the appearance of two extra letters on the back of the XJ-S — HE, for 'high efficiency'. This impressive chrome badge was not just a meaningless addition in an attempt to boost the model's sales, but a sure sign that Michael May had been at work.

In some ways, May is another Weslake; like the English cylinder-head magician, he has his own private laboratory and works strictly on a freelance basis for car manufacturers, without being under contract to any one of them. Michael May lives not far from Lausanne, in Switzerland, and he put in some hard work on the Jaguar V12 then reported back to Coventry. He supplied them with a thick file of his plans for a fantastic new head which would give improved performance with greater fuel economy... a manufacturer's dream!

May was by no means a beginner in the field for, apart from his impressive record as a motor-racing driver, he also had several more practical projects to his credit: a turbocharger for BMW and a high-output economy engine for the Ford Fiesta.

His new 'fireball' head worked on the principle of a very high compression ratio (12.5:1) combined with smaller exhaust valves and a special combustion chamber design which produced very high gas turbulence.

It is worth noting that, with its linear casting and its aligned parallel valves, the V12 head was the kind that any ambitious engineer dreamed of getting his hands on.

So how did Michael May get round the problem of spontaneous combustion with such a high compression ratio?

I shall try to explain. On the old cylinder head, if you compressed the mixture by 12.5:1 you had a 'diesel' mixture which would ignite as soon as the piston reached top dead centre, producing the kind of heat that would melt any piston crown which had not been designed to withstand such temperatures. In effect this would be a compression-ignition engine, where no spark is needed to ignite the fuel mixture, as opposed to the traditional internal combustion engine with which we — and Jaguar   are more familiar.

This is why your average car engine has spark plugs, for their purpose is to ignite the mixture just before the piston reaches this (top dead centre), so that the piston is not in a position of intertia at the crucial moment when the flame hits a very limited area of the piston's crown, because of the proximity of the spark to the piston.

If ignition occurs when the piston is at TDC it, and the valves, are under very intense fire and cannot stand such treatment for long! This, in fact, is what happens if you adjust your carburettors to provide too lean a mixture: the

Coming off the paint line, the XJ-S HE gets ready to be
fitted with what will make it into one of the fastest production cars in the world — its fuel-injection V12 engine. This
car is for export to America.

too-high temperatures produced during combustion have the same effect.

So, May's first problem was how to shift the ignited fuel as quickly as possible, so that the heat would be spread uniformly over the whole of the piston head. His solution is seen in the diagram on page   in which the arrows show the direction of gas turbulence. Tooling precision for these new heads was so vital that the company had to invest roughly half a million pounds in the installation of four new machines and a computerised milling machine.

This high compression ratio is synonymous with very high output, for it is well known that the more compressed the fuel mixture, the better it burns.

Another aspect of the design which is not to be sniffed at in these days of dwindling pocket-money is that you can use a very lean mixture and, consequently, the fuel injection system can be adjusted to provide less petrol. This is how it works out in hard petrol/air ratios. In an ordinary engine, this ratio lies somewhere between 12 to 15 parts of air to 1 of petrol. In an HE-head engine it can be as much as 23 parts of air to 1 of petrol.

If a leaner mixture means fuel economy, it also means problems with cold-starting and with combustion at certain engine speeds; Jaguar therefore had to ask Lucas for a high-tech ignition system with twin coils, electronic ignition and 'contact-less' distributor. Once this had been supplied, Jaguar was at last able to announce an XJ-S with a smaller appetite.

Here are a few figures for the statistics buffs: 300 genuine bhp; 155 mph (250 km/h); 302.5 lb/ft (44 m/kg) at just 3,000 rpm. What more could you want?

To make good use of the new power/torque curve, the final drive ratio went from 3.07:1 to 2.88:1, the highest ratio ever used on a series-production Jaguar. As it seemed obvious that owners would not know how to make the most of such impressive torque with a manual box, there was no manual option on offer and all the XJ-S HE were equipped with three-speed automatic transmission. The problems which might have arisen with manual transmission were wheelspin, rapid tyre wear and ignorance of how to cope with the rear-wheel drive on tricky surfaces, which could have proved mighty dangerous!

The fireball cylinder head was not the only new introduction in the 1981 JX-S HE. There was an even further improved Lucas-Bosch injection; new bumpers; new wheels; better brakes and new interior finish.

The XJ-S HE was the first new model under John Egan's chairmanship and he was determined that the car should have been tested to the limits to ensure reliability before it was offered to the Americans. He wanted the XJ-S HE to be perfect, because he saw it as the company's prestige four-wheeled shop window.

As for the works itself, John Egan wanted to put it back on a profitable footing through rationalisation and firm management. Fingers crossed, it seems as though his

Every car is given a 20-mile road test before delivery. This example is being checked before having its accessories fitted after the test drive.

policies are paying off, for the Americans have been taking all the Jaguars they can get in recent years.

During the gestation of the XJ-S back in the early 1970s, the American Authorities' vacillation over whether or not to ban convertibles outright prevented Jaguar from indulging any desire they might have had to provide an 'open' XJ-S.

Only latterly when the market potential became clear could Jaguar join an increasing band of European manufacturers and return to the manufacture of convertibles.

Jaguar's contribution to meet this trend was introduced in 1984: the XJSC. Not only did this cabriolet herald a return to a fine Jaguar tridition, providing sporting open-air motoring to its customers, but it also served as an introduction for the new all-aluminium six-cylinder AJ6 engine which is destined to power the first of a new generation of cars — the XJ40 saloon.

Some of the coachbuilding 'greats' have tried to outdo Jaguar with their rebodied XJ-Ss. These attempts have been made mostly by the Italians and the majority are simply styling exercises destined for exhibition at motor shows. This 'Spyder', designed and produced by the Pinin Farina house is a typical example.

XJ-S—TWR

Tom Walkinshaw is not a tyro in the world of automobile sport, and it is with good reason that his team bears his name: Tom Walkinshaw Racing, abbreviated to TWR.

Tom Walkinshaw and the XJ-S fell for each other and the relationship was blessed by John Egan himself, the chairman of Jaguar Cars Limited. The child of this marriage was known, naturally enough, as the XJ-S—TWR, and it showed the world that the concept of Jaguar as a racing marque was still very much alive.

It was in 1981 that Tom Walkinshaw had the idea of entering a race-tuned Jaguar in the new 'Group A', alongside BMW 528s, Audis, Alfetta GTV6s and Opel Monzas, to name but a few. In case you don't know, 'Group A' is a category for touring cars and it is one which attracts any manufacturer of cars with a sporting bias, for it is the best showcase in the world for his products. The regulations for this category stress that the cars should look just like the production models, and to all outward intents and purposes the automobiles which race in the European touring car championship events could have come virtually straight from the nearest traffic jam.

The manufacturer of the winning car reaps substantial commercial rewards, for potential customers, seeing what looks like an ordinary machine beat the rest of the world, turn into actual customers.

Of course, when it comes to the inside of the car, it is a different story. Where these engines are concerned, you're talking about 'hyper-performance'.

Tom Walkinshaw was not the first to want to race the XJ-S, which is unsurprising in view of that magic V12 engine. The XJ-S and Group A seem made for each other.

However, earlier experiments in this field (Broadspeed) did not attract much attention and were not renowned for their reliability. I am trying not to be too harsh, but this race-prepared version of the XJ-S was a flop because of lack of preparation and a too sophisticated approach.

So, when Tom Walkinshaw tried his idea out on various companies his proposals were received with polite bouts of throat-clearing and the odd sigh; no one was interested. Until he approached Motul, that is. They listened to him and, thanks to Chuck Nicholson's logistical support and the favourable reaction which came from Browns Lane, the TWR project began to take shape early in 1981.

Of course, the XJ-S' great problem, if you want to race it, is its weight — all 33 hundredweight of it. On the other hand, its most significant plus point is that V12 engine. Faced with those parameters, the way ahead seemed to be to give the V12 even more of a punch, to strip as much weight off as possible, and to improve the brakes so that you could be sure of stopping the car.

It seems simple enough in theory, but in practice it was somewhat tricky. Proof of this is that, as long ago as 1971, engineers were taking the V12 and trying to improve its performance, but they only succeeded at the expense of reliability.

This time was different, however. Tom Walkinshaw had signed an agreement with Jaguar which prohibited him from making any changes to the engine without the company's agreement. An identical clause was included to cover any problems with the engine; Tom had to notify the factory and was not to try any risky procedures without Jaguar's consent. Coventry's attitude is easily understandable. They wanted to cover themselves against any possibility of adverse publicity caused by carelessness. John Egan was not about to forget the Broadspeed XJ12 and its humiliating failure in 1977. This time a policy of 'sophistication at all costs' was out of the question and the watchword would be 'simplicity' instead. It was vital that any pit stops for repairs should be as short as possible, and a comprehensive supply of replacements parts on site was therefore imperative.

To return to the Group A category for a moment: it was an FIA introduction and the XJ-S, which qualified as of right for the old Group 1 (annual production of 5,000 plus), had to measure up to the new category's requirements. The most important regulation was that concerning weight/capacity; the lower weight limit was set at 1,400 kilos (27.5 hundredweight) for the XJ-S. The aim, therefore, was to slim down the XJ-S to as close to this limit as possible.

Another interesting aspect of Group A regulations is total freedom as far as the brakes are concerned. Tom Walkinshaw made full use of this and one of the most important introductions was in this area. The rear discs were no longer connected to the differential, but were sited in conventional fashion next to the wheels, which improved cooling. The brakes themselves were not as supplied on the standard XJ-S either. Tom Walkinshaw opted for big AP Lockheed calipers with huge 13-inch diameter and 35 mm-thick ventilated discs.

The BBS wheels were of magnesium alloy with dural rims, and consisted of three quick-release sections attached to the axle via a centre-lock hub, in Formula 1 style.

The centrepiece of this display — the V12 — had been simplified, ventilated and cured of the breathing problems which the emission programme had caused. It had more power, more torque and higher speeds.

The TWR experiment in the European championship may have been the beginning of a new official Jaguar racing programme. We can but hope!

XJS-TWR at Zolder. An impressive win... hopes of more... time will tell.

I should back up that statement with a few figures: 400 bhp compared with the original 300; 333.4 lb/ft (48.5 m/kg) compared with 294 (44); and 7,000 rpm compared with 6,000.

This was all produced by conventional means rather than by any secret new technology: new pistons, new high-lift camshafts, new connecting rods and modified fuel injection. And all without the slightest risk of a reduction in reliability!

As proof, I would draw your attention to Jaguar's record in the 11 events which make up the European touring car championship: five of the 11 were won by Jaguar, and the marque came second to BMW in the championship as a whole.

John Egan was bowled over by this performance and stated at Silverstone: 'I'm beginning to have great faith in it... this is one of the best days of my life.'

And, true enough, there is good reason to have faith in Jaguar's sporting renaissance; just read these 1982 results and you will see why the marque is showing more racing promise than it has for the last 25 years:

13 June 1982, European Touring Car Championship, Yugoslavia (Brno); First: Tom Walkinshaw/Chuck Nicholson.

27 June 1982, Austria; First: Tom Walkinshaw/Chuck Nicholson, second: P.Dieudonné/Jef Allam.

4 July, Germany (Nürburgring); First: Tom Walkinshaw/Chuck Nicholson.

12 September, England (Silverstone); First and second: Tom Walkinshaw/P.Dieudonné.

26 September, Zolder; First: Tom Walkinshaw, second: P.Dieudonné.

Time moves so slowly in the field of racing car development. Le Mans is a long way off yet and racing programmes are unbelievably expensive. We cannot bring back the past, but we can look forward to a future of Jaguar racing cars... perhaps.

One of the few Jaguar-engined single-seaters; Philippe Renault's HK Jaguar is set for a 400-metre dash. Alongside is a 600 cc Douglas motorcycle which took the world speed record in 1927 (Bugatti circuit, April 1973).

THE POWER HUNTERS

ONE CAN DREAM

Some motor racing enthusiasts will go to extraordinary lengths in an attempt to ginger up their engines, and all in the hope of an unattainable extra few miles per hour.

These power-hunters are a race apart and the results of their efforts more often make one shriek with fright than whistle with admiration. Give them their due — they add a little spice to life!

I can say without risk of contradiction that everything (or almost everything) has been tried in this field; Jaguar club newsletters from all parts of the globe are filled with hair-raising accounts of mechanical goings-on which are almost as crazy as the weird bodies which clothe these monstrous machines.

This fashion is as old as the XK generation itself for, almost before a new car had been run in, it was pounced upon by enthusiasts who could not let well alone. After four or five years, when the latest 'new' model was available on the second-hand market, increasingly outlandish modifications were effected to the poor engines, with every Tom, Dick or Harry thinking that he could do better than Lyons, Weslake and Heynes put together, and naively believing that he had come up with a completely original idea. Ignorance is bliss...

On the other hand, as well as these modified XKs' there were more sensible alterations to the standard XK, which were even of use to the Browns Lane team (this applies to

the liners for the 3.8-litre, fuel injection and oversized valves).

This 'mod' mania is as British as roast beef and one could write a sort of 'Jaguar Book of Records' on this subject alone.

The first, and most obvious, stage in modifying any car, and the one which any owner who is either a motor racing freak or a show-off can't wait to start, is the 'soup-up'.

Whether the approach to this operation is cautious, ambitious or hang-the-consequences, the improvement is minimal — if improvement there be. This applies to performance, top speed, torque and output, and the result is fairly likely to be a severe attack of engine failure. Anyone who has tried to emulate Harry Weslake has his own sob story to tell.

There is one basic premise which these searchers after 250 bhp from a 3.4-litre or 300 from a 3.8 do not seem to be aware of and that is that, whatever way you look at it, the XK unit's potential is limited both by its long stroke and its engine capacity. The factory always went as far as it could with its race-tuned engines without putting their reliability at risk, and there is no way that anyone could go further with safety. This is shown by the straight-port version of the XK unit in the XK 150S or the 3.8-litre E-type: 265 bhp was the ceiling. You will never wring any more out of the

XK without transforming your motoring outings into a series of infuriating and expensive breakdowns.

Since the XK engine's long stroke puts a limit on engine speeds because of the amazing linear speeds achieved by the pistons, it is not a good idea to go above 5,700 or 5,800 rpm — or perhaps 6,000 is feasible for a second or two — but above that you are really taking your engine's life in your own hands. All right, so there *have* been instances of cars which have survived higher speeds, but the exception proves the rule does it not? The case which everyone quotes is that of Tony Rolt who accidentally touched 8,000 rpm for a fraction of a second, and survived. But you must remember that his engine was so superbly balanced, with such excellent lubrication and top-end breathing that you really cannot compare it to a standard XK engine.

To produce additional horsepower you first have to improve the cylinder head breathing, on both the exhaust and induction sides.

The amount of fuel/air mixture breathed into the head is a direct function of the carburettor, the shape and diameter of the ports, the diameter of the valves and their seat angles, the shape of the cams which open the valves and, consequently, a function of the volumetric efficiency and the degree of vacuum created by the descent of the piston.

The most important part of the exhaust stroke is the speed with which the burnt gases can be discharged. The exhaust ports should therefore be as straight as possible, with a manifold consisting of gently curving pipes with no angular corners which might slow down the gases and, if possible, one exhaust pipe per cylinder to avoid the creation of turbulence which could have an adverse effect on cylinder re-charging during that vital moment when the valves 'cross', this enables induction to be accelerated thanks to the vacuum which is created on the opposite, exhaust, side.

Picking up the story where we left off, there is no doubt that all the carburation options have been covered — with or without superchargers. Enthusiasts set great store by the supercharger option with the SU carburettors which, of course, work on the 'constant vacuum' principle. We shall ignore the fuel injection option.

First of all there are the two 1¾-inch SUs with superfine needle, but you can also use three 1¾-inch SUs with a special manifold. Of course, I am not talking about the 2 H8 SUs which were originally produced for the C-type with a special inlet manifold, without which they would have no interest other than curiosity value, because of the too narrow passages in the standard pipe.

I shall spare you the three H8s option which some maniacs have tried out with a specially designed and cast manifold — a sort of early 'straight-port' design; I shall pass over the possibility of using two H10s, each with its own individual supercharger; and I shall not dwell on the two HD8s, used H8-style on the C-type heads and, with even more reason, on the three HD8 solution which is to the 3.8-litre what cream is to strawberries.

Some choosy enthusiasts have looked askance at Skinner Union's products and have opted instead for Italian Webers — either three 40DCOEs or 3 45DCOEs. An arrangement using two 50 DCO Webers is also possible if you use the special Oldham & Crowther pipe. Knowledgeable Jaguar men agree that this last shows a marked improvement on

Someone's idea of fun is this nightmarish monster based on an XK 120 chassis. There is no law against it, so why not?

No, this isn't 'Chitty-Chitty-Bang-Bang'. This astonishing car is an HWM belonging to the Jaguar enthusiast P.Lansard. HWM stands for Hersham and Walton Motors Ltd, managed by George Abecassis and John Heath. The car was fitted with Coventry's famous twin-cam unit.

any of the SU permutations. One notable supporter of the 50DCOs was John Heath who was the first to use this arrangement on his HWM in 1950.

If you like complexity, you might like to try Zenith-Strombergs, but this will lead to loss of horsepower, not gain.

Solex, the French carburettor manufacturer, has never come up with anything much in racing models, but you occasionally see a couple used with the 2.4-litre unit for economy reasons.

Some daring ex-motorcyclists have had a go with three Dell'Ortos, and you might find the odd photograph showing this set-up. As for using 6 AMALs, it is so difficult to get them all synchronised, that they are simply impracticable.

Supercharging via a centrifugal blower or turbocharging have always been fringe activities in the zany world of the power-hunters. However, in 1954, some Americans installed the massive Roots displacement blower in the radiator's traditional position, moving the radiator back into the luggage space.

Since the XK unit has a 'built-in' ceiling of 5,500 to 6,000 rpm, the only effect a supercharger would have is to smash the engine to pieces!

Petrol-injection is beyond the scope of most amateur mechanics, so I shall not dip into that hornets' nest!

If you want to go further than simply altering the carburettors, your next step is to take a look at the camshaft, for it is this which, by opening and closing the valves, indirectly feeds the fuel mixture into the cylinders.

Once again, it was racing development which brought about modifications to the height and shape of the cams. The lift on the 120 started out at 5/16 inch, and was increased to 3/8 inch on the competition C-type to provide improved volumetric efficiency. In theory, cam-lift cannot be much higher than 7/16 inch because, above that height, the pistons and valves act rather like castanets.

The cam profile is also a determining factor in valve timing and on the way the valve opens.

If the valve opens too early, the burned gases flow back towards the carburettor and impede the progress of the fresh mixture into the cylinder. If the valve opens late, the combustion chamber does not fill properly. The ideal point is at the valve 'overlap' stage, when there is a dynamic movement of the burnt mixture caused by the vacuum produced by the effect of the expanding burnt gases.

Since nothing is perfect in this world, you have to make a choice between flexibility and brute power. This is reflected in the choice of 'racing', 'road and racing' or 'full race' camshafts, depending on whether you want a longer overlap to improve performance at high engine speeds (but you lose out at low engine speeds, because all you will get is misfires and kangaroo hops), or whether you would prefer more flexibility in the middle range, in which case you have to sacrifice high-speed performance.

The perfect solution does exist, however, but it is a horrendously complicated system which frees the two camshafts and, through a vacuum-operated hydraulic device, enables you to have a variable overlap depending on engine speed. This system was devised by Bentley.

One last comment on camshafts. You can have various shapes: very or only slightly pointed, flattened with a little

point, rounded, etc. This is all worked out by a computer and, providing you have a solid engineering background, you can do almost what you like.

The inlet ports have a shape and a diameter (there's nothing like stating the obvious!). This passage from the carburettor to the valve opening plays a vital part in transporting the fresh mixture. If the port design is twisting and bending, you lose some of the momentum of the fuel/air mixture and the charge has to almost drag itself into the combustion chamber.

This prompts the question: 'How can you use only two carburettors on an in-line six-cylinder engine, where the gas has to travel such great distances?' This is a good question, because no two-carburettor solution can give a satisfactory result, since the inlet manifold design has to be very tortuous to connect with three valves.

Using three carburettors makes life much easier, since one carburettor per pair of cylinders means that the ports can be much straighter and can also be of identical length. This last is very important, for if gas has to travel along a longer port to reach its own particular cylinder, volumetric efficiency in that chamber is reduced. Engine modifiers who changed to Webers in 1952, or even earlier, can pat themselves on the head at this stage because they knew all about straight-port design!

One extra factor in improving gas flow to the cylinders: the interior surfaces of the inlet manifold should be smoothed and polished until there are no ridges which could slow down the fuel/air mixture.

Nowadays, if someone wants an immediate gain of 20 bhp or so in his 120, 140 or 150, all he needs do is to get hold of a cylinder head from a 3.8-litre E-type, 3.8-litre Mark X, or, even better, from a 420G, for the straight-port head in the E-types or 150s has one slight drawback: the three carburettors have to be perfectly balanced otherwise, if one of them is discharging a bit more or less than the other two, then the cylinder pair it feeds will be correspondingly sluggish. Because of this, if you own a 3.8-litre E-type, you have to make regular checks on the piston damper, the free linear movement of the piston, the needle adjustment, jet centering, synchronisation of the throttle-valves, and the exact balance of the fuel richness produced by each carburettor.

The 420G has a slightly improved induction pipe which comprises a manifold linking the three pairs, so that if one carburettor is out of kilter the gas is still shared out equally between the three pairs of cylinders. This system is ideal for anyone who has not got the time, or who cannot be bothered, to go through the weekly check drill.

There is little to say about the exhaust manifold, since there is little room for improvement on Jaguar's already excellent design. The C-type's exhaust ports are as level as they can be, with gentle curves to avoid slowing down the exhaust gases. The only minor problem is that, on an XK or an E-type, you have to do a lot of work on the interior of the head to enable the exhaust pipe to be set into the structure.

If you know a good metal-worker, he might be able to shape and weld a piece of the correct diameter tubing so that you can have some 'made-to-measure' pipework. Anyone who considers himself to be a genuine 'mod' enthusiast will go to these lengths, but any supplementary horsepower achieved by this operation is more than offset by the added weight of all that new piping.

Inlet valve diameters have expanded at a tremendous rate since 1948, since these valves work on roughly the same

This very 'special' XK 120 is owned by the well-known Jaguar enthusiast John Harper. This veritable bomb was entrusted to Ron Beaty's Forward Engineering for race preparation. (Croix-en-Ternois circuit, 1978.)

principle as an inverted bottle: the wider the neck, the faster the liquid comes out.

This diameter started out at 1¾ inches (43 mm) on the standard 120, and was then increased to 1⅞ inches (45 mm) on the C-type head. With the development of the wide-angle head, Jaguar was able to use a 2-inch (50-mm) diameter, and even a 2 3/32-inch (53-mm) one on some light-weight E-types. There is a limit to this procedure however, and it is set by the combustion chamber itself, since the two valves must never knock against one another.

Some people have managed to fit 2-inch (50-mm) inlet valves in standard heads — in other words, not the wide-angle variety. They include Conrero, and Peignaux, Jaguar's concessionnaire in Lyons.

The giant-valve solution is not really satisfactory, how-ever, as it is difficult to make them seat properly, and the only other possibility is one which Jaguar has never con-sidered because of the expense involved, and that is to have three valves per chamber — two for induction and one for exhaust. This gives the highest possible volumetric effici-ency. To the best of my knowledge, no one has attempted this arrangement yet.

There is no point in discussing valve seat angles, since Jaguar has researched that aspect in depth. I can hardly imagine an amateur tackling this subject with a PhD in the phenomena of turbulence and in relative torque values as a function of the valve seat angle.

Anything else to do with valves has already been perfec-ted by the manufacturers and is way beyond any amateur: special alloys for valve seats and stems; liquid sodium cooling, etc.

Let's move on to a more likely topic: pistons and compression ratios. As far as piston types are concerned,

All glass, and most of it fibre! Even the hood of this XK 120 is made out of glass fibre, using the original erected hood as a mould. Because of its lightweight body, it is one of the fastest XKs in the world. It belongs to John Pearson and is pictured at Beaulieu in 1970.

everyone seems to have his own pet design; light-alloy, slotted, bottom-ringed, double top-ringed, mini-skirted pistons — you name it. You will hear people arguing the case for double-sided crowns, dynamic turbulence crowns... but the most important factors are a piston's weight, resilience and compression ratio.

As you know, compression ratios have been increasing as fast as valve diameters. Jaguar started with a cautious 7:1, then tried a bolder 8:1. As soon as better-quality petrol was available, they could think of 9:1 and even 10:1. When they started using 11:1 and 13:1, even the best Saudi Arabian five-star was not up to such a challenge and a methanol-based fuel was needed to prevent detonation.

At such high ratios you have yourself a compression-ignition, or diesel, engine as the more compressed the fuel/air mixture, the more efficiently it burns, but beyond a certain limit it ignites spontaneously and at the wrong time. If you are running on four-star from your local service station, you would be advised to fix your compression ratio ceiling at 10:1.

The first engine feature to get the private enterprise treatment was capacity. The first such famous attempt was that of John Heath, who produced a 3.8-litre engine in his HWM back in 1952. Jaguar itself waited until 1957 before bringing out its 87 x 106 bore/stroke engine, which seems rather dilatory of the factory. But this 'make-haste-slowly' approach was due mainly to petrol supplies which were not that reliable in the post-war period, and the Suez crisis which followed soon after.

Some very talented motorists have made liners so that they could increase their engine's capacity from 3.4 litres to 3,996 cc (or 4 litres if you will), and a 4.2 engine to 4.5. Adding 600 cc to a 3.4-litre capacity takes some doing.

Because of its long-stroke geometry, the XK unit seemed to be calling out for an increase in its bore to give better breathing and volumetric efficiency. The limit for this increased bore was about 88 mm (giving an approximate 4-litre capacity), because any further reboring would make the liners too thin to withstand the stresses they have to take.

An engine-preparer's two weapons are lightening moving parts and balancing rotating parts. This lightening can bear on the pistons, but must not be carried too far, otherwise the piston head would soon be wrecked by the constant explosions it has to cope with. Another component which can be lightened is the flywheel. The first option is to turn it off on a lathe, making sure that you do not weaken it. The second option is trickier, in that you have to make a flywheel out of a light alloy, then fix a toothed steel ring round the outside — I'm sure you don't need to ask why the teeth should be made of steel!

Lightening the flywheel produces a marked improvement, since higher engine speeds are achieved more quickly than with the considerable inertia produced by the original heavy model. You find you have amazing acceleration power and, in addition, your speed falls as soon as you take your foot off the throttle and you can change gears at lightning speed.

The drawback with a lightened flywheel is that you get uneven running at idling speed because of the lack of inertia, the engine tends to miss, and you can even end up with a broken crankshaft.

There are two stages in the balancing process — the first static and the second dynamic. Balancing is a vital and delicate operation and it ensures that the engine can be run at high speeds without danger. In theory, a crankshaft such as that used on the XK engine can turn at over 10,000 rpm quite safely. The reason why such speeds cannot be reached in practice is that it is impossible to achieve a perfectly balanced engine and the slightest imbalance sets up vibrations which can lead to breakage. This imbalance is all the more difficult to resolve the more the crankpins are off-set from the crankshaft axis. Since the longer the stroke the more these crankpins are off-set... there you have it! The longer your piston stroke, the harder it is to balance the engine. So you are better off with a 53-mm 12-cylinder engine than with a 106 mm stroke 6-cylinder engine. In the first case, you can watch the needle rise to 8,000 rpm without turning a hair, but in the second case you exceed 5,700 rpm at your peril.

Lubrication at high engine speeds has to be ultra-efficient, for the least break in the oil film between two metallic parts which are rubbing together inevitably leads to a rapid rise in temperature. When this happens to a metal like that used in bearings, the result is a fusion of the two metal parts and you're off the road!

Oil has to work hard in all parts of an engine, so it has to be cooled quickly, filtered, and fed under pressure to the crankshaft, camshaft and small-ends of the connecting-rods.

It has been known for experienced amateurs to build themselves a separate oil sump fitted with a high-pressure pump, rather in the style of the inaccurately described 'dry sump' system used in the D-types.

An oil cooler is optional, depending on the quantity of oil in the sump. If yours will take 22 pints (12½ litres) you don't need a cooler but, if there is only room for 14 pints (8 litres), a little caution wouldn't go amiss.

Sometimes you will see a pipe running from one cam-cover to the other. This is an accessory which began to appear on the last C-types and which gives a better lubrication and balanced breathing in the top end of the engine at high speeds.

If you do not have an auxiliary oil sump, you can always polish the con-rods and any rough pieces on the crankshaft casting. It is always essential to have an adequate oil supply, so you must make sure that the precious fluid falls back into the sump as quickly as possible and does not stick on any protruding bits of metal. The highest estimate of the quantity of oil which gets 'stuck' in the engine at high speeds is about 5 pints. If your oil capacity is 22 pints, that is almost a quarter which is permanently out of action.

If you do everything I have suggested, with thoroughness and care, you have plenty to keep you occupied for the next few years and, rather than go through other possibilities in minute detail, I would rather tell you about two modifications which prove that there are no limits to what you can do with an XK.

The first involves an XK 120 drophead coupé, property of John Pearson and without doubt the fastest XK in the world. You might almost ask youself whether it can still be called an XK 120.

Pearson was well aware that he could not exceed certain limits in the engine's nominal power, so he began by doing

A 1950 XK 120 with 15-inch wheels, triple HD8 carburet-tors and straight-port head. Its 'Brooklands'-type aero-screen and louvred bonnet show that the owner was after speed rather than originality.

away wholesale with the steel body and building a glass-fibre replica. This even applied to the hood, where he used a glass-fibre casting of the original erected hood to form a fixed head. Aluminium sheet was chosen for the floor pan and transmission shaft. The only alteration in the body design was flaring of the wheel arches to accommodate the wide-profile tyres.

To say that the suspension was revised would be an understatement: negative rake and very slack torsion bars.

He retained the bottom end of the engine, but an E-type big-valve cylinder head came into play with triple Weber carburettors fed by a Tecalemit-Jackson pump.

The discs were virtually those of a 150, so there were no surprises there.

His first outings were frankly disastrous; his rev counter was malfunctioning and, although it showed 7,000 rpm, the poor engine was in fact turning over at 7,600. Luckily, there were no audible signs of protest under the bonnet.

He persevered and eventually managed to ruin the engine, whereupon he installed a hyper-tuned Mark X. Power-boosting continued thanks to some financial assistance from Duckhams and Dunlop; he had now reached 290 bhp and, at the back of the car, coil springs had replaced the leaf ones.

This side view of the XK engine shows the inlet porting from two Arnott superchargers.

The power:weight ratio enabled him to reach frightening speeds — up to 168 mph (270 km/h).

But Martin Oldham went much further than this on his 120, registered WPU 207. It now has absolutely nothing in common with the original car, has been modified as far as is humanly possible, but it is this kind of exploit which shows that there is truly no limit to what people will try to do with a Jaguar.

At the beginning the modification hinged on some very unusual Weber carburettors. They were 2 5/16-inch (58-mm) sand-cast ones and were very rare, being used mainly on experimental engines; their name was 58DCO3, the 'DC' standing for *doppio corpo* (double body). These mammoth carburettors were the cornerstone of Oldham's engine, on which was founded a lightweight E-type unit, assembled entirely from spare parts. This was a Herculean task in itself, since none of the parts was marked to assist the assembler; not even the lightened flywheel or the full race camshaft with its seemingly interminable open-valve phase. He had to start by re-inventing the fuel-supply and ignition diagrams, followed by machining the block and head so that it would fit the 51 mm bronze-seated tulip valves, and the proportional compression return springs.

The Webers were connected to a hand-worked manifold made out of sheet steel and especially designed for this engine. Fuel was pumped from the aluminium tank by two Mitsubishis through a pipe as thick as your thumb. The jet speed was 40 gallons an hour! There were lightened, reinforced con-rods, Powermax pistons with special rings, an oil sump flanked by two auxiliary reservoirs to increase the quantity of lubricant. It was insane!

The projected output was 360 bhp at 7,000 rpm, but 7,900 seemed to pose no problems, and the needle even nudged 8,200 for a second or two! Anyone who can get that much power out of an XK unit deserves a gold medal.

A multi-plate Borg and Beck clutch was needed to cope with this power, and the Moss Box was given a thorough working over.

The chassis had to be reinforced with a massive wishbone system and equally huge arches were needed to offset any tendency to flexing of the sidemembers.

Although the torsion-bar system was retained for the front suspension, all the 'Metalastik' bushes were taken out and replaced by bronze ones. At the rear, one single, very thick, leaf replaced the previous seven.

The shock absorbers were shifted, the recirculating ball

This arrangement of two H10 carburettors, each connected to an Arnott supercharger, should theoretically produce a flying car! The SU carburettor is the ideal one for use with superchargers since the piston lift is linked directly to the vacuum in the inlet manifold.

steering was replaced by a 140/150 Alford rack and pinion arrangement, disc brakes were borrowed from the 150, but with two independent circuits. The rest goes without saying: wide-profile tyres, lightweight body.

It is amazing what some people will do in their hunt for power!

Everyone thought that there was nothing left that had not been tried on an XK 120, until one day the world was faced with an XK 120 sporting the XJ-S' V12 engine! This astonishing car was the work of the German Hans Glaser. It was great fun, but really no more than that — rather like Count Zborowski's famous 'Chitty-Chitty-Bang-Bang' which used to set the crowd alight at Brooklands back in the 1920s with its 27-litre Maybach engine. All work and no play...

APPENDICES

SPECIFICATIONS

MODEL: SS 1 1932-35

(1934 model)

BODY		FHC	COACH & DHC	TOURER
CAPACITY		2,663 cc	ditto	ditto
BORE AND STROKE		73 x 106	ditto	ditto
CYLINDERS		6	ditto	ditto
COMPRESSION RATIO		6:1	ditto	ditto
MAXIMUM POWER		69 bhp at 3,800 rpm	ditto	ditto
MAXIMUM TORQUE		not available	ditto	ditto
CYLINDER HEAD		cast iron	ditto	ditto
VALVES		side valves	ditto	ditto
INDUCTION		1 or 2 RAG	ditto	ditto
FRONT DRIVE		beam axle	ditto	ditto
TRANSMISSION		4-speed box	ditto	ditto
REAR AXLE		live, 4.25:1	ditto	ditto
WHEELBASE		9 ft 11 ins	ditto	ditto
TRACK	front	4 ft 5 ins	ditto	ditto
	rear	4 ft 5½ ins	ditto	ditto
LENGTH		15 ft 6 ins	ditto	ditto
WIDTH		5 ft 3½ ins	ditto	ditto
WEIGHT		25¾ cwt		
ACCELERATION 0-60 mph		28.4 secs	ditto	ditto
TOP SPEED		75 mph	ditto	ditto
PRODUCTION STARTED		1932	ditto	ditto
PRODUCTION FINISHED		1935	ditto	ditto
CHASSIS NUMBERS RHD		135000 to 249500	ditto	ditto
NUMBER BUILT RHD		2,479*	ditto	ditto
NOTE: * 2,479 includes all body styles				

MODEL: SS 2

	1932-1933	1934-1936	
BODY	FHC	FHC	
CAPACITY	1,052 cc	1,343	
BORE AND STROKE (mm)	60.2 x 88	69.5 x 106	
CYLINDERS	4	4	
COMPRESSION RATIO	5.8:1	6:1	
MAXIMUM POWER	28 bhp at 4,000 rpm	38 bhp at 4,000 rpm	
MAXIMUM TORQUE	not available	not available	
CYLINDER HEAD	cast iron	cast iron	
VALVES	overhead	overhead	
INDUCTION	1 Solex or 1 SU	1 or 2 RAGs	
	or 1 RAG		
FRONT DRIVE	beam axle	beam axle	
TRANSMISSION	3-speed box	4-speed box	
REAR AXLE	live, 4.80:1	live, 5.29:1	
WHEELBASE	7 ft 6 ins	8 ft 8 ins	
TRACK front	3 ft 8¼ ins	3 ft 10½ ins	
TRACK rear	3 ft 8¼ ins	3 ft 10½ ins	
LENGTH	12 ft	13 ft 8 ins	
WIDTH	4 ft 6 ins	4 ft 8 ins	
WEIGHT	15½ cwt	20 cwt	
ACCELERATION	not available	not available	
TOP SPEED	60 mph	60 mph	
PRODUCTION STARTED	1932	1934	
PRODUCTION FINISHED	1934	1946	
CHASSIS NUMBERS RHD	300001	301000	
NUMBER BUILT RHD	549	1,247	
NOTE: The 4-cylinder SS 2s are described as a reminder			

MODEL: SS 90

	BODY	OPEN TWO-SEATER		
CAPACITY		2,663 cc		
BORE AND STROKE (mm)		73 x 106		
CYLINDERS		6		
COMPRESSION RATIO		7:1		
MAXIMUM POWER		72 bhp		
MAXIMUM TORQUE		not available		
CYLINDER HEAD		light alloy		
VALVES		side		
INDUCTION		2 RAGs		
FRONT DRIVE		beam axle		
TRANSMISSION		Moss box		
REAR AXLE		live, 4.5:1 or 3.7:1		
WHEELBASE		8 ft 8 ins		
TRACK	front	4 ft 6 ins		
	rear	4 ft 6 ins		
LENGTH		12 ft 6 ins		
WIDTH		5 ft 3 ins		
WEIGHT		22½ cwt		
ACCELERATION	0-60 mph	17 secs		
TOP SPEED		89 mph		
PRODUCTION STARTED		March 1935		
PRODUCTION FINISHED		November 1935		
CHASSIS NUMBERS	RHD	248246		
NUMBER BUILT	RHD	23		
NOTE:		18-inch wheels		

MODEL: SS 100   2.5 litres   3.5 litres

		BODY	OTS	OST	
CAPACITY			2,663 cc	3,485 cc	
BORE AND STROKE (mm)			73 x 106	82 x 110	
CYLINDERS			6	6	
COMPRESSION RATIO			7:1	7:1	
MAXIMUM POWER			102 bhp	125 bhp	
MAXIMUM TORQUE			not available	not available	
CYLINDER HEAD			cast iron	cast iron	
			push rods	push rods	
VALVES			overhead	overhead	
INDUCTION			2 H4 SUs	2 H4 SUs	
FRONT DRIVE			beam axle	beam axle	
TRANSMISSION			Moss box	4-speed Moss box	
REAR AXLE			live, 4:1	live, 3.8:1	
WHEELBASE			8 ft 8 ins	8 ft 8 ins	
TRACK	front		4 ft 6 ins	4 ft 4½ ins	
	rear		4 ft 6 ins	4 ft 6 ins	
LENGTH			12 ft 6 ins	12 ft 9 ins	
WIDTH			5 ft 3 ins	5 ft 3 ins	
WEIGHT			23 cwt	23¼ cwt	
ACCELERATION	0-60 mph		12.8 secs	10.9 secs	
TOP SPEED			94 mph	101 mph	
PRODUCTION STARTED			Sept 1935	Sept 1937	
PRODUCTION FINISHED			March 1941	Nov 1941	
CHASSIS NUMBERS	(1936-37)	RHD	18001 +		
	(1938-41)	RHD	49001 +	39001 +	
NUMBER BUILT		RHD	190	118*	
NOTE: * Andrew Whyte gives a figure of 166 for the 3.5-litre			18-inch wheels		

MODEL: XK 120

	BODY	OTS	FHC	DHC
CAPACITY		3,442 cc	3,442 cc	3,442 cc
BORE AND STROKE (mm)		83 x 106	83 x 106	83 x 106
CYLINDERS		6	6	6
COMPRESSION RATIO		7, 8 or 9:1	7, 8 or 9:1	7, 8 or 9:1
MAXIMUM POWER	std	160 bhp	160 @ 5,000	190 @ 5,500
	SE	180 bhp	180 @ 5,300	210 @ 5,750
MAXIMUM TORQUE	std	195 lb/ft	195 lb/ft	195 lb/ft
	SE	203 lb/ft	203 lb/ft	203 lb/ft
CYLINDER HEAD		A or C-type	A or C-type	A or C-type
VALVES		twin ohc	twin ohc	twin ohc
INDUCTION	std	2 H6 SUs	2 H6 SUs	2 H6 SUs
	M.C.	2 H8 SUs	2 H8 SUs	2 H6 SUs
FRONT SUSPENSION		ifs	ifs	ifs
TRANSMISSION		4-speed Moss	4-speed Moss	4-speed Moss
REAR AXLE (live)	ENV	3.64, 3.27, 3.92, 4.30, 4.56	ditto	ditto
	Salisbury	3.77, 4.09, 4.27	ditto	ditto
WHEELBASE		8 ft 6 ins	8 ft 6 ins	8 ft 6 ins
TRACK	front	4 ft 3 ins	4 ft 3 ins	4 ft 3 ins
	rear	4 ft 2 ins	4 ft 2 ins	4 ft 2 ins
LENGTH		14 ft 6 ins	14 ft 5 ins	14 ft 5 ins
WIDTH		5 ft 1½ ins	5 ft 1½ ins	5 ft 1½ ins
WEIGHT (incl fuel)		26 cwt/25½ cwt		
		alloy	27 cwt	27½ cwt
ACCELERATION	0-60 (std)	10 secs	9.9 s, 3.77 fdr	9.5 s, 3.54 fdr
	0-100	27.3 secs	28.2 secs	31 secs
TOP SPEED		124.6 mph	120.5 mph	119.5 mph
PRODUCTION STARTED		22 Oct 1948	March 1951	April 1953
PRODUCTION FINISHED		Sept 1954	Sept 1954	Sept 1954
CHASSIS NUMBERS	LHD	670001 +	679001 +	677001 +
	RHD	660001 +	669001 +	667001 +
NUMBER BUILT	LHD	6,437	2,484	1,471
	RHD	1,175	194	294
NOTE: 244 alloy-bodied		16-inch wheels	16-inch wheels	16-inch wheels

MODEL: XK 120C (C-type)

	PRODUCTION	WORKS-RACING	
CAPACITY	3,442 cc	3,442 cc	
BORE AND STROKE (mm)	83 x 106	83 x 106	
CYLINDERS	6	6	
COMPRESSION RATIO	8:1	9:1	
MAXIMUM POWER	205 bhp @ 5,800 rpm	220 bhp @ 6,000 rpm	
MAXIMUM TORQUE	220 lb/ft	227 lb/ft	
CYLINDER HEAD	C-type	C-type	
VALVES	twin ohc	twin ohc	
INDUCTION	2 H8 SUs	3 Weber 40s	
FRONT SUSPENSION	ifs	ifs	
TRANSMISSION	4-speed Moss	4-speed Moss	
REAR AXLE (live)	Salisbury + torsion bars	Salisbury + torsion bars	
WHEELBASE	8 ft	8 ft	
TRACK front	4 ft 3 ins	4 ft 3 ins	
TRACK rear	4 ft 3 ins	4 ft 3 ins	
LENGTH	13 ft 1 ins	13 ft 1 in	
WIDTH	5 ft 4½ ins	5 ft 4½ ins	
WEIGHT	20 cwt	20 cwt	
ACCELERATION 0-60 mph	8.1 secs	7.7 secs	
ACCELERATION 0-100 mph	20.1 secs	19.5 secs	
TOP SPEED	143.7 mph	146.6 mph	
PRODUCTION STARTED	August 1952	June 1951	
PRODUCTION FINISHED	August 1953	June 1953	
CHASSIS NUMBERS RHD	XKC 001 —	XKC 001, 002, 003	
	XKC 054	004, 005, 011, 012	
		038, 051, 052, 053	
NUMBER BUILT RHD	43	11	

MODEL: XK 140

	BODY	OTS	FHC	DHC
CAPACITY		3,442 cc	3,442 cc	3,442 cc
BORE AND STROKE (mm)		83 x 106	83 x 106	83 x 106
CYLINDERS		6	6	6
COMPRESSION RATIO		7, 8 or 9:1	7, 8 or 9:1	7, 8 or 9:1
MAXIMUM POWER	std	190 bhp @ 5,500 rpm	ditto	ditto
	SE	210 bhp @ 5,750 rpm	ditto	ditto
MAXIMUM TORQUE	std	210 ft/lbs	210 ft/lbs	210 ft/lbs
	SE	213 ft/lbs	213 ft/lbs	213 ft/lbs
CYLINDER HEAD	std	A-type	A-type	A-type
	SE	C-type	C-type	C-type
VALVES		twin ohc	twin ohc	twin ohc
INDUCTION		2 H6 SUs	2 H6 SUs	2 H6 SUs
		2 H8 SUs	2 H8 SUs	2 H8 SUs
FRONT SUSPENSION		ifs	ifs	ifs
TRANSMISSION		4-speed Moss OD option	4-speed manual OD with automatic transmission	manual + OD or automatic
REAR AXLE (live)	Salisbury	3.54, 3.31, 4.09 (OD), 4.27	ditto	ditto
WHEELBASE		8 ft 6 ins	8 ft 6 ins	8 ft 6 ins
TRACK	front	4 ft 3½ ins	4 ft 3½ ins	4 ft 3½ ins
	rear	4 ft 3⅜ ins	4 ft 3⅜ ins	4 ft 3⅜ ins
LENGTH		14 ft 8 ins	14 ft 8 ins	14 ft 8 ins
WIDTH		5 ft 4½ ins	5 ft 4½ ins	5 ft 4½ ins
WEIGHT (incl fuel)		28 cwt	28 cwt	29 cwt
ACCELERATION	0-60 (std)	8.5 secs	11.1 secs	11 secs
	0-100 mph	26.5 secs	29.5 secs	29 secs
TOP SPEED		121.1 mph	128.6 mph	127.4 mph
PRODUCTION STARTED		Oct 1954	Oct 1954	Oct 1953
PRODUCTION FINISHED		Feb 1957	Feb 1957	Feb 1957
CHASSIS NUMBERS	LHD	810001 +	814001 +	817001 +
	RHD	800001 +	804001 +	807001 +
NUMBER BUILT*	LHD	3,281	1,965	2,310
	RHD	73	843	479

NOTE: O/D optional; automatic transmission optional

* Paul Skilleter estimates a total of 8,951;
  Andrew Whyte 8,884

MODEL: D-type and XK SS

		PRODUCTION AND WORKS D-TYPE	XK SS	
CAPACITY		3,442 cc	ditto	
BORE AND STROKE (mm)		83 x 106	ditto	
CYLINDERS		6	ditto	
COMPRESSION RATIO		9:1	ditto	
MAXIMUM POWER		250 bhp @ 5,800 rpm	ditto	
MAXIMUM TORQUE		242 ft/lbs	ditto	
CYLINDER HEAD		35/35 D-type, or 35/40 wide-angle	ditto	
VALVES		twin ohc	ditto	
INDUCTION		3 45DCOE Webers	ditto	
FRONT SUSPENSION		ifs	ditto	
TRANSMISSION		4-speed manual	ditto	
REAR AXLE (live)		Salisbury, ratio options	ditto	
WHEELBASE		7 ft 6⅝ ins	ditto	
TRACK	front	4 ft 2 ins	ditto	
	rear	4 ft	ditto	
LENGTH		12 ft 10 ins	ditto	
WIDTH		5 ft 4½ ins	ditto	
WEIGHT		17 cwt (dry)	18 cwt (dry)	
ACCELERATION	0-60 mph	4.7 secs	5.2 secs	
	0-100 mph	12.1 secs	13.6 secs	
TOP SPEED		162 mph	149 mph	
PRODUCTION STARTED		June 1954	Jan 1957	
PRODUCTION FINISHED		August 1956	Feb 1957	
CHASSIS NUMBERS	short-nose	—	—	
	long-nose	XKC...		
		XKD...		
NUMBER BUILT	short-nose	53	16 + 2	
	long-nose	6	6	
NOTE: The D-type was given a 3.8-litre engine towards the end of its life (late 1957)		dry-sump lubrication	dry sump	

MODEL: XK 150 3.4 litres

	BODY	OTS	FHC	DHC
CAPACITY		3,442 cc	3,442 cc	3,442 cc
BORE AND STROKE (mm)		83 x 106	83 x 106	83 x 106
CYLINDERS		6	6	6
COMPRESSION RATIO		7, 8 or 9:1	7, 8 or 9:1	7, 8 or 9:1
MAXIMUM POWER	(std @ 5,500)	190 bhp	190 bhp	190 bhp
	(SE @ 5,500)	190 bhp	210 bhp	210 bhp
MAXIMUM TORQUE	(std @ 2,500)	210 ft/lbs	210 ft/lbs	210 ft/lbs
	(SE @ 3,000)	216 ft/lbs	216 ft/lbs	216 ft/lbs
CYLINDER HEAD		B-type	B-type	B-type
VALVES		twin ohc	twin ohc	twin ohc
INDUCTION		2 HD6	2 HD6	2 HD6
FRONT SUSPENSION		ifs	ifs	ifs
TRANSMISSION		Moss box (OD option)	Moss box (OD option)	Moss box (OD option)
REAR AXLE (live)	Salisbury	3.54, 4.09	3.54, 3.31, 4.09 (OD) or 4.27	3.54, 4.09
WHEELBASE		8 ft 6 ins	8 ft 6 ins	8 ft 6 ins
TRACK	front	4 ft 3¼ ins	4 ft 3¼ ins	4 ft 3¼ ins
	rear	4 ft 3¼ ins	4 ft 3¼ ins	4 ft 3¼ ins
LENGTH		14 ft 9 ins	14 ft 9 ins	14 ft 9 ins
WIDTH		5 ft 4½ ins	5 ft 4½ ins	5 ft 4½ ins
WEIGHT		28.1 cwt	28.75 cwt	31 cwt
ACCELERATION	0-60 mph SE	8.5 secs	8.5 secs	8.6 secs
	0-100 mph SE	25.1 secs	25.1 secs	25.5 secs
TOP SPEED — SE		123.7 mph	123.7 mph	121.2 mph
PRODUCTION STARTED		March 1958	May 1957	May 1957
PRODUCTION FINISHED		Oct 1960	Oct 1961	Oct 1960
CHASSIS NUMBERS	LHD	830001 +	834001 +	837001 +
	RHD	820001 +	824001 +	827001 +
NUMBER BUILT*	LHD	2,173	3,094	2,009
	RHD	92	1,368	662

NOTE: * includes 3.4, 3.4S, 3.8 and 3.8S;

Disc brakes make their first appearance on an XK

MODEL: XK 150S 3.4 litres

	BODY	OTS	FHC	DHC
CAPACITY		3,442 cc	3,442 cc	3,442 cc
BORE AND STROKE (mm)		83 x 106	83 x 106	83 x 106
CYLINDERS		6	6	6
COMPRESSION RATIO		8 or 9:1	8 or 9:1	8 or 9:1
MAXIMUM POWER (5,500 rpm)		250 bhp	250 bhp	250 bhp
MAXIMUM TORQUE (4,500 rpm)		240 lb/ft	240 lb/ft	240 lb/ft
CYLINDER HEAD		straight-port	straight-port	straight-port
VALVES		twin ohc	twin ohc	twin ohc
INDUCTION		3 HD8	3 HD8	3 HD8
FRONT SUSPENSION		ifs	ifs	ifs
TRANSMISSION		4-speed Moss box + OD	4-speed Moss box + OD	4-speed Moss box + OD
REAR AXLE (live)	Salisbury	3.54 or 4.09	3.54 or 4.09	3.54 or 4.09
WHEELBASE		8 ft 6 ins	8 ft 6 ins	8 ft 6 ins
TRACK	front	4 ft 3¼ ins	4 ft 3¼ ins	4 ft 3¼ ins
	rear	4 ft 3¼ ins	4 ft 3¼ ins	4 ft 3¼ ins
LENGTH		14 ft 9 ins	14 ft 9 ins	14 ft 9 ins
WIDTH		5 ft 4½ ins	5 ft 4½ ins	5 ft 4½ ins
WEIGHT (incl. fuel)		28½ cwt	28¾ cwt	30.9 cwt
ACCELERATION	0-60 mph	7.3 secs	7.8 secs	7.9 secs
	0-100 mph	21.4 secs	20.3 secs	21.9 secs
TOP SPEED		136 mph	132 mph	130 mph
PRODUCTION STARTED		March 1958	May 1957	May 1957
PRODUCTION FINISHED		Oct 1960	Oct 1961	Oct 1960
CHASSIS NUMBERS	LHD	830001 +	834001 +	837001 +
	RHD	820001 +	823001 +	827001 +
NUMBER BUILT*	LHD	2,173	3,094	2,009
	RHD	92	1,363	662
NOTE: * includes 3.4, 3.4S, 3.8 and 3.8S				

404

MODEL: XK 150S 3.8 litres

BODY	OTS	FHC	DHC
CAPACITY	3,781 cc	3,781 cc	3,781 cc
BORE AND STROKE (mm)	87 x 106	87 x 106	87 x 106
CYLINDERS	6	6	6
COMPRESSION RATIO	8 or 9:1	8 or 9:1	8 or 9:1
MAXIMUM POWER @ 5,500 rpm	265 bhp	265 bhp	265 bhp
MAXIMUM TORQUE @ 4,000 rpm	260 lb/ft	260 lb/ft	260 lb/ft
CYLINDER HEAD	straight port	straight port	straight port
VALVES	twin ohc	twin ohc	twin ohc
INDUCTION	3 HD8	3 HD8	3 HD8
FRONT SUSPENSION	ifs	ifs	ifs
TRANSMISSION	Moss box OD option	Moss box OD option	Moss box OD option
REAR AXLE (live) Salisbury	3.54 or 4.09	3.54 or 4.09	3.54 or 4.09
WHEELBASE	8 ft 6 ins	8 ft 6 ins	8 ft 6 ins
TRACK front	4 ft 3¼ ins	4 ft 3¼ ins	4 ft 3¼ ins
TRACK rear	4 ft 3¼ ins	4 ft 3¼ ins	4 ft 3¼ ins
LENGTH	14 ft 9 ins	14 ft 9 ins	14 ft 9 ins
WIDTH	5 ft 4½ ins	5 ft 4½ ins	5 ft 4½ ins
WEIGHT (incl. fuel)	28.2 cwt	28.75 cwt	30.9 cwt
ACCELERATION 0-60 mph	7.5 secs	7.6 secs	7.7 secs
ACCELERATION 0-100 mph	18.8 secs	19 secs	21 secs
TOP SPEED	137 mph	135.5 mph	131.7 mph
PRODUCTION STARTED	Oct 1959	Oct 1959	Oct 1959
PRODUCTION FINISHED	Oct 1960	Oct 1960	Oct 1960
CHASSIS NUMBERS LHD	830001 +	834001 +	837001 +
CHASSIS NUMBERS RHD	820001 +	824001 +	827001 +
NUMBER BUILT* LHD	2,173	3,094	2,009
NUMBER BUILT* RHD	92	1,363	662
NOTE: the most powerful of the XKs * includes 3.4, 3.4S, 3.8 and 3.8S			

MODEL: XK 150 3.8 litres

	BODY		OTS	FHC	DHC
CAPACITY			3,781 cc	3,781 cc	3,781 cc
BORE AND STROKE (mm)			87 x 106	87 x 106	87 x 106
CYLINDERS			6	6	6
COMPRESSION RATIO			8 or 9:1	8 or 9:1	8 or 9:1
MAXIMUM POWER @ 5,500 rpm			220 bhp	220 bhp	220 bhp
MAXIMUM TORQUE @ 3,000 rpm			240 lb/ft	240 lb/ft	240 lb/ft
CYLINDER HEAD			B-type	B-type	B-Type
VALVES			twin ohc	twin ohc	twin ohc
INDUCTION			2 HD6	2 HD6	2 HD6
FRONT SUSPENSION			ifs	ifs	ifs
TRANSMISSION			Moss box	Moss box	Moss box
			OD option	OD option	OD option
REAR AXLE (live)	Salisbury		3.54, 4.09	3.31, 3.54,	3.54, 4.09
				4.09 (OD), 4.27	
WHEELBASE			8 ft 6 ins	8 ft 6 ins	8 ft 6 ins
TRACK	front		4 ft 3¼ ins	4 ft 3¼ ins	4 ft 3¼ ins
	rear		4 ft 3¼ ins	4 ft 3¼ ins	4 ft 3¼ ins
LENGTH			14 ft 9 ins	14 ft 9 ins	14 ft 9 ins
WIDTH			5 ft 4½ ins	5 ft 4½ ins	5 ft 4½ ins
WEIGHT			28.2 cwt	28.75 cwt	30.9 cwt
ACCELERATION	0-60 mph		7.6 secs	7.6 secs	7.8 secs
	0-100 mph		19 secs	19 secs	21.8 secs
TOP SPEED			136.3 mph	136.3 secs	128.6 mph
PRODUCTION STARTED			Oct 1959	Oct 1959	Oct 1959
PRODUCTION FINISHED			Oct 1960	Oct 1961	Oct 1960
CHASSIS NUMBERS	LHD		830001 +	834001 +	837001 +
	RHD		820001 +	824001 +	827001 +
NUMBER BUILT*	LHD		2,173	3,094	2,009
	RHD		92	1,363	662
NOTE: not many of this model were made * includes 3.4, 3.4S, 3.8 and 3.8S					

MODEL: E-type Series 1 3.8-litre

BODY	FHC	OTS	
CAPACITY	3,781 cc	3,781 cc	
BORE AND STROKE (mm)	87 x 106	87 x 106	
CYLINDERS	6	6	
COMPRESSION RATIO	8 or 9:1	8 or 9:1	
MAXIMUM POWER @ 5,500 rpm	265 bhp	265 bhp	
MAXIMUM TORQUE @ 4,000 rpm	260 lb/ft	260 lb/ft	
CYLINDER HEAD	straight port	straight port	
VALVES	twin ohc	twin ohc	
INDUCTION	3 HD8	3 HD8	
FRONT SUSPENSION	ifs	ifs	
TRANSMISSION	Moss box, no OD	Moss box, no OD	
REAR SUSPENSION	irs, 3.31:1	irs 3.31:1	
WHEELBASE	8 ft	8 ft	
TRACK front	4 ft 2 ins	4 ft 2 ins	
TRACK rear	4 ft 2 ins	4 ft 2 ins	
LENGTH	14 ft 7.3 ins	14 ft 7.3 ins	
WIDTH	5 ft 5.2 ins	5 ft 5.2 ins	
WEIGHT (incl fuel)	24.1 cwt	24 cwt	
ACCELERATION 0-60 mph	6.9 secs	7.1 secs	
ACCELERATION 0-100 mph	16.2 secs	15.9 secs	
TOP SPEED	150.4 mph	149.1 mph	
PRODUCTION STARTED	March 1961	March 1961	
PRODUCTION FINISHED	Oct 1964	Oct 1964	
CHASSIS NUMBERS LHD	885001 +	875001 +	
CHASSIS NUMBERS RHD	860001 +	850001 +	
NUMBER BUILT LHD	5,871	6,885	
NUMBER BUILT RHD	1,798	942	
NOTE: this was the same 265 bhp engine as on the 150S.			

MODEL: E-type Series 1 4.2-litre

	BODY	FHC	2+2	OTS
CAPACITY		4,235 cc	4,235 cc	4,235 cc
BORE AND STROKE (mm)		92.07 x 106	92.07 x 106	92.07 x 106
CYLINDERS		6	6	6
COMPRESSION RATIO		8 or 9:1	8 or 9:1	8 or 9:1
MAXIMUM POWER @ 5,400 rpm		265 bhp	265 bhp	265 bhp
MAXIMUM TORQUE @ 4,000 rpm		283 lb/ft	283 lb/ft	283 lb/ft
CYLINDER HEAD		straight port	straight port	straight port
VALVES		twin ohc	twin ohc	twin ohc
INDUCTION		3 HD8	3 HD8	3 HD8
FRONT SUSPENSION		ifs	ifs	ifs
TRANSMISSION		Jaguar box, no OD	Jaguar box, no OD	Jaguar box, no OD
REAR AXLE		Ind. 3.07:1	Ind. 3.07:1	Ind. 3.07:1
WHEELBASE		8 ft	8 ft 9 ins	8 ft
TRACK	front	4 ft 2 ins	4 ft 2¼ ins	4 ft 2 ins
	rear	4 ft 2 ins	4 ft 2¼ ins	4 ft 2 ins
LENGTH		14 ft 7 ins	15 ft 4½ ins	14 ft 7 ins
WIDTH		5 ft 6 ins	5 ft 4 ins	5 ft 6 ins
WEIGHT (incl. fuel)		24.1 cwt	27.7 cwt	24.2 cwt
ACCELERATION	0-60 mph	7 secs	8.9 secs	7 secs
	0-100 mph	17.2 secs	19.1 secs	17.2 secs
TOP SPEED		150 mph	136.2 mph	150 mph
PRODUCTION STARTED		Oct 1964	March 1966	Oct 1964
PRODUCTION FINISHED		Sept 1968	Sept 1968	Sept 1968
CHASSIS NUMBERS	LHD	1E30001 +	1E75001 +	1E10001 +
	RHD	1E2001 +	1E50001 +	1E1001 +
NUMBER BUILT	LHD	5,813	4,220	8,366
	RHD	1,957	1,378	1,182
NOTES:		automatic optional	ditto	ditto

MODEL: E-type Series 2 4.2-litre

BODY	FHC	2 + 2	OTS
CAPACITY	4,235 cc	4,235 cc	4,235 cc
BORE AND STROKE (mm)	92.07 x 106	92.07 x 106	92.07 x 106
CYLINDERS	6	6	6
COMPRESSION RATIO	8 or 9:1	8 or 9:1	8 or 9:1
MAXIMUM POWER @ 5,400 rpm (except US models)	265 bhp	265 bhp	265 bhp
MAXIMUM TORQUE @ 4,000 rpm	283 lb/ft	283 lb/ft	283 lb/ft
CYLINDER HEAD	straight port	straight port	straight port
VALVES	twin ohc	twin ohc	twin ohc
INDUCTION	3 HD8	3 HD8	3 HD8
FRONT SUSPENSION	ifs	ifs	ifs
TRANSMISSION	Jaguar box, no OD	Jaguar box, no OD	Jaguar box, no OD
REAR AXLE	Ind. 3.07:1	Ind. 3.07:1	Ind. 3.07:1
WHEELBASE	8 ft	8 ft 9 ins	8 ft
TRACK front	4 ft 2 ins	4 ft 2¼ ins	4 ft 2 ins
TRACK rear	4 ft 2 ins	4 ft 2¼ ins	4 ft 2 ins
LENGTH	14 ft 7 ins	15 ft 4½ ins	14 ft 7 ins
WIDTH	5 ft 6 ins	5 ft 2½ ins	5 ft 6 ins
WEIGHT (incl. fuel)	24.1 cwt	27.7 cwt	24.2 cwt
ACCELERATION 0-60 mph	7 secs	8.9 secs	7 secs
ACCELERATION 0-100 mph	17.2 secs	19.1 secs	17.2 secs
TOP SPEED (except US models)	150 mph	136.2 mph	150 mph
PRODUCTION STARTED	Oct 1968	Oct 1968	Oct 1968
PRODUCTION FINISHED	Sept 1970	Sept 1970	Sept 1970
CHASSIS NUMBERS LHD	1R25001 +	1R40001 +	1R7001 +
CHASSIS NUMBERS RHD	1R20001 +	1R35001 +	1R1001 +
NUMBER BUILT LHD	3,785	4,286	7,852
NUMBER BUILT RHD	1,070	1,040	755
NOTE:		automatic optional	

MODEL: E-type Series 3 V12

BODY	2 + 2	OTS	
CAPACITY	5,343 cc	5,343 cc	
BORE AND STROKE (mm)	90 x 70	90 x 70	
CYLINDERS	V12	V12	
COMPRESSION RATIO	9:1	9:1	
MAXIMUM POWER @ 5,850 rpm (except US models)	272 bhp	272 bhp	
MAXIMUM TORQUE @ 3,600 rpm (except US models)	304 lb/ft	304 lb/ft	
CYLINDER HEAD	light alloy flat-head x 2	light alloy flat-head x 2	
VALVES	sohc per bank	sohc per bank	
INDUCTION	4 x Zenith Stromberg	4 x Zenith Stromberg	
FRONT SUSPENSION	ifs	ifs	
TRANSMISSION	Jaguar manual or automatic	Jaguar manual or automatic	
REAR AXLE (3.31:1 with manual box)	Ind. 3.07:1	Ind. 3.07:1	
WHEELBASE	8 ft 9 ins	8 ft 9 ins	
TRACK front	4 ft 6½ ins	4 ft 6½ ins	
TRACK rear	4 ft 5 ins	4 ft 5 ins	
LENGTH	15 ft 4 ins	15 ft 4 ins	
WIDTH	4 ft 1 in	4 ft 1 in	
WEIGHT	29.5 cwt	28.8 cwt	
ACCELERATION (not US models) 0-60 mph	6.8 secs	6.4 secs	
ACCELERATION (not US models) 0-100 mph	16.4 secs	15.4 secs	
TOP SPEED (except US models)	142 mph	146 mph	
PRODUCTION STARTED	Apr 1971	Apr 1971	
PRODUCTION FINISHED	Sept 1973	Sept 1973	
CHASSIS NUMBERS LHD	1S70001 +	1S20001 +	
CHASSIS NUMBERS RHD	1S50001 +	1S1001 +	
NUMBER BUILT LHD	5,182	6,119	
NUMBER BUILT RHD	2,115	1,871	
NOTE: There are 4 Series 3 4.2s	autom. option	autom. option	

MODEL: XJ-S and XJ-S HE

	BODY		XJ-S	XJ-S HE	
CAPACITY			5,345 cc	5,345 cc	
BORE AND STROKE (mm)			90 x 70	90 x 70	
CYLINDERS			V12	V12	
COMPRESSION RATIO			9:1	12.5:1	
MAXIMUM POWER			285 bhp	300 bhp	
MAXIMUM TORQUE			280 lb/ft	302 lb/ft	
CYLINDER HEAD			light alloy flat-head x 2	May fireball x 2	
VALVES			sohc per bank	sohc per bank	
INDUCTION			electronic injection	electronic injection	
FRONT SUSPENSION			ifs	ifs	
TRANSMISSION			automatic (mostly)	automatic	
REAR AXLE			Ind. 3.07:1	Ind. 2.88:1	
WHEELBASE			8 ft 6 ins	8 ft 6 ins	
TRACK	front		4 ft 10 ins	4 ft 10 ins	
	rear		4 ft 10½ ins	4 ft 10½ ins	
LENGTH			15 ft 11½ ins	15 ft 6½ ins	
WIDTH			5 ft 10½ ins	5 ft 10½ ins	
WEIGHT			33.1 cwt	34.5 cwt	
ACCELERATION	0-60 mph		6.7 secs	6.6 secs	
	0-100 mph		16.2 secs	16 secs	
TOP SPEED			153 mph	155.5 mph	
PRODUCTION STARTED			Sept 1975	June 1981	
PRODUCTION FINISHED			June 1981	still in production	
CHASSIS NUMBERS		LHD	2W50000 JNAEW 100000	JNAEW 4BC 105000	
NUMBER BUILT		RHD	ditto	ditto	
		LHD	8,002	still in production	
		RHD	6,992	still in production	

411

MODEL: XJ-S 3.6 and XJ-SC

	BODY	XJ-S 3.6	XJ-SC	
CAPACITY		3,590 cc	3,590 cc	
BORE AND STROKE (mm)		91 x 92	91 x 92	
CYLINDERS		6	6	
COMPRESSION RATIO		9.6:1	9.6:1	
MAXIMUM POWER		225 bhp	225 bhp	
MAXIMUM TORQUE		240 lb/ft	240 lb/ft	
CYLINDER HEAD		—	—	
VALVES		dohc	dohc	
INDUCTION		electronic injection	electronic injection	
FRONT SUSPENSION		ifs	ifs	
TRANSMISSION		5-speed manual	5-speed manual	
REAR AXLE		3.54:1		
WHEELBASE		8 ft 6 ins	8 ft 6 ins	
TRACK	front	—	—	
	rear	—	—	
LENGTH		15 ft 7½ ins	15 ft 7½ ins	
WIDTH		5 ft 10½ ins	5 ft 10½ ins	
WEIGHT		32.7 cwt	32.7 cwt	
ACCELERATION	0-60 mph	7.6 secs	8.0 secs	
	0-100 mph	19.6 secs	19.7 secs	
TOP SPEED		145 mph	137 mph	
PRODUCTION STARTED		Sept 1983	Sept 1983	
PRODUCTION FINISHED		still in production	still in production	
CHASSIS NUMBERS	LHD	—	—	
	RHD	—	—	
NUMBER BUILT		still in production	still in production	

When you lift up a Jaguar bonnet, you should be able to identify the engine version by a few vital signs, such as the colour o the cylinder head.

TYPE	YEAR	FOUNDRY REF.	INL.VAL. DIAM.	I.V.SEAT ANGLE	EXH.VAL DIAM.	E.V.S. ANGLE	OVERLAP OPEN INLET CLOSE EXHAUST	CAMLIFT
'A' 1st series	1948 1950	B143	1¾"	30°	1½"	45°	OI 10° CE 15°	5/16"
Production 'A'	1950 1955		1¾"	30°	1½"	45°	OI 15° CE 15°	3/8"
'B' 3.4-litre and 2.4-litre	1955 1968	WM351	1¾"	45°	1 5/8"	45°	OI 15° CE 15°	3/8"
'C' pre-series	1951	RJ27	1¾"	30°	1 5/8"	45°	IO 15° CE 15°	3/8"
Production 'C' Skinner Union	1951 1957	RJ32	1¾"	30°	1 5/8"	45°	IO 15° CE 15°	3/8"
Production 'C' Weber	1953 1957	RJ47	1¾"	30°	1 5/8"	45°	IO 15° CE 15°	3/8"
'D' 35/35	1954	AK535	1 7/8"	30°	1 5/8"	45°	IO 30° CE 30°	3/8"
'D' wide-angle 35/40 Weber	1955	A32	1 29/32"	45°	1 11/16"	45°	IO 35° CE 35°	7/16"
'D' wide-angle 35/40 Weber	1955	A44	2"	45°	1 11/16"	45°	IO 35° CE 35°	7/16"
'D' wide-angle 35/40 p.injection	1956	A23	2"	45°	1 11/16"	45°	IO 35° CE 35°	7/16"
'D' wide-angle 35/40 p.injection	1958 1964	A70	2 3/32"	45°	1 11/16"	45°	IO 35° CE 35°	7/16"
'SP' straight-port	1959 in prod.		1¾"	45°	1 5/8"	45°	IO 15° CE 15°	3/8"

CYLINDER HEADS
1968

Learn to recognise these five colours: silver (aluminium); sky blue; metallic blue; red; gold

HEAD COLOUR	C.R.	POWER (bhp)	INDUCTION	MODELS CONCERNED	NOTES
silver	7:1	152 to 160	2 chimney H6 SUs	XK 120 early models Mk VII early models	No studs on the front of the cam-covers, twinned spark-plug holes
silver	8:1	160 to 180	2 H6 SUs	XK 120, XK 140, Mk VII, Mk I 2.4	Some minor differences in the casting compared with the previous block
sky blue	8:1	190	2 HD6 SUs	XK 150, Mk VIII, Mk II 2.4, 3.4; 3.4-litre S	
metallic blue	8:1	220	2 HD6 SUs	XK 150 3.8, Mk IX, Mk II 3.8, S-type	
silver, then red	8.5:1	205	2 H6 SUs	XK 120C	
red	8:1	205 to 215	2 H6 SUs or 2 H8 SUs	XK 120, C-type, XK 140 MC, Mk VIIM (SE)	Cam-cover breathers on the inlet side on the Le Mans models. 'C' badge appears
red	8:1	220, 230	3 4ODCO3 Webers	Le Mans C-type	Twin breather with inter-connected camshafts
silver	9:1	250	3 45DCOE Webers	3.4-litre D-type + derivatives	Petrol injection was tried on an experimental basis
silver	9:1	277	3 45DCOE Webers	3.4-litre D-type + specials	Facility for dual ignition
silver	9:1	300	3 45DCOE Webers	3.4-litre D-type + specials	One of the most amazing heads; most frequently used on specials
silver	9.3:1	306	Lucas injection	Le Mans D-type	
silver	10:1/ 12.5:1	317	Lucas injection	3.8 D-type, LW E-type + derivatives	The largest diameter inlet valve used
gold	9:1	220 250 265	2 HD6s 3 HD8s 3 HD8s	340 (and 240) XK 150S 3.4-litre XK 150S 3.8-litre, 3.8 & 4.2 E-types	This is identical to the B-type head with the exception of much straighter ports

JAGUAR — CHASSIS AND ENGINE DETAILS

DATE	MODEL	TYPE	SPE	CHASSIS	ENGINE	BODY	COLOUR	INTERIOR	COMMENTS	
22.03.53	XK 120	M	SE	S[1] 6[2]80 667	W 7261 8[3]S[4]	J[5] 2674	battleship	red	Michelin test car	XK 120
24.05.56	XK 140		C	S[1]81[6]8 547 DN[7]	G 7786 8[3]S	P[5] 4947	chestnut	beige		XK 140
17.07.57	XK 140			A 819 051 BW	G 9134 8	P 5530	battleship	red		
26.07.56	XK 140		C	S[1] 815 741	G 8376 8S[10]					
05.12.60	XK 150	3.8	S	S[11] 832[12] 086 DN T[17] 826 900 DN	V[13] 7475 8 VS[14] 2086 9[15] VA[16]1994 8 VAS[18] 1264 8	J 11275				XK 150

1. The prefix S indicates Special Equipment: SE (chassis column).
2. The 6 is the number prefix for Mark IVs, Mark Vs and XK 120s (chassis column).
3. The number suffix indicates the compression ratio (engine column).
4. The suffix S indicates a 190 bhp engine (engine column).
5. J prefixes FHCs, F prefixes OTSs, P prefixes DHCs (body column).
6. 1 indicates a left-hand-drive model (for 140s).
   2 indicates a right-hand-drive model (for 140s).
7. The DN suffix signifies overdrive.
8. The prefix 8 indicates that it is either an XK 140 or a 150 (chassis column).
9. The BW suffix stands for Borg Warner (automatic box).
10. The S suffix indicates that the engine has a C-type cylinder head (engine column).
11. The S does *not* mean that it is an XK 150S!
12. The 3 indicates left-hand-drive (for 150s).
    The 2 indicates right-hand-drive (for 150s).
13. V indicates a standard 3.4 litres (A-type head).
14. VS indicates a triple-carb, straight-port head 3.4 litres.
15. The 9 indicates the compression ratio (engine column).
16. VA indicates the standard 3.8 litres (A-type head).
17. The T prefix means that it is an XK 150S (chassis column).
18. VAS indicates a triple-carb, straight-port head, 3.8 litres S.

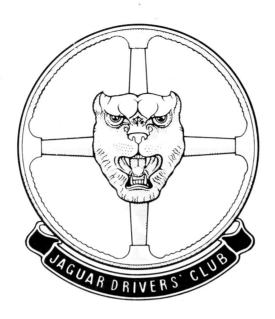

The Jaguar Drivers' Club

The tremendous enthusiasm for the Jaguar marque is reflected in the vitality of Jaguar Driver's Club, which is one of the largest one-make clubs in the UK. Formed in 1956 the club has over 7,000 members and offers a comprehensive range of activities, both social and sporting, and a monthly magazine.

Within the club are various 'Registers' which cater for particular models; those being of special interest to lovers of the Jaguar sports car being for the SS; XK 120, 140, 150 (which includes the C- and D-type and Lister-Jaguars); E-type; and XJ.

The JDC headquarters is at: Jaguar House, 18 Stuart Street, Luton, Bedfordshire, England LU1 2SL.

JAGUAR AT LE MANS

Since its very first participation in the event, many years ago, the Jaguar marque has always been associated with the Le Mans 24-Hours endurance race.

The reason for this association is Jaguar's enviable record in the event and the result is the increased sales of series production cars as a happy spin-off from the Le Mans victories.

Jaguar works cars participated on 14 occasions and produced five first places. This record speaks for itself and, what is more, anyone could buy a virtually identical Jaguar that same year.

It is a matter of record that every Jaguar model which competed on the Sarthe circuit also featured in the manufacturer's catalogue; for example, the XK 120, XK 140, C-type, D-type and E-type.

In addition, we know that the story of Jaguar at Le Mans has not yet ended, for Jaguar intends to return to Sarthe one day. When it does, the rest had better look to their laurels!

This was Jaguar's first outing at Le Mans.

Three XK 120s (the model had made its début at the 1949 London Motor Show) acquitted themselves well, with the Johnson/Hadley team's car holding steady in third place before it retired after 21 hours, with clutch problems.

No	Model	Drivers	Result
15	XK 120	P.Clark/N.Haines	12th
16	XK 120	P.Whitehead/J.Marshall	15th
17	XK 120	L.Johnson/B.Hadley	Retired (clutch)

The first Jaguar to finish was the number 15 XK 120 of Peter Clark and Nick Haines which came home 12th.

Jaguar's first visit to Le Mans. The three XK 120 open two-seaters are lined up together, just before the start.

Jaguar worked at record speed to have a new model ready for the following year. This was the XK 120C (more commonly, C-type) which had nothing in common with the XK 120 except for its engine and front suspension.

Heynes had designed a new tubular chassis and body, and 'Lofty' England, Jaguar's racing manager, had produced the perfect tuning for victory.

No	Model	Drivers	Result
20	XK 120C	P.Walker/P.Whitehead	1st
21	XK 120C	R.Lawrie/I.Waller	11th
22	XK 120C	S.Moss/J.Fairman	Retired (gasket)
23	XK 120C	L.Johnson/C.Biondetti	Retired (oil pump)

Robert Lawrie and Ivan Waller drove their XK 120C at an admirably regular pace to finish 11th overall.

Stirling Moss/Jack Fairman's C-type was forced to retire by a blown gasket.

'Lofty' England, Jaguar's racing manager, brings Peter Walker/Peter Whitehead's C-type out in front of the pits. Twenty-four hours later this car would cross the finishing line in first place.

The long, very fast Hunaudières straight is a key section of the Sarthe circuit. Jaguar had made some far-reaching modifications to the C-types in an attempt to give them more straight-line speed.

Unfortunately the new bonnet design soon produced engine overheating, and not one C-type finished the race.

No	Model	Drivers	Result
17	C-type	S.Moss/P.Walker	Retired (con rod)
18	C-type	A.Rolt/D.Hamilton	Retired (gasket)
19	C-type	P.Whitehead/I.Stewart	Retired (gasket)

The 'droop snoot' C-type. Low wind resistance is not necessarily the be all and end all as this car, driven by Stirling Moss and Peter Walker, proved when it had to retire soon after the start because of engine overheating.

Tony Rolt and Duncan Hamilton were also put out of the race by the same overheating problems, which may have been caused by the redesigned bonnet.

This was the C-type's redesigned back end which was intended to reduce drag. Number 19, driven by Peter Whitehead/Ian Stewart, was to be the first victim of the dreaded overheating.

This year's 24-Hours was memorable for an absorbing battle between the Jaguars, Alfa Romeos and Ferraris.

Running with more powerful engines, the C-types were almost back to their 1951 form.

A new rear suspension, lighter body and disc brakes were the other trumps which gave Jaguar a winning hand.

No	Model	Drivers	Result
18	C-type	T.Rolt/D.Hamilton	1st
17	C-type	S.Moss/P.Walker	2nd
19	C-type	P.Whitehead/I.Stewart	4th
20	C-type	R.Laurent/ Ch. de Tornaco	9th

Below: A fabulous year for the C-type Jaguars which had regained their old form; four cars started and four finished. That of the overall winners, Tony Rolt (seen here at the wheel at Arnage) and Duncan Hamilton, created history by being the first to exceed 4,000 kilometres in 24 hours.

Bottom: Stirling Moss (here at Mulsanne) and Peter Walker were to finish second, 29 miles (40 kms) behind the winning Jaguar.

Clearly visible on the raised bonnet of the Peter White-head/Ian Stewart C-type is the extra air vent which was given to all three works cars to feed the new Weber carburettors. Another characteristic of the works C-types was their disc brakes.

Fitted with disc brakes and SU carburettors, the C-type of the Équipe Nationale Belge finished ninth in class, driven by Roger Laurent and Charles de Tornaco.

1954

The C-types were showing their age, but Jaguar was ready with a replacement model. The fabulous D-type made its first Le Mans appearance. It was a completely new concept in racing car design and became a classic car. Despite a spirited duel with Gonzales/Trintignant's Ferrari, Tony Rolt and Duncan Hamilton had to settle for second place. Stirling Moss was fastest along the Hunaudières with 172.97 mph (278.37 km/h).

No	Model	Drivers	Result
14	D-type	T.Rolt/D.Hamilton	2nd
16	C-type	R.Laurent/J.Swaters	4th
15	D-type	P.Whitehead/K.Wharton	Retired (gearbox)
12	D-type	S.Moss/P.Walker	Retired (brakes)

Three D-type Jaguars made their début on the Sarthe circuit this year. The car assigned to Stirling Moss/Peter Walker was the first to retire (with brake trouble) after having put up the fastest time on the Hunaudières straight. Behind their number 12 is an identical D-type of Peter Whitehead/Ken Wharton which was put out of the race by gearbox trouble.

Tony Rolt and Duncan Hamilton drove the third works D-type and finished a brilliant second, only about 2½ miles (4 kms) behind the Gonzales/Trintignant Ferrari.

Jacques Swaters (sitting on the back of the C-type) and Roger Laurent (in the white shirt) brought the model's Le Mans career to an impressive end with a third overall placing.

1955

1955 is remembered as a year of mourning in the automobile sport world, but, despite the tragic circumstances, Jaguar won the event. The new long-nosed D-types had a new head design with a 280 bhp output and an extra 6 mph (10 km/h) along the Mulsanne Straight.

No	Model	Drivers	Result
6	D-type	M.Hawthorn/I.Bueb	1st
10	D-type	J.Swaters/J.Claes	8th
7	D-type	A.Rolt/D.Hamilton	Retired (gearbox)
8	D-type	D.Beauman/N.Dewis	Retired (crashed)
9	D-type	P.Walters/W.Spear	Retired (distributor)

Jacques Swaters, the pillar of the Équipe Nationale Belge, and his co-driver Johnny Claes seem worried and tired. They were nevertheless to take their yellow D-type into a brilliant third place at the end of the day.

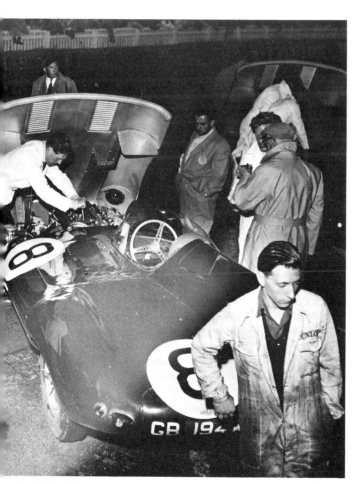

In 1955, the Le Mans week began with night-time practice sessions. Here the mechanics are working on the factory D-type of Don Beauman and Norman Dewis which was to meet a sticky end in the 11th hour.

Resplendent in its American livery, Briggs Cunningham's D-type, driven by Phil Walters and William Spear, was to be Jaguar's first casualty, only seven hours into the race, when it encountered fuel supply problems.

Right: The privately entered fixed-head 140 of Walshaw/Bolton.

Mike Hawthorn and Ivor Bueb brought Jaguar its third victory in the Le Mans 24-Hours. Their long-nose D-type set a mean speed record of 106.99 mph (172.18 km/h) and covered 2,580 miles (4,153 kms).

Winners in 1953, second in 1954, Tony Rolt and Duncan Hamilton had a less happy Le Mans in 1955 with this long-nose D-type which gave up the ghost after 15 hours.

1956

Following new ACO regulations, this year's Le Mans saw new full-width windscreens.

The works D-types now had fuel injection which should have given them the edge over the other 'D' entries but, nevertheless, an Écurie Écosse car won the day. A privately entered XK 140 fixed-head coupé also took part.

No	Model	Drivers	Result
4	D-type	N.Sanderson/R.Flockhart	1st
5	D-type	J.Swaters/F.Rousselle	4th
1	D-type	M.Hawthorn/I.Bueb	6th
6	XK 140	P.Walshaw/P.Bolton	Retired (fuel supply)
2	D-type	P.Frère/D.Titterington	Retired (accident)
3	D-type	J.Fairman/K.Wharton	Retired (accident)

All the 1956 Le Mans D-types are seen here in the Place des Jacobins, after being given the technical once-over. From right to left are cars Nos 5, 4, 3, 2 and 1, and the reserve car which was to start with the number '2'.

1957

Five cars started and five finished. This was Jaguar's greatest ever Le Mans triumph. Écurie Écosse also came up trumps. Jaguar's clean sweep of the top four places was all the more impressive in that the field included some very powerful Ferraris, Aston Martins and Maseratis set on showing the D-types the way home.

No	Model	Drivers	Result
3	D-type	R.Flockhart/I.Bueb	1st
15	D-type	N.Sanderson/J.Lawrence	2nd
17	D-type	J.Lucas/'Mary'	3rd
16	D-type	P.Frère/F.Rousselle	4th
4	D-type	D.Hamilton/M.Gregory	6th

Driving short-nosed 3.4-litre 'D's the French private entrants Lucas/'Mary' (number 16) and the Belgians Paul Frère/Freddy Rousselle (number 17, opposite) made Jaguar's cup overflow by finishing third and fourth overall respectively.

A new regulation for 1957 made full-width windscreens obligatory. This view of the Duncan Hamilton/Masten Gregory 3.8-litre 'D', which went on to finish sixth, shows how Jaguar solved the problem.

Écurie Écosse took second place with the Ninian Sanderson/J.Lawrence team's 3.4-litre D-type.

The 1957 Le Mans was an out and out triumph for Jaguar with its cars taking five of the first six places. What is more, Ivor Bueb and Ron Flockhart averaged more than 110 mph (180 km/h) over the 24 hours.

1958

Among other changes in the rules, the ACO applied the new CSI standards which limited engine capacity to 3 litres. Jaguar was therefore forced to produce a new engine, and shortened the stroke on the famous 3.4-litre XK unit.

The results of their modifications were not very convincing and engine failure led to the two retirements.

A series of accidents also put paid to Jaguar's chances, and the Hamilton/Bueb car was put out of the race after 19 hours, while they were lying second.

No	Model	Drivers	Result
8	D-type	D.Hamilton/I.Bueb	Accident
11	D-type	'Mary'/J.Guelfi	Accident
57	D-type	M.Charles/J.A.Young	Accident
6	D-type	J.Fairman/M.Gregory	Engine failure
7	D-type	N.Sanderson/J.Lawrence	Engine failure

The D-type entered by Écurie Écosse, with J.Lawrence and Ninian Sanderson as drivers, had a very short race, being brought to a halt by engine failure just 15 minutes after the start.

The Écurie Écosse's other D-type, driven by Jack Fairman and Masten Gregory, was to retire shortly afterwards with the same problem.

An accident during the third hour put paid to the Écurie Écosse's short-nose D-type, driven by J.A.Young and M.Charles.

The French driver 'Mary' was killed at the wheel of his own D-type which is seen here in the pits while, in the background, the Gendebien/Hill Ferrari drives on to victory.

Driving his own D-type, Duncan Hamilton, with the American Masten Gregory as back-up, lasted out longer than the other Jaguars, conceding defeat four hours before the finish.

1959

The 3-litre limit still applied and was still posing problems to the manufacturers, since it is very difficult to produce a new high-performance engine in such a short time. This is why there was only one Jaguar at Le Mans in 1959.

No	Model	Drivers	Result
3	D-type	I.Ireland/M.Gregory	Retired (piston)

This 3-litre D-type was the only Jaguar in the 1959 Le Mans. Driven by Masten Gregory and Innes Ireland, it retired at the end of the 70th lap, another victim of the 3-litre XK engine.

This was the last year that a D-type was entered for Le Mans.

As the result of an agreement reached between the works and Briggs Cunningham, the American motor racing enthusiast acquired the E2A prototype which was never put into production, but which was the forerunner of the later E-type generation of grand touring cars.

No	Model	Drivers	Result
5	D-type	R.Flockhart/B.Halford	Retired (engine)
6	E2A	D.Gurney/W.Hansgen	Retired (engine)

The E2A, the pre-E-type prototype, entrusted to Dan Gurney and Walt Hansgen, was put out of the race after nine hours by piston problems.

The 1960 regulations called for a proper windscreen. This is how the Écurie Écosse's faithful D-type turned out. Driven by the 1956 winner, Ron Flockhart, and by Bruce Halford, it fell by the wayside with a broken crankshaft in the 14th hour.

This was a transitional year for Jaguar. The 1960 E2A prototype had not been chosen for series production, and the new E-type had not yet been homologated in the grand touring category. Consequently, there were no Jaguars at Le Mans in 1961.

1962

Since Jaguar had shelved its racing programme indefinitely, it was up to the privately entered E-types to pick up the baton, as the model had now received its grand touring homologation. Briggs Cunningham's E-types did Jaguar proud, even though they did not win.

No	Model	Drivers	Result
10	E-type	B.Cunningham/ R.Salvadori	4th
9	E-type	P.Sargent/P.Lumsden	5th
8	E-type	M.Charles/J.Coundley	Retired (engine)

The Briggs Cunningham/Roy Salvadori E-type was to finish fourth: a great achievement for the new Jaguar model.

Peter Sargent and Peter Lumsden finished just behind, in fifth. Their E-type had a very unusual body, mid-way between the roadster and the fixed-head coupé.

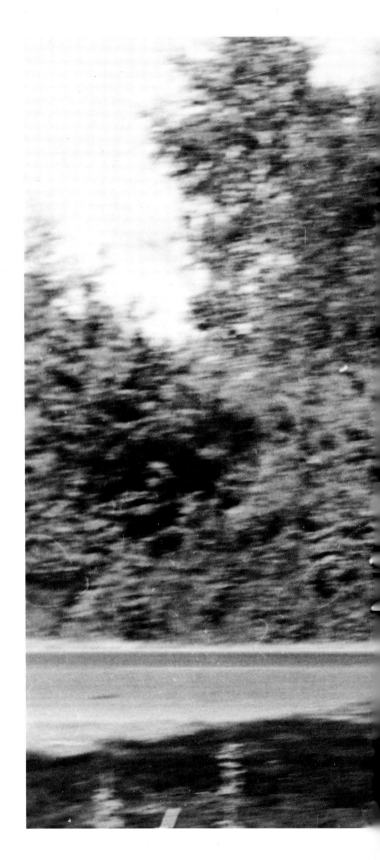

In actual fact, there were very few differences between a Le Mans E-type and the series version. The number 8 of Maurice Charles and John Coundley is a fine example of *this. Unfortunately it did not survive to the four-hour stage.*

1963

The lightweight E-type made its official début.

This much lighter high-performance version of the series E-type was ordered by Briggs Cunningham, who wanted to enter three in the 1963 24-Hours.

His aim was to achieve as high a placing as possible in the GT class.

No	Model	Drivers	Result
15	LW E-type	P.Richards/R.Grossman	9th
16	LW E-type	R.Salvadori/ B.Cunningham	Accident
14	LW E-type	W.Hansgen/A.Pabst	Retired (gearbox)

This Lightweight E-type, entered by the Cunningham team and driven by Walt Hansgen and Augie Pabst, would fall prey to transmission problems not long after the start.

The third lightweight E-type in the Cunningham armada, driven by Paul Richards and Bob Grossman, had its share of trouble but still managed to finish in ninth place.

The car driven by the team boss and Roy Salvadori had similar problems, but it held out until Roy Salvadori skidded on an oil patch.

This was the last time that an E-type was seen at Le Mans. The model had no need of further publicity to boost its already booming sales, so two privately entered E-types contested the event.

No	Model	Drivers	Result
16	E-type	P.Lindner/P.Nocker	Retired (engine)
17	LW E-type	P.Lumsden/P.Sargent	Retired (gearbox)

ACKNOWLEDGEMENTS

Our thanks go to the following, who have helped to make this book more interesting and attractive:

The motoring magazines: *L'Automobile, L'Argus, L'Action-Automobile, L'Auto-Journal, Autocar, Motor.*

Jaguar Cars Ltd: John Morgan, David Boole, Chris Butler, Alan Hodge, Roger Clinkscales.

The marque's historians: Andrew Whyte, Paul Skilleter, Chris Harvey.

Car owners: Peter Come, Max Demagny, Jany Crouzat, Patrick Lansard, Hubert Maechler, Jean-Claude Pruvot.

British Leyland France: Bernard Lamy.

The presidents of the French Jaguar Drivers' Club: Philippe Renault, Roland Urban.

ILLUSTRATION CREDITS

Auschitzki: pages 64/65, 122/123.
Autocar: (John Ferguson) pages 22/23, 60/61; (Harry Hodge) pages 110/111; (V.R. Berris) pages 146/147, 223, 242/243, 330/331, 364/365; 174/175, 190.
Autopresse (Archives D. Pascal) : pages 43, 52, 56, 70, 71, 75,77, 80, 81, 82, 83, 94, 98, 99, 102, 104, 105, 106, 107, 125, 149, 164, 165, 168, 169, 170, 171, 182/183, 199, 201, 207, 219, 230, 254, 255, 256, 257, 260, 269, 271, 275, 276/277, 279, 438, 439, 440, 442, 443, 444, 445, 446.
Fred Bayet: pages 380, 381.
Beroul : page 69.
G.Blanchet: page 205.
Borremans: pages 72/73.
Neill Bruce (Nigel Dawes Collection) : pages 130/131, 140/141, 144.
Coppieters: pages 78/79, 158/159, 167, 181, 206, 254, 257, 258/259, 261, 263, 264, 266, 272/273, 278, 441.
Deschamp: pages 316/317.
DR: pages 59, 121, 145, 176, 178/179, 224.
J.-M. Dubois-Autopresse: pages 129, 132 to 139, 142/143, 322 to 333.
Dumage: page 185.
Photo Germain: page 84.
Alberto Martinez: page 336.
Motor: pages 238/239.
Mourreau: page 318.
Presse-Sports: pages 100/101, 160, 274.
Puytorac: page 253.
Vachon: page 150.
Others documents are part of the author's collection.
Lay-out: Dominique Pascal.
Production: Anne-Marie Veujoz and Gilles Blanchet.

Achevé d'imprimer sur les presses de Berger-Levrault
à Nancy en avril 1985
Dépôt légal : juin 1984
Imprimé en France